ADVOCACY

ADVOCACY

Inns of Court School of Law
Institute of Law, City University, London

OXFORD
UNIVERSITY PRESS

Great Clarendon Street, Oxford OX2 6DP

Oxford University Press is a department of the University of Oxford.
It furthers the University's objective of excellence in research, scholarship,
and education by publishing worldwide in

Oxford New York

Auckland Bangkok Buenos Aires Cape Town Chennai
Dar es Salaam Delhi Hong Kong Istanbul Karachi Kolkata
Kuala Lumpur Madrid Melbourne Mexico City Mumbai Nairobi
São Paulo Shanghai Singapore Taipei Tokyo Toronto

and an associated company in Berlin

Oxford is a registered trade mark of Oxford University Press
in the UK and certain other countries

Published in the United States
by Oxford University Press Inc., New York

A Blackstone Press Book

British Library Cataloguing in Publication Data

Data available

Library of Congress Cataloging in Publication Data

Data available

ISBN 0-19-925496-6

1 3 5 7 9 10 8 6 4 2

Typeset by L. K. Murdoch, Tonbridge, Kent
Printed in Great Britain
on acid-free paper by
Ashford Colour Press, Gosport, Hampshire

FOREWORD

These Manuals are designed primarily to support training on the Bar Vocational Course, though they are also intended to provide a useful resource for legal practitioners and for anyone undertaking training in legal skills.

The Bar Vocational Course was designed by staff at the Inns of Court School of Law, where it was introduced in 1989. This course is intended to equip students with the practical skills and the procedural and evidential knowledge that they will need to start their legal professional careers. These manuals are written by staff at the Inns of Court School of Law who have helped to develop the course, and by a range of legal practitioners and others involved in legal skills training. The authors of the manuals are very well aware of the practical and professional approach that is central to the Bar Vocational Course.

The range and coverage of the manuals have grown steadily. All the manuals are updated annually, and regular reviews and revisions of the manuals are carried out to ensure that developments in legal skills training and the experience of our staff are fully reflected in them.

This updating and revision is a constant process and we very much value the comments of practitioners, staff and students. Legal vocational training is advancing rapidly, and it is important that all those concerned work together to achieve and maintain high standards. Please address any comments to the Bar Vocational Course Director at the Inns of Court School of Law.

With the validation of other providers for the Bar Vocational Course it is very much our intention that these manuals will be of equal value to all students wherever they take the course, and we would very much value comments from tutors and students at other validated institutions.

The enthusiasm of the publishers and their efficiency in arranging the production and publication of these manuals is much appreciated.

The Hon. Mr Justice Elias
Chairman of the Advisory Board of the Institute of Law
City University, London
August 2002

CONTENTS

PART 1
INTRODUCTION

ONE

INTRODUCTION

1.1   Why Should You Read a Manual on Advocacy?

Advocacy is one of the skills that form the core of the Vocational Course for the Bar. It is actually composed of several disparate skills which, when merged, produce the person recognisable as 'the competent barrister'. When you begin reading this Manual, and especially this chapter, you may have little idea what constitutes this 'competent barrister'. You will have seen actor/barristers in films, in plays, on television and heard them on the radio. Do not confuse dramatic effect with reality. These players are addressing themselves to audiences measured in hundreds, thousands or even in millions. As a real barrister, you will address your words to an audience often as small as one and rarely larger than a dozen. Furthermore, these films and plays can never show the constant consideration, and rejection, of alternating courses of action and even of words which precede the final performance of the barrister. You should spend some time in a barrister's chambers and the courts on a mini or a full pupillage. Then, you will start to experience for yourself the effort and planning that goes into producing what the public sees in court. Until you do this, you may find it difficult to judge whether a barrister is competent or not.

The early parts of the Manual are designed to introduce you to those skills which are necessary in order to perform competently as a barrister. When you have some grasp of them you should be better equipped to 'think on your feet', to maintain your composure and fluency when a witness gives a 'difficult' answer to your question or to recall at the end of a trial what a witness said three days earlier. These are skills that the competent barrister has and which, if you do not possess them already, can be acquired.

1.2   What this Manual Cannot Do

It is not expected that this Manual alone can render you competent to represent someone in court (it would be nice if things were that easy!). Armed with the Manual and having completed the Vocational Course, you will have some experience and understanding of the practices and procedures which constitute the professional life of the barrister. You will then be going into pupillage and that offers something that no classes or Manual can — daily access to a practising barrister, with the chance to read all the case briefs that your pupil master receives, perhaps to do some 'devilling' work on them and go into court and observe what goes on, fully informed about the issues in each case and its background. It is likely, though, that if you have worked through this Manual diligently your experience of pupillage may be enhanced by the awareness you have already of certain techniques or practices; equally, pupillage should improve and sharpen your understanding of what is demanded of an advocate. The sooner that you start visiting courts and see how the rules are used and what the advocates do, you will accelerate your own development.

1.3   How to Use the Manual

As stated above, a competent performance by a barrister draws on a variety of skills and abilities. It would be possible to write a Manual that simply told you about those skills but that would not be particularly helpful. Experience has shown us that you will understand and acquire these skills more easily if you can do two things. First, obtain some criteria by which to assess your own performances and those of others that you see (whether fellow beginners or practitioners in court). It is not enough to watch someone who is an acknowledged leader — you must have the ability to evaluate what you see. To say that a speech was 'compelling' or 'obviously persuasive' does not really help you to see what made it so. We have developed a set of advocacy training criteria, which we use as the basis for feedback in all of our advocacy classes (see **Chapter 8** and **Part 4**). If you read them carefully now, and always try to apply them later, you will be able to learn a lot more when you observe others or review your own performances. It should be noted that, while these training criteria are written with advocacy skills in mind, they largely represent transferable skills which are extremely useful in many areas of an advocate's practice (and beyond).

Secondly, it should help comprehension if you see the skills presented in the practical situations where they are likely to occur in reality. This Manual has several chapters which deal with the typical transactions in a courtroom — making speeches and questioning witnesses — see **Parts 5** and **6**. **Part 5** looks at opening *and* closing speeches. This has been done because, although in the courtroom they would be separated by all of the evidence in the trial, you would start to plan both how to start and how you intended to end the trial within a short time of receiving the papers in the case. As planning for the two should not be viewed as two separate processes but as a single coherent approach to the case, we have put them in the same section. **Part 6** looks at witnesses and the evidence they give. The chapters there explain, with practical examples, the techniques and objectives of questioning witnesses. At the end of **Part 6**, **Chapters 22** and **23** deal with the more 'mechanical' aspects of two applications or submissions which are often made to courts and are directly relevant to the evidence (either actual or potential) in the trial — namely, the voir dire and the submission of no case to answer.

After these Parts, which mix skills and tasks to show you the skills in commonplace or recognisable situations, comes **Part 7**. This has several short chapters which are more like guides to specific transactions, telling you how to do it. They reinforce and repeat the skills which are involved in the earlier chapters but the emphasis has shifted so that you are learning as much about the transaction as about the skill. These chapters look at particular applications or submissions that you could make in court, or particular procedures that you might use. The objective when selecting topics for inclusion here is to show those matters which the junior advocate (or pupil) will encounter most often in practice.

Please remember to refer to this Manual **throughout** the course. It is always useful to refresh your memory or even rework a topic in the light of experience. Soon, practice should ensure that many of the techniques and skills become more familiar and almost habitual. In particular, **Part 2** deals with some ancillary skills without which we will never succeed in gaining competence as advocates, while the **Appendices** offer some general assistance in several basic areas and all contain exercises to help you.

1.4   The Importance of Thorough Preparation

You should note now that preparation is as important as the 'performance' in court. Your objectives and how you may achieve them will differ from case to case and even within a single case. You need to identify what you are being asked to do at the outset — only then will you be able to plan the means of fulfilling those objectives. In particular, your lay client's needs and wishes are paramount. You must be able to discover what they are as efficiently and effectively as possible, then agree on an appropriate solution and the means of achieving it. To do all of this competently, you should become as familiar with other essential skills as you are with those in advocacy. Important examples are those of legal research, fact management and conference skills. Without a fluency in these sorts of skills to assist you in preparing for an appearance in court, you will always be working in court 'flying by the seat of your pants'. For any barrister this is an uncomfortable position to be in — anything that you can do to avoid it should be done. You must appreciate that when you make your first few appearances in court for real clients, you are bound to find these moments both nerve-wracking and intimidating, as well as very exciting. There are some simple steps that you can take in order to minimise the worst effects of your nerves. Arrive early at court, go into the courtroom in which you will be appearing. Stand where you will be standing when acting as an advocate. Make yourself as comfortable as you can. Try your voice out. Arrange your papers as if you are beginning the case. When the court is sitting and you are due to begin, take two or three deep breaths to counteract the breathlessness you will feel. If you can, arm yourself with a glass of water to deal with the dryness in the mouth you will experience. The pounding in the chest, the roaring in the ears, the loss of your stomach to an area adjacent to your shoe laces you can do nothing about. You are not odd. You are not alone in experiencing all this. Everyone does.

But do not add to your problems by a sudden realisation that you have not mastered your brief thoroughly. If you do, then you will be adding to the problems of your client, the very person you are in court to assist. You ought to use this Manual (and its companions) as a guide during the Vocational Course and to help you make a more comfortable transition from student to practitioner.

1.5   A Cautionary Note

Please remember that certain practices and procedures used by barristers are governed by rules. Sometimes these are legal rules, sometimes they are customary in origin (for example, wearing wig and gown in open court). Whatever their basis, the rules mean that these procedures always occur in the same manner (until the law is changed or someone thinks up a better method which then becomes the custom).

It is not the function of either this Manual or the Advocacy course to challenge accepted practices at the Bar but you should note that, sometimes, there is more than one way of doing something. The aim may be the same but two barristers may differ, quite properly, on how best to achieve that aim. So long as you abide by the legal rules and the rules of professional conduct, you are able to develop your own style and preferences as an advocate. If the method that you choose suits you and the particular situation, then that is acceptable. Do not do something in a particular way simply because someone else has told you to. They may know better than you — if so, you should follow their advice. Never do so unquestioningly.

1.6   Objectives and Teaching Theory for the Advocacy Course

It may be helpful for you, when reading this Manual, to understand what the Inns of Court School of Law is doing on its advocacy course because this Manual exists primarily to support that course. What we aim to do, for everyone on the advocacy course, is as follows.

1.6.1   TRAINING OBJECTIVES

(a) to demonstrate that competence in advocacy can be understood by reference to skills-based criteria;

(b) to familiarise students with the essential criteria by which competence in advocacy should be judged;

(c) to enable students to observe performances of advocacy and judge what is and is not competent;

(d) to allow students as much practice of advocacy skills in the classroom as can practically be arranged;

(e) to encourage students to practise their advocacy skills as much as is reasonably practicable;

(f) to offer students criteria-referenced feedback on their performances of advocacy skills, whether in the classroom or on video;

(g) to demonstrate to students various practices and procedures encountered by an advocate, either on video or through live performance;

(h) to familiarise students with basic techniques for advocacy, including questioning techniques and preparation for court;

(i) through all of the foregoing, to enable students to perform one or more advocacy tasks with a degree of competence that shows they are ready for pupillage and are likely to benefit from pupillage through their continued practice and observation of advocacy.

1.6.2 TEACHING THEORY

Our teaching theory for advocacy, although it also applies to the other legal skills, is:

People learn skills best through practice. Such practice is most useful if it is preceded by thorough preparation and followed by specific and informed feedback.

This theory leads us to abide by the following guidance, for the purpose of course design:

(a) Preparation should be as thorough as circumstances allow. Particularly, one should know the facts or allegations in the case and understand the relevant laws, substantive and adjectival, in order to determine which facts, allegations and evidence are material to the present task. By the end of the course, a student should be able to analyse factual material and have such existing knowledge of substantive and procedural law that an informed decision can be taken as to any appropriate advocacy tasks that may be undertaken.

(b) Preparation may be general and, in the early stages of learning advocacy skills, may need to be repeated often. Examples might be control over breathing and nerves, the ability to speak clearly and fluently and the ability to construct a logical argument. At a less general level, examples are the ability to use different questioning techniques in appropriate situations, to emphathise with witnesses or judges and to listen with eyes as well as ears. Preparation may also be specific (that is, related to a particular case or task) and this type of preparation should complement general preparation during the early stages of learning. By the end of the course, the competent student should have mastered the basic skills needed for general preparation and be able to demonstrate them, whenever called upon to do so.

(c) Unless very basic skills are to be practised or demonstrated, it is best to practise or demonstrate in the context of a specific advocacy task, using a particular set of case papers. This should assist in showing the relevance of the exercise and may encourage an insight into the application of an individual basic skill in many varied situations, that is, transferability.

(d) Learning may occur through a variety of ways. It may be through performance, or observation of oneself on video or of one's peers or of

6

experienced demonstrators. Such observation may take place in class or through video but will always be of maximum benefit when the performance is accompanied by feedback and explanation. Learning may also occur through reading a book or working through a computer-led lesson, but neither format is likely to be as effective as observing others or performing a skill personally, with explanation and feedback.

(e) A student will learn best how to improve their skills, as well as identifying strengths and weaknesses, if he or she performs a skill (usually in the context of an advocacy task) and that performance is reviewed (either instantly or later) by an observer who is able to apply skills-related criteria to the performance and articulate the degree to which that performance satisfied each of those criteria.

(f) Any skill **may** be learnt through sheer repetition alone and untutored. It may not be learned well, though. Many of the greatest advocates were effectively self-taught but it may now be agreed that early learning is done best with supervision. The student should be guided by an instructor who can demonstrate and observe, provide explanation and feedback. Self-tuition should be left until later, when the advocate's own professional experience, and familiarity with the criteria that should be used to judge competence, can replace the instructor.

(g) Students learn best in small groups with one or more instructors. While they learn most about their own abilities by performing in groups of one or two plus an instructor, they should experience larger groups as these will expose them to a variety of methods and thinking, as well as examples of good and bad practice. The student sometimes needs to see bad practice since it may be that only by being told it is bad and why, will the student know and understand that some aspect of the performance was faulty. The group has become too large when one or more students are denied the opportunity to perform and to discuss a particular skill or task in the class, for whatever reason.

(h) Feedback should be based on clear and objective criteria which are relevant to the skill and/or task, and are made known to the student in advance. Giving useful feedback is itself a skill which can be learnt and should be practised often. An infrequent instructor may not have great familiarity with the relevant criteria and may not refer to them at all when giving feedback. New instructors (or occasional instructors) should be trained to give feedback and, if resources permit, be accompanied in classes by experienced instructors.

(i) In the course of offering feedback, an instructor should have an opportunity to illustrate certain points by a brief demonstration. It should be possible to check that the feedback has been understood by observing an improvement when the student next performs.

(j) Feedback may be limited to a single issue, for reasons of time or because the student is at a very early stage on the course. Single issue feedback will work best when the student has many further opportunities to perform and those will occur in a short space of time. If future performances will be separated by a considerable period (say, a week), it may be better to offer 'multi-issue' feedback to the student, indicating a variety of strengths and weaknesses as the student will have ample time to reflect on each issue.

1.7   General Bibliography

You may find helpful information and techniques in the following books:

Bergmann, P. *Trial Advocacy*, West Publishing Inc., 1979.
Bevitt and Stanton, *Criminal Advocacy: a Practical Guide*, Cavendish 1997.

Crowther, E. *Advocacy for the Advocate*, Sweet & Maxwell, 2nd edn, 1990.

Du Cann, R.L.D., QC. *The Art of the Advocate*, Penguin, 1993, revised.

Evans, K. *Advocacy in Court*, Blackstone Press (OUP), 2nd edn, 1995.

Fridd, N. *Basic Practice in Courts and Tribunals*, Sweet & Maxwell, 3rd edn, 2000.

Hyam, His Honour Judge Michael *Advocacy Skills*, Blackstone Press (OUP), 4th edn, 1999.

Murphy, P. and Barnard, D. *Evidence and Advocacy*, Blackstone Press (OUP), 5th edn, 1998.

Nathanson, S. *Non-trial Advocacy: A Case Study Approach*, Cavendish, 2001.

Pannick, D. *Advocates*, OUP, 1993.

Popat, Bourne and Gilliatt, *Civil Advocacy: a Practical Guide*, Cavendish, 1997.

Shaw, *Effective Advocacy*, Sweet & Maxwell, 1996.

Sonsteng, Haydock and Boyd, *The Trial Book*, West Publishing Inc., 1984.

Stone, M. *Cross-Examination in Criminal Trials*, Butterworths, 2nd edn, 1995.

Stone, M. *Proof of Fact in Criminal Trials*, W. Green & Son, 1984.

(Other books and articles may also be referred to within the following chapters.)

TWO

THE QUALITIES OF THE ADVOCATE

2.1 Introduction

The barrister is known as a person of integrity, someone who judges can trust. The best barristers are also known for the qualities they display in the courtroom. They have mastered their briefs — they know the evidence and the contentious issues in each case, how to handle a 'difficult' witness and, perhaps above all, how to get the triers of fact to see the case from the standpoint of their client.

These practitioners have accumulated several of the disparate qualities that make up the able barrister. Some of these qualities are to do with personality and this course is unlikely to change that. Either you are the sort of person who will stand up to an unpleasant judge to safeguard your client or you are not — all that can now be attempted is to encourage you to use your latent strength of character. Similarly, no one can make you behave in an honest fashion, they can only stress the vital importance of doing so. Honesty is important — to you professionally; to your client in a case where your dishonesty might harm his or her interests; and to ensuring public confidence in the judicial system.

Other qualities can be acquired or improved, for example, eloquence and detachment. There are others. Although opinions may differ as to the entire spectrum of such qualities or as to their relative importance, those qualities or skills set out in the rest of this chapter are particularly important. Considerable reliance has been placed on Richard Du Cann QC's excellent book *The Art of the Advocate*.

2.2 The Essentials of Advocacy

2.2.1 PRACTICE AND HARD WORK

You may not currently have much experience in public speaking. The idea of being the only voice heard in a court room may fill you with a sense of dread as well as great anticipation. Two things are certain though. First, you should get better with practice so never miss a chance to gain experience — debates, moots or mock trials, for example. These opportunities may occur infrequently. All your fellow students will, at least should, read this Manual, so you may encounter some competition. So practise with your friends, better still with your relatives for they will be more long-suffering. Force yourself to listen to what you are saying. Force yourself to criticise yourself as you are speaking. Ask yourself all day and everyday: 'Was that the best word, was that the best way of expressing myself?'. Never be content with the answer: 'Well, that's how I always do it.'. In due course, your performance is going to be judged by the audiences you are to face and address. Their opinion will be based on their assessment, not yours.

Secondly, you must be prepared thoroughly for every case you take. The need for solid preparation and planning is emphasised in every skills Manual for this course, but it is important to stress that the conduct of an application or trial, the handling of an examination-in-chief or a cross-examination, in a competent fashion will not happen by some magical process. It is the product of hours of hard work or, as Richard Du Cann puts it, industry.

The advocate, as Lord Hewart said, must 'claw the facts'. If he or she does not, all the virtues and brilliant improvisations will not help him or her. The facts must all be retained in his or her memory, so long as the case lasts: dates, names, times, exhibit numbers. Then as fast as they were mastered they must be forgotten so that others in the next case he or she does can take their place. Memorising facts of this kind is sheer drudgery. To do it properly the advocate must be prepared to forgo the pleasures of private life at the most inconvenient moments and for indefinite periods.

2.2.2   TENACITY, COURAGE AND SELF-CONTROL

Tenacity and self-control are two distinct but related qualities — both depend upon you having the strength of character necessary to do a good job in adverse circumstances. Tenacity is needed when you encounter a difficult witness — perhaps one who is out to show the court he or she is smarter than you or is just wilfully contrary. As Richard Du Cann says:

> Counsel must expect to cross-examine many witnesses whose evidence he will fail to destroy. He must also expect to come across a number who believe that attack is the best method of defence and who will do all they can to embarrass him . . . Two qualities are required on these occasions more than any others: tenacity and a form of question which allows no opportunity to the witness to score.

You also need self-control in such circumstances — the advocate who is readily embarrassed or angered into an obvious flush will show signs of losing control of himself or herself and the case. The position is worse if your reaction is more than a mere blush; one of the most unpleasant sights in a court room is to see a barrister and a witness engaged in a row (unless, of course, to do so is part of a deliberate plan on your part). To quote Du Cann again:

> Control of his feelings there must be, in particular of his temper. If he cannot, he will not keep control of his tongue and he will not keep control of the case. Forensically simulated emotion should be one of the armaments of the advocate. Personal sensitivity is not.

Finally, you will require courage. You will sometimes find that those in a position of authority seek to test you, occasionally to dominate or bully you. On such occasions make sure of your position. If it is untenable, abandon it. As stated in Du Cann:

> It is always right to be seen to admit wrong. To fail to do so can do immense harm.

But if, on checking, you are satisfied that you are right, press on and stick to your point even if it means confronting a judge. You should be fearless in promoting or defending your client's interests. Remember, though, that judgment is also a quality possessed by the competent advocate. As Du Cann says:

> There is a time to stand and a time to sit for every advocate, and unless he can solemnise some form of marriage between courage and judgment he will never reach the first rank of the profession.

Your point may have been made the first time. To persist in pressing a matter may do more harm than good. Such judgment cannot be taught, it must be acquired through experience and reflection. Never be afraid to ask your colleagues, especially senior ones, for advice on such matters.

2.2.3 HONESTY

The rules of professional conduct require the barrister to maintain a sense of etiquette in court but the quality of honesty is one which is essential. If you have made a mistake — for example, referred inaccurately to some evidence in your closing speech; forgotten to put a point in cross-examination — never be too egotistic to admit your error. Also, never mislead the court. If you have said anything which may have done so, always retrieve the matter before anything irremediable occurs. This must be adhered to no matter what the cost to one's reputation or self-esteem and sometimes, regardless of the cost to your client. Richard Du Cann gives a memorable example from the libel action brought by Harold Laski. (Note that Slade is the QC appearing for the [claimant], Laski; Hastings and Wentworth Day are leading and junior counsel for the defence.)

> In the Laski case Slade contended that the plea of justification (the claim that the words printed in the newspaper were true) included the claim that Laski had been guilty of cowardice by remaining in America during the First World War since this was the suggestion made by Wentworth Day's question to Laski. If this was right it meant that Hastings also had to prove that Laski was a coward. If he did not, Laski was bound to succeed. During Slade's final speech to the jury Lord Goddard interrupted to raise a matter of law, then Hastings intervened:

> HASTINGS: . . . I distinctly recollect hearing Mr Slade say that he was not making a substantive claim in respect of that [i.e. that Laski was a coward] and therefore I have not even addressed my mind to it.

> After further legal argument Slade left the point saying:

> SLADE: I shall be very astonished to find that . . . I have allowed this case to proceed on a footing that the jury could find the whole of these words to be true, which would mean that Mr Laski had been guilty of cowardice.

> Half an hour later Hastings intervened again. He had found a passage in the transcript when Sir Valentine Holmes, Slade's junior in the case, had said during an exchange with the judge: 'We are not asking the jury as regards the part relating to cowardice to give Mr Laski damages . . .'. In that possibly ill-considered sentence, which was not vital to the argument then taking place, the whole of Slade's point, one upon which he believed he could win the whole case, was swept away in the middle of his final speech. Whatever the obligations to his client and whatever the personal feelings he had himself, Slade recognised the most important single fact of the situation: Hastings had already addressed the jury on the basis that the point was abandoned. So he told Goddard:

> SLADE: . . . I am not going back on anything Sir Valentine Holmes said, any more than I should go back on anything I said myself; and I therefore prefer to err on the side of fairness, and I shall not ask the jury to deal with that part of the libel at all.

2.2.4 LANGUAGE AND HUMANITY

Given the possession of the qualities of tenacity, courage, self-control, judgment and honesty, the advocate requires an understanding and a love of language, and the trial advocate requires also an understanding of and love for humanity. These latter qualities cannot be taught. You have either got them or you have not. But you can be alerted to the need to value both. You can be taught the need to demonstrate that you value both. Take language first.

Throughout your future professional life, words will assume a dominant position. Some, boringly, will be inflexible because the practice of law and human affairs has made them so: 'mens rea', 'bills of exchange', 'charterparty', 'Scott schedules', 'maliciously', the list is endless. From these you will be unable to escape. It is not so with the rest of the natural English vocabulary. But you will find when you are on your feet that you use one word and can then become a prisoner of it. Words like 'situation' and 'relationship' once used become traps. This can only be avoided if you train your mind concisely to be a movable *Roget's Thesaurus*, alert to the use of alternative words apt both for the occasion and the different clients, witnesses and audiences that you will face. Your language, as Lord Chesterfield said in 1750, must be 'the language for them all'. Take the simple example used by Du Cann from *R v Gardiner*. Ernest Wild QC is cross-examining a labourer who claims to have seen the accused entering a building with the victim.

> WILD: Where did you see him [the defendant] first?
> WRIGHT: Against Church Lane.
> WILD: So he saw you?
> WRIGHT: Yes.
> WILD: You were loitering about.
> WRIGHT: No, I was going down the road.

But the youth was leaning against the edge of the witness-box, his hands in his pockets. 'Loitering' was what the jury were going to remember. Wild continued:

> WILD: When did you see him the second time?
> WRIGHT: He came down the road.
> WILD: He saw you then?
> WRIGHT: Yes.
> WILD: And the third time too?
> WRIGHT: Yes, he spoke to me.
> WILD: He must have seen you all the time?
> WRIGHT: Yes.
> WILD: And he must have known you were about?
> WRIGHT: Yes, he spoke to me.
> WILD: Do you represent that, knowing you were about, he went into the chapel and behaved in the way you state?
> WRIGHT: Well, he did.

When striving to hit your target in this fashion, it is essential to keep one eye on the judge/jury/magistrates to see if they have taken your point. Also, try to observe the witness as much as possible — something in their demeanour may be very useful. In short, be alert and be observant.

Finally, always remember to whom you are talking. In the first instance, this may be the witness but, through him or her, you are talking to the triers of fact. Try to see whatever you do in terms of how they will see it and understand it. Almost the last word goes to Richard Du Cann — this time referring to Marshall Hall.

> He had an understanding of human frailty which enabled him to catch the throats of all who heard him speak. When he was quite young he defended a prostitute charged with murdering one of her clients. She was forty-seven, her former attraction devoured by the life she had been forced to lead. At the end of his speech as he was about to sit down, he caught sight of her sitting hunched in the dock. On the spur of the moment he added these words:
>
> > Look at her, gentlemen of the jury. Look at her. God never gave her a chance — won't you?

You might note that this style of advocacy seems a little dated now — indeed that has sometimes been said to the writer. A more recent example of a celebrated advocate is George Carman QC. He was criticised by opposing counsel in a libel trial (*Mona Bauwens* v *The People Newspaper*) for:

> painting a rather crude picture of Mr Mellor [then the Government's Heritage Secretary] behaving like an ostrich and putting his head in the sand 'thereby exposing his thinking parts'.

Maybe rather than consider whether styles of advocacy have 'dated', one should simply ask at the end of each case, 'did it work?'.

PART 2
BEFORE WE START

THREE

MEMORY AND RECALL

3.1 Introduction

At the start of the last chapter, the point was made that the able barrister has a wide variety of skills, several of which may need to be deployed at any one time. Some of these can be honed to your advantage so that they become almost second nature. One example is the ability to take accurate notes swiftly. Another is the ability to remember in a trial what a witness said five minutes/hours/days before.

It is of vital importance that the barrister can recall what a witness actually said in his or her testimony. An accurate note will help but, sometimes, you may not have the time to find your note. Also, in a trial you may be faced with a question like 'Isn't there an authority on this point? A recent decision of the Court of Appeal?'. It will be to your advantage to show that you are knowledgeable on current law but you cannot carry around an entire library. You have to rely on your memory.

This chapter contains some ideas on how you might improve your memory and recall, while **Chapter 4** has some tips on note-taking and shorthand.

3.2 Memory and Recall Techniques

You need to remember what you hear so that you can ask further questions in examination-in-chief, ask the right questions in cross-examination and re-examination and, if you are making a closing speech, so you can emphasise those aspects of the oral evidence which support your theory of the case. Developing a good aural memory requires practice.

What can you do to help you remember what you hear? The following techniques can improve your ability to recall oral communications accurately.

Try to understand what you hear. Process the information you hear as you hear it. One of the problems which arises in processing the information as you hear it is that you may let your mind wander away from the speaker when the speaker is between words. This happens because you can think faster than anyone can speak and you will have processed the information as soon as, or even before, the last word is spoken. The pause in the speaker's communication to you then gives your mind time to dwell on other things which can interfere with the processing of the next piece of information. Try to keep your mind fully on the speaker even when the speaker pauses for thought. One way of maintaining your concentration is to predict what the speaker will say next and record mentally when you are correct and when you are wrong.

Trace the development of the ideas being communicated. Concentrate your attention and interest continuously on the speaker and what he or she is saying. Mentally repeat or summarise key ideas or statements, or associate related ideas as they are being communicated. Always remember that you can get the witness to summarise what he or she has said or to repeat what has been said. If possible, and a 'must' when you are cross-examining, take notes of the key ideas or facts. But do not take extensive notes as this will divert your attention away from what has been said. In the context of the cut and thrust of advocacy, you may not have time to refer to your notes of what the witness has said, before you need to retrieve the information to use in examining another witness or in your closing speech.

3.3   Memory and Recall Exercises

The following exercises contain a number of passages taken from *Total Recall: Successfully Boost Your Memory Power* by J. Minninger (Thorsens, 1987), pp. 206–209. Ask a colleague to read one to you and then see if you can list accurately the main points of the passage.

3.3.1   EXERCISE 1

Your wife or husband says:

> We have a lot to do before the party tonight. I don't know if we have enough glasses. Could you call your brother, George, and ask him to bring ice when he comes if he's coming before 7.00. If he won't get here until later, ask Harriet to pick it up on her way home from work. The tablecloths are still in the dryer, and the folding chairs have to be brought up from the basement. I suppose George can do that if he comes early. I don't know if we have enough glasses. I better go get those tablecloths out of the dryer before they get wrinkled. Do you think your brother and Harriet will hit it off?

You have a lot of extraneous information. Your goals here are to decide what you were being asked to do and arrange them in proper sequence. Here's what you should have 'heard':

Call George and see if he is coming before 7.00 pm.

If yes: (a)   Ask him to bring ice.

(b)   Tell your wife he will be early, so he will bring the ice and can help carry the chairs up from the basement.

If no: (a)   Call Harriet and ask her to buy ice on her way home from work.

(b)   Tell your wife that Harriet is bringing the ice, and you will have to carry the chairs up from the basement.

Optional: Count the glasses.

3.3.2   EXERCISE 2

That was a typical family situation. Now try one that you may have run into in your business life. Your boss, Mr Fickle, also likes to 'think out loud'.

Mr Fickle says:

> I need some cigarettes from the drugstore downstairs. Get me a pack of Camel Lights and charge it to my wife's account. Try to get Steve to take care of you because the older guy may give you a hard time. Before you go down, take this report to Mr Samson on the 13th floor in the annex and give it to his secretary. If she's not there, get somebody to sign for it. Last month some jerk lost the report and I got my ear bent. Make two Xeroxes of it just to be safe. One of those copies has to go to headquarters today, so drop it off at shipping, but tell them to send it second class. Mr Samson says we're spending too much on postage, so if it takes longer to get there, that's his sweet problem. Do you think something's wrong in his department? He's been crabby as the devil lately.

This was a hard one, but typical of many busy offices. Most of what was said were instructions, spoken and implied, but they certainly were not in order. You might even have had to grab a pencil and write down what was wanted to be sure you got it all.

Here's what you were being asked to do.

(a) Address an envelope to headquarters (implied).

(b) Make two photocopies of the report. Place one copy in the envelope you just addressed.

(c) Deliver the original report to Mr Samson's secretary on the 13th floor in the annex. If she is not there, leave the report with someone else and get a signed receipt.

(d) Deliver the 'headquarters' envelope containing the photocopied report to shipping and ask them to send it second class.

(e) Buy a pack of Camel Lights at the drugstore and charge them to Mrs Fickle's account. Try to be waited on by the younger assistant.

(f) File the second photocopy of the report as a backup, in case one of the other copies is lost (implied).

3.3.3   EXERCISE 3

Remember that the skills acquired in one context will serve you equally well in another. Getting instructions from a teacher, colleague or sales assistant can be tricky. See how much of the following you actually need to remember, and try to organize it into a sequence.

The paint store sales assistant says:

Put the stain on with a soft brush and really rub it in. If you try to put it on too thickly, the surface will dry while the underneath part is still wet. Then you'll get a rippled surface because the hard top skates over the wet bottom. Did I tell you that you have to mix it well before you start? Don't use your best screwdriver. The lighter colours really look good in this finish, but I think the dark colour you've chosen will be OK. You have to seal it afterwards with two or three coats of polyurethane varnish, otherwise the rain will soak in and warp the wood. Oh, but you're using it inside, so that's not a problem, but be sure you clean the wood first to free it of dust and dirt.

You had to discard some of the information you got here. If you put the remainder in a working sequence, it should come out like this:

(a) Clean the wood first.

(b) Stir the stain if necessary.

(c) Rub the stain into the wood thoroughly with a soft brush.

(d) The sales assistant doesn't like dark stains.

As the exercises illustrate, an excellent means of ensuring that you remember things is to start by analysing and reorganising the information you need to remember.

There are many books which describe such techniques, including: *Use Your Memory*, Tony Buzan, BBC Publications, 1995; *Total Recall: How to Maximize Your Memory Power*, Joan Minninger, Fine Communications, 1997; *The Brain Book*, Peter Russell, E P Dutton, 1979.

3.4   Witnesses and the Court

The exercises in **3.3** were designed to start you thinking about exactly how adequate your memory is and how you might set about improving it, as you almost certainly need to do. As advocates, though, we also rely on other people's memory skills.

3.4.1   WITNESSES

If a witness cannot recall the events, words or documents that led to their being called as a witness, then it may be that some vital information is being lost to the court. While one might expect a witness who is being cross-examined to suffer a little from problems of memory, the same should not normally be said of a witness during their examination-in-chief. However, problems certainly do arise in-chief and one of the main causes is the requirement that you do not ask leading questions of your own witness. That is, you cannot ask the witness questions which suggest the desired answer to the witness. This frequently produces very open questions such as:

'What happened next?' or

'Did anything else happen?' or (just about the worst question you could ask)

'Is there anything else that you would like to say to the court?'

While the advocate who asks questions like these cannot be guilty of suggesting the desired answer to the witness, they are certainly not providing much help to them either. Let us suppose that a witness has already told us part of what they remember of an incident. You might ask a 'What happened next?' question but it does not specifically take the witness to that part of their story that you want them to talk about now. So, since the testimony of the witness might be compared to a spool of audio tape (or video film) gradually unwinding from their memory, you could offer some sort of marker to let them know where on the tape you want them to go. How about:

You have told the court that the claimant's car swerved across the road and onto the opposite carriageway. What happened next?

Now the witness has an idea of where you want him or her to take up the story, although still you have not indicated a particular incident or topic to him or her. If the witness is still stuck for an answer, you might then try (assuming it is not in dispute):

Were there any cars travelling along the road in the opposite direction from the claimant's car?

If you particularly want the witness to continue to talk about the claimant's car, you could ask:

Once the claimant's car crossed to the opposite carriageway, could you still see it?

Let's assume the witness answers 'Yes'; she now should have in her mind's eye that car across on the wrong side of the road. So you might risk:

Q.   Did you see what happened to the Claimant's car then?

A.   Oh yes, a white van drove into it and pushed it off the road completely.

Now the incident has come back to life for the witness and you should be able to get them talking more fluently. Witnesses' memories are like anyone else's, they sometimes need a bit of prodding to get them working and, like everyone else, they are more likely to respond to questions which give little bits of (non-contentious) information and start them visualising the incident at a particular point in what they saw or heard.

3.4.2   JUDGES, JURIES AND MAGISTRATES

You may be the greatest advocate since Marshall Hall but if the people who have to find the facts cannot recall your arguments or the important pieces of evidence when the time comes for their adjudication, you are in trouble (and so is your client). As with witnesses, the court will remember something best if they can visualise it. It is obviously more difficult for the court to do this than it was for the witness since the court may be unfamiliar with the scene, for example, and anyway the judge wasn't there when the incident happened and engraved itself on the witness's mind. This is an acid test of your skills as an advocate because you must bring the incidents to life for the court: not for nothing do we say that part of the function of an opening speech is to 'set the scene'. The better the court can get inside the head of the witnesses and almost see through their eyes, hear through their ears, the better your chance that the court will remember the evidence. Witnesses who are allowed the freedom to tell their own story are much more memorable than one who just has to answer 'Yes' or 'No' to a series of questions. Witnesses whose testimony is largely uninterrupted (or whose answers are not cut off by the advocate) are likely to be more clearly recollected later by the court, as well as probably seeming more credible. In your speeches or submissions to the court, try to concentrate on your strongest points: first, there won't be too many, which always makes things easier to remember, and secondly, you can get away with repeating yourself on a couple of points but not on a dozen. Repetition, whether of a word or phrase, or a verbal snapshot of a moment during an incident, always helps people to remember. If the court can remember your arguments, then you stand a chance of succeeding in the case; if it can't remember them, you have wasted your time and your client's money.

FOUR

NOTE-TAKING

4.1 Note-taking in Practice

Of course you can take notes. You did it at school, let alone at university. You don't need to learn about notes now.

Fair enough, but:

(a) How often have you taken a note that did not make sense when you reread it?

(b) How often have you taken a note that was not even legible later?

(c) How often have you not been able to find a particular point in your notes when you reread them later?

(d) How often have your notes missed out an important point?

This sort of problem is irritating, but in the past it has probably been no more than that. You felt slightly less secure because your notes were not very good. You may not have understood something properly because a note did not make sense, or you may have lost a few marks in an exam because your notes on a particular point were not very good.

However, as a professional barrister there is far more at stake for you than simply being irritated or not understanding a point very well. If your skills in taking notes are not good enough the result may be that you fail to remember an important point that a client has told you, that you spend extra hours in a library because you cannot remember where you looked something up, or that you do not have a good enough basis on which to make a closing speech or a cross-examination.

From now on bad notes will cost time and money, and will have a real impact on how good a job you do for the client. In going into a profession where the accurate and efficient use of words is vital you can no longer afford to make do with inadequate notes.

Recall problems that you have had with notes you have taken in the past. Look back at notes you took as a student and examine them critically. Were they as good as they could be? Try to identify what the weaknesses were.

Taking good notes is not something that will magically happen when your first real client walks in the door. You will have to be ready in advance. So analyse now what the weaknesses in your note-taking are, and start working on them **now!**

Even if your existing note-taking techniques are not too bad, they could still be more polished. In any event, you will still need to adapt your note-taking abilities for practice. Taking notes as a student is not the same as taking notes as a professional lawyer. In the past you could always complain or miss out bits if the lecturer was going too fast, but you are not going to be able to do that when a judge is giving judgment — you have to get it all and you have to get it right first time!

The rest of this chapter on notes is for guidance. It provides suggestions on how you might develop your own skills. There are also some comments on how basic note-taking skills can and should be adapted for different purposes. As with so much in learning skills, the point is not simply whether you can understand the need for good notes, but whether you can produce them.

4.2   Essentials of Good Notes

The following check list has some obvious ingredients, but it should still be useful for reviewing how good your note-taking is, and may suggest some points on which you could work. A good set of notes needs to have:

(a)   *Reasonable legibility*   It is not easy to improve bad handwriting, but there may be something you can do to improve or speed up the way you write.

(b)   *Good organisation*   You must be able to find something in a set of notes. Points should be dealt with in groups.

(c)   *Clear layout*   Subheadings, underlinings, indentations, etc. for easy reference.

(d)   *Comprehensive coverage*   Every important point must be included. It is more important to get the sense and the understanding than to get every word down.

(e)   *Selectivity*   You cannot write down everything, you must get down what matters without wasting space on what does not. If the exact wording does matter it must be recorded.

(f)   *Abbreviation*   To be able to get words down fast when necessary some form of coherent abbreviation, shorthand or speedwriting technique is essential. (See **4.9**.)

4.3   Research Notes

These are probably the notes with which you are most familiar. If you are serious about building a successful career as a lawyer, you should already have good experience of taking notes of cases and statutes or notes from textbooks. However, techniques for taking research notes in practice are not quite the same as those for taking notes in university or college.

The objective in taking the notes is different. In learning law the objective is to cover an area of law comprehensively — the cases, the statutory sections, the rules and the exceptions — but in practice the objective of research is very specific rather than general, and the need is not to cover the whole area but to cover only those points which arise in the client's case. You need to prepare properly for research, defining very carefully what needs to be looked up. If you do not plan your research properly, you may waste lots of time on unnecessary notes.

Having planned your research for a particular case, you need clear notes of what you look up. It is easy to ignore this need — you find the point you want and just jot it down on a piece of paper that happens to be handy. But all too often when you come to write the opinion or to present the case in court you find that your note is inadequate and you have to go and look up the point again, or you cannot quite remember what your note means! Never let this happen to you.

4.3.1 VITAL POINTS IN TAKING NOTES OF RESEARCH

(a) *Be systematic*   Never retain a point you have researched in your head or put it on whatever paper is handy. Boring though it may be, all research should be properly and systematically recorded.

(b) *Always keep clear references*   When researching an area of law in a textbook or in *Halsbury*, always make sure that you clearly note which book you are using and which page of the book the note comes from, or you may not be able to find it again. When researching a case, make sure you write the name of the case and the reference at the top of the note. It may be useful to quote references to the solicitor so that he or she can look the point up. If you are researching electronically, keep a precise note of the web page, not just the web site.

(c) *Make full notes from each source*   Make sure you note all cases, statutes, etc. that are mentioned in one source that will need to be followed up in another. If part of a judgment is particularly important, make sure you note down which judge gave the judgment and the page number of any quotation. In researching a statute, make sure you note the section and subsection exactly, and note whether you have written down the exact words of the statute or just a summary.

(d) *Note all points, not just those in your favour*   Although you are researching your client's case, always note points against you. Although you may not want to use them you must be prepared to meet them, and you must not mislead the court as to the effect of an authority.

(e) *Anticipate the future use of sources you research*   Make a clear note of which authorities you may actually wish to refer to in court. In some cases, as in magistrates' courts, it may be necessary to have photocopies of an authority that you wish to refer to if it is not likely to be easily available at the court.

(f) *Make careful use of photocopies and printouts*   Photocopying sources is a useful and time-saving way of gathering research material. If you take copies or a printout, ensure each is clearly labelled with the case to which it is relevant. Never assume that you have researched a topic simply because you have taken a photocopy of a relevant page and put it in the file — you must read it!

(g) *Make up clear and coherent summaries*   Sometimes the original notes of research are clear, but in a complex case they may be confused and may need to be copied out more coherently for use. Again this may be boring, but if you don't do it you will sooner or later have a case where you wish you had!

(h) *Always keep notes of research*   Never throw your research notes away. The case may come back or a similar case may come in. Using existing notes saves time, and it is pointless to have to start again with a point you have researched. Do not send the notes back to the solicitor with the brief or they may get lost.

One way of keeping notes efficiently is always to take notes of research in the same notebook, starting a new page for each case you research and heading it clearly. If these research notebooks are kept together it is then easy to refer back. If you do use separate pieces of paper for research in each case, make sure that you have an efficient filing system.

Your notes of research should be good enough to be worth keeping. Good research notes ultimately save time and can become not only a resource but also a source of confidence and strength in constructing a case.

4.4 Notes made in Preparing a Case

Methods of information management in the preparation and presentation of a case are fully dealt with in the appropriate chapter of the **Case Preparation Manual**. Only a few points are emphasised here. Even more than with research, there is a tendency in preparing a case simply to make rough notes and throw them away as soon as they have been used. This shows a real lack of appreciation of how important a resource good notes can be to the practitioner, and what a sound basis they provide in the preparing of a case properly.

Having said this, the first notes made on reading a brief or on reading a document may well only be of temporary use—they are simply first impressions of what is relevant and first notes for full chronologies. There is no reason why these notes should not be on the back of an envelope! However, in all but the simplest case, much fuller notes about the case should follow. A full set of notes that are clearly written, clearly set out, and properly filed so that they can easily be found, will be the best possible basis for preparing a case.

4.4.1 VITAL POINTS IN TAKING NOTES IN PREPARING A CASE

(a) *Prepare brief and clear notes on each aspect of the case*   Each aspect of a case should be summarised for easy reference. For example, most cases would need the following: a full chronology, a list of *dramatis personae*, lists of events, lists of documents, lists of evidence available and evidence required, etc.

(b) *Take care with layout*   A good layout will enable you to find a point quickly, and sooner or later you will appreciate how important that can be in court!

(c) *Appreciate the importance of good notes as a basis for a case*   Clear notes are the basis of the good and confident presentation of a case, in terms of advocacy and of writing and drafting. You must have a case at your fingertips if you are to present it clearly and coherently, and clear concise summary notes will be the best basis for this.

(d) *Appreciate the extent to which good notes save time and money*   Making good notes on all aspects of the case will make it much easier and quicker to look things up and will save having to duplicate work on a brief when points have been forgotten.

(e) *Appreciate the extent to which good notes clarify thinking*   The more complex a case, the more difficult it is to get on top of it. Making good sets of notes about a case helps to bring it into focus.

(f) *Always keep a full set of notes*   As with legal research, it is important to put one's notes on a case together in a coherent and legible form, and to keep them for future reference. Although it is quite tempting to throw notes away the moment a brief goes back to the solicitor, it is important to keep them as the case may come back again. Notes made in preparing to write an opinion can be invaluable in getting into a case quickly when the case comes back to be prepared for trial.

4.5 Notes made in Preparation for Writing

If you make good notes in the course of preparing a case the thorough understanding gained will give you the soundest possible basis for clear writing. If you have good preparation notes you do not need to riffle through the papers continually while you are writing an opinion or preparing a draft. If you have good notes of all the basic detail there is much less chance that there will be errors in your writing.

You should have all the notes that you made in preparing the case to hand while you are writing an opinion or a draft, so that you can refer to them easily. In addition, it is good practice to make special outline notes for the opinion or draft prior to writing it.

4.5.1   VITAL POINTS IN MAKING NOTES PRIOR TO WRITING AN OPINION OR DRAFT

(a) *Appreciate the importance of notes in ensuring clarity and coherence* By making notes you can check that you have identified everything that should be included in the opinion or the draft.

(b) *Appreciate the importance of notes in providing a clear structure* Making notes can help to give the clarity of structure that is vital, and should avoid the waste of time that often occurs if you start writing and then suddenly realise that you have left something out or failed to deal with it in the right place. The notes should also give you a framework for order of paragraphs and the proposed contents of each.

(c) *Appreciate the importance of notes for accuracy* It is vital that an opinion or draft is completely accurate, or it will at least create a bad impression, and may weaken a case. Good notes should provide an easy source of reference to ensure accuracy.

4.6   Interview Notes

There are particular difficulties in taking notes of an interview or conference, and yet such notes are important as they may be the only record of what was actually said. The requirements of note-taking during an interview are rather different from those of taking notes from research or for written documents, but people do not always remember this to start with, and often take inadequate notes as a result. In addition, it is important that note-taking supports the interview rather than making it more difficult, the problem being that you must concentrate primarily on the client rather than on the notes.

(a) Attention tends to centre on getting everything on paper rather than on making sure that everything is said.

(b) In making notes, you will look down quite often, losing eye contact with the client, and therefore possibly making the client feel less involved and less communicative.

(c) In making notes, you may miss visual signs of how the client is reacting.

(d) You cannot write down everything, and must make instantaneous decisions about what is important enough to write down.

(e) In writing down one point you may miss what is said next.

(f) Sometimes there will simply be physical difficulties in taking notes, for example, when you talk to the client outside court and there is not even anywhere to sit down, let alone a table to lean on. The difficult circumstances do not make the notes any less important!

(g) The points that need noting will not necessarily come out in the right order.

(h) The points that need noting will not necessarily come out with the right degree of emphasis.

(i) There is only one chance to take notes. Although you can to some extent go over notes to check that they are correct, there is only a limited extent to which this can be done without undermining the client's confidence.

Because of some of the difficulties of taking notes during interviews, there is a tendency to try to find alternatives, but the drawbacks of potential alternatives must be appreciated.

Using a tape recorder for an interview to avoid the need to take notes is not necessarily a good idea. You cannot refer back to points easily — it may be difficult to rewind to the right point and you cannot really do that during the interview. If you want the interview in a form in which you can more easily refer to it then the whole tape must be typed out, which takes time and will produce a long manuscript which will take some time to read, especially if the client is verbose or wandering. It is generally preferable to have written notes which can concentrate on the main issues without repetition and be easily referred back to.

You can get someone else to take the note. A barrister taking a conference will often ask a solicitor or a pupil to take a note. This may well be a good decision as it leaves the barrister free to deal with the client, but the main drawback is that it is often done in a rather offhand manner, and the resulting notes often fail to contain some items that the barrister needs. If someone else is to take the note it must be made absolutely clear what points they should concentrate on, what form the notes should take and so on.

4.6.1   VITAL POINTS IN TAKING NOTES OF AN INTERVIEW

(a) *Use a framework for the notes*   It may well be possible to have a framework in mind for the interview before it starts if you know what it will be about. This can provide a basic framework for the notes. If you have not had the opportunity to get a framework in mind, form one as soon as possible.

(b) *Decide who will take the note*   If a solicitor and a barrister are at a conference they do not both need to take a full note. There may also be a pupil or a trainee solicitor present who could take the note. Whenever there is a choice, it must be made clear who will take the full note. The barrister taking the conference may well still wish to take a few notes of particular points personally.

(c) *Have proper materials ready for taking notes*   This is easy enough in chambers, but may be more problematic if the interview is in a cell or a corridor. A proper notebook or paper with something to lean on should be carried, and notes taken fully and systematically however difficult the circumstances.

(d) *Keep a relationship with the client*   Try to avoid taking notes at the very start of the interview. It is important to establish a relationship with the client before starting to take notes, and to maintain it while taking notes. Explain to the client what you are taking notes of and why, and ask the client to pause while you write something down. However important the notes are, the client is more important.

(e) *Make selective notes*   You cannot write down everything the client says. You must be intelligently selective. When you do start taking notes, try to note the main issues briefly and clearly. Make notes on the main points with large gaps which you can then fill in later in the interview. However, beware the generalised summary where detail is required.

(f) *Note appropriate details*   Do not try to write down too much. The details that matter, be it descriptions or figures, can often be recorded with few words. If the actual words said matter, do make sure you get them down.

(g) *Make notes at the right time*   Try to judge when to write things down. It may not help if you take notes while a client is dealing with something he or she finds painful to deal with — knowing that everything is being taken down may discourage the client from speaking at all.

(h) *Check the notes before the interview ends* Check your notes with the client before the interview ends. This will not involve pedantically running through every point, but summarising issues and checking details to ensure the notes are accurate.

(i) *Check the notes after the interview* Try to reread your notes of the interview as soon as possible after it takes place to ensure that they are comprehensible and include all the relevant information. At that stage you may still remember enough of the interview to be able to make corrections, later you will not!

(j) *Keep a proper copy of the notes* Do not leave the notes of an interview on odd pieces of paper, unless the original notes are very clear. Make a copy of the notes with everything set out clearly and in a suitable order. When you are preparing for trial, a note of an early interview can help to recall the details of the case that might otherwise be forgotten. Also keep a note of advice given—you may need to refer back to it later.

4.7   Notes in Court

Taking notes during a court case may sound strange — the barrister is in court to talk, not to write. But there are various aspects of the case that will need recording for different purposes, and good advocacy is based on proper preparation and good notes.

Although some barristers do make full notes for what they will say in court, it is generally better for good advocacy to make brief and clear notes to which you can refer quickly and easily just to remind yourself what comes next. You should know your case well enough for this to be sufficient, and the advocate who is always shuffling papers and who appears to be just reading out notes will rarely look or sound convincing. You can also miss a lot if you are looking at papers rather than at people in court. Only a framework and the most important questions should generally be noted in advance. (See, for example, **18.2.2**.)

4.7.1   OPENING SPEECH

An opening speech will often be based on notes. You need to make notes for the speech itself, separate from notes on the case. These should be summary notes. Writing the speech out in full is not advisable as you will tend to look as though you are reading an essay.

There are again some special techniques for taking these notes.

(a) An appropriate order is vital.

(b) Make the notes big and clear for easy use.

(c) Some form of highlighting must be used so that the notes can be glanced at quickly. You should know the case well enough for that glance to be sufficient.

(d) The points that must be made must be clearly emphasised so that none are forgotten.

(e) The notes should have some system for emphasising the changes of area and thought so you can use them to best advantage.

4.7.2   DEALING WITH WITNESSES

Examination-in-chief There are two basic approaches that tend to be taken by student barristers preparing an examination-in-chief of a witness. The first is to write out every question fully, and the second is simply to use the witness's witness statement without making notes. Both approaches have real weaknesses. If you write out every question you will soon encounter the difficulty of not getting the answer you expect and not knowing how to proceed, or you will ask your next question rather than reacting properly to the witness's answer. The process is easier where a witness statement will stand as the evidence-in-chief.

So an examination-in-chief should be based on notes properly prepared expressly for the purpose:

(a) Identify the areas on which the witness should be questioned and put them in a suitable order. These may be areas only where there is additional information.

(b) Each of these areas and each change of issue should be emphasised in the notes to be easily followed.

(c) Identify the basic point of each question you consider asking and include that in the notes, but never write out whole questions unless there are particular points where the exact wording is vital.

(d) Annotate the notes with points about how to ask a question or what you are really trying to achieve by asking it.

(e) Always be ready to depart from your notes if reality requires it!

Cross-examination There are also two fairly common reactions to learning cross-examination. One is to write out long lists of hostile questions and the other is simply to panic! In fact for the vast majority of people a good cross-examination is again most likely to be based on good notes.

In preparing notes for a cross-examination:

(a) List all the points that you need to put to the witness, either because they undermine the witness's testimony or because they are part of your own case.

(b) Put these points into a suitable order.

(c) Note ideas for questions under each point.

(d) For cross-examination there may be some point in writing out whole questions, as there is more importance in the exact form of the question to make the point you want.

(e) Include in the notes some indication of how hard to push a point, depending on how important it is to your case.

(f) Review your notes in detail during the examination-in-chief, being ready to add to them, delete from them or reorder them to most effect.

(g) Make sure your notes are clear enough for easy reference. For effective cross-examination it is especially important that you do not constantly refer to your notes. To be effective your concentration must be on the witness, not on a piece of paper.

(h) It is particularly important to be prepared to depart from your notes when the reaction of a witness demands it, but beware of being lured into a departure that may do your case harm!

Taking notes of what witnesses say As well as making notes for questions to ask witnesses, it is also important to take notes of what a witness says. This point often does not occur to the student barrister — you just listen to what the witness says and hope it is what you want! You need to become adept at compressing a question and answer to note down what you need, and sometimes it is useful to note down verbatim what a witness says. In taking notes, however, never forget that watching the witness is important.

There are various purposes for which you may wish to take notes of what a witness says. First, while a witness is giving evidence-in-chief you may need to note a point for cross-examination, or for your closing speech, as appropriate. This might be needed where a witness says something that did not appear in any written statement, or where some point can be made about the exact words that a witness uses. Secondly, during a cross-examination you may need to note what the witness says for re-examination or for your closing speech. Remember that you may need to note what a witness says while you are questioning them, as well as asking questions and dealing with replies.

4.7.3 CLOSING SPEECH

Basic notes for a closing speech will often be made while you are preparing the case for court — you can note what the main lines of argument and the main strengths of the case are, and organise a suitable order for dealing with them. Some notes must be made in advance as you will often have limited opportunity to work on your closing speech while the case is in progress, especially early in practice. In addition, these notes will need to be reviewed during the case, in the light of arguments made by the other side and the evidence that is produced.

Some people say that good advocacy stems from a good closing speech — you decide what you will say and everything else is then constructed to build up to it. This is probably only true for big criminal cases, but it does emphasise the importance of coherent and detailed case planning.

4.7.4 SUMMING-UP

While it is not necessary to take full notes of the summing-up, you should be ready to take notes of important points, not least because you may wish to refer to what the judge said on an appeal. While it may be possible to get transcripts from court, this will take time, and it can be valuable to have your own note to work with. On drafting grounds of appeal based on a summing-up, see the *Drafting Manual*.

4.7.5 JUDGMENT

Judgments are written out in law reports, and in most courts are recorded, so why should a barrister ever need to write them down personally? You only need to know if you won or lost, how much, and what is to happen about costs.

This reaction is to some extent true. You do not need notes of a whole judgment. But you frequently need some notes from a judgment, for example:

(a) to explain the details of a judgment to the client,

(b) to decide whether to appeal,

(c) to decide on what basis to appeal, if some grounds turn on precisely what the judge said.

Even when transcripts of judgments are available they take time and cost money, so you may well need a sufficient note on which to give basic advice and take decisions. Notes may also be important for drafting grounds of appeal.

4.8 Note-taking in other Contexts

The note-taking skills described in this chapter may be applied to other aspects of the lawyer's work. There is, for example, the need to take notes in carrying out a negotiation. It is important to make notes in advance of what your options are, what is the most and least you might achieve and so on. You also need to take notes during the negotiation, of anything that the other side reveals and of anything that is agreed.

There is also the need to take a proper note of a telephone conversation. It is increasingly common for barristers to give advice over the telephone, but all too often the barrister does not write anything down and has to be reminded of the whole case if the solicitor comes back for further advice. When advising by telephone, or simply using the telephone to get further information, taking a full and clear written note is important.

Finally, there are two particularly important possibilities for the young barrister. First, your pupil master will almost certainly ask you to take notes during conferences, and a clear note that you can refer to quickly to check points or that you can hand over to be kept with the brief will impress. Secondly, in early practice one is often asked to do devilling work on a brief, which will frequently involve organising and making notes. Again, if this is done well it will impress.

4.9   Shorthand

The importance of an ability to take good notes in almost every skill the barrister uses has been outlined already. One central element of note-taking is a need to write quickly. You may already be able to write shorthand, or you may already have devised your own methods of abbreviation. However, many students will not be familiar with a speed-writing system, and others may well be able to improve their approach. This chapter gives guidance on speed-writing. It is adapted from *Self-Shorthand* by C. G. L. Du Cann (London: Council of Legal Education, 3rd edn, 1982).

4.9.1   WHY CREATE YOUR OWN SYSTEM OF SELF-SHORTHAND?

It will enable you to take notes much more rapidly than, and just as accurately as, longhand. It may enable you to dispense with the drudgery of learning an established shorthand system, and yet gain for yourself all the advantages you personally need of shorthand. It will lessen your labours and save your time for more important use than mere transcription.

4.9.2   ELEMENTS OF A SYSTEM OF SELF-SHORTHAND

4.9.2.1   Initials
You already know, and probably use, hundreds of nationally recognised initials. This is the foundation of your extended use of initials.

Read the list given in any good dictionary, once or twice if you wish.

In general, you will find that such as you need will 'stick'. Besides, most of them speak adequately for themselves and cannot be confused with anything else.

These accepted initials are permanencies. That is a great advantage. Another great advantage is that they are generally understood.

Use initials with discretion. So long as it is not going to mislead, confuse, puzzle or delay you, they are invaluable. Remember that context is everything. If the word 'government' occurs over and over again and no other word such as 'God', which might be confused with it in interpretation and transcription, the letter 'G' will stand very well for 'government' and save the writing of nine letters wherever it occurs. In one piece of writing, hundreds of letters may be saved.

4.9.2.2   Abbreviations: national and professional
Abbreviations are of the utmost importance. Some which are nationally recognised you know already and have probably more or less accepted before you ever thought of self-shorthand.

'Abbreviate the abbreviations wherever practicable' says self-shorthand. Very often it **is** practicable. For the nationally recognised abbreviations were not scientifically thought out to the best advantage; they grew like a wild plant.

Applying the important principle of 'abbreviating the abbreviations' to the weekdays, for example, we can get down to 'MWF' for 'Monday, Wednesday and Friday', but 'T' and 'S' would equally stand for 'Tuesday' and 'Thursday' and 'Saturday' and 'Sunday'. Clearly then, you cannot abbreviate down to initials in this instance.

But by the aid of another principle, the small-letter principle — to be explained below — we may overcome this difficulty. M^y, T^y, W^y, Th^y, F^y, St^y, S^y will do very we$^{ll\ indeed}$.

Make a habit of this abbreviated abbreviation and think of the time and labour saved in a lifetime.

Never use an abbreviation, however conventional and nationally recognised, where a briefer and equally intelligible abbreviation exists. Be on the look-out for abbreviations which can be abbreviated, and cut them ruthlessly.

The set of professional abbreviations of the greatest general importance to the ordinary person is that of the journalistic and printing occupations.

There is a well recognised list of these in all publishing, journalistic and printing establishments. Most of these were agreed as long ago as the International Shorthand Congress of 1887.

List of abbreviations for longhand

A	a	.(a dot on the line)
	about	abt
	according	acc
	account	acct
	advertisement	ad
	affectionate	aff
	affectionately	aff^{ly}
	afternoon	aft^n
	again	ag^n
	against	ag^{st}
	American	Amer
	among	am^g
	amount	am^t
	ance (suffix at end of words)	-ce
B	because	b^{ec}
	been	b^n
	between	b^{tn}
	brought	bro^t
C	caught	ca^t
	chairman	ch^m
	circumstance	cir^{ce}
	committee	com^e (or cte)
	could	c^d
D	difference	dif^{ce}
	different	dif^t
	difficult	dif^{clt}
	difficulty	dif^{clty}

E	-ence	-ce
	England, English	Eng.
	especially	esp
	evening	ev^g
	ever	-r
	every	ev^r
	excellent	exc.
F	faithfully	ff^y
	for	f
	Friday	Fri
	from	f^m
	further	fur^r
G	general	gen
	generally	gen^y
	good	g^d
	government	gov^t
	great	g^t
H	had	h^d
	have	h
I	importance	imp^{ce}
	important	imp^t
	-ing	g
	-ion	n
L	large	lge
M	manuscript	Ms
	meeting	m^{tg}
	-ment	m^t
	Monday	Mon
	morning	m^g
N	notwithstanding	notw^g
O	objection	obj^n
	occasion	occ^n
	o'clock	o'c
	of	o
	opinion	op^n
	opportunity	pp^y
	other	o^r
	ought	o^t
P	page, pages	p. pp.
	particular	part^r
	popular	pop
Q	query	q^y
	question	q^n
	quotation	quot
S	said	s^d
	Saturday	Sat
	several	sev^l
	shall	sh
	should	sh^d
	-sion	n

	specially	spec
	Sunday	Sun
T	that	t
	the	/ (the first stroke of t)
	their, there	th^r
	though	tho
	through	thro
	Thursday	Thurs
	-tion	n
	together	tog^r
	truly	ty
	Tuesday	Tues
V	very	v or v^y
	very good	vg
W	Wednesday	Wed
	whether	wh^r
	which	wh
	with	w
	without	w^t
	would	w^d
Y	yesterday	$yest^y$ or y'day
	you	y
	your	y^r
	yours	yrs

These handsomely repay learning by heart. Many of them are self-suggestive so they are easy to master. Many of them, as already pointed out — notably the days of the week — can be further abbreviated.

But they will not only repay learning. They repay being studied. Note the *principles* behind them. Our initial principle is here. So is small-size and positional writing. So is the use of symbols like the dot for an 'a' and 'an' and the simple down-stroke for 'the'.

4.9.2.3 Conventional spelling

Like the Americans, take the needless 'u' out of words like 'labour' and 'honour' at all times. But, of course, such words as these you can abbreviate further, for lab' and hon' are intelligible beyond confusion or mistake.

Cut suffixes like -ette to 'et'. So write 'cigaret', 'suffraget' at the most, while you can at the least write 'cig' for 'cigar' and 'ci^{gt}' for 'cigarette'.

You will have noted the superfluous apostrophe in words like 'don't' and 'can't' and others. It reminds us — unnecessarily — that a letter has been eliminated. In rapid writing the reminder is inopportune and distracting. So cut out the apostrophe as a set policy. Write 'cant', 'dont', 'wont', 'shouldnt'.

4.9.2.4 Fast-writing habits

Practice is the chief secret of success. But some people's writing lends itself to rapidity. A cursive or running style of handwriting is best. If you have a slow, crabbed hand through wrong teaching or wrong imitation when young, it may be difficult to adopt a new hand.

So eliminate unnecessary loops, for instance, both top and bottom. Journalists, who are fast-writers from professional necessity, have a habit of joining words. This helps speed. It is a habit worth adopting, as it obviates delay caused by lifting the pen from the paper.

4.9.2.5   Small and large-letter principles

In **4.9.2.2** you met the small-letter principle. It spoke for itself at once, and showed how useful and important it was.

The large-letter principle will cause you no difficulty.

For example, take the letter 'A':

Archbishop	Ab^p
Abridge	Ab^r
Absolutely	Abs^{ly}
Acceptance	A^{cc}
Acknowledgement	Ack^t
Affirmative	$Afft^{ive}$
Aeroplane	A^{pln}
Affidavit	$Aff^t t$
Agriculture	Ag^{ture}
Agent	Ag^t
Appendix	App^x
Archdeacon	$Arch^d$
Astronomy	Ast^y
Assistant	Ass^t
Average	Av^{ge}

Positional and small-size writing are useful in calling attention to abbreviated forms. You met with it in **4.9.2.2** at the ends of words like 'should' being written 'sh'. But it can be applied to beginnings as well as to ends of words, just as advantageously. Use it for prefixes as well as suffixes.

Thus the prefix 'con' — or 'com' — is frequent and can be indicated by a small 'c' positionally written, for example:

content may be written ctnt
compromise may be written cprme

And 'circum' can be equally well written by a small 'c'. If you feel you must distinguish it from the symbolic letter 'c' for 'con' or 'com' you can use 'cstroke' thus: 'c/'.

circumference — c/fmce
circumflex — c/flx

Other prefixes can be similarly reduced. Further examples are the very frequently occurring 'per' and 'pro'. Thus:

proposition — p/pstn
proposal — p/psl

while 'per' can take the small raised 'p' as in:

perspicuity — ^{p}spct

thus clearly distinguishing it from:

prospect — p/spct

Prefixes and suffixes, in fact, are one of the most fertile fields for the ingenuity of the self-shorthand writer.

4.9.2.6   Eliminations

Often the words 'a', 'an' and 'the' can be omitted without loss. So can formal words like 'the member' or 'this ancient and honourable society', for the transcriber will recollect such formal adjectives.

Thus write 'hm' and 'hr' for 'him' and 'her', for such contractions cannot be mistaken for any other word.

Sometimes two or even more vowels can be dropped with real safety. Thus:

'plain' can be written 'pln'
'contentment' can be written 'ctmtt'.

4.9.2.7   Key words and recurrent expressions

This should remind the student that in self-shorthand one must always have regard to the context. It is the context which governs key words and recurrent expressions and how they are represented.

For example 'deft' is the recognised legal abbreviation for 'defendant', and a very useful abbreviation it is. But a note-taking judge, magistrate, barrister or non-phonographic reporter in court will not keep writing four letters when one will do all that is wanted. A capital 'D' is enough here — though on other occasions a capital 'D' might well mean something other than 'defendant'.

4.9.2.8   Arbitrary symbols

Do not be afraid of using arbitrary symbols, even if they are algebra to other people. Use them freely according to your convenience. But recollect that the more they spring naturally from the word or phrase they represent, the easier they are to decipher and to remember.

4.9.2.9   The commonest words

The self-shorthand writer needs, of course, to pay special attention to the commonest, that is to say, the most frequently occurring words in the English language. Obviously to make and learn abbreviations for these is of special importance. The 12 commonest words are also 12 of the shortest. These 12 words, it is authoritatively stated, make up 25% of all normal English, whether written or spoken.

1. a or an	7. that
2. and	8. in
3. the	9. any
4. of	10. to
5. be	11. is
6. it	12. his

4.9.3   WARNING

Never get so involved in taking notes of what is being said by a client or witness that you fail to listen and watch for the non-verbal clues which will help you understand what is being said and whether it can be believed.

FIVE

MODES OF ADDRESS

5.1   Introduction

Whenever you appear as an advocate you should always know the correct way to address the person or people who are in court to decide the issues of law and fact. Using an incorrect title is a sign of possible disrespect or inexperience. Most judges and magistrates will not object strongly to being addressed by an incorrect title, so you may not realise until later, if then, that you had risked upsetting the court. Of course, some judges do mind and will soon let you know if they think that your choice of title is inappropriate. You may find that their chosen response is to say, rather obscurely, 'I can't hear you, Miss Jones.' Your response may be simply to talk louder, assuming that either you are speaking too quietly or the poor old judge is a little deaf! What they mean by this expression is not that they can't hear you but that they won't — you sometimes get a similar response if a judge thinks you are dressed inappropriately for their court. With luck, your opponent will realise what the judge's objection is about and help you out, if possible.

If you are unlucky, the judge won't tell you about your gaffe, but will simply sit there and smoulder! Your chances of persuading the judge to decide in your client's favour may be diminishing with every fresh example of the slight. As a novice advocate, you will get much of your early experience in the magistrates' court or County Court, so you will become used to addressing the court as 'Sir/Madam' or 'Your Honour'. Problems may then arise if you are sent to the High Court, and confusion may increase if your appearance there is before a circuit judge, sitting as a judge of the High Court!

A few years ago, a very junior barrister appeared at the Old Bailey in a hearing with several more experienced barristers. He was the last one to address the judge and his task should have been a simple one; sadly, although most of what he said made sense, he addressed the judge several times as 'Sir'. This was a considerable slight since any Crown Court judge is entitled to be called 'Your Honour' and, even worse, anyone sitting as a judge in the Old Bailey is entitled to be addressed as 'My Lord/Lady'. The judge said nothing but sat there and glowered fiercely at the young barrister. The barrister eventually realised that something was up but could not think what, until he noticed that counsel sitting by his side was muttering something. The young barrister's first reaction was to think, 'How rude'; his second was to listen to what his colleague was muttering. It was 'My Lord — **my Lord**'. Realising his error, the barrister apologised at once, the judge recovered his previous complexion and everything went as planned thereafter.

In order to avoid similar embarrassment yourself, read the rest of this chapter with care.

Figure 5.1   Modes of address

Youth Court **and** **Magistrates' Court**	District Judge (formerly Stipendiary Magistrate): Chairman of Lay Bench: Members of Lay Bench:	'Sir/Madam' 'Sir/Madam' 'Your colleagues'
Tribunals	Chairman: Other members:	'Sir/Madam' 'Your colleagues'
County Court	Circuit Judge: Recorder or any person sitting as a deputy Circuit Judge: District Judge:	'Your Honour' 'Your Honour' 'Sir/Madam'
Crown Court	High Court Judge: Circuit Judge: Recorder or any person sitting as adeputy Circuit Judge: Exceptions [see: PD [1982] 1 All ER 320]: Central Criminal Court – any person sitting as a Judge: Recorder of Manchester/ Liverpool:	'My Lord/My Lady' 'Your Honour' 'Your Honour' 'My Lord/My Lady' 'My Lord/My Lady'
High Court	Judge: Any Circuit Judge sitting as a Judge of the High Court: District Judge: Master:	'My Lord/My Lady' 'My Lord/My Lady' 'Sir/Madam' 'Master'
Court of Appeal	Lord Justice:	'My Lord/My Lady'
House of Lords	Lord of Appeal in Ordinary:	'My Lord'

5.2   Using the Correct Form of Address

5.2.1   VOCATIVE/ACCUSATIVE

The way in which you address the court may vary depending upon whether you are using the vocative case (i.e., calling upon the judge as if by name) or the accusative case (i.e., in place of 'you').

   (a)   Where the correct form of address is 'Sir/Madam', 'Master' or 'Your Honour' there is no real distinction between addressing the court in the vocative or accusative cases.

       Examples:

       Vocative:
       '*Sir/Madam*, the defendant is content for the matter to be dealt with today.'
       'In my submission, *Master*, the claimant has failed to show a total failure of consideration.'
       '*Your Honour*, there are three affidavits in this case.'

       Accusative:
       'May it please you, *Sir/Madam*.'
       'If you look at the document marked "A", *Master*, you will see that ...'
       'Does *Your Honour* have a copy of the defendant's antecedents?' (Note: you should avoid calling a Circuit Court judge 'you'.)

(b) There is, however, a marked difference between the appropriate use of 'My Lord/My Lady' and 'Your Lordship/Your Ladyship'. Use 'My Lord/My Lady' whenever you are addressing the judge in the vocative sense. Use 'Your Lordship/Your Ladyship' in place of 'you'.

Examples:

Vocative:

'*My Lord*, the third defendant has taken no part in these proceedings.'
'I am obliged, *my Lady*.'

Accusative:

'May it please *Your Lordship*.'

'I am happy to tell *Your Lordship* that the parties have reached terms in this matter.'

'Does *Your Ladyship* have the claimant's affidavit sworn on the 13th March 2002?'

(c) It is perfectly acceptable to combine both forms of address in one sentence.

Example:

'*My Lady*, if I may deal with the points which *Your Ladyship* has raised ...'

(d) Use 'His Lordship/Her Ladyship' and 'His Honour/Her Honour' in place of 'him' or 'her', i.e., when referring to the judge in the third person.

Examples:

'Describe the layout of the room to *His Lordship*.'
'Tell *Her Honour* what you saw when you entered the room.'

5.2.2 HYBRID SITUATIONS

Figure 5.1 shows the way to address a person who is sitting as a deputy Circuit or High Court judge. Some confusion, however, arises where a Circuit Court judge is sitting also as a deputy judge of the High Court in order to hear a mixed list, i.e., some County Court and some High Court cases. In these circumstances, it is the case itself which determines the mode of address. If your case is a County Court matter, address the judge as 'Your Honour'. If the case is a High Court matter, address the judge as 'My Lord/My Lady'. Note, however, that if a High Court judge hears a case which is listed as a County Court matter, he or she must still be addressed as 'My Lord/My Lady' and not demoted!

Another hybrid situation occurs when it is necessary to see the judge in his or her private room, e.g., to seek an indication regarding sentence (for the limited circumstances in which this might be appropriate see *R* v *Turner* [1970] 2 QB 321). In this situation, address the judge as 'Judge'.

5.2.3 REFERRING TO ANOTHER JUDGE

It is often necessary to refer the court to (the judgment of) another judge. In so doing, use his or her proper title.

Examples:

Refer to 'Roper J' as 'Mr Justice Roper'.
Refer to 'Roper LJ' as 'Lord Justice Roper'.

5.2.4 SOCIAL OCCASIONS

Occasionally, you may meet a judge socially, for instance, on the train to court. The proper form of address in these circumstances is simply 'Judge'.

SIX

QUESTIONING TECHNIQUES

6.1   Introduction

This chapter provides a brief introduction to the different types of questioning and techniques that you will need to grasp and be able to apply when conducting the examination of witnesses.

6.2   The Open-ended Question

This is a question that does not limit the scope of the answer. The witness will usually give a narrative answer.

Examples:

Q: 'What happened after he struck you?'
Q: 'Why did you telephone her?'
Q: 'Where did you go after you left the police station?'
Q: 'How did you cope at work with one arm in plaster?'

This type of question is particularly useful when you want the witness to tell the story or part of it in his or her own words. It helps to move the story along. It can, however, allow the witness too much scope for 'rambling' off the point and overuse of open questions risks a loss of control.

6.3   The Closed Question

This is a question which limits the scope of the answer. It is particularly useful when you are seeking to elicit a particular piece of information or detail from a witness. It allows much greater control of the witness than an open question.

Examples:

Q: 'What time was it?'
Q: 'How far away were you at that point?'
Q: 'In which hand was he holding the gun?'

6.4   The Transition

Transitions are a means of moving the witness from one piece of evidence or topic to another. They are like paragraph breaks or headings. They communicate a change of topic or place to the witness and also to the court. They may take the form of a statement such as 'I want to turn now to the moment when the ambulance arrived', or a question (either open or closed) such as 'After that day, when did you next see the defendant?' Transitions are a useful way of structuring the testimony, controlling the witness and pruning irrelevant details at the same time.

Suppose, for example, you wish to elicit two pieces of evidence from the witness:

(a) that she was present in the doctor's surgery on the day in question; and

(b) approximately 20 minutes after her arrival, she heard the defendant threaten the doctor.

After establishing the witness's presence in the waiting room at the doctor's surgery, you might ask:

Q: 'What, if anything, happened then?'
A: 'Well, I picked up a magazine from the table, you know one of those fancy ones, I think it was *Country Life*. As I was reading it, they have such beautiful pictures in it you know, Mrs Reid from down my road came in with her Sandra who had this awful chest cold. Mrs Reid was telling me about the arthritis in her hands and the pain she was in. Then we heard this commotion and all of a sudden, Brian Peters came storming out of the doctor's room shouting that he'd be back and that next time he'd make sure the doctor never practised again ...'

Although you got there in the end, it would have been much more effective if you had used a transitional question instead, for example:

Q: 'Did there come a time when something unusual/unexpected happened while you were sitting in the waiting room?'
A: 'Oh yes. I was sitting chatting to Mrs Reid about her arthritis' (there is a limit to the extent you can control some witnesses!) 'when we heard this terrible commotion. All of a sudden, Brian Peters came storming out ...'.

6.5 The Point of Reference (or 'Piggy-Back Question')

This is the method of including in your question a fact or facts which have already been elicited from the witness. It provides a context for the question and is a useful technique for emphasising an important fact, clarifying the evidence, obtaining greater detail from the witness, controlling the witness and/or providing a transition.

Examples:

Q: 'What happened directly after you heard Miss Jones scream?' — emphasis and detail.
Q: 'When you said he left, to whom were you referring?' — clarification.
Q: 'Describe the knife you saw in the defendant's hand' — emphasis and detail.
Q: 'Did you see Mr Green again after he left your office that afternoon?' — transition and control.

Note that a point of reference can be included in either an open or closed question and form part of a transitional question.

6.6 Leading Questions

A leading question is one that suggests or tends to suggest its own answer. It usually calls for a 'yes' or 'no' response. It often assumes a fact that has not yet been established.

Examples:

'Were you in Manchester on 5 May 2002?'
'Did you see the knife in his hand?'
'Was she standing three feet away from you?'

A non-leading question in the same circumstances would have been:

'Where were you on 5 May 2002?' (date not in dispute).
'What did you see?'
'How far away was she?'

A leading question undermines the witness's credibility. It leaves the impression that you are afraid to let the witness open his or her mouth. It allows you to give the evidence yourself—that is not your function! It is for the witness to tell his or her account to the court. As a general rule, it is therefore not permitted to elicit evidence in **examination-in-chief** by the use of leading questions. There are two exceptions to this general rule.

6.6.1 CIRCUMSTANCES IN WHICH A LEADING QUESTION MAY BE ASKED DURING EXAMINATION-IN-CHIEF

6.6.1.1 A leading question may be asked when the subject matter is not in dispute

Example:

There is no dispute that the parties met at the claimant's office on the evening of 10 March 2002.
Q: 'Did you meet the defendant at your office on the evening of 10 March 2002?'

Sometimes one piece of information is agreed while another is not.

Example:

There is no dispute that the parties met on the evening of 10 March 2002. The time of the meeting is in dispute.
Q: 'Did you meet the defendant on the evening of 10 March 2002.'
A: 'Yes.'
Q: 'What time did you meet?'

Example:

There is no dispute that the parties met one evening at the claimant's office. The date is in dispute.

Q: 'Do you recall an evening when you met the defendant at your office?'
A: 'Yes.'
Q: 'When was that?'

Counsel often use a leading question when the subject matter is unlikely to be contentious. For instance, where there is unlikely to be any dispute that a conversation took place, counsel might ask 'Did you have a conversation with the defendant?'. It is important to differentiate between the fact of a conversation taking place and what was said during that conversation. One may be in dispute while the other is not. If in doubt, check with your opponent.

6.6.1.2 A leading question is permitted when you are seeking to elicit a denial from your own witness as to his or her own alleged conduct

Example:

Q: 'Did you tell Mr Smith on 4 January 2002 that he was "dead meat"?'
A: 'No.'

What is in reality a leading question may appear to be non-leading by the simple device of offering the witness limited choices. As a matter of common sense, the answer must be one or the other.

Example:

Q: 'Were you in this country or abroad on 6 February last?'

In this example, the answer is suggested in the question, in the sense that the witness will select one or other option. This type of question, although leading in its strictest sense, is rarely objectionable. It has the advantage of enabling you to guide the witness where you want him or her to go. Note that the non-leading version is to ask 'Where were you on 6 February last?'.

6.7 Non-leading Questions

How then do you formulate your questions so as to avoid asking your witness a leading question? There are two basic methods you can use:

(a)   Start your questions neutrally with one of the following interrogatories:

Who ... ?
What ... ?
Why ... ?
When ... ?
Where ... ?
How ...?

Or with a neutral invitation:

Tell	Describe
Explain	Demonstrate

These will enable you to elicit the answer from the witness. Generally avoid asking questions which start with the words 'Did you ... ?', 'Were you ... ?', or 'Was it ... ?' — these will normally contain suggestion(s) and tend to lead!

(b)   Another basic way is to think of the answer you wish your witness to give and then omit any reference to the answer when framing the question. The question should come quite naturally.

Examples:

Answer required: 'Sunday'.
Q: 'What day was it?'
NOT (a leading question):   'Was it a Sunday?'

Answer required: 'Blue jeans and a white t-shirt'
Q: 'Describe what he was wearing.'
NOT: 'Was he wearing blue jeans and a white t-shirt?'

Answer required: '(He left) three weeks ago.'
Q: 'When did he leave?'
NOT: 'Did he leave three weeks ago?'

The above illustrations show the advantage of preparing by using short headings or points. You should see the benefit of a simple form of 'bullet point' preparation such as: 'Setting the scene — Sun/8 pm/wet?'.

6.8   Combining Questioning Techniques

If you use too many open-ended questions you run the risk of losing control of the witness and too much irrelevance clouding his or her testimony. If you use too many closed questions, you will leave the court with the impression that the witness is a robot whom you have pre-programmed. Instead, achieve a balance by combining these techniques for the maximum effect:

(a)   ask open questions to allow the witness to tell his or her story;

(b)   ask closed questions to elicit details from the witness or emphasise part of the story;

(c)   ask open questions to enable the witness to continue with the next part of the story;

(d)   ask closed questions to elicit details, and so on.

This is sometimes referred to as the funnel technique.

6.9   In Summary

Leading questions	Non-leading questions
(Avoid in examination-in-chief; use in cross-examination)	(Use in examination-in-chief; avoid in cross-examination)
Did you?	Who?
Didn't you?	What?
Were you?	Why?
Weren't you?	When?
Was it?	Where?
Wasn't it?	How?
You saw/did/said . . .	Tell/Describe
	Explain/Demonstrate

SEVEN

THE ADVOCATE AS A STORYTELLER

7.1   Introduction

We can often remember quite easily the earliest stories we were told and, if we have children, we are quite confident that we can recall and tell those stories to them. It may be that we can remember those tales just because we were young and our memories were very absorbent; it may also be because the stories were clear and had a simple structure. Also, the storyteller seemed to be familiar with the story so that they were fluent, had a confident manner and perhaps were able to do other things at the same time as telling the story (for example, monitor the listener's attention — 'Are you listening to me?').

We don't remember those stories because we can easily identify with their situations — mermaids and flying horses, talking animals and sentient toys — but the good storyteller will engage the listener's imagination. They are transported into a form of acceptance and we might call this a form of **persuasion**.

When telling a story, it is always a good idea to have a clear leitmotif (or recurrent theme associated with a particular person, idea or situation) and our childhood stories are full of those, even down to the names of the characters. What does the listener recall of the story later? All of it or just bits and pieces? If the 'story' is the evidence at a trial, then the advocate may want to ensure that the listener does indeed recall only bits and further that only those bits which favour the client are recalled. How might the advocate do this?

Perhaps the most important step is to decide whether the story is acceptable to the listener; does it 'fit' with the listener's idea of how the world and humankind work? Everyone who sits in court to adjudicate on competing versions of the 'facts' in a case brings with them some prior knowledge and beliefs about how things work, what makes people act in certain ways or what they mean when they say certain things. If your client's story fits better into that wealth of knowledge and beliefs than your opponent's story, you have the advantage in persuading your audience to find the facts as you allege them to be. Alternatively, since you are likely to have to present your client's story as it is, rather than as you might like it to be (an ethical requirement), you may need to think about strategies to adopt in order to alter the mindset of your listener, so that the story becomes more acceptable and so more credible.

Much has been written on the importance of story-telling as a part of the persuasive process. The rest of this chapter tries to put this into context for advocates.

7.2   Why Should an Advocate be Able to Tell a Story?

It is important for an advocate to be able to tell a story well. You must, of course, obey the rules of professional conduct (e.g., not to mislead the court) and you must always use information supplied by your instructing solicitors (usually from the lay client), rather than making it up for yourself (!). But the essence of proceedings in the courts of England and Wales is their oral nature. For a barrister, this is most obvious when you are called on to make a speech in a trial. This is your opportunity to present your story to the court. When you look at the chapters on speeches, bear this in mind.

The section on fact management in the *Case Preparation Manual* (**14.6.2**) refers to the concept of **themes** as part of the preparation for trial. For example

> The theme . . . may be defined as that part of the 'story' presented in court which the lawyer selects and presents because of its particularly persuasive effect in relation to the ultimate conclusion which the lawyer wants the tribunal of fact to draw.

Much of the story which is involved in a trial cannot be told, maybe because of:

(a) lack of witnesses at the time of trial; or

(b) rules of evidence (e.g., rule against hearsay); or

(c) it is legally irrelevant to the issues in dispute at the trial.

A good example is the Bodkin Adams prosecution at the Old Bailey in the 1950s. Several books have since been written about the case and its defendant, Dr John Bodkin Adams. This, in itself, might suggest that the whole story did not emerge at the trial. In what is perhaps the most authoritative work on the topic, by the trial judge (then Devlin J), Lord Devlin devotes several pages to a consideration of the opening speech for the Crown by the Attorney-General. He then concludes:

> . . . the whole story of Dr Adams was not told at the trial. The story emerges from his long years in practice at Eastbourne during which he acquired a curious reputation as a legacy hunter. It slips through the death of Mrs Morrell in 1950 which passed unnoticed at the time. It bursts into the news in August 1956 after an inquest has been held on the body of another wealthy patient, Mrs Hullett. After that the rumours spread to cover many other names, including that of Mrs Hullett's husband who had died six months before her.

> So it came as no surprise to the public to hear in December 1956 that Dr Adams had been arrested and charged with murder. What was a surprise was that he was charged with the murder, not of Mrs Hullett, but of Mrs Morrell who had died so long before [1950]. Then, when the preliminary proceedings in the Morrell case were begun before the Eastbourne magistrates in January 1957, the public learnt that the Crown would be calling evidence to show that Dr Adams, although not formally charged with the murder of either Mrs or Mr Hullett, had in fact murdered both of them. But when the trial began at the Old Bailey nothing at all was said about the Hulletts. The name was not mentioned until the last day after Dr Adams had been acquitted. Many people believe that, if the doctor had been tried for the murder of Mrs Hullett instead of Mrs Morrell, he would have been convicted.

Good advocates can make an implausible story sound credible; even a poor orator will benefit from having a good story to tell.

7.3   The Story

Plausibility is often a good foundation in telling a story. Do all your facts fit together? What was the defendant's motive for committing the act? Is that how most people behave? Is it how the court might believe someone in your client's position might behave? This represents the contents of your story. You will need to consider these contents before starting a trial. In choosing your theory of the case before trial, you have to consider the cause of action; the issues that you must prove; and the admissible evidence at your disposal.

7.3.1 EXAMPLE

Let us take an example. At the end of **7.5** there is a criminal case, *R* v *Heath*. Take 15 minutes to read it now.

Now consider the evidence which is available to both prosecution and defence. From the standpoint of prosecuting counsel, what is your story? An everyday story in these depressing times, of mindless violence out of all proportion to any provocation? Or is it an argument, started by an over-reaction from the landlord and ending with an unreasonable piece of self-defence from the accused? Has this been a row simmering for months, since Heath was convicted and barred from the pub? Is Heath a simple lager lout or a more cunning thug with a preconceived plan? Was the glassing done on the spur of the moment? Or was this another episode in the continuing jealousy of Heath and John Bull in their rivalry for the affections of the barmaid, Tracey Croft?

To a large extent, these matters and the choices you make have nothing to do with what we are concerned with at the trial. That is determined by the counts on the indictment and the criminal law. But to be plausible, to be persuasive, the evidence that you use at trial must make sense in human as well as legal terms. It really is not enough to call witnesses to say they saw Kevin Heath push a beer mug into a publican's face — if at all possible, your story should explain why this happened.

To return to a trial mentioned earlier, *R* v *Bodkin Adams*, it may be that the indictment was too restrictive to allow a truly credible story to be told (see Lord Devlin's observations cited above). But you must work with whatever material you have to convince the triers of the facts that your story is the correct one. It matters not whether your trial is in the magistrates' court, in front of a jury or a High Court judge — your audience is always more likely to accept a story which fits in with their beliefs, knowledge, experiences and prejudices.

7.4 The Telling

Our focus is shifting now, away from the story itself to the listeners. They will judge (quite literally) whether you have told a good story or not. In part they will be assessing the story but also they will be assessing you and the way in which you told the story.

Since story-telling can occur at the start of the trial (or your client's part of it) as an opening speech or at its conclusion, as a closing speech, you may find that the 'ideal' story you told at the start has had to be modified by the end because of the evidence that has emerged or the demeanour of certain witnesses in giving their evidence. What you can and should do is: repeat key words or phrases throughout the case, use them frequently so that they can be leitmotifs of characters, places or situations. Choose the elements of your story with care, e.g., if you are relying on a particular interpretation of an incident, how likely is it that your audience will accept that interpretation as likely or credible? If a 13-year-old tells her headmaster that she was late for school because she was abducted by aliens from Alpha Centauri, she is unlikely to be believed. If she repeats the story to a meeting of the local UFO society, she may well be believed. Although the ability to adduce hard evidence to back up our stories always helps, the more the story fits in with the way our listeners see the world, the more likely they are to accept it. So, the point to remember is, know your audience.

Always use language that your listener will understand easily. Barristers in a trial often use only a few documents; information is communicated by word of mouth so your meaning must be readily comprehensible to your listener. If you want the audience to absorb your points, don't rush and don't become prolix. The most memorable points are often the shortest ones. Be fluent, making sure pauses are deliberate and have some purpose. Use short simple sentences. Avoid subordinate clauses like the plague. They are very tempting, especially when while uttering one thought another occurs to you and you have a concern that unless you fit the idea within the sentence you are delivering you will forget it. Sometimes you can. Generally, however, you will lose the proper impact of both ideas. You may lose your main verb. You are likely to lose your subject and your object. By then you will have forgotten how you started the sentence and will not have the faintest idea how to finish it. Your aim must be to construct sentences which are grammatically correct. They are so much easier to listen to and consequently much more likely to persuade.

Be sparing with gestures. Arms flailing like the sails of a windmill do not add to the force of any argument and they are tiring to watch. Any gestures used should be deliberately chosen solely to add emphasis to the words you are using. Above all, stand still. Do not fiddle with papers or with the keys in your pocket or your buttons or anything. Such constant, restless, mindless movement distracts and will eventually irritate your audience.

7.5   Exercises

You may want to practise your story-telling abilities; after all, anyone can read a good story but it takes a lot of practice and hard work to be able to transport your listeners into your story — for example, to take the jury at Croydon Crown Court back to Christmas Eve 2000, in the bar of The Cutpurse pub in New Addington (*R* v *Heath*); or to the homes of the rich and elderly in Eastbourne who were the (now deceased) patients of Dr Bodkin Adams.

It may be quite useful to start practising story-telling in a non-legal context. Choose a situation with which you are more familiar and which does not have the same restrictions as a legal trial. The following exercises are suggested.

EXERCISE 1

Using one of the following scenarios, devise a short story (no longer than five minutes). Try to commit it to memory so that, when you try to relate it to a colleague, your performance is fluent.

Consider the information that you want to convey, whether there are any key words or phrases that you could use. Perhaps most important, think about your audience — who are they, what sympathies might they have, what might their 'official' attitude be towards you or your story?

(a)   You are a pupil at school who has missed 'gym' and are about to go before the Head Master to explain your absence (your third missed class this term).

(b)   You are an employee of a large company. Yesterday you were late for work (fifth time this month) and you are now waiting to see the Supervisor who has asked you to explain your latest absence and why it keeps happening.

(c)   You have been charged with stealing property from a car on 3 September 2000. You are about to keep an appointment with your solicitor. You told her on the telephone that you are not guilty and have an alibi, with potential witnesses. She asked you to come and give her the details of the alibi.

(d)   Your bicycle is in collision with a van on the road. The van driver does not seem injured; you have several cuts and grazes and a terrible pain in one of your arms. The police have been called and now an officer wants you to tell her what happened.

EXERCISE 2

Find a set of statements and instructions in a case that you can use (perhaps the *Heath* case at the end of this chapter, or from one of the other Manuals or from a cooperative barrister). Study the papers for, say, an hour then report the case orally to a friend in

45 minutes. The following day, present your report in 25 minutes and, on the third day, tell it in 15 minutes to someone who knows nothing about the case. Each time, see if this 'stranger' has grasped the essential points of the case. This will help you to distil your stories to their essence; it should also ensure that your stories are ones that stay in the mind(s) of your audience. These times may be varied according to the size and complexity of the case (e.g., if you use the following case the times would be considerably shorter).

A Criminal Case: *R* v *Heath*

<u>BRIEF FOR THE PROSECUTION</u>

R

v

KEVIN HEATH

Counsel has herewith:

(1) Indictment

(2) Committal statements

(3) Defendant's antecedents and previous convictions

(4) Witnesses' previous convictions

(5) Statement of Defence in accordance with the Criminal Procedure and Investigations Act 1996.

Counsel is instructed in the prosecution of the above-named Defendant who faces the 2 counts shown on the indictment.

The facts emerge clearly from the statements. The reviewing lawyer takes the view that a plea to s. 20 GBH would not be acceptable.

Counsel will note that two of the prosecution witnesses have previous convictions. The defence must be told of these, whether or not they ask for them, in accordance with the decision in *R* v *Collister and Warhurst* (1955) 39 Cr App R 100.

IN THE CROWN COURT AT CROYDON

THE QUEEN

v

KEVIN HEATH

INDICTMENT

Kevin HEATH is charged as follows:-

COUNT 1   STATEMENT OF OFFENCE

Causing grievous bodily harm with intent contrary to section 18 of the Offences Against the Person Act 1861.

PARTICULARS OF OFFENCE

Kevin Heath on the 24th day of December 2001 unlawfully caused grievous bodily harm to John Bull with intent to do him grievous bodily harm.

COUNT 2   STATEMENT OF OFFENCE

Inflicting grievous bodily harm contrary to section 20 of the Offences Against the Person Act 1861.

PARTICULARS OF OFFENCE

Kevin Heath on the 24th day of December 2001 unlawfully and maliciously inflicted grievous bodily harm on John Bull.

Date: 17 March 2002   John Collison
                                                Officer of the Crown Court

STATEMENT OF WITNESS

Statement of: JOHN BULL

Age of witness: Over 18

Occupation of witness: Publican

This statement consisting of one page, signed by me, is true to the best of my knowledge and belief and I make it knowing that, if it is tendered in evidence, I shall be liable to prosecution if I have wilfully stated in it anything which I know to be false or do not believe to be true.

Signed: *J. Bull*
Signature witnessed by: *R. Maybury*   Statement dated: 28th December 2001.

I am the landlord of The Cutpurse public house and have been so for 5 years.

On Monday, 24th December 2001 I was serving behind the bar throughout the evening together with Tracey CROFT, my permanent barmaid and a number of part-time staff.

Being Christmas Eve the pub was very busy and in general the atmosphere was noisy but pleasant.

At about 9.00 pm I had reason to speak to a youth who I know as 'Ferret'. He is in his early twenties, about 5′7″ with dark hair and a pointy face. He had been in the pub since opening time and at this time he was being difficult and abusive towards Tracey who was serving at the part of the bar near the pool table. He was waving a pool cue around. I told him to pack it in or go home. I have had trouble with him in the past and banned him from my pub in June last year following a fight in my garden. I know he has been in trouble with the police plenty of times and is always playing 'Jack the Lad'.

All was well until about 10.30 when a group of carol singers arrived to sing in the public bar. This was by invitation and is something of which I am particularly fond.

The carol singers were grouped around the door. They had just begun to sing when they were interrupted by foul chanting from near the pool table. Although I could not at this stage actually see who was doing it, I had no doubt who was responsible. I felt very angry and upset and decided to take swift action as I am entitled to do by law. I went along the bar to the pool table where I could see Ferret and his friends chanting and yelling and once again Ferret was waving his pool cue about. I could see other people were getting upset. I called to him 'Alright you foul mouthed lout, shut it, and out'. I then left the bar by the hatch and went to eject him. At this Ferret came over to me and said, brandishing the cue, 'I'm going to stuff this . . .' I said 'Don't mess with me Ferret' and fearing an attack took the cue from him and threw it behind the bar, turning away from Ferret as I did so. As I turned back I heard the words 'You've had this coming, fat man'. After that, everything went blank, although I dimly remember hearing screaming.

I woke up in hospital and found out that I had been hit in my face with a glass beer mug. I have cuts to the left side of my face from my eye to my chin which needed 50 stitches. I am in considerable pain.

At no stage did I provoke this attack. I am 6′1″ and weigh 16 stones.

I made a sketch of the layout of the Public Bar which I produce as JB/1.

I am willing to attend court and give evidence, if required.

Signed by: *J. Bull*   Signature witnessed by: *R. Maybury*

JB/1

SERVING AREA

BAR

FRUIT MACHINE

HATCH ↑

POOL TABLE

ENTRANCE → MENS' W.C.

STATEMENT OF WITNESS

Statement of: TRACEY CROFT

Age of witness: Over 18

Occupation: Barmaid

This statement consisting of one page, signed by me, is true to the best of my knowledge and belief and I make it knowing that, if it is tendered in evidence, I shall be liable to prosecution if I have wilfully stated in it anything which I know to be false or do not believe to be true.

Signed: *T. Croft*
Signature witnessed by: *R. Maybury*   Statement dated: 25th December 2001

I am a barmaid at The Cutpurse public house, On Christmas Eve I was serving behind the bar, together with John BULL and other part-time staff. It was very crowded and lively and lots of people bought drinks for John and me. There were a lot of regulars in the pub, as well as a boy called Ferret. I think his real name is Kevin something but everyone calls him Ferret. He was banned by John for a while in the summer, but has been in a lot ever since. John doesn't like Ferret very much because he's mouthy and a show off. Before the fight, the only time I heard John speaking to Ferret that evening was a couple of hours earlier. I was serving near the fruit machine. Ferret was playing the machine and wanted change. He was being a bit loud and cheeky about my dress — just being silly and nothing nasty. John was next to me and seemed to take offence. He is very protective about me, and told Ferret to 'sod off'. Ferret seemed quite annoyed and went back to his friends who are always around the pool table. He had quite a lot to drink — I served him at least 5 pints of Tennants.

Nothing else happened until the carol singers came. John had booked them and was really looking forward to it. John said that if there was any trouble from Ferret and his lot then either they'd be out or he'd sort them out. I can't remember which.

Shortly after the carols started, Ferret and his mates started singing disgusting words and upsetting everyone. John turned very red and walked across the room from the bar over to the pool table. I ran round behind the bar to see what was happening. John yelled at Ferret to get out. Ferret picked up his pool cue and stood facing John. John grabbed the pool cue and they struggled with it. Eventually John broke it in two, turned round and flung it behind the bar. As he did this I saw Ferret pick up an empty pint beer mug from the table and as John turned back Ferret said something and smashed it into John's face. I screamed 'look out', but it was too late. John fell to the ground and his face was pouring with blood. There was a lot of screaming and shouting. Ferret tried to run off but other men held onto him. I waited until the police and ambulance came.

John is a lot bigger than Ferret who is about the same size as me. I am 5′ 7″ tall.

I am willing to attend court and give evidence, if required.

Signed: *T. Croft*   Signature witnessed by: *R. Maybury*

STATEMENT OF WITNESS

Statement of: DAVID DRAY

Age of witness: Over 18

Occupation of witness: Builder

This statement consisting of one page, signed by me, is true to the best of my knowledge and belief and I make it knowing that, if it is tendered in evidence, I shall be liable to prosecution if I have wilfully stated in it anything which I know to be false or do not believe to be true.

Signed: *D. Dray*
Signature witnessed by: *R. Maybury*   Statement dated: 25th December 2001.

On Christmas Eve I was in The Cutpurse pub. Everyone was very merry and we was all having a good drink.

At about 11.00 pm the carol singers arrived. Shortly after they started I was in the men's having a pee. When I came out I looked over the pool table and saw some sort of scrap going on between big John and some little geezer. I saw the little one get a clout round the ear and John took his pool cue off of him. As John turned round the other one picked up his beer mug and smashed it into John's head. John fell like a stone. The bloke who hit him tried to slip out but I got him and held him, as what he done was well out of order.

Signed: *D. Dray*   Signature witnessed by: *R. Maybury*

STATEMENT OF WITNESS

Statement of: IAN MICHAEL FIRM

Age of witness: Over 18

Occupation of witness: Police Constable 2212

This statement consisting of one page, signed by me, is true to the best of my knowledge and belief and I make it knowing that, if it is tendered in evidence, I shall be liable to prosecution if I have wilfully stated in it anything which I know to be false or do not believe to be true.

Signed: *I. M. Firm*
Signature witnessed by: *R. Maybury*   Statement dated: 3rd February 2002.

On Monday, 24th December 2001 I was on duty in full uniform in a marked police vehicle. At 11.20 pm as a result of information received I went to The Cutpurse public house, New Addington. It was very crowded when I arrived. Lying on the floor between the pool table and the bar was a man I now know to be John BULL. He appeared to be unconscious and was bleeding heavily from wounds to the left side of his face and I proceeded to give Mr Bull first aid. Shortly after this the ambulance arrived and Mr Bull was taken to hospital.

As a result of enquiries I spoke to a youth who I know to be Kevin HEATH. I noticed that he had blood on his right hand and spots of blood on his jacket. He was slightly dishevelled and his breath smelt strongly of drink, although he was not drunk.

I said to HEATH 'From what I have been told you hit the landlord, is this true?' And I then cautioned him. He replied 'He went for me'. I then told HEATH I was arresting him on suspicion of causing grievous bodily harm. After caution, he was taken to Croydon Police Station by other officers.

After the pub had been cleared I briefly examined the public bar area. Behind the bar near the pool table I found 2 pieces of pool cue which I produce as Exhibit IMF/1. Between the bar and the pool table I found a broken pint beer mug with jagged edges which appeared to have blood on it. This was placed in a bag and sealed. I produce this as Exhibit IMF/2.

Signed by: *I. M. Firm*   Signature witnessed by: *R. Maybury*

STATEMENT OF WITNESS

Statement of: RONALD MAYBURY

Age of witness: Over 18

Occupation of witness: DS Croydon CID

This statement consisting of one page, signed by me, is true to the best of my knowledge and belief and I make it knowing that, if it is tendered in evidence, I shall be liable to prosecution if I have wilfully stated in it anything which I know to be false or do not believe to be true.

Signed: *R. Maybury*
Signature witnessed by: *S. Gent*   Statement dated: 26th December 2001.

At 9.30 am on Christmas Day 2001 I was on duty at Croydon Police Station. There I saw a man I now know to be Kevin HEATH. I reminded him that he was under caution to which he replied 'I know all that — let's get on with it'. In the company of DC Tibbs I then interviewed HEATH in the interview room at the police station between 9.32 and 10.00 am. The interview was tape-recorded using two tapes. At the conclusion of the interview I sealed one of the copies and signed over the seal. I produce this as my Exhibit RM/1. I later prepared a written summary of the interview, which I produce as my Exhibit RM/2.

Later that day at 11.30 am HEATH was charged with wounding John BULL with intent to do him GBH. The charge was read over to him, he was again cautioned and replied 'No I've really done it this time though haven't I?'

Signed: *R. Maybury*   Signature witnessed by: *S. Gent*

RECORD OF TAPE RECORDED INTERVIEW

Person Interviewed: Kevin HEATH   Exhibit no: RM/2

Place of Interview: Croydon Police Station   No of Pages: 3

Date of Interview: 25th December 2001

Time Commenced: 9.32 am   Time Concluded: 10 am

Duration of Interview: 28 minutes   Tape Reference No: RM/1/1234

Interviewing Officer(s):   DS Maybury

Other persons present: DC Tibbs

Tape Counter	Person Speaking	Text
0001	RM	(Introductions) I must remind you that you are under caution. You do not have to say anything. But it may harm your defence if you do not mention when questioned something which you later rely on in court. Anything you do say may be given in evidence. Do you understand?
0008	KH	Yeah.
0015	RM	Do you object to being interviewed without a solicitor being present?
0025	KH	Well, I ain't going to get one this morning, am I? Anyway, I've done this a few times before.
0038	RM	Well, if you change your mind at any point, stop and tell me.
0049	KH	Yeah OK.
0055	RM	Now, what do you know about the glassing in The Cutpurse last night?
0066	KH	Well, not much really. That fat bastard of a landlord went for me with a pool cue. He hit me over the shoulder with it and it broke. He looked really angry as if he was going to do me again with the thick end of the cue so I punched out at him. He dropped like a stone, the girls started screaming and the geezer I know as Wally grabbed me and said that's out of order, you're staying here until Old Bill get here.
0081	RM	Were you drunk when you hit Big John Bull?
0089	KH	No — well merry really.
0096	RM	Are you a regular drinker?
0101	KH	Yeah.
0110	RM	What's your tipple?
0119	KH	Lager top.

0127	RM	How many do you drink on average when you go to the pub?
0131	KH	About 5/6 a night.
0144	RM	How many did you have last night before you hit John?
0150	KH	About 3/4.
0157	RM	Pints?
0163	KH	Yeah.
0170	RM	Any shorts?
0174	KH	No.
0181	RM	What were you doing before John, the publican came up to you?
0194	KH	Drinking with my mates.
0200	RM	Which ones?
0211	KH	I don't know — there were lots of them around.
0223	RM	So you must have had a pint glass in your hand?
0229	KH	Well, yeah.
0237	RM	So you must have realised when you punched out that you would hit John with the glass?
0242	KH	Well — no.
0250	RM	Come off it, you don't just forget you're holding a pint glass
0265	KH	Well I did.
0273	RM	Do you know Tracey Croft?
0278	KH	Yeah.
0288	RM	Well?
0294	KH	Yeah — she's my bird — well sort of anyway.
0304	RM	Does John fancy her?
0310	KH	Yeah he does a bit.
0321	RM	I put it to you that you are jealous of John because of Tracey and ...
0323	KH	(*interrupted*) Bollocks.
0335	RM	I'll continue, you are jealous and when John told you to get out of the pub in front of your mates you felt small and decided to do him.

0342	KH	Rubbish.
0351	RM	Please let me finish.
0360	KH	Sorry.
0374	RM	You had a glass in your hand and smashed it into his face quite deliberately?

(*Silence*)

0380	RM	Well he didn't hit you with a pool cue did he?
0388	KH	I suppose not.
0397	RM	You got cross and did him with the glass knowing full well you had it in your hand didn't you?
0405	KH	Well yeah, I'm sorry really, it's that bloody Tracey, she's a tart.
0412	RM	But that doesn't justify you putting all those stitches in John's face does it?
0424	KH	No — as I've said I'm sorry, are you going to charge me?
0430	RM	I'm afraid so but you've done yourself a bit of good by being so frank.

INTERVIEW TERMINATED

Previous convictions of KEVIN HEATH

d.o.b. 1.6.77

Date of Conviction	Court	Offence	Sentence
1.8.89	Croydon Juvenile	Theft	Conditional Discharge 1 year
12.11.90	Croydon	Burglary × 3	Supervision Order 1 year
1.3.91	North London Juvenile Court	Threatening words and behaviour	Attendance Centre 12 hours (no order on the breach of S.O.)
6.11.94	Liverpool City Mags.	Threatening words and behaviour	80 hours' Community Service
2.10.95	Inner London Crown Court	Handling	120 hours Community Service
1.9.96	Wallington Magistrates	ABH, Criminal Damage	£200 fine/7 days £200 fine/7 days *14 days served
3.8.01	Croydon Magistrates	ABH (at Cutpurse P.H.)	28 days' imprisonment

Previous convictions of JOHN BULL

d.o.b. 6.6.40

Date of conviction	Court	Offence	Sentence
12.5.76	Maidstone Crown Court	ABH	£150.00 fine
17.3.92	Inner London Crown Court	s. 20 Malicious Wounding	£200 fine/£100 compensation

Previous conviction of TRACEY CROFT

d.o.b. 2.6.82

Date of conviction	Court	Offence	Sentence
1.1.01	Croydon Mags.	Theft (shoplifting)	Conditional Discharge 12 months

<u>IN THE CROWN COURT AT CROYDON</u>

THE QUEEN

v

KEVIN HEATH

_____

DEFENCE
STATEMENT

_____

Defence Statement under the provisions of Section 5 Criminal Procedure and Investigations Act 1996

The Defendant is not guilty of either count 1 or 2 on the indictment.

The Defendant acted in self-defence.

The Defendant acted with reasonable force in the circumstances in self-defence to protect himself against John Bull.

Dated: 12th April 2002

Signed: *Kevin Heath*

Keymon & Keymon
147 Sutton Place
Croydon

Solicitors for the Defendant

BRIEF FOR THE DEFENCE

R

v

KEVIN HEATH

Counsel has herewith:

(1)   Indictment [see prosecution brief]

(2)   Prosecution Statements [see prosecution brief]

(3)   Proof of Kevin Heath

(4)   Previous convictions of Kevin Heath [see prosecution brief]

(5)   Statement of the Defence disclosed to Prosecution [see prosecution brief]

Instructing Solicitors act for Kevin Heath who faces an indictment alleging s. 18 Grievous Bodily Harm with s. 20 GBH in the alternative.

Mr Heath admits his presence at The Cutpurse on Christmas Eve but says that he hit the landlord in self-defence in the form of a pre-emptive strike.

As Counsel will appreciate, there is quite a lot of background history to this matter, including the fight with Mr Bull in the summer of 2001 for which he received a sentence of 28 days' imprisonment. Mr Heath remains adamant that on the previous occasion, as on this, he was the victim and not the aggressor. Instructing Solicitors are aware of rumours concerning Miss Croft and Mr Bull. Mr Heath is an old client, though inclined to be headstrong and tends to 'want his say' in the witness box.

Instructing Solicitors do not know whether or not any of the prosecution witnesses have previous convictions. No doubt, any such convictions will be disclosed in due course.

If convicted, Mr Heath would be willing to undertake community service or be placed on probation. The Rev. Thanet is prepared to give character evidence on his behalf. Would Counsel please use his best endeavours on behalf of Mr Heath.

CALL KEVIN HEATH of 21 Tree Avenue, New Addington

Who will say:

On Christmas Eve I was in The Cutpurse with Sharon and her sister, Debbie Wood. I used to go there quite a lot until one day last summer when I was having a bit of a laugh with Tracey Croft in the garden (Sharon does not know this). John, the landlord, came over and turned nasty and smacked me in the mouth. I tried to defend myself but I got nicked and was found guilty by the Magistrates, even though I wasn't. I got a prison sentence for this and John banned me for 3 months. On Christmas Eve I got to the pub about seven. I was drinking pints of Tennants. I suppose I had about 7 or 8 pints.

About 9.00 pm I was over playing the fruit machine. I asked Tracey for some change and made a couple of comments about her dress which was very low cut. Sharon was over at the pool table. Next thing John came over and told me to 'sod off' and leave Tracey well alone. Although I felt angry I just turned and walked back to the pool table. I never picked up a pool cue like he said. I didn't even swear at him. It's ridiculous the way he carries on — he must be almost 60 but Tracey is a young girl, not 20 yet.

When the carol singers came I was over near the pool table with Sharon and Debbie and a couple of others. When they started I suppose we were taking the mick a bit. Suddenly John was barging through everyone yelling at me to get out. I did have a pool cue in my hand, it's my own. John just came up to me, hit me round the left ear with his right hand. I tried to block him with the cue but he broke it in two and turned away and threw the bits behind the bar. As he turned back I thought he was going to attack me, so I picked up my pint mug and hit him across the head with it. I never said anything to him.

After this I panicked and tried to run off but some big geezer held onto me. The police came and I was arrested. I was then taken to the Police Station.

Since being charged I have seen Tracey Croft and she won't give evidence against me.

PERSONAL CIRCUMSTANCES

I am 25.

I have a number of previous convictions.

I live with my girlfriend, Sharon Wood, and she is expecting a baby in six months' time.

I do casual work as a roofer and take home £100 a week.

7.6 Further Reading

Armour, J. 'Stereotypes and Prejudice: Helping Legal Decisionmakers Break the Prejudice Habit', *Calif. Law Rev.*, 1995, pp. 733–772.

Baron, Jane B. 'Intention, Interpretation and Stories', *Duke Law Journal*, 1992, pp. 630–678.

Bennett, W.L. and Feldman, M.S. *Re-Constructing Reality in the Courtroom*, Tavistock, 1981.

Devlin, P. *Easing the Passing; the trial of Dr John Bodkin Adams*, Faber & Faber, 1985.

Evans, K. *Advocacy in Court*, Blackstone Press (OUP), 2nd edn, 1995.

Lopez. 'Lay Lawyering', *UCLA Law Review*, Vol. 32 (1984).

Ohlbaum, Edward D. 'Basic Instinct: Case Theory and Courtroom Performance', *Temple Law Rev.*, 1993, pp. 1–57 and appendices.

Sarmas, L. 'Storytelling and the Law: a case study of *Louth v Diprose*', *Melb. U. Law Rev.*, 1994, pp. 701–728.

Stone, M. *Cross-Examination in Criminal Trials*, Butterworths, 2nd edn, 1995.

***Case Preparation Manual* (Chapter 14).**

EIGHT

HOW TO RECOGNISE COMPETENCE WHEN YOU SEE IT

8.1 Introduction

Isn't this a rather strange chapter to put in a book of this sort? After all, any time that you go into a court or tribunal, you should see people acting as advocates and (usually) being paid to do so. Aren't they all competent advocates? And isn't it safe simply to mimic their techniques and style? Well, 'No' is the answer. When you see an advocate in court, it may be their first time in such a court, or it may be that they have good points and bad points (regardless of how much experience they have). The latter is more likely to be the case.

The point is that you cannot afford simply to adopt wholesale and uncritically whatever you see being said and done by advocates in court. It would be fantastic if you could do so but that is not the case. As a novice advocate, you will be tempted to regard all other advocates as more experienced than you (probably true) and therefore better advocates (not necessarily true) and highly competent in everything they do (almost always not true). All of us have strengths and weaknesses, things we do well and things we do badly. It is a fact that when advocates appear in court, they very seldom receive any feedback on the quality of their performance. You might say that they learn whether they are potential silks or should start looking for another job by the amount of work they are sent to do. Unfortunately, that may depend on a number of factors, only some of which are connected to the advocate's ability. Even then, there may be things that the (soon-to-be-ex-) advocate does well. There is no formal system for helping advocates to monitor the standards of their advocacy, more is the pity. Indeed, most practitioners would look aghast if you (or anyone else) offered them some constructive criticism after seeing them in court.

So until there is some such monitoring system in place, the best that can be done is to look out for yourself the best way you can. How can you do this? One of the best methods is to have a set of criteria that you can take into any court or tribunal. Then, when you watch other advocates in action, you can judge for yourself how well (or otherwise) they are performing all of their functions and be confident that you have identified those functions and the proper standards to be attained.

8.2 How should we Define Competence?

8.2.1 DIFFERENT THINGS TO DIFFERENT PEOPLE?

It is plain nonsense to suggest that the degree of expertise that we should expect from an experienced advocate is the same as that which we are likely to find in a beginner. Nevertheless, it is a fact that a professional advocate must be capable of achieving a certain minimum level of competence, no matter what their experience. This is an essential requirement; one need only point to the public interest in litigation being conducted by competent advocates (for the avoidance of miscarriage of justice and achieving an efficient and effective system for litigation, for example) to see that there must be a basic level of competence that must be achieved before it is safe to employ someone to be an advocate in court.

8.2.2 A BASIC LEVEL OF COMPETENCE

What should we expect of any advocate, regardless of expertise or experience? This could be defined in terms of knowledge, perhaps.

8.2.3 KNOWLEDGE

We might say that any advocate should know and be able to make effective use of the rules of procedure (i.e., those rules which govern the way that the relevant court functions). We should not expect an encyclopaedic familiarity with all such rules but the advocate should know all those rules of general, common relevance — on costs, for example. The competent advocate should also know when he or she is confronted by a more unusual rule, where to find it and how to apply it. The same goes for the rules which govern the evidence that can be put forward in court. So we can say that a competent advocate should have a good accurate knowledge of the rules of evidence and procedure, those matters which are adjectival to the subject matter of the litigation.

In a similar fashion, we can say that any competent advocate should have a good working knowledge of various, commonly-met, bodies of substantive law. Examples might be the criminal law, the laws governing contracts and the laws governing liability for negligence. In addition, the advocate should have a thorough knowledge of the laws that are relevant to the particular matter that is before the court (i.e., the subject of the present litigation). That knowledge may have been acquired through previous experience of such litigation, it may have been acquired through post-qualification study or it may have been acquired specifically for the purposes of this litigation. Any competent advocate should know (and have the ability to research, if necessary) the substantive legal rules which are or may be relevant to the current litigation.

It is a fact that professional advocates in this country (that is, barristers and solicitors) will have spent a considerable amount of time in learning a large body of law, before they ever obtained their professional qualification. The vast majority of advocates will have law degrees and the rest will have a non-law degree and have gone through a shorter, intensive law course. There are certain core law subjects in which all would-be professional advocates must have passed examinations (there is no need to rehearse them here). Furthermore, during their training period for their professional qualification, they must have passed examinations on the rules of procedure and evidence (see the BVC and LPC requirements). We might be safe in assuming a basic level of competence as far as legal knowledge is concerned. How about the application of that knowledge? And what about factual knowledge? Advocates must be familiar with the allegations in the litigation, the available evidence and, combining legal and factual knowledge, the advocate must know in every case what facts need to be proved in order to achieve the outcome which their client seeks.

These intellectual qualities must be gained **in advance** of the hearing where the advocate is to perform. How the knowledge was gained is irrelevant although we can learn effective techniques for both the law and the facts. What we need, as an observer in court, is a criterion that relates to **preparation**. Often, we will not know exactly what the advocate has had to do in order to be prepared for this piece of litigation (although a trainee or pupil connected with the advocate should have observed the advocate's preparation). What we can do is observe what the advocate says and does in court, and judge whether those words and deeds are appropriate and relevant to the laws and allegations in this particular piece of litigation. That relates to the **content** of the advocate's performance and we should have a criterion to judge that, too. Since we are beginning to look at this in terms of what the competent advocate should be able to say and do, we can see it as the definition of a skill. Or rather, as the definition of a collection of skills which might be summed up as advocacy skills.

8.3 Advocacy Skills

This part of the chapter follows the standard ICSL philosophy of separating out the bundle of related but disparate skills which typically are used together to produce a competent performance in the court room. The ICSL has spent a great deal of time looking into what makes for a competent piece of advocacy. We have looked at those skills which are required for a submission or application to a court, as these are the tasks on which most advocates cut their teeth. We have also analysed the skills that advocates use when questioning witnesses; we think that slightly different skills are used or objectives set, depending upon whether one is engaged in examining one's own witness or one called for the opponent. We have produced sets of criteria which can be used to produce an objective critique of an advocate's work, whatever the context.

The training criteria for making (or opposing) an application to a court are set out in **8.3.1**; the criteria for handling a witness are set out in **8.3.2** (for examination-in-chief), and **8.3.3** (for cross-examination). Some criteria are always relevant — such as the ability to speak clearly and fluently — others are relevant either to making a submission or to questioning a witness but not to both (for example, the use of appropriate questioning techniques). In the main, we are looking at *transferable skills*, that is, skills that can be used in more than one context.

8.3.1 ADVOCACY TRAINING CRITERIA FOR APPLICATIONS

In order to be regarded as competent, the advocate should show his or her ability to:

(a) prepare a skeleton argument for the application and refer to it in the application when necessary and appropriate;

(b) make an application which is appropriate, relevant and legally and factually sound and is consistent with the skeleton argument;

(c) structure the application in a clear and logical way;

(d) deliver the application clearly and fluently, using appropriate language and manner, referring to notes when necessary or desirable;

(e) make an application which is effective and persuasive and responds appropriately to the intervention of the judge.

Remember that the rules of professional conduct should always be observed.

8.3.2 ADVOCACY TRAINING CRITERIA FOR EXAMINATION-IN-CHIEF

In order to perform this exercise satisfactorily, you must show your ability to:

(a) Prepare the case effectively, understanding:

   (i) the case that has to be proved;

   (ii) the issues in the trial;

   (iii) the issues on which this witness can give evidence;

   (iv) the rules of evidence and procedure;

   (v) the principles of examination-in-chief.

(b) Ask questions which:

   (i) seek to elicit only admissible evidence;

    (ii)   seek to elicit only relevant evidence whether to an issue or to credit;

    (iii)   enable the witness to establish all of the evidence he or she can give (including the production of exhibits).

  (c)   Structure the questions in a way which:

    (i)   is clear and logical to the witness and the tribunal;

    (ii)   is responsive to the witness's answers;

    (iii)   takes into account the relevance of this witness to the case as a whole and the client's interests.

  (d)   Speak clearly and fluently, at an appropriate pace, using appropriate language and manner, referring to notes when necessary or desirable.

  (e)   Control the witness and elicit evidence using appropriate questioning techniques which:

    (i)   enable the witness to give his or her evidence in as coherent and persuasive a way as possible;

    (ii)   respond as appropriate to the witness's answers.

Remember that the rules of professional conduct should always be observed.

8.3.3   ADVOCACY TRAINING CRITERIA FOR CROSS-EXAMINATION

In order to perform this exercise satisfactorily you must show your ability to:

  (a)   Prepare the case effectively, understanding:

    (i)   the case that has to be proved;

    (ii)   the issues in the trial;

    (iii)   the issues on which this witness can give evidence, in particular those on which this witness is helpful, damaging or neutral to your client's case;

    (iv)   the rules of evidence and procedure;

    (v)   the principles of cross-examination.

  (b)   Ask questions which:

    (i)   seek only admissible evidence;

    (ii)   seek only relevant evidence (whether to an issue or to credit);

    (iii)   cover all relevant evidence of the witness (including that relating to exhibits);

    (iv)   enable the witness to assist your client's case in so far as he or she is able to do so;

    (v)   in so far as it is necessary to do so:

        (1)   put your client's case to the witness;

        (2)   undermine the testimony of the witness;

        (3)   undermine the credibility of the witness;

(vi)   make appropriate use of contradictory material.

(c)   Structure the questions in a way which:

   (i)   is clear and logical to the tribunal;

   (ii)   is responsive to the witness's answers;

   (iii)   takes into account the relevance of this witness to the case as a whole and your client's interests.

(d)   Speak clearly and fluently, at an appropriate pace, using appropriate language and manner, referring to notes when necessary or desirable.

(e)   Control the witness and elicit evidence using appropriate questioning techniques which:

   (i)   confine the witness's testimony appropriately to the evidence you seek to adduce;

   (ii)   respond as appropriate to the witness's answers.

Remember that the rules of professional conduct should always be observed.

8.3.4   ADVOCACY TRAINING CRITERIA FOR SUBMISSIONS

After the court has heard oral evidence, counsel will make a submission (akin to a closing speech at the end of a trial). Because it is impossible to predict with certainty what evidence will be before the court following testimony, it is difficult to submit a skeleton argument which can deal comprehensively with the issues and arguments before the court. Frequently, for this reason, such closing submissions will be made without a skeleton argument. It is also likely that the judge will not intervene whilst counsel is addressing the court. The training criteria which would otherwise apply (for applications to the court) need to be recast as follows, to meet this situation.

In order to perform this task satisfactorily, you must show your ability to:

(a)   Prepare the case effectively, by understanding the relevant law, facts and procedure and planning your submission.

(b)   Make a submission which is appropriate, relevant and legally and factually sound, and in which you respond appropriately to points made by the other side.

(c)   Structure your submission in a clear and logical way.

(d)   Deliver your submission clearly and fluently, using appropriate language and manner, referring to notes when necessary or desirable.

(e)   Make a submission which is effective and persuasive.

Remember that the rules of professional conduct should always be observed.

8.3.5   THE TRAINING CRITERIA IN MORE DETAIL

Those criteria are explored in more detail in **Part 4**, with one exception. Professional conduct and ethical behaviour is the subject of the separate *Professional Conduct Manual* and it is better to look at that Manual for expert coverage of the topic. For present purposes, we might say that the advocate is bound by a code of conduct established by the legal profession. A simple understanding of (and adherence to) the standards that the courts, clients and the public are entitled to expect from an advocate should enable you to do the right thing in most situations.

PART 3
A CASE TO PRACTISE WITH

NINE

R v FRANK SMITH

9.1   Introduction

This chapter contains parts of a case for you to practise some of your advocacy skills. You have the brief for the prosecution in a Crown Court trial, where the accused man, Frank Smith is alleged to have dishonestly received some items of jewellery, knowing or believing them to be stolen, contrary to the Theft Act 1968, s. 22(1).

You have the Instructions to Counsel and a copy of the indictment, together with a collection of witness statements for the prosecution. In addition, you have a transcript of what Frank Smith said in his examination-in-chief. With these you should be able to practise an opening speech, the planning for which should test your preparation skills of case management and legal research and the delivery of which should enable you to work on your presentational skills. You will need to evolve a case theory, think about the themes which you might use in relation to each prosecution witness and also consider exactly what story to tell the jury to enable them to 'see' and understand what you allege was going on in the period surrounding this offence.

You can use the witness statements to practise your witness handling skills in the context of examination-in-chief; your planning can be done at any time but you will need to arrange with someone else, preferably two other people, to practise the examination-in-chief. Ideally, one colleague can play the role of the witness and the other can play the judge or defence counsel to object to questions, when necessary. For cross-examination, it is suggested that you plan your cross-examination of Frank Smith simply by considering your theory of the case and assuming that your witnesses all said what you anticipated they would say. Have a colleague prepare to play the role of Frank Smith by reading the prosecution papers and the transcript of Smith's testimony-in-chief. Don't look at that transcript until very shortly before you are going to perform the cross-examination, since in a real trial you would not know exactly what the accused would say in evidence until he was actually saying it. Your opportunity to refine your preparation for cross-examination is necessarily of very short duration but nevertheless you must make the most of it — see how well you do with Frank Smith. Try to get a third person in again, to play the judge or defence counsel.

If you have the time, and a little imagination, you can use the papers in *R v Smith* for a complete trial. It is to be hoped that Smith's case theory emerges quite clearly from his evidence-in-chief, so it should not be too hard to construct some simple instructions to defence counsel. Smith may well be the only witness for the defence. If you had enough people willing to take part, you could start with the prosecution opening speech, followed by the evidence for the prosecution (with both examination-in-chief and cross-examination, possibly re-examination), then the evidence of Smith himself (set the transcript to one side and actually have someone to perform the examination-in-chief, as well as having someone to cross-examine him), then perhaps closing speeches from advocates representing the prosecution and defence.

9.2   *R v Frank Smith*: the Case for the Prosecution

In the Maidsbury Crown Court
Indictment No. 1542/02

Regina v Frank Smith

INSTRUCTIONS TO COUNSEL
TO PROSECUTE

Counsel is instructed to conduct the case for the Crown against Frank SMITH at his trial. Mr Smith is indicted on a single count of handling, contrary to s. 22(1), Theft Act 1968. The allegation is that he dishonestly received a gold and emerald necklace and matching pair of earrings, knowing or believing them to be stolen.

On Sunday 3rd February 2002, a farmhouse — Toy's House, near Maidsbury — was burgled. The house owner, Miss Vera Fanshawe, clearly places the burglary between the time she left for church on Sunday morning and the time she returned from church. She states that various items were stolen; the most important for this case were the necklace and earrings set referred to above.

As Counsel will see from the papers, Mr Smith is not alleged to be an habitual receiver or 'fence'. Rather, this was an isolated incident where Mr Smith had a great incentive to acquiesce in the original theft occurring, knowing that he would derive particular benefit from it. It appears, by his statement to the police during interview, that he expected to receive the jewellery at a specific time on a specific day. The Crown say that he knew or believed that the goods would have to be stolen in order for him to receive them and that he acted dishonestly. Mr Smith does not seem to deny receipt, rather he has put forward a story to explain his possession, superficially consistent with acting honestly and not knowing or believing that the goods were stolen. The Crown say that this 'explanation' is a pure fantasy on his part.

Mr Smith paid a large sum of money for the goods but nothing like as much as they are worth (Counsel is referred to the statement of Mr Chisolm); further, we can establish when the goods were stolen and Mr Smith admits coming into possession very rapidly thereafter. It seems very unlikely, if not impossible, that Mr Smith burgled the premises himself, given the statement of Miss Fanshawe, the victim of the burglary.

The Crown say that Mr Smith admits receipt of property which can be proved to have been stolen, and that the circumstances show beyond a reasonable doubt that, at the moment of receipt, he knew or believed the property to be stolen. His lies (there can be no other description) during the interview are blatant and also demonstrate clearly his guilty knowledge, as does his refusal to name his 'supplier'.

Crown Prosecution Service
Maidsbury Division, April 2002

Indictment

In the Maidsbury Crown Court   No. 1542/02

Regina v Frank SMITH

Statement of Offence
Handling stolen goods contrary to s. 22(1) of the Theft Act 1968

Particulars of Offence
Frank Smith on or about the 3rd day of February 2002 dishonestly received stolen goods, namely a gold and emerald necklace and matching pair of earrings belonging to Vera Fanshawe, knowing or believing the same to be stolen goods.

E. Brown

Officer of the Crown Court

Date: 26th April 2002

<u>STATEMENT OF WITNESS</u>

<u>Name</u>: Vera Fanshawe

<u>Age</u>: Over 18

<u>Occupation</u>: Farmer

This statement, consisting of 2 pages, each signed by me, is true to the best of my knowledge and belief and I make it knowing that, if it is tendered in evidence, I shall be liable to prosecution if I have wilfully stated in it anything which I know to be false or do not believe to be true.

<u>Dated</u>: 25th February 2002

<u>Signed</u>...........   <u>Signature witnessed by</u>...........

I own and farm 1,600 acres of mixed dairy and beef farmland around the village of Downham, near Maidsbury in Kent. My family has owned this land for many generations. Since 1865, my family has lived in the house which I now live in, on the farm. The farm is known as Toy's Farm, after a local landmark, and the house is called Toy's House. I live alone at Toy's House with my dogs and cats; I inherited the house and farm in 1991 on the death of my uncle, Frank Fanshawe. He was my father's elder brother and he died with no legitimate children. For many years before his death, he had been close to a man named Frank Smith. Frank Smith was Frank Fanshawe's illegitimate son and the family had been given to understand that Toy's Farm would go to Frank Smith on the death of my uncle Frank.

The two of them fell out in 1990 and uncle Frank told me that he had altered his will so that I, not Frank Smith, would succeed him. That was indeed the case. Since uncle Frank's funeral, I have tried to restore good relations with Frank Smith. I have no children and Frank has two young sons, Adam and John. I would like Toy's Farm to stay in the family and thought that Frank would be happy to take it on after I am gone. Unfortunately, Frank was upset when I explained matters to him last August and lost his temper with me, saying that Toy's should have been his all along. Since then, with one exception, he has refused to talk to me.

Toy's Farm has been experiencing financial difficulties for some years now and with the recent 'mad cow disease' scare, beef prices have fallen very low. Income from the dairy herd has also dropped since the Milk Marketing Board was abolished. During storms last Autumn, one of the milking parlours was badly damaged and the milking equipment was put out of action. I needed to repair the parlour and equipment quickly but lacked the cash to do so. The cost was £9,850.00 and the bank agreed to lend me the money over a short period while I tried to sell some assets to pay for the loan.

I decided to auction some jewellery which had been in the family for about a hundred years but which no-one seems to have liked. This was a set of a gold and emerald drop pendant necklace with matching earrings. Because of its age and quality, I had previously had this set valued for insurance purposes and knew it to be worth around £5,000.00. The balance of the money I intended to raise from auctioning off various old pieces of furniture. I contacted the local firm of auctioneers, Chisolms, and they agreed to handle the sale as a 'country house' auction. They placed advertisements in various newspapers and magazines. These advertisements always made specific mention of the gold and emerald jewellery set. While we were making arrangements for the auction, Chisolms confirmed that the jewellery set should fetch at least £5,000 at the auction.

Shortly after the local newspaper carried an advertisement for the auction, I was telephoned by Frank Smith who seemed very annoyed about the auction. In particular, he said that under no circumstances was I to sell the necklace and earrings as these had some sort of sentimental value to him. I insisted that the money had to be raised to repay the loan, that I did not care for the jewellery and would go ahead with its sale;

he put the telephone down very abruptly. The auction was set for Tuesday the 5th of February 2002 and, as usual, I went to Downham parish church for communion on the Sunday before. When I arrived there, I saw Frank Smith was also in the congregation. That was unusual for him. He didn't speak to me but looked at me from his seat several times and smiled.

At the end of the service, I saw Frank go off with some other people to the 'Red Cow', a local pub. I drove straight home and found that my front door had been broken open. I went inside but there was no-one there. I rang the police and then went upstairs to check if anything had been taken. I found that a few pieces of silver were not there but also the gold and emerald jewellery set was gone. I am sure that all of these items were in their usual place when I left for church and I am sure that the front door was shut and locked.

When the police came, I told them what had happened. They asked if I could think of anyone who might have stolen the items, either people with the opportunity or the motive. The only person I could think of was Frank Smith and I told them so. I was upset by that, so I also told the police that Frank could not have done it as I had seen him at church and it would not have been possible for him to get to Toy's House and break in and get to church before me. That was comforting to me as I did not want to think that Frank might stoop so low.

On Tuesday the 5th February, I was asked to attend Maidsbury Police station. On my arrival, I was shown several items by Detective Constable Matlock. Amongst them were my gold and emerald necklace and earring set which had been stolen on the previous Sunday. The other things I did not recognise.

Detective Constable Matlock explained that the police would need to retain the jewellery as evidence so they have not been sold at auction yet. The auction itself had to be cancelled and I am still paying interest on the bank loan.

Signed..........   Signature witnessed by..........

<u>STATEMENT OF WITNESS</u>

<u>Name</u>: Gwen Matlock

<u>Age</u>: Over 18

<u>Occupation</u>: Woman Detective Constable, Kent Constabulary

This statement, consisting of 1 page, signed by me, is true to the best of my knowledge and belief and I make it knowing that, if it is tendered in evidence, I shall be liable to prosecution if I have wilfully stated in it anything which I know to be false or do not believe to be true.

<u>Dated</u>: 4th March 2002

Signed..........   Signature witnessed by..........

Acting on information received, on Monday 4th February 2002 at 2.25 pm I went to Thorneybrook Cottage in Downham. The door was opened by a man I now know to be Frank SMITH and I asked if he was the owner of the house. He said he was and then identified himself.

I asked Mr Smith whether he knew Miss Vera Fanshawe of Toy's Farm and he replied, 'Yes, she's sort of my cousin'. I asked him where he had been on Sunday 3rd February and he replied, 'Here and there, you know. I went to church in the morning, then off to the pub for a pint and back home for Sunday lunch'. I said, 'Did you go anywhere else on Sunday?' and he replied, 'Yes, I went back to the pub for a few jars on Sunday night. I was there until closing time.' I asked him if he had been to Toy's Farm at all on that Sunday and he said, 'No'. I then asked if he knew that Miss Fanshawe had been burgled on Sunday and he looked surprised but said nothing.

I then said to him, 'Some valuable items were taken from the house, including jewellery'. I saw him immediately look towards a cupboard on a nearby wall. I said to him, 'Would you mind if I looked in that cupboard?'. He replied, 'There's nothing in there, you know'. I said, 'If there is nothing in there, it won't hurt to look, will it?'. He still made no move towards the cupboard so I said, 'If you don't open it now, I shall have to go and get a warrant and then you will open it'. Smith replied, 'It's not what it seems, you know. I knew nothing about any burglary'. He then opened the cupboard, which was locked, using a key from a chain attached to his trousers. I looked inside the cupboard and saw a package wrapped in oilskin. I asked Smith to take the package out and he unwrapped it on the table in front of the cupboard.

Inside the oilskin were two gentlemen's gold hunter-style fob watches, a gold and emerald clasp and a gold and emerald necklace in very similar style. Also in the package was a pair of earrings which appeared to match the necklace and clasp.

I said to Smith, 'I believe that some or all of these items came from the burglary at Toy's Farm on Sunday and I am arresting you for receiving stolen property'. I then cautioned him and he replied, 'You don't understand. All of these things belong to me. They are mine'. I took Smith back to Maidsbury Police Station. I subsequently interviewed him there, accompanied by PC Barnet and Smith's solicitor, Roger Hatley.

At 6.10 pm on the 4th February 2002, I was present when Smith was released on unconditional bail to return on Wednesday 6th at 10.00 am. I was present on the 6th February at 10.12 am, when Smith was charged with handling stolen property knowing or believing it to be stolen, namely the gold and emerald necklace and earrings. Smith was cautioned and said, 'I don't know who has made the bigger mistake — you lot or me'. He was then released on unconditional bail to surrender to Maidsbury Magistrates' Court at a later date.

Signed..........   Signature witnessed by..........

STATEMENT OF WITNESS

Name: Warren Barnet

Age: Over 18

Occupation: Police Constable, Kent Constabulary

This statement, consisting of 1 page, signed by me, is true to the best of my knowledge and belief and I make it knowing that, if it is tendered in evidence, I shall be liable to prosecution if I have wilfully stated in it anything which I know to be false or do not believe to be true.

Dated: 6th March 2002

Signed...........   Signature witnessed by...........

On Monday 4th of February 2002, I was present during an interview with Mr Frank SMITH at Maidsbury Police Station. The interview was conducted by WDC Matlock and I recorded this interview. Also present was Mr Roger HATLEY, Smith's solicitor. I produce the record of interview as WB/1.

Signed...........   Signature witnessed by...........

RECORD OF INTERVIEW   Exhibit WB/1

Person interviewed   Frank SMITH

Place   Maidsbury Police Station

Date   4.2.02

Times   Interview began: 17.45 am/pm and ended   17.55 am/pm

Interview recorded by   PC Barnet

Other persons present   WDC Matlock, Roger Hatley (Defendant's solicitor)

Woman Detective Constable Matlock reminded Smith that he was under caution, then said:

Q.   You told me that you are Vera Fanshawe's cousin. That's not right is it?
A.   Well, I am. It's just that I was born on the wrong side of the blanket, you know.
Q.   You are not a member of the Fanshawe family?
A.   Not formally. Vera's uncle Frank was my dad but he never married my mum.
Q.   Did you live with Frank Fanshawe?
A.   No. But we were close, given the circumstances. He bought Thorneybrook Cottage for my mum after I was born and sometimes he would visit us there.
Q.   Is Frank Fanshawe named as your father on your birth certificate?
A.   No. It says 'Father unknown' but the whole village knew he was my dad.
Q.   That is Downham, is it?
A.   Yes.
Q.   You must have been upset when your father left his farm and home to someone else, then?
A.   Of course. It was not a complete surprise, we'd fallen out a few months before he died over some silly argument and he said that everything would go to his niece Vera. I had never met her at that time and thought he might just be saying it out of spite. It turned out that he meant it, though.
Q.   How did you come to have the gold necklace and earrings in your house?
A.   This is going to sound silly.
Q.   Go on.
A.   Look, everyone in Downham knows that farm should have been mine, and everything that went with it. The Fanshawes are my family and it is my inheritance. I could not believe it when I saw that advert in the paper about the auction.
Q.   Why not?
A.   She was going to sell off my mum's jewellery. [Pause] You know, my father would bring the necklace and the earrings to our house when he came to visit my mum. He would set them out on the table and get her to put them on. I was only a child then but I can remember that clearly. She looked beautiful in them. My father said that he would give them to her, only they were family heirlooms and he needed to sort it out so he could do it legally. He never did give them to her. He always took them with him when he left us. Then Mum died and I never gave them much thought until my father died. It was upsetting that he never even left me the emerald jewellery in his will. Still, Vera told me that when she's dead, Toy's will come to me. That should have been all right — I'm still a young man and she must be in her sixties. I've got time on my side.
Q.   So what about the advert?
A.   Well, I couldn't believe that she was going to sell my mum's jewels. At least, what should have been my mum's. And mine.
Q.   They were going to auction. You could have bought them.
A.   You're joking. Do you know how much they are worth? I don't have that sort of money to spare. Anyway, why should I buy them? They are my inheritance. She has no right to sell them. No moral right anyway.

Q. So you decided to steal them?

A. No way. Listen, I was in the pub in Downham one night, the Red Cow. I got a bit tight and told everyone what a rotten stunt it was, her selling off my mum's jewels in an auction.

Q. When was this?

A. I think it was last Thursday, the last day of the month. It might have been the Wednesday, though. I can't quite recall now.

Q. Go on.

A. Well, after I'd said my piece, one of my mates suggested that he had a solution to my problem. He said that he could approach Chisolms, the auctioneers, privately and offer them money in a private sale before the auction. Guaranteed sale, that kind of thing. Once he'd got that, he'd let me have the necklace and earrings.

Q. What, free?

A. No. He said that I would have to pay him but the amount would depend on what sort of deal he could strike with Chisolms.

Q. You were prepared to pay up to £5,000 for them?

A. No way. I have said, I don't have that much spare cash. He said that he thought he could get them for £2,000 or less.

Q. How was he going to do that?

A. I don't know. He said he had a friend in the trade — jewellery, that is.

Q. So what happened?

A. We arranged to meet again in the Red Cow on Sunday lunch-time.

Q. The 3rd?

A. Yes. He came in about 1 o'clock and we went into the saloon bar. There was no-one else around and he took a bag out of his pocket. He put the necklace and earrings on the table and told me his friend had struck gold. We had a laugh about that. He said that Chisolms had agreed to accept £1,500 for the set, as his friend was in the trade and prepared to pay cash. I could manage that so we went back to Thorneybrook and I gave him the money. I asked him how much his friend wanted for helping me and he said nothing, that he'd been able to pick up some other pieces while he was doing the deal and they had made it worth his while. All the same, I gave him another £100 for his mate and £100 for himself.

Q. Making £1,700 in total?

A. That's right.

Q. Who was this friend of yours?

A. I can't say, can I? I know there's been a burglary now and I've been conned a bit, but he was just a good mate who tried to help me out over something I was really upset about. Everyone in Downham knows about Frank Fanshawe being my dad, they all think I should have got Toy's and not Vera. They are my friends and they sympathise.

Q. But you say you paid £1,700 for jewellery which you admit is worth £5,000? To a man in a pub who you're not prepared to name? What's the name of his friend in the jewellery trade?

A. He never said.

Q. This whole story is a sham. A pack of lies, isn't it?

A. No. It all happened just as I have said. If you don't believe me, I have nothing else to say.

Interview terminated at 17.55 pm.

<u>STATEMENT OF WITNESS</u>

<u>Name</u>: Thomas Chisolm

<u>Age</u>: Over 18

<u>Occupation</u>: Auctioneer and antiques seller

This statement, consisting of 1 page, signed by me, is true to the best of my knowledge and belief and I make it knowing that, if it is tendered in evidence, I shall be liable to prosecution if I have wilfully stated in it anything which I know to be false or do not believe to be true.

<u>Dated</u>: 6th March 2002

<u>Signed</u>..........   <u>Signature witnessed by</u>..........

I have been in the antiques business for 15 years. I run the family auction company which is based in Maidsbury. I have considerable experience of valuing and selling antiques, including antique jewellery, both at auction and through our shop.

On 10th December 2001, I was telephoned by a Miss Vera Fanshawe of Toy's Farm, Downham. She was very keen to raise some money quickly. I visited her home on 14th December and saw she had some excellent pieces.

The top item was a set of emerald jewellery, set in 18 carat gold. It dated from the late nineteenth century and she could establish its provenance within succeeding generations of her family to date. It was a charming set and I advised her that it could fetch in excess of £6,000 and we should have a reserve of £5,000. This meant that if bidding stopped before £5,000, the set would be withdrawn.

Miss Fanshawe also had some large pieces of furniture from various centuries that she wished to dispose of. I advised her that we were likely to maximise prices by holding the auction at her house and she agreed. We agreed that it was appropriate to leave the furniture in situ and Miss Fanshawe was insistent that the jewellery should stay in the house too.

We fixed on a date of Tuesday 5th February 2002 and my firm placed advertisements in newspapers and magazines, both national and local. Some were to run over several weeks, others just single issues, depending on the publication. There would have been three advertisements in the local Maidsbury and West Kent Gazette over the January–early February period.

In all of the advertisements, we used photographs, either colour or monochrome, of the jewellery set to promote the auction at Toy's Farm. We never publish price guides or reserve prices in our advertisements but the auction catalogue included price guides for all items in the sale. Copies of the catalogue were freely available throughout January 2002 by post or to personal callers at my firm. We had 500 copies printed and distributed most of them. I have no idea who received copies as we keep no records of that information.

<u>Signed</u>..........   <u>Signature witnessed by</u>..........

Kent Constabulary
Criminal Antecedents Form

C.R.O. no 841/9/80

Accused: Frank SMITH

Age: 32 (d.o.b 12.11.69)

Offences: Handling stolen goods

Court: Maidsbury Crown Court

Previous convictions

1.   11.6.89 Maidsbury Magistrates Court Taking a motor vehicle Fined £100

2.   2.4.90 Maidsbury M/C Driving w/o due care Fined £120, licence endorsed

3.   11.9.91 Wealden Crown Court Causing death by reckless driving 6 months' imprisonment, disqualified from driving for 12 months

Prepared: 16.3.02
at   : Maidsbury Police Station

<u>IN THE CROWN COURT AT MAIDSBURY</u>

THE QUEEN

v

FRANK SMITH

DEFENCE STATEMENT

Defence Statement under the provisions of Section 5 Criminal Procedure and Investigations Act 1996

The Defendant is not guilty of the count on the indictment.

The Defendant at no time knew or believed the goods to be stolen property.

Dated: 22nd March 2002

Signed: *Frank Smith*

Wrench and Jemmy
12 High Street
Maidsbury

Solicitors for the Defendant

9.3   Frank Smith: Examination-in-chief

<u>Frank SMITH</u>

TRANSCRIPT OF EVIDENCE-IN-CHIEF

[The Defendant entered the witness box and took the oath]

My name is Frank Smith. I live at Thorneybrook Cottage in Downham. That is just outside Maidsbury.

I have lived there virtually all my life. I live there now with my wife, Muriel, and my two sons, Adam and John. I currently work as a sales representative for an agricultural feed merchant in Maidsbury.

I was raised at Thorneybrook Cottage by my mother, Elsa Smith. My father was Frank Fanshawe. He was not married to my mother. He lived at Toy's Farm. It is a cattle farm just outside Downham village.

Frank Fanshawe died on August the 10th 1991. He left Toy's Farm to his niece, Vera Fanshawe, and everything that went with it.

That was a surprise to me. I was Frank Fanshawe's only child. He was getting on in years when he met my mum. When I was a teenager, I would visit him at his home quite regularly and when I was 18 I worked for about a year on the farm.

Sometime after that, we fell out. He said he would leave everything to Vera but it was still a surprise when he did.

I tried to get on with Vera Fanshawe when she moved into Toy's House. I invited her to my house several times or for drinks in local pubs but she never seemed very keen to come. She seemed to think she was better than me and my family. She kept herself aloof.

There was a time when she contacted me. She asked me to see her at Toy's House. When I got there, she said she was going to leave Toy's House and farm to me, with all personal effects, when she died. She has no children or other family that I know of. She is much older than me so I think we both expect that I will outlive her by many years. I found that an acceptable solution to the situation but, when I asked if I could manage the farm in the meantime, she got angry and told me not to be so presumptuous. She more or less threw me out and since then has refused to speak to me, even on the telephone. That conversation took place in July 1996.

There seemed to be nothing I could do except accept the situation. I'd already lost the farm once and I didn't want it to happen again. She would ignore me when our paths crossed but I could live with that.

Something did happen that I couldn't live with. In February this year, adverts started appearing about an auction which was to take place at Toy's Farm. It was to be run by Chisolms. They are a local firm who regularly hold auctions, usually at their sales rooms in Maidsbury.

All of these adverts made a big thing about the fact that the auction included three items of jewellery and there was a photo, too. There was a gold necklace with inset emeralds and a matching pair of earrings.

I had seen them before, like I told the police. My dad, Frank Fanshawe, promised them to my mother but never gave them to her. I often saw her wear them when he came to our house. He did give her a gold and emerald clasp, which he said he had got a London jeweller to make especially for my mum. It was a good match for the design of the necklace and earrings.

I could not accept that Vera Fanshawe was going to sell the emerald jewellery set. I did not know what it was worth but I could see no way that I could afford to buy them. At auction you expect dealers to be there and they'd drive the price right up.

One night, the week before the auction — I can't remember which night — I was in my local pub, the Red Cow in Downham. I was complaining to my mates about how unfair it all was and how my inheritance was being sold off.

One friend — I'm not prepared to name him — said that he had a friend who might be able to strike a deal with the auctioneers. That he would buy the jewellery set and maybe get it for less than it might fetch at the auction.

He didn't say exactly how much the set might be worth — I don't think he knew. He had a friend in the jewellery trade, he said. He said I might pay less than £2,000. I told him it would have to be a lot less for my pocket.

We met again in the Red Cow on the Sunday lunch-time, as arranged. He was alone. We went somewhere a bit private because you don't want everyone to know your business. He told me the price was £1,500. That was a lot but within my limits. We went to my house and I paid him the money.

I also paid him another £200, half for him and half for his friend. He never told me his friend's name. He left the jewellery at my house. I put it in the cupboard for safe-keeping.

I have learnt since that the jewellery came from a burglary at Toy's Farm. If I had known that earlier, I never would have bought the set. I had no idea that a burglary was being planned.

PART 4
THE BASIC COMPONENTS

TEN

PREPARING FOR COURT

10.1   Introduction

This is a job that has to be done sometime and by someone; you can only hope that it is you doing it in plenty of time before you are due in court. Of course, life doesn't always work out like that and you may be heavily reliant on someone else's notes of interviews with the client, background research on the law and the evidence, etc. That does not mean that you can simply breeze into court with little preparation. A classic example of how things can suddenly go wrong is when you are asked to go to court on some simple matter and ask the court to make 'the usual order'. Somehow, courts have a knack of discerning those advocates who are working to someone else's script and when you stand up and ask for 'the usual order', you may be asked, 'And what is that then?' or 'Why do you say you should have it?'. The competent advocate has considered these points in advance and has a reply ready; the incompetent advocate will become flustered and begin searching amongst their papers in the vain hope that the answer wil magically appear there.

Of course, there is a third category of advocate, too. Neither wholly competent nor wholly incompetent, this category is perhaps best described by the label 'beginner'. Anyone just starting out on their career as an advocate will be only too well aware of the high profile nature of the job. It matters not that there may be only three people in the room to witness your performance — you, your opponent and the district judge, perhaps — in your eyes, that's two too many! You will prepare the case to the best of your ability, devoting far more time to it than your more experienced colleagues seem to spend on their preparation. When someone passes you a file or brief and says, 'Just ask him for the usual order, and don't worry, he's a pussy cat', you won't accept that. You will read books, ask people to explain, try to be prepared. Then you go to court and everything falls apart; that great point you discovered at 2 a.m. last night is never argued in court because:

(a)   you were too nervous about it; or

(b)   you were too intimidated by the judge or your opponent or the situation to raise it; or

(c)   you couldn't find it in your notes; or

(d)   you forgot it.

This has happened to every advocate at one time or another but it happens to some more than most and it happens to beginners more than to experienced advocates. What can you do to stop it from happening to you?

There are three basic lessons to learn. First, prepare thoroughly for your appearance in court. Secondly, deliver the performance that you have prepared. Thirdly, be prepared to adapt in court to a fluid situation. Let's consider these in a little more depth.

10.2 Thorough Preparation

When you go into any court or tribunal, in fact whenever you want to speak on someone else's behalf, you should be prepared. You should be familiar with the relevant procedure and rules that apply in that court; you should be familiar with the law that is relevant to the case; you should be familiar with the evidential material that is (or might be) available for this hearing.

For example, you are sent to argue for summary judgment in a hearing before a Master in the Queen's Bench Division in the High Court. Before entering the room, you should know the procedural rules set out in Part 24 of the Civil Procedure Rules, together with any related rules, for example those dealing with the possible costs orders that may be made. You should be familiar with any rules governing the evidence that you (or your opponent) wish to use, for example, has your client's affidavit been served on your opponent in good time? If not, are there any rules that you can use to seek extraordinary permission to use that evidence? You should also know the relevant substantive law, that is, the law which deals with the claim. Since your claim is for summary judgment, more likely than not your client alleges that the defendant has no defence to the claim. In order to substantiate that allegation, if required to do so, you should be familiar with the relevant legal principles, first, as to why the claim should succeed and secondly, why there is no viable defence to it.

It follows that you must be familiar with the factual allegations made in the case (for which you will need to know the statements of case and your client's affidavit in support), because it is the synthesis of the legal framework with the specific factual allegations in this case which produce the argument that your client's claim must succeed and there is no reason why the case should go to a full trial.

Once you have gone through all of this preparation, you may need to write a skeleton argument to submit to the court in advance. These are increasingly used, both in civil trials and interim applications. What you put into a skeleton argument will depend partly on your style and preferences and partly what you learn suits the court. However, it should cover the following matters:

- The nature of the application or submission.

- What the case is about (where necessary).

- The issues between the parties (if necessary).

- The argument in the form of a series of legal propositions and submissions supported by authority and evidence (with references to pages and paragraphs as necessary).

The skeleton argument should also:

- Assist the court to assimilate your argument easily.

- Persuade the court to grant the order that you seek.

- Identify precisely what you are asking the court to do.

It may also be appropriate to hand in a separate chronology to the court.

Is that all you need to do in order to be fully prepared for this application? I'm afraid it is not that easy. Let's go back to the first two of our three basic lessons. First was thorough preparation and second was deliver the performance that you had prepared; in sporting parlance, don't leave your performance in the dressing room! It makes little difference to the outcome whether you prepared the case poorly or prepared yourself poorly for court. What you have done with your preparation so far is to work on the

content of your advocacy performance; the necessity to do that will never change from one case to another. What you must do now is to prepare the **delivery** of your performance.

10.3 Prepare your Delivery

Delivery will be the subject of an in-depth exploration in **Chapter 13**, so what you have here is a summary of the points that you will need to work on.

For many people, the advent of the video camera and, more recently, the camcorder has meant that many of us now know what we look like to others, much more realistically than we would by simply looking into a mirror. The video camera shows us what we look like when we move, stand or sit, it reveals our gestures to us and it tells us how we sound to others. Because of the fairly common ownership of such cameras, you may have already seen the picture that you present to others, the value of which was once described by Robert Burns, in 'To a Louse', as follows:

> O wad some Pow'r the giftie gie us
> To see oursels as others see us!
> It wad frae mony a blunder free us,
>   An' foolish notion.

If you have seen yourself, you may have been minded to make some changes but that is unlikely to have been done if the video was made on a social occasion. What you need to do now is record yourself delivering a piece of advocacy. Try to create the sort of conditions that will be present in court, for example, dress in formal court clothes, and deliver a straightforward speech or submission to the camera. Five minutes' worth should be enough to start with! Then review it. How do you look? Are you standing up straight or slouching? Are your hands in your pockets or fiddling with a pen? Can you hear yourself? Are you speaking too fast? Are you looking at the camera or away from it?

All of these points, and others, will be addressed in **Chapter 13**. For now, it is enough that you appreciate that, for many lawyers, preparing the law and the evidence for each case is relatively straightforward. After all, you have a law degree, are used to working on researching legal points in a law library, have a fund of basic legal knowledge; you have read the statements of case in this case (and maybe many others during your training), you have seen the evidence (in witness statements, affidavits and the like) and can remember it. If you can't remember it, now is the time to re-read **Chapter 3** of the Manual. What is not straightforward is the transition from **lawyer** to **advocate**.

10.4 From Lawyer to Advocate

On the face of it, this transition should be simple. After all, don't we all advocate almost every day of our lives? When you are at the supermarket and debating with your partner which brand of breakfast cereal to buy, if you want the cornflakes you will argue in favour of buying them and your objective will be to persuade your partner of the merit of your choice. What is so different about 'advocating' something in a courtroom?

Perhaps it is the fact that you are now arguing for someone else, so there is a sense of responsibility. Perhaps it is because you are now being judged on the quality of your argument by someone who has power, over both you and your client. Perhaps it is the public nature of the advocacy; whereas you may be happy and relaxed to debate points on a private level and at a private volume, when called on to do so with an audience and at much greater volume, the situation becomes less familiar and more uncomfortable. It should be clear that the more appearances that you make as an advocate, the more familiar and less uncomfortable it should all become. How do you survive until then?

Practice is the answer. You will find things becoming easier as you get more and more appearances under your belt. What you need to do is to increase your number of performances artificially, by using the video camera and working with others in a similar situation, as well as with more experienced advocates who can point out things that you may have overlooked. In the same way that pilots train on a flight simulator, so you can clock up more hours by working on advocacy simulations and getting more experience that way.

At various places around the Manual, for example **Chapter 9**, you will find an entire case to use as a vehicle for some advocacy work.

10.5   Being Adaptable

The third basic lesson that has to be grasped is that you must retain the ability to adapt and respond to a changing situation. It is sometimes said that advocates are quick-witted and have the ability to 'think on their feet' in court. What that really means is that the advocate is sufficiently well-versed in the relevant law and evidence that, even if something unexpected happens, the advocate can cope with it. The unexpected may be just being asked a question by a judge in the middle of your submission to the court; the judge wants to know about a particular point and wants to hear your answer now. For all the judge knows, you were just about to deal with that point. If so, it should be no problem for you to tackle it now. If you were going to deal with it later on in your submissions, you should know the answer even if you have to think about it a little more carefully. When that happens, you then have to make a judgment on whether to go back to the topic you were dealing with before the question or carry on from the point that your answer has now taken you to. The choice you make depends on what points you had to skip past to get the answer: were any of them important to your case, or contentious? If so, it's probably better to go back and deal with them. If not, carry on from the point which interested the judge.

It is a little different when you are questioning a witness. Here, the witness is meant to be under your control inasmuch as they are in the witness box to answer your questions. There is more chance that something unexpected will emerge from a witness than there was with the judge (at least we can expect the judge to appreciate concepts like legal relevance, admissibility and know the relevant legal framework for the case). So when the unexpected, and possibly inadmissible, answer is given, you should be prepared with your response. First, don't let your mouth open wide with surprise, don't flush with embarrassment and don't start stumbling over your words. If the answer was irrelevant to the issues in the case, you might ignore it or perhaps admonish the witness to listen carefully to your questions and simply answer them (this is likely to draw more attention to the unexpected answer). If the answer was relevant to the issues in the case, you may want some time to consider your response, in which case say something like:

> Perhaps we will return to that later, Mr Jones. For now, perhaps you could tell the court . . .

Having bought some time, you may want to leave the subject well alone but, if the answer came from a witness you were cross-examining, you might decide it has to be squashed. You could do that by attacking the credibility of the answer, for example, why is this the first we've heard of that? Is it something the witness has just made up? If they have made written statements some months (or even years) ago and the subject is not raised in the statement, why not? An alternative is to challenge the witness's memory of events that may have happened a long time ago; another might be to suggest that the witness, however innocently, is enhancing their account in a bid to help the court.

The central point is that you should be ready with an array of possible responses to the unexpected, like a collection of arrows in your quiver, so that you can calmly select the appropriate one to use in any given situation. Problems start when you don't expect the unexpected; you approach the trial or hearing with the mental equivalent of blinkers on and you are so focused on your own case and how to present it that anything that upsets your planned strategy pushes you completely off course. If you can remember that things seldom turn out exactly the way you anticipated before going into court, then you won't be so shocked when that prediction comes true.

10.6 Planning a Route to your Destination

We have looked at the need to understand (and perhaps research) the relevant law, to acquire a thorough grasp of the allegations, the evidence and the areas of dispute between the parties. We have also looked at the need to present yourself clearly in court and to be adaptable. The last hint is that before you finally start out on your journey through this case, you must have a clear idea of where you want to be at the end of it. You have to identify your client's objectives: what does he or she want out of this litigation? A judgment that they are not liable to the claimant? An award of damages? A verdict of not guilty? Then, what might you need to do in order to achieve those objectives? To answer these questions you will need to predict the arguments that you want to present to the court at the end of the case. Only then can you start to work backwards to consider how you can best guarantee that those arguments are in fact available to you at the end of the case.

It is often said that the advocate needs to start planning the closing speech for a trial before setting foot in the court. Really, you need to have a very clear picture in your mind of how the hearing will work — who will be there, what they are likely to say — so that you can start to see the time spent in court as a whole, rather than a series of isolated events. In a trial, what counsel says in opening the case may present a certain version of the case; the opponent needs to know whether that version might be challenged. As each witness appears in the witness box, the advocate cannot ignore what preceding witnesses have said, their answers will help to determine the questions that **this** witness is asked. At the start of a trial, a judge's notebook is blank, apart from the names of the parties perhaps. By the end of the evidence and speeches, it will have been filled up and the advocates cannot change its contents but they had a large role in determining what was written in it. During the course of the hearing, the thorough advocate has to keep in mind what he or she **wants** to have in the notebook, what is **actually** going into it, and what **might** still be put in.

10.7 Planning to Work with Witnesses

In this section, we examine the matters that the advocate should consider before going into court for a trial, or other hearing which involves calling witnesses.

10.7.1 THINKING ABOUT THE EVIDENCE

As with any appearance in court, you must identify several matters:

- What are the appropriate legal tests that will be applied?

- What are the facts in issue in the case? (In a civil case these should be clear from the statements of case; in a criminal case, a plea of not guilty requires proof of all the elements of the offence and one should then consider the possible/probable defence case as disclosed by the defence statement.)

- What evidence do you intend to adduce to ensure each issue is resolved in favour of your client?

- How do you intend to adduce that evidence?

This final point lies at the nub of how we start to prepare for calling witnesses. Will the evidence be in the form of answers given by a witness to questions asked by the advocate? Will the evidence emerge from a document, such as an affidavit, or from examination of an exhibit, such as a sketch plan or the alleged weapon, stolen property, etc.? If so, who will produce the exhibit in court? Might the admissibility of the evidence be challenged?

What you need to do is to plan how the evidence, needed to prove each material issue, can be put before the court. Look at your papers critically to determine each place where a material fact can be proved with the use of a witness and/or an exhibit. You can set out your conclusions in tabular form, using a column to identify each fact in issue, then another to show that there is evidence to prove that fact (maybe just a tick would do), then a third to identify the source(s) of that evidence. There could be more than one source — for example, several eye-witnesses to an accident who can each speak about what they saw happen. If one source is open to challenge — for example, a confession in a criminal trial might be excluded — that point should be recorded and alternative sources to supply the same evidence should be shown. That way, you can identify in advance all the possible ways to prove your case (or attack the opponent's case), consider the arguments for and against issues of admissibility, and think about your best response if your preferred source of evidence on an issue fails to do the job that you wanted.

In the court room, when questioning witnesses, try to be as flexible and responsive as you can be. We have just considered one way to do this — by plotting different routes by which you can reach the same conclusion. Another way to resist inflexibility is to avoid using a detailed list of questions. By all means, have a concise note of those facts that you want the witness to tell the court about, and an idea of how you want to present this witness to the court (if it is your witness, they should appear to be reliable, truthful and accurate).

You should have a structure when working with witnesses. You need to think about the order for calling the witnesses, if you have more than one, and you always have to think about the structure of each witness's testimony.

10.7.2 STRUCTURING THE TESTIMONY IN YOUR CASE

There are some conventions that are used in deciding the order in which several witnesses may be called into court to give their evidence. In criminal cases, it is usual to call the victim first. In cases of violence, they will usually establish that the assault took place, what injuries were suffered and perhaps identify the assailant. In cases of dishonesty, where property has been taken, the victim can assert that they did not give permission for their property to be dealt with in that fashion. In cases involving illicit drugs, the prosecution will need to prove the nature of the substance, requiring expert evidence of the testing of a sample recovered from the accused. They will also need to prove that the sample of substance tested by the expert was the one taken from the accused — this requires the prosecution to show a chain of possession, with the substance being taken into lawful custody, put into a sealed container, labelled and initialled and then transported through various pairs of hands until it reached the expert. The prosecution should be ready to call every person who provides a link in this chain, if it becomes necessary to do so.

The order of witnesses for the defence in a criminal trial is not wholly a matter of choice for the advocate and the client. The Police and Criminal Evidence Act 1984, s. 79, prescribes that if the defendant is to testify at trial, they must be the first witness to be called for the defence. This is subject to the court's discretion to allow another defence witness to be called into the witness box before the accused testifies; the discretion is only likely to be used where the other witness will talk about non-contentious facts and there is some good reason for taking their evidence out of the usual order. Generally, witnesses in criminal cases are kept out of court until the time comes for them to testify. The objective that lies behind s. 79 is that, as this rule cannot be applied to the accused, there is a risk that the accused may modify his or her testimony to 'fit' what evidence has already been given. This risk (which arises because the accused can see and hear all of the testimony in the case, up until he or she testifies) can be kept to a minimum if he or she is the first defence witness. Defence witnesses who will talk only about the character of the accused should always be called after the accused has testified.

Within these limitations, the advocate must still consider the best running order for the presentation of the evidence which he or she will rely upon. One excellent rule of thumb is to put yourself into the position of the trier(s) of fact — what would best enable the tribunal of fact to understand your client's case? Will the court be able to see how each witness contributes to your case? Will the significance of their testimony be clear? How do you want the story to unfold? These are all important questions but perhaps the most practical one is — who is available? Witnesses sometimes fail to turn up at court when they should. This may be due to nerves, illness, or even forgetfulness. Unless you are granted an adjournment by the court to secure the witness's attendance, you will have to do the best you can with what you have. That is one reason why you should have identified already the various alternative sources of evidence which you could use to establish each contentious issue in the case. Now you are able to stay calm and use your flexibility to your advantage — your advance planning is already paying dividends!

10.7.3 STRUCTURING THE TESTIMONY OF INDIVIDUAL WITNESSES

Having determined the (probable) sequence for calling the witnesses, we must now look at each witness individually. The order in which you explore topics with a witness will depend in large measure upon whether they are called to support your client's case or that of the opponent.

10.7.3.1 Structure for examination-in-chief

For examination-in-chief of 'your' witness, you will be concerned to see that:

(a) the witness is encouraged to recall the events;

(b) he or she can express their recollection clearly;

(c) the witness can talk about matters in the required degree of detail; and

(d) the court can follow and recall the testimony easily.

You can usually achieve these aims by helping the witness to go through the material events in a chronological order. After all, that is the sequence in which the events occurred so it should seem quite natural to the witness and the court to talk about them in that order. It may be that you do not get the necessary amount of detail about a particular matter from the witness when they talk about it for the first time. That can happen because you must not 'lead' your witness but use open questions which prompt them to tell the story in their own words. This will mean that, from time to time, you will need to interrupt their narrative in order to go back and cover a topic in more detail. For example, 'You have told the court that you arrived at the bus stop at about 10.30 am. Can you recall what the weather was like then?' and then, 'After you arrived there, how many people were at the bus stop?' If the witness is the first to be called for your client, you may want to get their story out quite swiftly, so that the court can see what happened, in broad terms. Having established the backdrop, as it were, you can then back-track and enable the witness to fill in more of the detail.

Sometimes, you will decide that the court will have a better understanding of events (or perhaps be more sympathetic to your client) if they learn first what happened to bring the parties to court at all, and then find out what events led up to that conclusion. Having settled the witness with the usual questions, such as, 'Please tell the court your full name' or 'What do you do for a living?', you might then ask the witness, 'Do you know why you are in court today?' When the witness replies affirmatively, you can then ask, 'Please tell the court what happened'. The witness is likely to start talking about the conclusion of a sequence of events, for example, 'My car was stolen' or 'I was hit over the head and had to go to hospital' or 'This man came up to me in the club and said I'd been talking to his girl'. You can then concentrate on those events with the witness, before turning to more preliminary matters.

Finally, we should also consider the use made of witness statements in civil cases. In both civil and criminal cases, witnesses usually provide statements to the parties calling them, in advance of the hearing. Generally, these statements will be exchanged between the parties before the trial, so that there are no surprises at the hearing itself (one significant exception to this is with defence witnesses in a criminal trial). In criminal cases, such statements will usually be disclosed only to the parties and their lawyers, and the judge in Crown Court trials; the witness's evidence at trial will be what they say in the witness box rather than what they said in the previous statement. In civil cases, the witness's previous statement will often be ordered to serve as their evidence-in-chief (see e.g., Civil Procedure Rules, r. 32.5). This has consequences for any examination-in-chief by the advocate.

The start of the (civil) examination-in-chief will look something like this:

Having asked the witness to identify themselves, the advocate will have the court usher show the witness 'a document'.

Advocate:	'Do you see a signature on the document?'
Witness:	'Yes.'
Advocate:	'Whose signature is it?'
Witness:	'Mine.'
Advocate:	'When did you make that statement?'
Witness:	[replies]
Advocate:	'Were its contents true when you made it?'
Witness:	'Yes.'

At this point you may sit down, leaving your witness to be cross-examined. However, you may wish to ask the witness to augment the evidence that is in their statement. You will need to ask the judge for leave to do so. The judge may refuse and suggest that you can pick up any points during your re-examination of the witness, after cross-examination. If you are given permission, then you may build on the witness's earlier statement. For example, 'Mr Smith, in paragraph 3 of your statement, you say that, "Because the weather was so hot, I took the safety guard off the machine that I was operating." What did you do with the safety guard?'

Because, in effect, you are combining the written statement with the oral testimony, you can be more selective with the topics that you ask the witness to deal with in the witness box. Concentrate on those topics which are central to your case, and which will help the court to form a view of the witness's reliability and recollection. It is probably helpful to work through those topics in the order in which they appear in the written statement. As you will often use the statement as the 'springboard' for a question, the witness should understand clearly what you want them to talk about. Another reason to question your witness in court is where their statement is now out of date. Here, strictly speaking, you do not need to get leave from the court before asking questions but you should tell the judge what you are proposing to do. The judge may be concerned that a second, up-to-date, statement should have been taken from the witness and served on your opponent before the trial. Since your aim now is to bring out new information, rather than looking at known events in greater detail, you should probably follow a chronological sequence, as we saw earlier.

10.7.3.2 Structure for cross-examination

Your aims are rather different when you question the witnesses that have been called by your opponent. For one thing, you do not expect that they will support your client's case (although they may do in some topics). It is usual for a cross-examiner to want to undermine either the testimony of the witness (or the credibility of the witness) or to show its irrelevance to the issues in the trial. Further, as the witness's recollection of events is likely to be significantly different from the one that you seek to establish, you want to make their recollection more obscure than clear. You are also under a duty to question the witness on issues where your client's case differs from their recollection (known as 'putting your case to the witness'). In cross-examination, you are allowed to ask questions which suggest things, or put propositions, to the witness. So, you might say, 'But the man in the green jacket never had a knife in his hand, did he?' or 'You never saw his hand.' or 'The man in the green jacket had left by then.' In other words, you have a different story to tell and you do not want to give the witness a second chance to repeat their evidence-in-chief.

In cross-examination, then, your order of topics should be clear to the **court**. You want the tribunal of fact to understand why you are asking the questions that you use: you want the court to appreciate the discrepancies between the competing versions of events. But you do not always want the **witness** to see where you are going or what you are trying to do. The order of topics needs careful consideration, as does the order of questions on a particular topic.

You may wish to try to bait a trap for the witness, rather than immediately confront them with the proposition that you would like them to accept. So, for example, you may want to cast doubt on a witness's earlier testimony that when they saw the man in the green jacket, he was holding a knife in his hand. If you simply say to the witness, 'The man in the green jacket never had a knife in his hand, did he?', the likely answer you will get is, 'He did'; blatant confrontation seldom produces agreement. If you begin by exploring the circumstances in which the observation took place, you may find either that the witness accepts that your proposition is reasonable or the court may well decide it is reasonable and not accept the witness's testimony on the matter. So, you might suggest (if to do so is consistent with your instructions) that the venue was dark, or busy, or the witness's attention was distracted, or something of that sort which might lead on to the witness acknowledging at least the possibility that they might be mistaken, in all the circumstances.

10.8 A Work Plan for a Criminal Trial and Conference

10.8.1 INTRODUCTION

The remaining paragraphs of this chapter contain a short, simple plan to use when preparing for a trial in the Crown Court, either as the prosecutor or for the defence. It is intended to act partly as a check list of the things you should cover in your preparation and also as a guide to organising your materials.

There is also a plan for a conference with the defendant in a criminal case and some points to consider when questioning witnesses in court and making speeches. Some of these will be covered in greater detail in other chapters.

You could try to create your own check lists after studying a particular situation, perhaps add your points to the one given here for the defence conference. Remember, what you find here is always open to improvement or adaptation. This section of the chapter provides a start for you — build on it!

10.8.2 WORK PLAN

On receiving Brief:
Read the instructions: What am I being asked to achieve?

10.8.2.1 Defence brief

(a) Look at the *indictment.* **Never** prepare a case without the indictment. Compare the counts with the committal charges. Are they the same? If they differ, ask yourself why. Always consider what alternative convictions could be recorded.

(b) Read prosecution statements and exhibits: do the papers disclose a prima facie case?

(c) Are my instructions a plea of *guilty* or *not guilty?*

Not Guilty

(a) Is that supportable on my instructions? If not, conference/advice.

(b) Is a conference required in any event? (Desirable in all but the simplest of cases.)

(c) Are my instructions adequate? If not, request further and better particulars.

(d) Points of law: PACE 1984; CJA 1988; CJA 1991

what additional evidence may be needed?: e.g., custody record and relevant police officers; medical reports of any examination of victim/defendant.

(e) Additional evidence required generally: e.g., proofs to be taken from potential witnesses; plans; photos.

(f) Expert evidence: must be served on prosecution if intended to be relied upon at trial.

(g) Alibi: (i) is it an alibi case?

(ii) if so, has anything been done about it — defence statement?

(h) Notices of additional evidence: do we require the witnesses to attend?

(i) Unused material. Has this been requested/served?

(j) As a result of my instructions/conference can I offer any sensible pleas to the prosecution. If so, solicitors should write at once.

Note: most of the above points are far better covered in a written Advice than in a chat over the telephone.

Guilty

(a) On my instructions is that a proper plea or equivocal?

(b) On my instructions is a *Newton* trial likely on issue(s) of fact? If so, consider a discussion in advance with prosecution so that witnesses can be warned to attend, thus avoiding need for adjournment.

(c) Any evidence required in support of mitigation? e.g., proof of job.

(d) Any character witnesses, references, service records, etc.?

(e) Request extension to legal aid for psychiatric/medical report (if appropriate).

(f) Research authorities on sentence for type of offence and assess likely range, or talk directly to the prosecuting advocate to find out what, if any, pleas of guilty might be acceptable to the prosecution, or possibly if the prosecution would be willing to allow the court simply to bind the defendant over to keep the peace.

(g) Advise solicitors to inform court of fact of guilty plea. Always prepare for a best and a worst result. If best, an acquittal, be ready to argue costs. If worst, be ready to make a speech in mitigation of sentence **and** to advise on appeal.

10.8.2.2 Prosecution brief (not guilty)

(a) *Indictment:*
draft it if requested;
if already drafted, check it is correctly drafted and that there is evidence to support it.

(b) *Advice:*
additional evidence if needed and photos;
disclosure/non-disclosure in accordance with the Criminal Procedure and Investigations Act 1996 and relevant case law;
disclose any previous convictions of any prosecution witness.

(c) *Opening note:*
contents must be borne out by reference to admissible evidence;
plan structure: enough law/fact to help the jury, not confuse them;
visual aids: OHP, video, graphics, schedules — will they help?

(d) *Preparation of jury bundle:*
only what's really necessary;
make sure it's legible;
include plans, agreed schedules, glossaries, etc.;
folders/binders, etc.

(e) *Order of witnesses:*
defence (and judge) always want to know this.

Tight preparation = Strong presentation.

10.8.2.3 Defence conference

(a) Keep requisite degree of formality: avoid use of first names with client and (during conference) with solicitor (often difficult to do!).

(b) Put client at ease: explain what you are going to discuss: be prepared to **listen** and not just **talk**.

(c) Explain what the charge means.

(d) Explain strengths/weaknesses in the defence ⎫ be frank: this avoids the 'why

(e) Explain possible sentence upon conviction ⎭ didn't you tell me?' afterwards.

(f) If this is the defendant's first Crown Court trial: explain what will actually happen at court.

The idea of points (a)–(f) is that they remove uncertainty in the client's mind and help to make the client confident that:

(i) you understand the case; and

(ii) you are in charge and capable of running it.

10.8.2.4 Examination-in-chief

(Much harder than cross-examination in many ways because you are not allowed to lead the answers from the witness.)

In advance

(a) Be clear in your own mind what it is that you want to adduce from the witness.

(b) A statement is often badly put together and you may well not want to follow its sequence. As a result a plan/check list of sequence and content may be helpful. (Note: if you are going to ask questions on matters not covered at all then a further statement should be taken and served on the defence.)

(c) Try to put the witness at ease — courtrooms can be very intimidating. A relaxed witness is far more likely to come up to proof.

(d) 'Difficult' witness: **Don't** rush to make him **hostile** in law: try 'going round again'; if it's a memory problem, seek a short adjournment so that he can refresh his memory — a trial is not a memory test (Note: there will almost always be an argument over this in the absence of the jury.)

10.8.2.5 Cross-examination

(a) You have a duty to put your main challenges to the witness during cross-examination, e.g., it never happened: you've made it up; you're mistaken, etc.

(b) From the statement and your instructions, **plan** what you're going to ask in order to try to **assist** your case: i.e. are there obvious areas where the witness is vulnerable and you can make a good point? Are there obvious areas where the witness is strong and will simply be 'firmed up' if pressed by the defence?

(c) Don't try to get the witness to make comments: he or she is unlikely to want to help you and you can make the comment in your closing speech without fear of getting the wrong answer.

(d) When you have got a favourable answer: **stop**. Many cases have been lost by pushing a question too far.

(e) Don't be frightened **not** to ask questions: if a witness has been favourable to you or failed to identify/mention your client **leave well alone**, however tempting to try and score a few points.

Both in examination-in-chief and cross-examination:

(a) make sure that the witness is keeping his voice up;

(b) don't go too fast: follow the judge's pen;

(c) let the witness answer before asking your next question;

(d) try to keep questions short: nothing is worse than when your clever but convoluted question is met by blankness and 'Sorry, I don't understand what you're getting at'.

10.8.2.6 Speeches

(a) Speeches should be as short as possible: juries do not need 20 minutes on the burden and standard of proof.

(b) Make your good points and sit down: don't spoil them by waffle and numerous bad points.

(c) If you feel your client won't feel you have 'had a good go' if you make a very short speech, explain to him or her beforehand why you're doing so — they normally understand.

(d) Prosecution:

    (i) fair presentation and comment on evidence;

    (ii) not duty to secure conviction at all costs;

    (iii) not duty to 'sum up' case to them by rehearsing all the law and facts (again).

Note: prosecution of a 'Guilty' plea is covered in **Chapter 39**.

ELEVEN

WHAT TO SAY IN COURT

11.1   Introduction

To a certain extent, the answer to the question implied in the title of this chapter must
be found in **Chapter 10**. It is unlikely that you will be able to say the right things at
the right times unless you have prepared for your appearance very thoroughly. So,
hasn't the job been done? Well, the proof of the pudding comes when it is eaten and
even the best preparation in the world is just wasted effort if you cannot say the right
things and take the right decisions once you get into the courtroom. Every advocate
has to make use of their knowledge of the law and put it together with their analysis
of the evidence and issues in dispute to produce what the court requires, namely a
performance which is appropriate, relevant, legally sound and factually sound. It is
worth looking in more detail at these requirements, in particular to see how they might
apply to the range of tasks which the advocate may be asked to perform.

11.2   The Content of Submissions

In a sense, the four requirements set out in **11.1** are the wrong way around: if the
advocate does not put forward arguments on a submission which are 'legally sound
and factually sound', there is little chance that the arguments will be 'appropriate and
relevant'. Although the twin requirements of appropriateness and relevance are more
important than simply being sound on the law and facts, the advocate must first know
the 'facts' and the necessary law in order to construct the legal and factual framework
within which it becomes possible to gauge whether an argument is appropriate or
relevant.

11.2.1   APPROPRIATE AND RELEVANT

11.2.1.1   Your submission
Whenever you are called on to make an application or submission to a court, one of
your earliest steps in preparing will be to digest exactly what appears in the statements
of case. Of course, it is a little different in criminal cases but there will still be a charge
sheet, summons or indictment to consider. Looking at these will help you to discover
the issues between the parties, who alleges what, when and who bears the burden of
proof. It will also be the start of your legal analysis, when the causes of action are
disclosed or the elements of the offence revealed.

'Relevance' denotes some sort of relationship between things; what you say in court
must be directed to identifying the issues in the case and how they should be resolved.
When you dissect a set of papers prior to going into court with them, you have to learn
a lot of things which you did not know before. Someone else may have been through a
sorting process already, so that if you are instructed on behalf of Mr Smith in his
careless driving prosecution, you don't suddenly find a lot of documents to do with his
pending divorce. Similarly, when you open your mouth in court, you should not just
say anything that appeared in the case papers (or your instructions). You must
regularly gauge whether what you are about to do, whether it be drawing the court's

attention to some factual allegation or addressing an argument to the court, is connected to the issues that are of concern to the court.

If 'relevant' means that you should talk only about matters that are likely to be (and should properly be) considered by the court when adjudicating in the case, what does that leave for 'appropriate' to do? Appropriate means that you are sensitive to your surroundings, the context in which you are operating. For example, in a prosecution for grievous bodily harm it may be clear that the victim has suffered nasty injuries. A defence advocate who has to allege that in fact the 'victim' was the protagonist and the accused was simply acting in self-defence must appreciate that the court is likely to feel a considerable sympathy for the injured person. That may make it necessary to adopt certain tactics or arguments which acknowledge that sympathy and appreciate that, when putting forward the defence case, there may be a lot of resistance. Again, it may be 'appropriate' in a hearing seeking an interim payment of damages for personal injury to tell the court what the claimant requires the money for, even though the legal test for making the interim payment doesn't require you to do so. A piece of factual information or an argument may be 'appropriate' without strictly being 'relevant' in a legal sense.

11.2.1.2 Opposing a submission

When a court hears a submission or application, it is generally the case that the advocates and the judge all have the same documentary information (affidavits and statements of case have been served on the opposing party in advance). No-one is usually taken by surprise at the hearing. However, just because the advocates have access to the same information it does not follow that they will make the same use of it. Different people see different arguments, disagree over what is a strength and what is a weakness in the case. When you are opposing a submission or application, your task is twofold.

First, you must prepare to respond as best you can, so you should try to anticipate your opponent's arguments. What will the other side be emphasising? Which of the weaknesses in your case will they seek to exploit? When preparing to respond, it is tempting to plan for every eventuality and that has some sense to it. But you must be ready to adapt your strategy or your arguments to meet the situation on the day; you must not present your case like an automaton, blithely assuming that everything is going just the way you thought it would. Suppose that you spotted a weak point in your evidence while preparing the case, then you should work out a tactic to deal with it but you must still listen in court. If your opponent does not raise that topic, for whatever reason, you should consider very carefully whether you now need to say anything about it when you respond. If you do, you may just remind your opponent of a forgotten argument or alert your learned friend to the existence of a weakness (they may not have seen the point in those terms until now). Thus, what is relevant and appropriate can change quite rapidly in the course of competing arguments on a submission. The second part of your task, then, is to monitor constantly what the other side is saying and the response of the court, and to tailor your arguments to suit the circumstances as they are at the moment.

11.2.1.3 Skeleton arguments

In a civil case, your application or submission may be supported by a skeleton argument. This document will be prepared by you in advance of the hearing and supplied to both the court and your opponent. Assume that both have read it before the application starts. Clearly, the content of your skeleton argument should fulfil the same criteria as your oral argument — it should be appropriate, relevant and sound in fact and law. It may be that there is adequate coverage of a point in your skeleton and you can therefore either take it very shortly in addressing the court orally, or perhaps simply refer the court to the passage in the skeleton. For further guidance on skeleton arguments, see the ***Drafting Manual*, Chapter 23**.

11.2.2 LEGALLY AND FACTUALLY SOUND

Whatever you say in court as an advocate, it must be a fair and accurate representation of the facts in the case and the law relating to the case (or the particular hearing at least). You should never knowingly mislead the court on the law or the evidence (whether going to a disputed fact or not). If you do so innocently and in good faith, then as soon as you realise your error you should draw the court's attention to it and correct yourself.

Let's look at how your submission might be legally and factually sound. In an application for summary judgment, the test is to be found in the Civil Procedure Rules (CPR), r. 24. No judge will need you to tell him or her that but they will expect you to base your arguments, for or against summary judgment, on an accurate understanding of what the criteria are for summary judgment. For that, you need the current text of CPR, r. 24, to hand. As this (new) rule is interpreted and applied by the courts, some elements may assume greater or lesser significance. You will need to be as up-to-date as you can be, on how the courts are using CPR, r. 24, and be able to use that knowledge as the basis of your arguments to the court.

As for being factually sound, you should know the number of affidavits in the case, who swore them, when they were sworn and, most importantly, what they say (and don't say). Anything you say to the court of a factual nature must be accurate: don't say the unpaid debt is £12,500 if it is £15,200, for example. On a more mundane level, if one of the witnesses is named John Tyler, don't refer to him as Jack Taylor. We all make little slips like that from time to time but the important thing is to listen to yourself. Even if you know the witness is called John Tyler, it may not always come out like that. As stated, that slip is probably quite inconsequential but for one thing — it may plant a seed of doubt in the court's mind whether you know what you are talking about. If you can make an error over something as simple as a name, especially when it is on a document in front of you, what else might you be mistaken about?

11.2.3 REFERENCE TO LEGAL SOURCES

On most applications or submissions, your court will probably be legally qualified (a judge, a district judge, a Master) and the last thing such people want is a lecture on the law. After all, they may know it as well as you, if not better, and use it more frequently too. What the court wants, then, is not copious references to the legal sources for your arguments, it wants you to have extracted the legal principle from the case of *Smith* v *Jones*, say, and apply it to the allegations and evidence in the present case. On an application by the defence advocate in a Crown Court trial to exclude an interview between the police and the accused from being heard by the jury, the judge will not want to hear from counsel about the legal history of the Police and Criminal Evidence Act 1984, s. 76. The judge will want the advocate to have identified the relevant part(s) of s. 76 — maybe 'oppression' — and then present the arguments, based on a synthesis of the relevant law and evidence.

11.3 Content when Questioning Witnesses

'Content' is a more complex topic in relation to witnesses than it is for submissions. You might want to turn to **Chapter 8** and read the advocacy training criteria on examination-in-chief and cross-examination in **8.3.2** and **8.3.3**.

11.3.1 YOUR WITNESS

What you ask a witness will be governed by several considerations. First, you must not ask your witness leading questions (see **Chapter 18**). If you do, then although the subject matter of the question may be 'relevant' and based on a sound understanding of the law and allegations, it may not be 'appropriate'. Thus, you should use appropriate questioning techniques.

In any hearing where witnesses are called to testify, you should have identified what evidence they can give which will help to establish your client's case. This will decide the relevance of your questions and their answers. If you don't ask questions to make the optimum use of the witness and get all of the relevant evidence that they could give, you probably have not conducted an examination-in-chief which is wholly appropriate to the circumstances of that case. Further, you should not ask a question which requires the witness to speak about inadmissible matters; such questions may be logically relevant but are not legally relevant (see for example *R v Blastland* [1986] AC 41). Finally, you should try to insulate your witness from attack by your opponent in cross-examination. That may mean getting the witness to talk about topics relevant to your opponent's case as well as your client's case. Such topics may not be of direct legal relevance to your client's case but it could certainly be appropriate to canvass them at this point.

11.3.2 YOUR OPPONENT'S WITNESS

As before, what is required here will be fact-specific to the individual case, as determined by the issues between the parties and what evidence the witness can give. You should use appropriate questioning techniques here, too, but what is appropriate has changed (see **Chapter 19**). In general terms, examination-in-chief is about **trust**, the advocate allowing the witness the freedom to tell their story in their own words, but cross-examination is about **control**. The cross-examiner doesn't want the witness to tell their story in their own words; instead, the cross-examiner asks leading questions designed to convey the story of the cross-examiner's client in words chosen by the cross-examiner. In one sense, it does not matter what answers most witnesses give in cross-examination because the cross-examiner never expected the witness to agree with the proposition in the question anyway. One of the functions of cross-examination is to put your client's case to the witness (see **Chapter 19**) and such 'questions' are unlikely to produce much agreement between the advocate and the witness. The degree of control exerted on witnesses in cross-examination can often be seen if you keep a note of the questions and answers; typically, the questions contain the detail while the answers are just 'Yes' or 'No'. Questions asked during examination-in-chief are generally not so detailed but can produce quite lengthy and complex responses from the witness.

Other aims of cross-examination, which make certain questions appropriate, are the need to use the witness to assist your client's case and the possibility of undermining the witness and/or their evidence. On the former point, it is not always the position that a witness called by the opposing party will be 100% damaging to your client's case, more often than not the witness may be a source of assistance on at least some topics. If you can see a way in which your opponent's witness could supply answers which help your client, it is appropriate to ask the questions which produce those answers; evidence given by opposing witnesses which supports your case always seems to be more persuasive. On the latter point, undermining, you might ask questions which attack the credibility of the witness themselves (for example, to show they are biased) or of their version of events (for example, comparing it with other evidence given in the cases which is inconsistent with their version).

TWELVE

STRUCTURING YOUR WORK

12.1 Introduction

The subject of structure needs to be seen in two distinct ways. First, you can deal with structure in the context of applications or submissions made to a court or tribunal. These may be applications at an ad hoc hearing (e.g., application for summary judgment) or in the course of a trial (e.g., voir dire). The second context is in the examination of witnesses, whether called by your client or by other parties in the litigation. This chapter looks at structure within these two contexts but it is important to note, at the outset, that there are three basic requirements that are relevant to structure, whatever the context.

12.1.1 THREE BASIC REQUIREMENTS

The three basic requirements for structure are:

  (a) be clear;

  (b) be logical; and

  (c) be responsive.

Remember, **clarity** is everything, obscurity is nothing. Your ultimate aim is to persuade and, to do that, you must communicate accurately with the tribunal. You are most likely to do that if everything you say and do is clear in its meaning. A clear structure is a good guarantee for that. Coupled with clarity is the need to be **logical**. Despite the critiques of the human reasoning process that have been made (see e.g., the works of Edward de Bono), it is a fact that the most common process for reaching conclusions relies heavily (although not solely) on logic.

When devising a structure for your work, you should choose one that 'makes sense'. To achieve that, it should make sense to others, too. That is not to say that there can only be one logical structure, although there may be a 'normal' or common structure to particular applications. One might present information on the basis of a chronological order, or a geographical order, or even 'best point first'. Perhaps the best general description is that individual points should flow clearly from one to another, rather than appear as a motley collection of unrelated data.

Finally, **respond** to the other players in the drama. Even when there are only two of you (maybe on an application when no-one appears for the opponent), you may still face questions from the court. Deal with them as they arise if at all possible. If you really cannot provide an immediate response, indicate that you will be doing so shortly. Whether making an application or questioning a witness, you cannot afford to stick to pre-conceived notions or a particular structure *regardless* of what others are saying or thinking. A script is almost useless in court for many reasons but here it hampers good advocacy by imposing a strait-jacket on the advocate. You must have a clear and logical structure certainly, but you must never adhere to it just for its own sake. If there is no need to amend or adapt it while you are in court, so much the better but your planning should have enabled you to be flexible in your work. You should be alert to what the tribunal or your opponent or the witness are saying, doing or thinking. They are communicating with you and each other either directly or indirectly and you cannot afford to ignore what they are saying.

12.2 Applications to a Court

12.2.1 CLEAR AND LOGICAL: YOUR APPLICATION

Your first consideration is, what stage of the proceedings are we at? Has the hearing been arranged primarily for the purpose of the application you are to make, or is the application merely incidental to a more wide-ranging hearing? For example, is this an application for summary judgment or is it an application, during a trial, to exclude evidence?

In the former situation, introductions are required. The court needs to know who the advocates are and courtesy dictates that you tell the court, even if it clearly knows their identities already. The court also needs to know who the parties are to the litigation and which advocate represents which party. The court may require you to tell it something about the case itself, before you launch into the application. In the latter situation, such introductions would be unnecessary at best and bizarre at worst.

12.2.1.1 The ad hoc hearing
A general structure for such a hearing could look like this:

(a) Introduce advocates, parties, the case, the application, all very briefly.

(b) Check that the court has all of the relevant documents. Be specific, don't just say, 'Have you got the papers in this case?'.

(c) Briefly state the order in which you propose to present the rest of your application.

(d) Explain the background to the application, if appropriate.

(e) The substance of the application:

  (i) Set out the arguments in support of your application, combining the specific evidence in this case with the relevant legal rules. Don't lecture the court on the law, or spend time stating what you understand the law to be in some abstract way. Always apply the law to the evidence and remember that the court has probably heard a great many of these applications, it does not need to receive the benefit of your legal research!

  (ii) If necessary, anticipate and deal with the arguments of your opponent. If these counter-arguments will be on points that you need to establish to succeed in the application, deal with the point as you interpret it first and then indicate why the counter-argument has no merit.

  (iii) For any application, there may be several legal requirements on which the court needs to be satisfied before your application can succeed. You should have an argument designed to deal with each such point.

(f) Summarise your strongest arguments, by way of a conclusion, and offer to assist the court with any questions that it may have.

(g) Allow your opponent to make his or her arguments to the court.

(h) Ask to be allowed to reply to those arguments, if necessary.

(i) The court announces its decision.

(j) You raise any supplementary points which are relevant now that the main decision has been reached.

That is fine as a framework but it may not turn out that way in practice. For example, suppose your opponent keeps interrupting your arguments? Or the judge keeps asking questions, none of which seem relevant to the point you are dealing with? The answer is to be flexible and responsive. You might suggest that it would be simpler for all concerned if you could present all of your arguments first and then give the floor to your opponent. That is responsive as it does not require you to carry on as if your opponent was saying nothing. If the judge asks a question, you should deal with it. You might then return to your previous point, or you could skip to that part of your plan which follows on from the judge's question. If in doubt, ask the judge.

12.2.1.2 The application within a trial

Typically, this type of application will arise after the beginning of the trial, perhaps concerned with an issue of evidence. Here, one can afford to be much more specific as the court should be fully aware of the context of your application. So, a general plan might work like this:

(a) State that an application now needs to be made. In circumstances where questions of law are decided by different people from those who decide questions of fact, this is all you should say at present, then wait for the triers of fact to leave the court.

(b) State what the application is (e.g., an application pursuant to s. 76 of the Police and Criminal Evidence Act 1984).

(c) If the application places the burden of proof on you (not always the case; see e.g., s. 76 of the 1984 Act), set out the allegations of fact that you rely on, relating each of them to the legal requirements on which you must satisfy the court. Do not deal with the relevant law unless you are applying it to the alleged facts.

(d) Allow your opponent to present any counter-arguments.

(e) Ask for an opportunity to reply, if you need one.

(f) The court announces its decision on the application.

(g) Carry on with the trial, at a point and in a manner consistent with the court's decision.

12.2.2 CLEAR AND LOGICAL: OPPOSING AN APPLICATION

Much of what concerns the advocate who is making an application is inapplicable to an advocate who must respond to that application. Typically, it will be unnecessary to introduce yourself when you first speak to the court as that should have been done by your opponent. Any relevant documentation should also be before the court by now and you can simply make use of it, without needing to introduce it.

Clarity here simply requires that each of your arguments is clearly differentiated. Do not conflate two separate points; keep your arguments as simple as they can be. Logic will often dictate that the order in which you raise issues and present your arguments on them is the same as the order adopted by your opponent. That may be unfortunate for two reasons. First, their order may differ from your preferred order for tactical reasons and, secondly, you may have to re-arrange your running order at the last possible moment. Even so, that is probably the best course of action rather than sticking to your own intended order unless the order chosen by your opponent was, in your opinion, defective for some reason. In this situation you may want to indicate that you will not be following the order of points used by your opponent, and perhaps explain why. Then you should go on and explain what your order will be, to minimise any confusion for the court.

It is not of great assistance to work on a framework when you are opposing an application, for reasons just stated. But you should have an order for the arguments, in case you want to substitute your order for that used by your opponent. Thinking about the appropriate order for your arguments also requires you to think about which arguments are your strengths and which are your weaknesses. This is an extremely useful process when preparing for court and should never be overlooked. The judge may have already asked your opponent some questions. These questions could indicate matters which the judge is concerned about. You might then concentrate on those matters in your submission.

12.3 Questions to a Witness

12.3.1 YOUR WITNESS

During examination-in-chief, you should be using each witness to tell the court what they know of the story of the case. In each trial there are one or more issues which the parties dispute and which the court must resolve; sometimes these are disputes of law but much more often they are disputes of fact. You should structure your sequence of questions to a witness with a primary objective of getting the witness to speak clearly and logically about the 'facts'. Your questions should assist the witness to achieve a good communication with the trier(s) of fact. That means that you go through topics in a sensible order, that the witness is enabled to give all of the evidence that they could give (and which is useful to your client's case) and they do so by telling their story in their own words, as much as possible. Studies of witness credibility have shown that juries are likely to find a witness much more credible (and persuasive) if they demonstrate a good understanding of what they are testifying about and appear confident in what they are saying. It also helps, apparently, if the advocate does not interrupt very often.

What you need to do to start the examination-in-chief is to settle the witness. They need to get used to their surroundings, to being the focus of attention, and to the sound of their own voice projected across the courtroom. So you start them with easy, short questions to which they know the answers and which allow them to talk a little. For example:

- Give the court your name and address?

- What is your occupation?

- Where do you work?

- How long have you worked there?

Such questions pose no major test for a witness and so they help to take the pressure off. Once the witness has relaxed, you can move onto the substance of their evidence. What sequence might you adopt there?

You will usually find that, as the witness is telling a story, they will recollect it best (and the trier(s) of fact will remember it better) if you enable the witness to work through their story in a chronological order. As this is your witness, you should not ask leading questions, even if you wanted to (see **Chapter 18**). Open questions which allow the witness some freedom to tell their story are the ones that should be in the majority at the beginning of the examination-in-chief. Obviously, the lack of direct control that you have when using open-type questions means that sometimes the witness says something ambiguous or obscure and further explanation is required. Then you have a choice; either you interrupt the 'flow' of the witness's narrative, as in:

> Stop there, please, Sergeant. You just said that Mr Jones was drunk. What led you to that conclusion?

and immediately seek the further clarification from the witness. Or you can let the witness continue to answer open questions until they have concluded their narrative, and then return to topics raised by the witness earlier, getting the detail through more specific questions. The former tactic is acceptable (it is sometimes called the 'funnel' technique; and see **18.3.7.12**) but you must be careful not to go into so much detail now, through over-use of closed questions, that the court cannot see the wood for all the trees.

As well as using your witnesses to establish your client's case, you may also want to use them to cast doubt on your opponent's case and you may want to protect your witness from a damaging attack in cross-examination. Both objectives are likely to result in you asking questions which are not an obvious part of your client's theory of the case. In order to minimise any confusion that may arise in these circumstances, it is usually better to leave these topics to later in the witness's evidence, after they have done their best to establish the evidence favourable to your client.

The other consideration is that you should be responsive to a witness's answers. You cannot simply plough on, appearing to others to pay no regard to the answers the witness is giving. The sequence of questions and answers should flow in a clear and logical fashion. When breaks occur, and there is a change of subject, that should be clear from the first question on the new topic, as in, 'I want to turn now to the moment when the ambulance arrived. What did ...?'.

So you see that, when thinking about the sequence of your questions for examination-in-chief, you should have a clear idea of the basic running order of topics through which to take the witness. The sequence in which specific questions are asked may be better left until you are actually on your feet questioning the witness, otherwise you risk being too tied to a plan and not responding appropriately to the witness's answers. (See also **10.7** and **Chapter 18**.)

12.3.2   YOUR OPPONENT'S WITNESS

When cross-examining a witness, your aims are a little different. Now you are likely to be less concerned with assisting the witness and allowing them to tell their story. In fact, you probably don't want them to tell their story (again). You won't be able to finalise your running order for the topics you need to cross-examine on until the moment that your opponent concludes the examination-in-chief. That doesn't give you a lot of time! Obviously you need a list of all the topics you might need to question the witness about, and you should think about a sensible order in which to raise those topics. But suppose the witness never gave an anticipated and crucial piece of evidence? A large part of your intended cross-examination may just have become redundant. You must be able to respond to the evidence actually given by the witness in-chief. If they haven't hurt your case, don't cross-examine them, leave them well alone.

You need to analyse each opposing witness to see on each issue in the case:

(a)   do they have evidence relevant to this issue?

(b)   if so, does it hurt my client's case? or

(c)   does it help my client's case? or

(d)   is the witness effectively neutral?

Once you have done that, you will have an overall picture of the witness as potentially harmful, helpful, neutral or a mixture of these depending on the particular topic. In turn, that will help you to decide on your likely running order for the topics. If you think the witness can help you on a particular topic, it might be best to deal with that at or near the start of your cross-examination, especially if you think you may have to attack them on other topics. They may be less willing to agree with your questions towards the end of your cross-examination if you have given them a tough time earlier on.

Finally, as with the examination-in-chief, listen to the witness's answers and respond to them. Your response will probably be different since the answer may be a damaging one, but you should constantly be reassessing what questions you need to ask this witness. One difference between the sequence of questions in examination-in-chief and in cross-examination is this: in examination-in-chief, you want to help the witness and so you raise topics in a clear and logical order (typically chronological). In cross-examination, you want your questions to be structured in a way that makes them clear and logical to the trier(s) of fact but maybe not so clear to the witness — at least until it is too late for them to do anything about it! The key here may be to have a gentle and patient build-up, through a series of relatively innocuous questions, until you have painted the witness into a corner. Then you ask the key question (probably putting some part of your client's case to the witness), saying something like, '. . . That must be right, mustn't it, Miss Smith?'. If you have built up the previous questions and answers sensibly and patiently, the court is likely to agree with your proposition even if the witness does not. (See also **10.7** and **Chapter 19**.)

THIRTEEN

SPEAKING AND DELIVERY

13.1 Introduction

Once again, as with several of these chapters, you will wonder why on earth we need a chapter on such an ordinary topic — isn't speaking something that you do everyday? Yes, like most of the skills that are used by a competent advocate, we all use our speaking skills every day. But now the circumstances are different; we are not speaking privately or personally, as we are used to doing, but we are to speak in public, on behalf of someone else and, in a sense, on the record. Our client is depending on our ability to speak well for him or her, and other people are judging us on our speaking ability, amongst other things. In short, we are now in the public eye and what we are engaged in is public speaking. You may have had a taste of this already, in a variety of situations as diverse as a debating society, a mooting competition or a wedding. If so, you will be familiar with the nerves that accompany your first efforts at speaking to an audience, with the strain you feel in trying to project your voice into a large room and with the problems you seem to be having with your breathing.

Speaking as an advocate imposes stress on the speaker and that stress manifests itself in several symptoms. These are most common in the novice and become more bearable (and thus less noticeable) with experience. However, it is much better to work on such matters before your first appearance as an advocate, so that your personal discomfort may be reduced and there is less danger of your client's interests suffering because of your inexperience.

Appendix C gives you some guidance on techniques to use for working on relaxation and breathing, as well as articulation and projection. We have tried to make this as 'law-relevant' as possible but some of the exercises may strike you as inappropriate. If so, please take the following steps. Get a video camera and a blank tape. Set the camera to record yourself and then spend a few minutes delivering a set speech (or reading from a favourite text) to the camera. Now rewind the tape and observe yourself. See if there are any nervous mannerisms that you can spot, are you including lots of ums, ers and ehs? Are you pausing in the right places to give the appropriate emphasis to your words? Is it too fast? Or too slow? Have you got to turn the volume right up on the monitor to hear yourself? Now imagine that you are doing the same thing again, but this time in a courtroom with other people present. Do you think your performance will be better, or any more comfortable, now?

It is time to realise that, although not all advocates are frustrated actors, the competent advocate requires many of the techniques which are commonly used in drama. Actors on a stage do not get themselves heard at the back of the auditorium if they use the same voice that they use when talking to a friend on the telephone. If you want to be heard in court, you need to be able to utilise the same techniques that actors use to ensure that their voices are heard and their words are clear.

13.2 Speak Clearly and Fluently

Communication is the name of this game. If you don't speak clearly, then your words might just as well have never been uttered. Worse still, they may be misunderstood and convey a wrong impression to your listeners. For the advocate must be both the creator and the performer: you have to think of the words and you have to say them. The first part calls for good language skills, a broad vocabulary and a basic understanding of grammar. The second part requires you to articulate those words so that your listeners can:

(a) hear your words;

(b) comprehend your words; and

(c) attach the correct interpretation to them.

So do not mutter, do not use a 'small' voice, do not look at the floor, do not speak at a pace so fast that your listeners cannot keep up nor so slow that they lose interest or concentration. Do look at your listeners, take care over your pronunciation, speak at a reasonable pace, use appropriate variations in tone and use pauses, too.

Writing as someone who has spent several years listening to people taking their first steps in training as advocates, I have found the common faults of speaking to be concerned with the following.

13.2.1 THE PACE OF SPEAKING

This can be too fast or too slow but typically it is too fast. Why? It seems that the appearance in court is an ordeal that the speaker wants to get over as quickly as possible. It also seems to be believed that, by speaking fast and maintaining a steady stream of 'noise', there may be less opportunity for anyone else to intervene and do anything unsettling such as asking a question, or changing the subject.

The more competent performer will speak at a more normal pace, will pause for breath whenever necessary and, indeed, will make positive use of **pauses**. What do I mean by that? A pause may be used for various purposes: to get your breath; to mark a transition between one point and the next; to give emphasis to the previous point; and finally to allow the listener to make a note if that is what they are doing. A competent advocate should feel able to use pauses in all of these ways and not be frightened that someone may intervene or 'take the floor' from them. If that happens, you should be prepared for it and respond, for example by answering a question. When that happens, you impress the questioner that you are in control, of both yourself and this case; that is a persuasive plus for you.

13.2.2 THE VOLUME OF YOUR VOICE

It is important to remember that you will often be addressing your listener over a distance of several feet. You may be across a table from, say, a district judge in his or her room or you may be twenty feet away from a judge in a courtroom. Both must be able to hear you, and neither should think that you are speaking too loudly or too quietly. It is likely that you will find less of a problem in speaking at the right volume to someone across a table, than across a room. Generally, we are unaccustomed to speaking over such distances, other than in a classroom during schooldays. You must be able to turn up the volume, whenever the situation demands it. That does not mean that you should start shouting, though!

13.2.3 FLUENCY

When required to speak in public, it is often the case that one's mind goes blank and ideas have almost to be forced out. Your voice becomes more staccato, less natural and the number of ums, ers and ehs increases dramatically. Try to eliminate these 'fillers' if you can; they can become very distracting to the listener. All they really are is a subconscious way of trying to disguise the fact that you have nothing better to say at present. Worse, they may have become a habit which is present whenever you speak, on a par with 'like' or 'you know'. These phrases are meaningless and should always be avoided. Although to eradicate them from your speech may require some attention, and the initial attempts to do so will simply result in your becoming more aware of them and self-conscious, the longer that you consciously try to do without them when you speak, the easier it will be for your listener to follow the words that really matter.

13.3 Use Appropriate Language and Manner

What is meant by the phrase 'appropriate language and manner'? Our aim, when talking, is to communicate with our listeners and we will do so most effectively when our vocabulary is a shared one and our listeners have no distractions.

When I say 'appropriate language', this does not include nor require anyone to use what critics sometime call 'legalese'. The competent advocate should always use a vocabulary which is suited to both the listener and the situation. So you should ask yourself, who am I talking to, who is listening to me? In many situations, the answers will be the same but that is not so when dealing with a witness, for example.

13.3.1 OBSCENE LANGUAGE

As an advocate, you must show respect for the court, there should be no place for obscene language or swearwords of any kind from you certainly, and if they come from a witness, you should stop them immediately. There is one exception to this, though, and that is where the evidence relevant to the litigation contains swearwords itself. An example might be found in *R* v *M, The Times*, 23 April 1996, where evidence was produced in a murder trial that the appellant had described 'cutting' her victim because he was 'acting like a fucking hero'. Here, the obscenity is an integral part of the appellant's words and it would be appropriate to present the court with the unexpurgated version, both as part of the evidence and within a closing speech in the trial.

13.3.2 VERNACULAR LANGUAGE OR SLANG

Again, this has to do with respect for the court, it also has to do with clarity. A single word may have a variety of different meanings and the way that words most quickly acquire new meanings is through the language of the streets. If we use (or allow others to use) words which have a slang sense and are being used thus, our listeners who do not share this vocabulary may lose the message that we are trying to convey.

Don't use vernacular words or phrases yourself unless, as before, they are a relevant piece of the evidence before the court. Even then, some explanation or clarification may be called for so that the correct interpretation can be put on the words by your listeners. Occasionally, you may find that your listeners needed no such explanation but it is better to err on the side of caution.

13.3.3 JARGON

Try to avoid this if you can. Perhaps, if you are appearing before a professional judge and another qualified advocate, you may use common spoken 'shorthand', as long as you are certain that there can be no misunderstanding by your listeners. Otherwise, there will be lay people present, your client, perhaps, or a witness, or even people in the public gallery in court and all of these people are entitled to understand and follow what you are saying. In those circumstances, while it may be tempting to abbreviate words or use Latin tags, for example, you would do much better to use plain English. Often, it is tempting to use jargon because you may think that it shows that you are on the inside, in the know, an experienced advocate. In fact, there are many other ways by which those who are experienced will judge whether you know what you are talking about; jargon alone will not convince them that you are experienced in your work if all of the other signs do not.

One particular situation which cries out for you to use jargon is when dealing with an expert witness. Now the temptation is to prove to others not that you are an experienced lawyer but that you are an expert in another field altogether. This is a tactic fraught with danger as the likelihood is that either you are not an expert and do not fully understand the expert's jargon, or the person deciding the facts in the case does not understand the jargon. In this latter situation, the fact-finder will feel, rightly, that he or she is being excluded from the dialogue between you and the witness. That may eventually result in some information not being communicated to the fact-finder successfully, at best, and in a feeling of hostility towards you (and maybe your client, too), at worst. The North Americans have a saying, 'Keep it simple, stupid' and this sums up (albeit rather brutally) what should be your guiding principle, both here and in other areas.

13.3.4 LABELS FOR PEOPLE

How should you refer to people in court? They fall into five basic categories:

(a) the tribunal itself;

(b) your fellow advocates;

(c) parties to the litigation;

(d) witnesses;

(e) everyone else.

13.3.4.1 The tribunal

Novice advocates are told how to address judges in various courts. A High Court judge is always 'My Lord/Lady' or 'Your Lordship/Ladyship'; these are not interchangeable. 'My Lord' is the equivalent of the judge's name (it represents the vocative case), while 'Your Lordship' is simply the equivalent of 'you' (the accusative case). Whilst wishing to adhere to the earlier injunction against using jargon, one must bow to what is standard practice in every court.

Don't use 'you' when speaking to a High Court judge, although I don't think anything adverse would happen if you did say, 'Have you got the Particulars of Claim in front of you?'. This sort of innocuous question, incidentally, can cause problems for even the most conscientious novice. The question coalesces in their mind as it appears above. It strikes them as a reasonable question to ask, little danger of it backfiring, so they engage first gear and start to ask it. As they do so, they remember that a High Court judge should be addressed as Your Lordship and not 'you'. The question emerges as 'Has Your Lordship [well done!] got the Particulars of Claim in front of . . .' and then their voice fades as they begin to see where this is leading them. Avoid a surfeit of 'My Lords' and 'Your Lordships', they are not necessary and can become extremely repetitive. The question would have been perfectly acceptable as 'Has Your Lordship got the Particulars of Claim?'. (For further help with addressing judges, see **Chapter 5**.)

Two other possible problem areas are juries and magistrates. Juries can be addressed as simply 'members of the jury' or, sometimes, 'ladies and gentlemen of the jury'. Statements to justices of the peace are usually addressed to the chairperson, who is referred to as 'Sir' or 'Madam'. For a reason obscure to me, it is quite common for police officers and solicitors to address magistrates as 'Your Worships', while barristers rarely if ever use the expression.

13.3.4.2 Fellow advocates

It is usual to refer to a barrister as 'my learned friend' and a solicitor as 'my friend' (in the vocative case), and to use 'him' or 'her', 'his' or 'hers' and 'you' wherever you would normally do so.

13.3.4.3 Parties to the litigation

The parties to the litigation are given titles, separate from their names. So the person who is suing in a civil claim becomes 'the claimant' while the person being sued becomes 'the defendant'. If many people are suing, they are 'the first claimant', 'the second claimant', etc. Typically, they are referred to by these titles, rather than as (say) 'Mrs Freda Barrett', when the advocate is addressing the court, but they are addressed as (say) 'Mrs Barrett' when appearing as a witness.

13.3.4.4 Witnesses

When talking to, or referring to, a witness, you should give them their full and correct title when first addressing them and usually do so thereafter. For example, a witness who, when asked to tell the court his name, replies, 'Eric Barrett', should be referred to subsequently as either 'Eric Barrett' or 'Mr Barrett'. To abbreviate this to 'Barrett' would imply a lack of respect for the witness; that in turn requires an exercise of judgment by you and that is never the function of an advocate.

13.3.4.5 Everyone else

What about everyone else? There aren't too many people left whom you might need to address but people associated with the court will usually be referred to by their job description, as in, for example, 'Usher, could you give this to the witness?'; 'I wonder if the stenographer could read the witness's previous answer to the jury?'; or 'I will hand this letter up to the clerk'.

13.3.5 APPROPRIATE MANNER

It is sensible to remember that, as an advocate, you are appearing in a court of law and important issues are being decided in the litigation (at least as far as the parties to the matter are concerned). This is not the appropriate place to look in detail at non-verbal language (see **Appendix F**) but do note that you need to give the appearance of taking things seriously, and of giving due respect to the court. Furthermore, your ultimate aim as an advocate is to persuade the tribunal to decide in your client's favour; you must appear to have confidence in the merits of your arguments or evidence and you must do nothing that may interfere with your communications with the tribunal.

It follows that:

(a) you will stand up when saying anything in open court, unless it is the practice in that court not to do so;

(b) you will stand up when being spoken to;

(c) you will not put your hands behind your head and lean back in your seat as if to convey an air of innate superiority;

(d) you will not speak to anyone in court with your hands in your pockets;

(e) you will not do anything discourteous at all (such as pick your nose, clean out your fingernails);

(f) when not speaking in court, you should be taking a note of what is being said or done (that should help to occupy your hands);

(g) when speaking in court, you should try not to distract your listeners from your words with any gesture or movement of the hands, unless it has some relevance to your words (so, no fiddling with pens, scratching your nose/ears/neck, stroking your chin, playing with keys, pocket snooker, etc.).

13.4 Refer to Notes when Necessary or Desirable

It is a fact that there are some very experienced advocates around who use very detailed plans for their work in court. One example is Brian Leveson QC who was noted by reporters to have used almost a script when appearing for the prosecution in the trial of Rosemary West for murder. That is perhaps a good illustration of the truism that what works for one does not necessarily work for all. If you or I tried to work to a script, the effectiveness of our advocacy might well fall sharply. Let us consider the pros and cons.

13.4.1 PROS AND CONS OF A SCRIPT

First, the pros:

- you have all of your preparation to hand;

- there is little danger of you missing something out if you stick to your script;

- you will deal with topics in the order you intended;

- your delivery is quite likely to be clear and fluent.

What about the cons?

- you will be reading from your script so your delivery may be flat or monotonous;

- because you are reading, you are looking at your notes, not at the judge or jury or magistrates or witness;

- you cannot respond easily or swiftly to questions or other unexpected deviations from your plan because:

    (a) although you may have the answer in your plan, you don't have it in your mind;

    (b) your plan is so full, it is time-consuming to find specific pieces of information within it; and

    (c) you may lose your place in your plan and lose your concentration;

- although you will deal with all of the points that you planned to, others may have arisen in the course of the trial or hearing which you hadn't planned for and those may now be overlooked.

On balance, I think that the evidence is strongly in favour of **not** using a script.

13.4.2 WHY YOU SHOULD NOT USE A SCRIPT

It is quite understandable that, when you are first on your feet as an advocate, one of your main fears is 'drying up', when your mind goes blank and all your careful preparation evaporates into thin air. That has happened to all advocates at one time or another. Another big worry is that you will overlook something important; although you had planned to deal with *argument x*, in all of the cut and thrust somehow you forgot to say it. So people often use plans to guarantee fluency and ensure a thorough coverage of the issues. That is understandable but the disadvantages are so great that very few advocates can overcome them.

Imagine what it is like to be spoken to by someone who never looks at you, indeed who never looks at anything except the pages clutched in his or her hands? Does that person inspire confidence? Do they look as if they have a good understanding of the case, or even their own arguments? Do you believe them? It is true in some cultures that it is considered rude to maintain eye contact and that it is more polite to look down when addressing someone in a position of authority. Plainly, in a multi-cultural society you should be aware of that **but** that will not help you if you do not come from such a culture or, if you do, the people that you are addressing are not aware of your cultural background. As a general rule, in this country many people rely, at least in part, on assessing credibility by measuring eye contact. Expressions such as 'looking shifty' and 'he couldn't even look me in the eye' are indications of the importance that is often attached to eye contact. There is at least a danger that by using a script you will begin to lose some of your credibility.

Imagine someone talking to you about something of interest to both of you. You ask them a question but they don't answer it. You might be puzzled. If it happened again, you might be annoyed. If it keeps happening, and you are a judge, you just might stop listening to what that person has to say — they are not talking to you but at you. The advocate has to be someone who responds to those around him or her. If you have a very short note or plan, that will force you to concentrate on holding all of your arguments in your head. If you know what you want to say but only decide exactly how to say it seconds before you do so, then your words will have a more natural ring to them. If you are watching your judge and see that a certain argument (or even a phrase or word) has the judge nodding in agreement, then you might want to make more use of that argument (or phrase or word) than you had intended originally.

The final nail in the coffin for scripts, I hope, is this. Suppose that you are due to question a witness. It is almost impossible to predict how a witness is going to behave in the witness box — whether they will be garrulous or monosyllabic, nervous or relaxed, helpful or not — until you actually see them in that box. That is one reason why examination-in-chief is so much harder than cross-examination: you haven't had time to gauge the witness's demeanour and ability to answer questions. In those circumstances, it is really very difficult to plan an exact sequence of questions and stick to them. The planning is easy of course, but witnesses seldom turn out quite the way you planned they would. To use a detailed script here (a bit like the notes of a police interview but with the answers still to be filled in) would almost certainly result in a total loss of flexibility, you would be unable to respond to the witness's last answer by adapting the next question to suit. That must suggest that you are not listening to the witness's answers and, if you appear not to be, why should anyone else?

13.4.3 WHY YOU DON'T NEED A SCRIPT

Remember what I said your two big worries were as a novice advocate? (See **13.4.2**.) The first was drying up and the second was overlooking some topic or argument. It might not seem like it when you are starting out but these are both easily overcome. As for drying up, this is simply a product of your nerves and what you need to do is relax. Your first move is to pause, this is quite natural and no-one will suddenly think that you are incompetent and don't deserve to be an advocate. Then take a deep breath or two and try not to think of anything for a second or two, if you can. If that doesn't work and you need longer, ask for it. 'If I might have a minute, Your Honour' is a phrase not unknown to Her Majesty's judiciary. The judge is unlikely to be unsympathetic, after all, it has probably happened to him or her more times than they care to remember.

Once you have relaxed a little, your mind is more likely to recollect what you wanted to say. Suppose that does not happen? Why not say, 'I should like to return to that point a little later, if I might' and move on to your next point? Your next point should not be hard to find, it is in your plan. Now we come to the second big worry, overlooking something. You should not have a script but you should have some sort of plan, its function is really that of a prompt. It is not there as a substitute for your memory, nor as a comfort blanket whose thickness clearly shows the number of hours' preparation you have put into this case. Your plan needs to be short and the points expressed concisely. A bullet point format is ideal. If you look down at your plan and see 'Negligence' or 'No serious issue to be tried', for example, that should act as a trigger for your memory and the relevant arguments (or questions) should come to mind. The bonus for you is that, as you carry on with the case, the point that you have dried up on, or forgotten, will often come back and you can deal with it a little later than planned. This is not usually fatal to your chances of success in the action. So be relaxed, have faith in your memory, use bullet points in your plan and you should have few hiccups; those that do afflict you will be less painful.

13.4.4   USING A SKELETON ARGUMENT

If you find that you are to make an application before a court and you are expected to prepare a skeleton argument, the points above may need some modification. First, the skeleton argument is written to support the application and the judge will normally receive and read it in advance of the application hearing. Typically, a copy will also have been supplied to your opponent. In this situation, it makes sense to acknowledge the existence of the skeleton in planning and making your application (or opposing one). A skeleton is not a script and the last thing the judge will want is you simply reading out large excerpts from it (let alone all of it!). Use it sparingly, make occasional references to it and regard it as a resource which allows you to take points more shortly where appropriate to do so. For example:

> Your Honour, clearly I must persuade the court that there is a serious question to be tried. I have addressed that matter in my skeleton at paragraph 4 and, unless Your Honour has any questions, I do not propose to add anything to that.

FOURTEEN

PERSUASION

14.1   Introduction

When we look at persuasion, we begin to explore what lies at the heart of 'advocacy'. Is it a skill, or a knack? Are great advocates born, not made, as some would assert? The *Concise Oxford English Dictionary* defines *persuade* as

to cause another to believe

to convince

to induce

to lure, attract, entice, etc.

These may (or may not) have been put in descending order but, as advocates, we might try to identify with the first couple of definitions, while hoping to avoid accusations of the latter pair.

When we watch advocates in practice, we often come to a conclusion about an individual's persuasiveness. Perhaps we should try to define in more detail exactly what we mean, in order that we may try to emulate it.

14.2   How do we Persuade?

It is beyond the scope of this Manual to devote the amount of space to this topic that it deserves. There are other books which concentrate wholly on this topic and you are recommended to go and seek them out. There are a couple of points to use as starters, though.

First, the more that your message is one that the trier(s) of fact can identify with and the more your proposition strikes the listener as just 'common sense', the more likely you are to persuade your audience that what you say is correct (we don't need to start exploring notions of 'truth' or what 'really happened' as we don't really look for these in court).

Secondly, your message must be memorable. If your judge (or jury or magistrates) cannot recollect your message at the important time, i.e., when coming to a decision, then you have lost the case. So your presentation of your case must be designed to give the maximum help to your audience to remember your points.

These basic points both refer to your 'message'. What we need to look at are your communication skills, a basic grasp of psychology (or understanding human nature, if you prefer) and a brilliant grasp of the facts of your case. The *Penguin Dictionary of Psychology* defines **persuasion** as 'a process of inducing a person to adopt a particular set of values, beliefs or attitudes'.

It goes on to say that a number of factors are likely to be used in this process, both rational and non-rational, for example, credibility and persuasive communication. Persuasive communication, the dictionary says, consists of both external aspects:

(a) the message itself;

(b) the arguments presented;

(c) the credibility of the source;

(d) the medium used,

and internal aspects:

(a) the person's original beliefs;

(b) the person's credulity.

As to communication skills, the ability to speak clearly and fluently is dealt with elsewhere (in **Chapter 13**) but it is understood that you must possess the ability to articulate at an appropriate pace, with suitable volume. If you are not heard (because you are too loud, too quiet or too fast), the message will not get through. But you need more than the ability to talk, you need a facility for language. Very often, what decides a case is the ability to choose the right phrase, or the best word, for the situation. There may be many ways to describe something or someone — an incident, a document, a witness — and part of being persuasive is the ability to select the description that 'fits' best. That means 'fits' for your listener, not for you. What is important here is getting your message across, communicating with the court. The choice of words or phrases is of great importance to success as an advocate.

What about understanding human nature? Well, that arises in various ways. For example, judges generally don't like to be lectured about the law. From time to time, you will have a case that requires argument on a point of law, but even then judges don't want a lecture on the history of the legal topic, what they want is help; whatever you say must be of direct and clear relevance to the dispute that the judge has to settle. Similarly, where someone has suffered some type of loss or damage (especially physical injury), any court is likely to have some sympathy for that person and the advocate representing the 'other side' must be sensitive to that. This doesn't mean that if, say, your case is that the 'victim' was in fact 100% contributorily negligent, you shouldn't say so; it does mean that you should appreciate that it may be a difficult message for the court to accept.

Last point, for now — having a brilliant grasp of the facts of your case. It does not matter if by 'facts' we mean the undisputed facts in the case, or a combination of what's not in dispute and your client's version of what is in dispute, you should have a clear understanding of both. Further, as far as it is possible to, you should have a clear understanding of your opponent's case, too. Lord Hewart CJ once said that the advocate must 'claw the facts' and indeed you should work very hard to have the fullest possible understanding of the detail in each case, from the microscopic (e.g., what the likely answer will be to **this** question) through to the macroscopic (e.g., which of the possible case theories is the best 'fit' here).

We should not leave this section without observing that you must have a good understanding of the law which is relevant to the case, too. Without it, all the other skills are useless. But gaining that understanding should be relatively straightforward for you; in many cases, you will already possess all the legal knowledge that you need before you receive the case papers. Legal knowledge is something that you can improve every day, with no reference to anything other than statutes, law reports, and text books. You should of course try to keep abreast of legal developments. What is different about each case and every client is not the relevant law but the facts: the names, dates, places and people. Those are the things that must be learnt, forgotten and then learnt afresh with every new case.

14.3   What's your Message? Developing a Case Theory and Themes

How do you prepare a case for a hearing in court? First, you sit down and read through the documents; there may be statements of case, statements from witnesses, a proof of evidence from your client, and documentary exhibits. Then, you check that your legal knowledge is up to scratch. You consider what else you need to know, or to have available for court, and write an advice on evidence, calling for extra statements, other documents and so forth. You also have a conference with your client, there may be things you need to tell the client, almost certainly questions that you want to ask. Having prepared as thoroughly as you can, you begin to see where you are likely to be at the end of the trial or hearing, what evidence will be before the court, which issues need to be proved and the probable strengths and weaknesses of both your client's case and that of your opponent. What you need to do now is consider your theory of the case.

I say **your** theory, because you will have evolved it but we must be aware of ethical traps here. It is sometimes said that advocacy trainers are good on advocacy skills but worse on ethics. You must not put forward a theory of the case just because it seems to have a good chance of success. It must be supported by the evidence, it must further the objectives of your client and it must not mislead the court. You should always explain your proposed case theory to your client and get their agreement to use it. That is not to say that your case theory must be carved in stone, though. One important thing a novice advocate soon learns is that, when you get into court, things don't always turn out the way you expected them to. As each trial develops, so the way things are seen may change, witnesses become more (or less) credible, an anticipated strong point becomes a weakness; the advocate must respond to these shifts and so must your case theory.

An experienced practitioner at the Old Bailey used to say that he would start several hares running at the beginning of a trial and see which one the dogs chased. It is permissible to have more than one theory of the case, perhaps intended to meet a variety of possible outcomes. What the practitioner meant was that an advocate must retain adaptability until the end of the trial when, finally, any ambiguities must be resolved. He hoped that, when he advanced the case theory in its final form, he chose the one he felt confident would have the most appeal for the jury.

14.3.1   THEMES

It is often said by prosecutors that the Crown does not need to show a motive, to explain why the accused committed the crime. There is no crime where the elements of the offence include greed, jealousy, revenge or anger. Nevertheless, when we are asked to determine whether a particular act was done, or a particular state of mind existed, then we automatically seek out clues that make such an act or state of mind more (or less) likely. If we can see a reason (i.e., motive) for someone saying or doing a particular thing, then we are more likely to find that the person did say or do that thing. Offering a reason is not necessarily conclusive when we have to persuade others, but it certainly helps.

Themes are often put forward to enable the trier(s) of fact to assess properly the witnesses they see and hear, the documents they read and the arguments of the advocates. A witness may be accused of lying in court, a proposition easier to believe if there is evidence to show jealousy, say, against the advocate's client.

Suppose you want to say that an apparently credible eye-witness to a road accident is not to be believed. You could just say so but that is not very persuasive. If your theme is that the witness was too far away to have a proper view and is doing her best to help the court (not the party calling her, because we'll run into problems of showing partiality) but is nevertheless wrong, your theme for that witness is that she is honest but mistaken.

Compare, for example, what prosecuting counsel, Timothy Langdale QC, was reported to have told the jury in opening the Crown's case against Sandra Wignall, charged with the murder of her husband, some 17 months after their marriage. Remember that the only elements of the offence that the Crown had to **prove** were that Sandra Wignall was a party to the unlawful killing of her husband and had an intention either to kill or to cause grievous bodily harm to him. Counsel told the jury (see *The Guardian*, 27 October 1993) that:

> ... lust and greed were the driving forces behind the murder ... Sandra Wignall was a woman to whom sex was all-important and although she might fall for a number of men, there was one man who was a special object of desire to her, one man who seemed to have a hold over her so she would do his bidding [one of her co-accused, and her alleged lover, B] ...

Later on during the trial, the prosecution called a witness, described in reports as a friend and neighbour of the accused woman, who testified that:

> Once she [Sandra Wignall] told me he [B] blindfolded her and tied her to the bed and brought a man in to have sex with her with ... [B] present.

It is clear that, subject only to some apparent latitude by the court as to the relevance of this information, the prosecution's theme for Sandra Wignall was that she was besotted by her lover and would do anything for him, including playing an intimate part in the murder of her husband. Subsidiary themes which supported the 'rightness' of this theme were that the deceased man had a life insurance policy which would pay Sandra Wignall £21,000 on his death, that B had heavy debts and that Sandra Wignall had previously discussed selling her house to raise money for him.

14.3.2   CASE THEORY

This should be a short and simple statement which sums up how the issues in the case should be decided, based upon the evidence, and how that results in a verdict favourable to your client. To take the case of Sandra Wignall again, the prosecution's case theory was that the murdered man was taken for a night-time walk in local woods by his wife, that she 'in the hope of lulling him into a false sense of security ... had gone so far as to perform oral sex upon him as the attackers came upon him' and that he was then set upon and stabbed three times with a knife, twice in the heart, dying before help could reach him. You can see there the essential allegations against Sandra Wignall:

(a)   a man was killed (her husband);

(b)   unlawfully (stabbed with a knife);

(c)   with intention to kill (inferred from her role in the attack).

In a different case, the prosecution in 1994 of Gordon Foxley for corruption, Foxley had been a senior civil servant at the Ministry of Defence when he allegedly took 'backhanders' of some £1.5 million from three foreign companies. Prosecuting counsel, Victor Temple QC, told the jury at Snaresbrook Crown Court that the trial, expected to last two weeks, was almost entirely concerned with documents. You may think that with that amount of documentary evidence, the jury needed a peg to hang the prosecution case on. Counsel gave it to them:

> The Crown say this defendant agreed to take a series of substantial backhanders, and in doing so took dishonest advantage of his position, breaching the trust bestowed upon him by his employers.

Again, the essential allegations are clear:

(a) this defendant (Foxley had already been identified as a senior official in the MOD: any person serving under the Crown would be covered by the relevant legislation);

(b) agreed to take (one can commit the offence of corruption by offering or receiving a bribe, in Foxley's case the latter);

(c) a series of substantial backhanders ('any gift or consideration' is what the law requires);

(d) took dishonest advantage of his position (the Crown did not need to show dishonesty, just that Foxley knew the payments were connected with the past or future performance of his duties, as reward or inducement but this is perhaps an example of a theme emerging within the case theory);

(e) breaching the trust bestowed ... by his employers (again, directed towards showing that Foxley acted corruptly, that is, purposefully doing an act which the law forbids as tending to corrupt, accepting any improper or unauthorised gift).

14.4 Delivering the Message

The advocate should present himself or herself and their arguments in such a way as to convince the court of their merits. Let's not delude ourselves, sometimes cases are won **despite** the best efforts of the 'winning' advocate, not because of them. But it cannot hurt your client's prospects of success if you appear to be confident and in control. If the court can feel that you are to be trusted, then your credibility is likely to increase. That may help your client. What is confidence? It includes acting naturally (and not sweating unduly, or looking shifty), speaking clearly and naturally (no unnaturally long pauses, no inappropriate language) with variations of tone and pace to maintain interest and emphasise certain points.

The advocate should be seen to have a clear idea of what they are arguing for and to have an understanding of the relative strengths of their possible arguments. Have they sorted the relevant from the irrelevant and then **re-sorted** to refine the available material down to what the court really wants to know about? The effective advocate is the one who does not throw in everything including the kitchen sink but who, having done all the preparatory legwork, is prepared to dump most of it and focus their energies on what lies at the heart of that specific case.

Having identified what the client wants from the proceedings, and compared that with what the court is likely to give, the persuasive advocate thinks about how to 'sell' their arguments to the court, how to make them share what your client wants. In his book on advocacy, *Advocacy in Court*, Keith Evans describes defence counsel in a jury trial as having to 'show the jury the way home', that is, how to arrive at the desired outcome by the least painful means. If you have a point that needs making but it is weak, then you should appreciate that and act upon it. Don't pretend it is not a weakness, you will be found out; better to acknowledge it as a weakness (again, you show you can be trusted and are acting practically), then produce supporting argument to bolster it. If you can do all of these things, then you have passed beyond the stage of novice advocate and are on the way to being really effective and persuasive in the courtroom.

14.5 Persuading a Judge on an Application

As the use of skeleton arguments becomes more and more widespread in civil hearings, advocates are finding that judges enter the courtroom rather more well-informed about the case and the arguments than perhaps they were in the past. Also, with the emphasis given in the Civil Procedure Rules to a pro-active judiciary, advocates are finding judges much more interventionist than has traditionally been the case. No longer are judges prepared to sit silently as the advocates present their carefully-crafted arguments. Now, judges have read the evidence, they have read the arguments in the skeletons and they have questions to which they want the answers.

Some people might regard an interventionist judge with trepidation. Won't they ask all sorts of difficult questions? Well, yes, they will, and that should be welcomed with enthusiasm! An enquiring judge is not a problem for the advocate but is of potentially great assistance. No longer need you stand there, arguing away with no clues as to whether you are addressing the judge's concerns until he or she announces the decision. When a judge asks you a question, it usually indicates an issue which is troubling him or her. You now have the opportunity to target your arguments to maximum effect. No need to waste time talking about matters that are already sorted — instead spend your time helping the judge on those topics which are still to be determined. Of course, the potential pitfall for the advocate is that the interventionist judge makes greater demands on the advocate in terms of his or her grasp of the facts of the case and the relevant law. The judge's questions may be on a part of your submission that has not yet been reached — too bad, the judge wants an answer — now! The advocate really must be on top of the case, with excellent preparation skills. This should always have been the aspiration of the advocate, now it is a necessity.

The flexibility that this demands from the advocate is nothing new really. It is surely better to spend five minutes addressing a judge's real concerns than fifteen minutes addressing everything that you think might possibly be of concern to the judge. Tackling the real issues and showing how to resolve them in a way that should ensure the success of your application must be what persuasion is all about. The opportunity to engage in the court in a dialogue should be seen as a tremendous asset for any advocate. It is only a threat for the un-informed and under-prepared, two things an advocate should never be.

PART 5
BEGINNINGS AND ENDINGS

FIFTEEN

OPENING SPEECHES

15.1   Introduction

The opening speech is the first opportunity that advocates have to set out the case theory which, in their opinion, will persuade the court to determine the issues in favour of their client. Very often, these days, the court will be quite familiar with the likely evidence in the trial — for example, in many civil trials now, there will have been a mutual exchange of witness statements. The judge will have a bundle of those and the statements of case in the case. Similarly, in the Crown Court the judge will have seen the indictment and the bundle of prosecution witness statements before the trial begins. The big difference is that the triers of fact in criminal trials are magistrates and juries. Crucially, they will have next to no knowledge about the case before the trial starts, apart from hearing the charges against the accused read out and hearing the pleas of not guilty entered. Thus, for the triers of fact in criminal trials, the opening speech is the first real chance to become acquainted with the issues; whereas, in civil trials, the judge already has a good idea of what the case is all about before the advocate ever stands up. This may mean there are certain differences of emphasis when opening a case to a judge, rather than to magistrates or a jury. Nevertheless, there are some general factors which should be ever present in an opening speech.

15.2   The Basic Purpose of an Opening Speech

The opening speech serves as an introduction to your client's case. It should set out the essential facts on which your case is founded; it should fill in a little background so that the triers of fact begin to see the 'bigger picture', otherwise there is a danger that the speech and the subsequent evidence will appear rather disconnected as if the witnesses were simply a group of people chosen almost at random; and, finally, the speech should introduce one (or more) possible case theories.

The opening speech comes at the very outset of the presentation of your client's case to the court. If you were writing a book, this speech would be an introduction or prologue to assist the reader and bring them up to speed with the plot and characters. If this were a restaurant and not a courtroom, the speech would be replaced by an enthusiastic *maître d'*, talking the diners through the delights of the menu and offering an hors d'oeuvre or two to whet their appetite. Last analogy! — the triers of fact are about to board a bus, driven by you. It could turn out to be a mystery tour, where everyone finishes up at your intended destination (the end of the trial) but no-one is quite sure how they got there or what they saw on the way. Indeed, some passengers may have seen different sights from the rest, some or all may have missed some very interesting sights along the way simply through ignorance. That's not what you want. Your opening speech must be like the very best guided tour — one where the travellers know from the off where they are going, how they are going to get there and what they are likely to experience along the way.

So, the speech is an outline and a guide. It is an introduction and it should introduce the circumstances that gave rise to the litigation, the parties who are involved in it, what your client seeks from the triers of fact and, most crucially, how the issues will be resolved in such a way as to make the outcome sought by your client the inevitable result of the trial. You should always take great care when preparing an opening speech, whatever the court, as what you say now will act as a template for the rest of the case. If you tell the court that a witness will say *x* in their evidence, and that witness fails to do so, your opponent is likely to draw the court's attention to that failure. It may not be a significant omission to you but the triers of fact may disagree. Also, if you advance a particular case theory in your opening speech and the evidence turns out not to support that but is fine for a different case theory which could also win the case for your client, you will have to work hard to persuade the court to let you walk away from your original theory.

This sounds like a recipe for caution, keeping things vague and talking in generalities. You can take this advice too much to heart but there is a great gap between what you **need** to say in an opening speech and what you **can** say by way of comment on the facts that you expect to prove. Too much caution is bad, but some caution is sensible, moderation is the rule. Never open a case 'higher' than you need to. It is a dangerous technique to be too bullish in your opening, bold assertions now that facts *x*, *y* and *z* will be proved may come back to haunt you later, what appear now as justified and confident predictions about the evidence may just turn out to be hostages to fortune. Take the example of prosecuting counsel in the obscenity trial concerning *Lady Chatterley's Lover* by DH Lawrence. Extracts from the speech to the jury show him saying:

> ... the heroine, Lady Chatterley, and the hero, the gamekeeper, are, you may think, little more than bodies, bodies which continuously have sexual intercourse with one another ...
> ... the story of the book ... is little more than padding ...
> ... sex is dragged in at every conceivable opportunity ...
> ... the book puts promiscuous sex on a pedestal ...

Each of the propositions was subsequently used by the defence as the basis for a question to the defence expert witnesses. They became ammunition for the defence to shoot back at the prosecution and no advocate can afford to supply his or her opponent with bullets. Of more concern, no client can afford to indulge an advocate who, through lack of foresight as to consequences (or maybe just lack of imagination), fails to see how what they perceive as strengths can swiftly become turned around into weaknesses. There is almost nothing your opponent will enjoy more than being given the chance to do this.

15.3   The Elements of the Speech

A competent opening speech consists of the following elements:

(a)   introducing your role as advocate in the case, and that of your opponent(s), to the court;

(b)   giving a clear summary of the facts of the case;

(c)   giving a clear statement of the disputed issues between the parties;

(d)   giving a brief outline of the evidence of witnesses, if the admissibility of that evidence is not challenged;

(e)   addressing the court on the law;

(f)   speaking clearly, using appropriate language;

(g)   delivering the speech without reading from a prepared script;

(h)   complying with the rules of professional conduct.

15.4   How to Structure your Opening Speech

What follows are several suggestions on how to structure an opening speech in various contexts. They are not intended to be prescriptive and, when you become more experienced as an advocate, you will find that you prefer to do things in your own way. That is as it should be but you must always remember that the purpose of the opening speech is to put the essential facts of your client's case before the court and the basis for liability or its denial. Always try to keep your speech as concise as possible, appear to be decent and honest in your dealings with the court now. Remember the rules of professional conduct.

15.4.1   CIVIL TRIALS

The structure of speeches in civil trials will be largely the same, whether taking place in the County Court or High Court (although in the latter forum, replace 'Your Honour' with 'My Lord/Lady'). The opening speech will usually be given by the advocate who represents the claimant but, occasionally, it may be the right of the defence to start the trial with a speech. It really depends upon who bears the burden of proof on the matters in issue in the trial.

It is quite usual in civil cases to have a skeleton argument prepared in advance of the trial. This will be a document which sets out, quite briefly, the issues which are in dispute between the parties (these may not be instantly clear from the individual statements of case and it requires an overview which can only be done after all statements of case are available). The skeleton argument should summarise the party's case on the issues and summarise the propositions of law which the party relies upon. Finally, it should contain cross-references to the statements of case, the court bundle (any documentary real evidence or witness statements), and the legal sources which support the propositions of law. The skeleton argument should underpin your opening speech; the written document is not intended to replace the oral speech. For more guidance on skeleton arguments — see the **Drafting Manual**, **Chapter 23**.

In your opening speech, you should ensure that you do the following:

(a)   **State the nature of the case**
For example, 'Your Honour, this is a claim for damages for personal injury arising out of a road traffic accident, caused by the defendant's negligence' or, 'Your Honour, this is a claim for damages based on an alleged breach of contract'.

(b)   **State the issues in the case, i.e., the areas of dispute between the parties**
For example, 'The issue between the parties is whether the car was of merchantable quality' or, 'The issue between the parties is whether the defendant fell below the standard of care expected of a reasonable prudent driver when he overtook the lorry on the roundabout' or, 'There are three issues in this case: first, has the respondent committed acts of violence against the petitioner and, if so, is there a danger that he will do so again? Finally, if there is such a danger, should the respondent be excluded from the matrimonial home?'

(c)   **Summarise the facts which have been established or will be established during the trial**
Thus, any significant factual matters which are relevant but not in dispute should be identified, you will want to identify the circumstances that gave rise to the events which are the subject matter of the litigation, as well as its aftermath.

For example, in a claim for damages for personal injury, you would want to set the scene, describe what was happening immediately prior to the injury being suffered, how the injury was sustained, what happened immediately thereafter and what the longer-term consequences were.

(d) **Read out the statements of case and the relevant parts of any documents whose use has been agreed by the parties**
This may seem unnecessary to you. After all, the judge has the statements of case and your skeleton argument. You may be right, the judge will often indicate that he or she will read the statements of case for themselves now or has already read them. If so, you should still take the judge to the key points in the statements of case (for example, the allegations of negligence in a personal injuries case) as it remains important to ensure the judge has absorbed these important allegations.

(e) **Refer to any relevant legal principles contained in statute, regulation or case law**
Again, this may seem unnecessary. The judge will have considerable experience of handling cases like this and may be thoroughly familiar with the relevant law. Indeed, often the legal position will be agreed between the parties, and the court has to resolve only issues of fact. This may be where the skeleton argument comes into its own, particularly as no judge ever welcomes a lecture on the law! Unless the relevant law is quite esoteric, it is probably best to keep such references to a minimum.

(f) **Briefly state why, on the law and facts as you understand them, the claimant should succeed.**

15.4.2 OPENING FOR THE DEFENCE IN A CIVIL TRIAL

It should be quite clear that much of what needs to be done in opening the case for the claimant need not be repeated by the defence. For example, the statements of case only need reading once. However, if the defence is calling evidence at the trial, it may be that an opening speech is desirable, in addition to any skeleton argument that the defence has prepared for the court. Remember that any opening speech for the defence will come after the evidence for the claimant has been presented to the court. Any defence opening should, therefore, concentrate on the matters which it is intended to establish through the evidence to be tendered on behalf of the defence, together with a summary of the case theory for the defence. This last point is important; up to this point in the trial, when defence counsel has cross-examined the claimant's witnesses, that has been done with two things in mind. The first is the statement of case entitled 'defence', which the judge has a copy of, the second is the defence theory of the case, which the judge does not have. A good judge can probably make a reasonably accurate guess as to the defence case theory, based upon the defence itself and the questions asked by defence counsel in cross-examination, but this is not the time to play guessing games with the judge. Use a short opening speech to clarify what your theory of the case is and why the defendant should succeed.

15.4.3 CRIMINAL TRIALS

A distinction must be drawn here between trials in the magistrates' court and trials in the Crown Court.

15.4.3.1 Magistrates' court
The basic rule here is that each side (prosecution and defence) is entitled to make just one speech to the magistrates. In certain circumstances, they may be allowed to make two speeches (in which case this must also be permitted to their opponent) but these situations are rarely encountered. The most typical scenario finds the prosecution advocate making an opening speech and the defence making a closing speech. So, we don't have to worry about a defence opening speech — there won't be one. What about the prosecution?

We have to remember that, although justices of the peace are not professionally qualified for their position, they do adjudicate on many cases every year. The upshot is that they acquire plenty of judicial experience and don't need long lectures on the law (or only rarely). Also, factually they may be familiar with most of the scenarios that are likely to be played out in a summary trial. So what does the prosecutor say in the opening speech? The answer is next to nothing. A typical opening might run thus:

> Sir (or Madam), in this case I appear on behalf of the Crown and my learned friend, Miss Smith, represents the accused. This is a simple case of driving without due care and attention, contrary to the Road Traffic Act. I will now call PC Jones.

You could expand this if you wanted to, perhaps to identify the witnesses and their part in the proceedings, but that will seldom be necessary. This advice — to err on the side of extreme brevity — should be redoubled if you find yourself prosecuting in front of a stipendiary magistrate. They **are** legally qualified as well as hearing perhaps in excess of a hundred summary trials each year; they really have heard it all and, as there is no statement of case to refer the court to (unlike a civil trial) except maybe a quite uninformative charge sheet, you might as well get on with calling the evidence.

15.4.3.2 Crown Court

The prosecution opening speech Here, the prosecution is entitled to open the case to the jury and should always do so in a full and proper way. What follows is intended only as a starting point. You should always assess in each case whether or not the suggested structure is appropriate and, if not, you must alter it to suit the circumstances of that case.

The jury will probably find it helpful if your opening speech starts by setting out, very shortly, the essential facts which are the prosecution case. You might want to refer to the indictment here and, if it is a complicated one (perhaps it contains alternative counts covering the same behaviour), you might want the jury to look at it while you explain the counts to them. You should have ensured there are sufficient copy indictments for all the jurors to have sight of one. In simple cases, the jury will have heard the count(s) read out to the accused and his plea(s), or they will have been told what the counts are by the clerk to the court, so you won't need to spend much time on this part of the speech.

Typically, the prosecutor will then go on to review the facts in more detail. Of course, at this stage there are no facts usually, only allegations. But what you try to do is to set the scene, establish some sort of context in which to place the bald facts of the crime itself. No offence occurs in a vacuum, crimes are committed by humans, acting on human impulses and emotions and with motives that other humans can understand. The jury need to be persuaded of the truth and, while the prosecutor is always there to see that justice is done rather than simply secure a conviction, the truth may become more identifiable if the jury are able to get a good feel for what was going on around the time of the offence. They may need to be given some understanding of the scene where the offence was committed, who was present and the relationship between them, and how the accused committed the offence. Into this (which is essentially a story-telling exercise), you could insert references to particular witnesses who will testify for the prosecution, as a prelude to their testimony. That is sensible and helpful but what you must avoid is overstating your case and in particular, appearing to rely too heavily on specific witnesses to establish particular points for your case. If you are only calling a single witness, then you may want to indicate in quite explicit terms what he or she will say on oath; after all, if they don't then your case will collapse anyway. But, where you are calling several witnesses, be wary of setting your stall too high for them. It is much better to leave yourself some flexibility since you can never be quite sure how the evidence is going to develop during the trial. This is one of the hardest things for a novice advocate to grasp, i.e., that a trial is a dynamic, growing process of discovery. Of course, as the advocate you should have a better idea than most of exactly where you are all going and what is likely to happen by the end of the trial but you are mistaken if you believe that advocates are never taken by surprise by what witnesses say and never have to adapt their case to meet the situation as it confronts them. Your ability to respond is compromised if you have been too specific (and optimistic) in opening the case. There is also a risk that too much detail now will result in you losing the jury's attention, after all they are here to listen to the evidence and find the facts.

When you refer to specific evidence in your opening speech, you should always check first that your opponent does not challenge its admissibility. Now, you don't have to do that with every single piece of evidence but some items are almost certainly going to be challenged (e.g., police evidence of an alleged confession by the accused). You should always check with defence counsel, preferably before going into court, whether there will be an objection. This may have been dealt with at a pre-trial hearing but you should double-check. If the answer is no, then you can mention the evidence in your speech. If the answer is yes, then you must omit any reference to that evidence from your opening speech. If the issue was *not* resolved at a pre-trial hearing, the judge will usually have to determine the question of admissibility later, in the absence of the jury, and if you mention the evidence now, that determination will be otiose. It may be that the confession is really all the evidence that you have against the accused; in that situation, you can ask the judge to take the admissibility point as a preliminary issue before your opening speech. If so, the jury will be excluded while the point is argued. If you win the argument, you open your case as intended and refer to the confession; if you lose, you will probably not make an opening speech but offer no evidence and halt the case instead.

On a similar note, it may be that the defence disputes the identity of the offender, saying that while a crime may have been committed, the defendant was not the offender. If identification is a live issue in the trial, then you should not say that the accused was seen at a particular time or place, you may only say that a man (or woman) was seen at that time and place and that your witnesses will say that the man (or woman) was the accused.

It may be that you can anticipate with some confidence what the likely defence case will be. For example, the accused may have offered an innocent explanation during an interview with police, such as self-defence or alibi. The defence statement may have shed more light. Now, the burden of proof for most defences in criminal trials rests with the prosecution. While it is for the defence to raise some evidence to suggest, say, self-defence, if they do so then it is for the prosecution to prove beyond reasonable doubt that the accused did not act in self-defence. In such circumstances, it might be thought sensible to mention any such defences in your opening speech, so that you can knock them down again. In practice, your confident guess as to the nature of the defence case could turn out to be just that — a guess. Most of the time it is not worth spelling out to the jury what you think the defence case is going to be. It is much better to keep your guess to yourself, while planning accordingly.

You should state the elements of the offence(s) which the prosecution has to prove (while also stating that anything you say to the jury about the law is subject to whatever the judge may say on the subject). You should state that the prosecution has brought the case and it is for them (i.e., you and your witnesses) to prove it; the defendant need prove nothing (burden of proof). Tell the jury that they must be convinced beyond a reasonable doubt of the defendant's guilt before they can convict (standard of proof) and that, if not, it is their duty to acquit.

Defence opening speech The defence is only entitled to make an opening speech if calling witnesses to testify on the facts (and the accused himself doesn't count for this purpose). So, you may not have the right to make an opening speech at all and, even if you do, you may decide that it is sensible not to. It may be better to leave your arguments to the closing speech. As a general rule, perhaps you should not make an opening speech if you are not confident of what your witnesses will say on oath; better to wait and see, then your speech can be based on what the witnesses actually said and so, more importantly, can your theory of the case. Conversely, the longer the time that defence witnesses will spend testifying, the greater the need for some guidance for the jury before the witnesses start their evidence.

If you are going to make an opening speech, you should indicate that you are entitled to do so by informing the judge, 'Your Honour, I shall be calling witnesses of fact in addition to the defendant'. Then proceed to knit together the following five strands:

(a) *Comments on the prosecution evidence* You may want to do this, especially because the prosecution could not. However, this is the sort of job that you will definitely want to do in your closing speech and the jury may wonder why you are just repeating yourself. It is usually best to keep your comments for your closing speech, then you can combine them with observations based on the evidence of the defence witnesses, too.

(b) *Outline the defence evidence* This is quite similar to the job that the prosecutor had. As then, you should be alert to the fact that witnesses sometimes fail to say what we expect them to (and some even say things we never expected them to!). It is best to paint your picture with a broad brush, that way you leave some room to adapt your case as the evidence is given, and you avoid giving too much advance information to your opponent.

(c) *Your theory of the case* Even applying a broad brush, you should still have a good idea of how the defence case is likely to unfurl in court. So you should have a case theory now (of course, you should have had a case theory before setting foot in the courtroom) and you may want to set it before the jury. A combination of the uncontested evidence in the case and your client's version of the matters in issue should enable you to present a theory of the case to the jury. You want to try to make the jury see that the only reasonable inference to be drawn from the evidence is that the defendant is not guilty and your case theory is the better/more appropriate/correct one. However, do this concisely and leaving some room for flexibility later, should the need arise. Of course, no-one expects the defence case to collapse, as witnesses fail to deliver their expected testimony, but even if they all 'come up to proof', the jury won't want to hear you simply repeat your opening speech at the end of the trial.

(d) *Weaknesses in your case* It is a very moot point whether you should mention these now. After all, you may be fortunate and the witness you had the least faith in does superbly. But in some instances you know that, even if everything goes well, a certain issue or incident will still be a source of potential danger for your case. Your choice is to say nothing now and try to deal with it when it arises in testimony and in your closing speech, or to raise it now. The latter strategy has a disadvantage in that you alert your opponent to the weakness, but it has the advantage of honesty. In the eyes of the jury, you will be seen as frank and open: the fact that you are prepared to acknowledge the flaws in your case, yet still demonstrate how the defendant is not guilty may be quite persuasive. Openness now also shows that you are not being taken by surprise when the weakness become manifest during testimony, it shows control and confidence. If you do decide to be frank, never describe a weakness in those terms; simply state the point that is the weakness and try to put it in the best light that you can.

(e) *Burden and standard of proof* You should take this opportunity, if making a speech, to remind the jury shortly that the prosecution brought the case and it is for them to prove it, beyond a reasonable doubt. The defendant does not have to prove his or her innocence, it is enough if they raise a question (or reasonable doubt) in the minds of the jury.

15.5 Dos and Don'ts

15.5.1 THINGS TO AVOID DOING IN AN OPENING SPEECH

You should not:

(a) argue — now is not the time to discuss the pros and cons, nor is it the time to persuade — that will come later;

(b) state your personal opinions — either on the facts or the credibility of any witness — frankly, no-one cares and it is not your job to waste time on this;

(c) overstate your client's case — the trier(s) of fact may remember what you say now, especially as they may be reminded of it by your opponent. Try to understate;

(d) read your speech from a prepared text — of course, you should have notes but if possible try not to look at them. If you are prepared properly, you should be able to make your speech with very little need to look at your notes; besides, there are other more important places to observe, e.g., the jury box or the Bench.

15.5.2   THINGS YOU SHOULD CONSIDER DOING IN AN OPENING SPEECH

You should:

(a) consider the best way to enable the trier(s) of fact to empathise with your client — a typical example is by using your client's name, rather than his or her title in the proceedings (e.g., 'Mr Smith' and not 'claimant', or 'accused');

(b) decide on the best way to minimise any empathy the court may have for the opposing party — for example, you may want to try to depersonalise them by using only a title when referring to them (e.g., 'the claimant');

(c) try to look at the trier(s) of fact — eye contact is desirable, although you don't want to stare. If addressing justices of the peace or a jury, try to make individual eye contacts rather than simply staring at a point on the wall above their heads. It is sometimes said that, for a jury trial, it is a good idea to forecast who the chairman of the jury will be and concentrate your efforts on them. I would not recommend that as you may be wrong and the other jurors may feel slighted.

15.6   Telling a Story

The opening speech is your first chance to acquaint the court with your theory of the case, and the themes which give depth and colour to the cold, two-dimensional allegations between the parties. First impressions are very important and this will be the time when the court has its first real impression of you. As an advocate, your job is **to persuade** and one of the best ways of doing this is to recreate the moments (or longer) leading up to the matters that gave rise to the litigation and assist the trier(s) of fact to 'see' what happened. Most cases are decided on their facts, not on nice questions of law, and the sooner you knit 'the facts' (that is, the uncontested facts and your client's version of those in dispute) into a single coherent story, the more likely it is to be remembered later. This 'story-telling' element of your speech is the best setting for your case theory to be introduced, but the story is more than just the theory. If your version makes sense as a story, it is likely to be persuasive. (See **Chapter 7**.)

15.7   Check List for Preparation

What should go into the introduction?

What are the main facts of the case? How will they be developed (that is, through the testimony of witnesses, or documentary evidence, or other exhibits)?

What are the issues in the case? Which 'facts' are in dispute? What are the legal principles on which you will rely to establish your client's case?

What are your main themes in the case?

What are your subsidiary themes in the case?

What is your theory of the case?

What weaknesses are there in your version of the case, in your client or in your witnesses?

15.8   Bibliography

Bergman, P. *Trial Advocacy in a Nutshell*, West Publishing Co., 1979.

Crowther, E. *Advocacy for the Advocate*, Sweet & Maxwell, 2nd edn, 1990.

Du Cann, R. *The Art of the Advocate*, Penguin, 1993, revised, pp. 72–91.

Evans, K. *Advocacy in Court*, Blackstone Press (OUP), 2nd edn, 1995.

Hyam, M. *Advocacy Skills*, Blackstone Press (OUP), 4th edn, 1999.

Mauet, F. *Fundamentals of Trial Technique*, Little Brown, 2nd edn, 1995.

Sonsteng, Haydock and Boyd *The Trial Book, A Total System for Preparation and Presentation of a Case*, West Publishing Co., 1984.

SIXTEEN

CLOSING SPEECHES

16.1 Introduction

You will almost certainly have seen some great closing speeches without going any-where near a courtroom. Many writers of stage plays, cinema films and television series have recognised the drama of the situation and the potential that it offers to stir the emotions with pleas for justice and the truth. Often these dramatic works are of American origin and involve jury trials. It cannot be denied that such scenes have tremendous appeal — they are exciting, moving and thrilling. How often is it like that at three o'clock on a hot June day in an airless courtroom in Acton? Not very often is the simple answer.

Although the closing speech does offer certain opportunities for counsel to indulge in an otherwise frustrated theatrical nature, it must be remembered that not every closing speech takes place in front of a jury (the vast majority will not), nor should every barrister try to be the next Humphrey Bogart or Henry Fonda.

What you, as a barrister, must do is to consider your audience and what you are asking them to do. Closing speeches can be made in criminal trials and civil trials; they can be made to juries or to magistrates, to Crown Court judges or judges in the High Court or County Court; they can be made for the claimant or the prosecution or for the defendant. What you have to do and the ways in which you seek to do it will vary, according to all of these factors. Your manner is also likely to be affected by the topic of the litigation — a closing speech to a judge in a personal injury claim may be quite different from another speech to the same judge when hearing a fraud trial. So, how should you go about making a closing speech?

16.2 The Purpose of a Closing Speech

16.2.1 PERSUASION

The purpose, at heart, never varies. You seek to persuade the person or people who have to decide the facts to come down in your favour. You should have put your theory of the case already, shown the court your story and your themes. Now you are trying to knit all these strands together into a coherent whole — to show them the picture as you want them to see it. This may sound like an incitement to distortion or deceit but it is not.

No barrister should ever mislead a court (specifically, whoever is responsible for determining the facts). You must never tell your audience that a witness said A when he or she really said B. You may need to remind the court of the times when a witness said something which made the going tough for your client, in order to explain it away (your opponent may remind the court without the favourable explanation!). But having said that, you are entitled to reinforce your client's story in so far as you have the evidence to back it up.

16.2.2 UNFAVOURABLE EVIDENCE

So the main purpose of a closing speech is to persuade your audience of the merits of your case, by interweaving your story with the appropriate evidence. Another major purpose has been alluded to — the necessity of dealing with the evidence that undermines your story, that knocks holes in your theory. Usually, this will be the evidence of your opponent's witnesses, perhaps unshaken by cross-examination. Sometimes, it will be evidence from your own witnesses — some damning admission made in cross-examination or an unexpected answer which just slipped out. Whatever its origin, do not ignore it. To do so runs the risk of misleading the court and since your opponent and/or the judge is almost certain to refer to this evidence, you will appear at best careless and at worst dishonest in the eyes of the court. If the court forms this opinion of your veracity, the client will be 'sunk without trace'.

16.2.3 THE LAW

Having dealt with themes, stories and the evidence, what is left? Usually the law. The length of time and the detail that you devote to the legal points raised in the case will obviously depend on the nature of the case. You should not duck making submissions on the law but you should remember a few important points.

First, in a jury trial the judge decides questions of law and will direct the jury accordingly. Anything you say to the jury about the law is subject to whatever the judge says. (If he gets it wrong, the place to correct it is in the appeal court — don't have a slanging match in front of the jury.) Secondly, in a trial where a professional lawyer is adjudicating, whilst you can make sophisticated legal points in your speech, remember that the audience is human — he or she will eventually cease listening to you; and he or she is legally trained — make your points on law succinct and keep to the point, the court does not want a lecture on the law of nuisance (for example). Thirdly, if you must quote from decided cases or statutes, you should do your utmost to ensure that the court has sufficient copies of the report to follow your remarks. (Curiously, it is not common to do this when addressing a jury, even though they are the audience most likely to be ignorant of the law.)

16.3 The Content of a Closing Speech

16.3.1 KEEP IT TO THE POINT

Keep things short and to the point. It is often unnecessary to reiterate a great deal of evidence from the trial. Take what you need to remind the court of your themes and theory — use the evidence to reinforce the validity of your arguments. Remind the court of those things that you said you would demonstrate in your opening speech (if you made one), then highlight the evidence which (you say) makes your points.

16.3.2 SETTING OUT THE THEORY OF THE CASE

If you did not make an opening speech, now is the time to set out your theory of the case, how the evidence knits together to substantiate your assertions. Distil your arguments to a minimum — concentrate the minds of your audience on those few essentials which, if decided favourably to your client, will mean that judgment goes in your favour. Never appear to express your personal opinion of the evidence or of a witness. You should preface any comment on the evidence with an objective phrase such as 'Members of the jury, you may think . . .'.

16.3.3 THE LAW

Deal with the relevant law but not in great detail or at length. When addressing an audience of non-lawyers (lay magistrates, jurors), remember that they may need points explained in quite straightforward terms. Do not labour any points. Always reiterate the appropriate burden and standard of proof. In a criminal trial, the defence barrister, when confronted by apparently watertight prosecution evidence which is directly contradicted by the defence, will remind the jury (or magistrates) that a 'Not Guilty' verdict does not mean that the defendant has proved his or her contentions, simply that they have been left in doubt and must give the defendant the benefit of it.

16.3.4 ORDER OF PRESENTATION IN YOUR SPEECH

It is normal in a civil trial to deal first with the claimant's case and then with that of the defendant, regardless of whether you are making a closing speech for the claimant or defendant. Similarly, in criminal trials your speech will usually start by reviewing the case for the prosecution and then that for the defendant. So you follow the sequence in which the evidence was presented. This is because, generally, it is the claimant or prosecution who has the legal burden of proof — their case will be lost if the evidence in their favour is not up to the requisite standard. Because the claimant (or prosecution) started the litigation, it is usually they who have defined the issues in the case or 'chosen the battleground' and it is sensible to set out those issues within the context of their 'case'.

16.3.5 PREPARATION

If possible, do not make a closing speech without a chance to prepare it fully. This is so obvious that you may think it does not need saying. In a trial, it is not always possible to predict precisely when you will be called upon to make your closing speech. Often it will be straight after the last witness has finished his or her testimony and the defence has closed its case. If you have been occupied in examining witnesses, you may not have your closing speech in anything like its ideal state. It now becomes important to see who has 'the last word'.

16.4   Order of Speeches

16.4.1 CIVIL TRIALS

Closing speeches always occur in an established sequence. In a civil trial, the defendant's counsel goes first, followed by the claimant's barrister. So, the barrister appearing for the claimant gets more time to marshal his thoughts and the evidence, and to perfect a plan. (If there is more than one claimant or defendant, speeches go according to numerical order — 1st defendant — 2nd — 3rd, etc.)

16.4.2 CRIMINAL TRIALS

In a criminal trial, the basic principle is that the defence closing speech goes last. After that, you must distinguish between trials with magistrates and with a jury.

16.4.2.1 Magistrates
Where magistrates are to decide guilt or innocence, the rule is that, normally, each side may make a single speech in the case. This usually works out so that the prosecution makes a short opening speech before any evidence is heard, then the defence makes a closing speech after all of the evidence is completed. If either barrister wishes to make a second speech (i.e., to close as well as to open the case), this can be done but only with the court's permission and your opponent must be given the same opportunity, where it is still possible.

16.4.2.2 Trial by jury
If you are in a trial by jury, then usually both the prosecution and defence can make a closing speech, regardless of whether an opening speech was made. The prosecution

barrister may forgo a closing speech if he or she made an opening speech and either there was no defence evidence or the only witness was the accused — counsel may feel that there is nothing to add to the opening. A defence barrister should never surrender the chance to make a closing speech. Often, the defence do not make an opening speech (either through choice or the rules) but, even if the defendant's case was opened with a speech, the chance to have the last word to the jury is generally seen as a vital asset.

16.4.2.3 More than one defendant

If there is more than one defendant in a criminal trial and each is represented separately, the closing speeches for them will take place in the order in which they are named on the indictment. The defendants have no say in determining this order: sometimes the least important defendant is last, sometimes the most important. Whoever's name appears last gets the plum position for their closing speech. (Note that in this situation, the prosecution makes a single speech, dealing with all the defendants.)

16.4.2.4 Value of the final speech

When making the final speech that the jury hear (subject to the judge's summing-up) before they consider the verdict, one can deal cogently with all the issues in the case, whether raised by the prosecution or any co-defendant. Those barristers who preceded your speech could only guess what you were going to say and how you would say it; you have the advantage of knowing what they said.

16.5 Planning your Speech

It should be clear that you need to think about the content and structure of your closing speech (if one is to be made) before the trial starts. It can only be a rough plan but you should have it ready for the beginning of the trial. As the trial progresses and witnesses substantiate (or undermine) the points you want to make, keep a record of what they said (highlight it in your notes or put an asterisk by it) so that it can be found easily. Try to refine and fill in the detail of your plan after each witness, or during adjournments. Such 'free' time is often limited in a trial, especially those lasting a day or less, so make the most of every chance you get to polish your speech. Even if you do so, you will inevitably have to carry a lot of material in your head.

This is no bad thing. You should be able to recall the really important pieces of evidence quite clearly. It will help you to do this if you have chosen a few key words or phrases (or even mental pictures) taken from your theory of the case and its themes. This will help you when making the speech to get your message over — as key words stick in your mind, so they will with the jury, judge, etc. The fewer points you ask your audience to think about, the more likely they are to do so and with reasonable recollection of the relevant evidence.

16.6 Delivering your Speech

'May it please you, Your Honour/Sir/Madam/members of the jury . . .' This is the traditional, courteous way to start a closing speech. Some judges deprecate use of the phrase 'may it please you'. After that, the manner in which you present your speech is really a question of individual style. You will develop your own style with time but it is a good idea to watch more experienced barristers when you go into court during your pupillage. You may see good and bad examples of a closing speech — be discriminating. Think about the sequence of events used in the speech, about the tone used by the barrister and the pace of delivery. Then consider how effective it was.

Just as you watched the judge's pen while examining a witness, so you must observe your audience during your speech. Make sure that you don't go so fast that they lose track of your arguments; but don't go so slowly that their eyes start to glaze over! Remember to look the jurors (or whoever is deciding the facts) in the eye but don't stare at individuals. Don't look wildly around the room — you are talking to a specific group of people and it is legitimate to concentrate on them. The best advocates will establish such a rapport with their audience that, for both sides, there is no-one else in the courtroom.

Some barristers like to use hand gestures, others don't. You will probably do whatever is natural to you; but remember, you want your listener(s) to recall your arguments and evidence, not the fact that you looked like a Punch and Judy man without the puppet! So if you are going to use gestures, do so sparingly and to emphasise your points. You will almost certainly 'lose' a judge if you indulge in too many gestures or any 'purple' prose. Judges generally prefer the more detached approach, with points made calmly and rationally, without appeal to the emotions. Remember that Horace Rumpole is a creature (of fiction and) of the Old Bailey — he works with juries, not in the Chancery Division of the High Court.

16.7 Bibliography

Du Cann, R. *The Art of the Advocate*, Penguin, 1993, pp. 189–218.
Evans, K. *Advocacy in Court*, Blackstone Press (OUP), 1995, 2nd edn, pp. 66–67, 80–87.
Murphy, P. and Barnard, D. *Evidence and Advocacy*, Blackstone Press (OUP), 5th edn, 1998, pp. 210–211, 226–227.
Stone, M. *Cross-examination in Criminal Trials*, Butterworths, 1995, pp. 209–214.

16.8 Check List for a Closing Speech

(a) Prepare a plan before the trial. (Once you know where you want to be at the end of the case, it will help you to concentrate on how you are going to get there.)

(b) Use key words or phrases to encapsulate the important points of your case. (Both you and your audience are more likely to remember a few simple phrases.)

(c) Remind the court (especially non-lawyers) of the appropriate burden and standard of proof on the contentious issues in the case.

(d) Make any concessions that seem appropriate in the light of the evidence given in the case. (It helps to focus attention on the real issues and may make you seem quite a reasonable person.)

(e) Using your key words, review the important points in a sensible order. Refer to the evidence which supports or undermines your case.

(f) If there is evidence which damages your case, deal with it. You might be able to offer an explanation for it which is consistent with your case; you might suggest that the witness is mistaken or lying; you might argue that, even if the evidence is accepted by the court, it does not prove what your opponent says it does.

(g) Watch your audience. Try to keep their attention. Think about how they might see the evidence and arguments, then try to present your speech in a manner that makes your points comprehensible to them.

(h) Decide before you begin what your closing words will be. If need be, write them down. Nothing reduces the impact of a speech more than the sight and hearing of an advocate who runs down at the end of a speech simply because he does not know how to end it. It saps the life out of everything that precedes it. It gives an unmistakable appearance of a lack of confidence in the advocate in the case he is presenting. It is easily avoided.

(i) Don't go on for too long.

16.9   Epilogue

'My poor client's fate now depends on your votes.'
Here the speaker sat down in his place,
And directed the judge to refer to his notes
And briefly to sum up the case.

But the judge said he never had summed up before;
So the Snark undertook it instead,
And summed it so well that it came to far more
Than the witnesses ever had said!

(From 'The Barrister's Dream' in Lewis Carroll's *The Hunting of the Snark*.)

Note: the Snark should not be used as a role model!

PART 6
WITNESSES

SEVENTEEN

THE TASK AHEAD

The following six chapters (**Chapters 18** to **23**) look at how advocates deal with witnesses. The chapters concentrate on the practical issues of technique and object-ives. Please read them all carefully and use case studies as the raw material to practise them on (see for example, **Chapter 9**). Try working with your friends and colleagues, taking turns to play the role of the witness.

At the Inns of Court School of Law, we have devised a set of advocacy training criteria by which we can measure the competence of an individual advocate when questioning a witness. These criteria are set out in full at **8.3**. You will get a better understanding of the following chapters if you refer to the criteria now. Whenever you practise questioning a witness, try to apply those criteria to your work and consider the results. Equally valuable will be the comments of your friends and colleagues if they can base their feedback to you on those criteria. Of course, you can also apply them to any example of questioning a witness that you see, for example while visiting a court or watching a training video. The best advocates reflect upon their work frequently and think about ways in which they might improve.

One of the criteria that you should pay particular attention to is that which deals with questioning technique. For an advocate to abide by professional rules and the rules of evidence, the questions that he or she asks should appear in an appropriate form. An example of this is that, when you question your own witness, you should not 'lead' them. This means that the witness should be enabled to tell their own story in their own words. **Chapter 18** explains more about that and other questioning techniques which are appropriate for examination-in-chief. Conversely, when you question an opponent's witness, you should aim to exert considerable control over the witness. In cross-examination, you should not give the witness an opportunity to repeat the damage they have just inflicted on your case when they were questioned by their advocate; nor should your questions allow the witness to elaborate or give more details in ways that simply strengthen the case against your client. Competent cross-examin-ation demands that you put your case to the witness, in an affirmative fashion, and that you exert control over the witness by asking plenty of closed, 'leading', questions. These questions should restrict the witness's freedom by severely limiting the range of answers that he or she can possibly give. **Chapter 19** tells you more about the techniques of cross-examination, and its aims and objectives. **Chapter 20** looks at the important, and often over-looked, skill of re-examination. This aspect of questioning is becoming even more important in civil cases as the opportunities to examine-in-chief are restricted. Re-examination often becomes the only significant chance which the advocate gets to question their witnesses at all, in court. We mentioned earlier the need for any advocate to abide by professional rules when questioning witnesses. This includes the need to comply with relevant rules of professional conduct, of course. It also includes the need to behave properly and sensitively towards witnesses. **Chapter 21** draws attention to these important matters, since to proceed in ignorance of them may affect not just your own professional obligations but also your client's prospects of success in the instant case.

At the end of this collection, you will find two chapters which set out how you might deal with evidence in the course of a trial. They are in this part of the Manual because they are closely connected with the work that the advocate has to do when planning for trial and then considering the sufficiency of the evidence at trial. **Chapter 22** looks at the issues, the procedure and some of the arguments that can arise in the context of an application to exclude evidence. **Chapter 23** takes you through the application that you might make to stop a case part-way through the trial, on the basis that there has been insufficient evidence adduced by the claimant or prosecutor to require the defendant to call evidence in rebuttal. Both of these chapters contain case studies as examples of how the applications could work in practice.

EIGHTEEN

EXAMINATION-IN-CHIEF

18.1   Introduction

Examination-in-chief is the process of eliciting evidence from your own witness. It is often the most difficult skill to acquire in practice yet its importance is frequently underrated. The novice dithers over whether a question is leading or not and ends up not asking it at all, while even the more experienced practitioner may overlook examination-in-chief in his or her eagerness to plan a devastating cross-examination! Examination-in-chief is the first opportunity the court has to assess the witness. A strong impression made at that stage will outlast many an attack in cross-examination.

18.1.1   THE AIMS OF EXAMINATION-IN-CHIEF

The aims of conducting any examination-in-chief should therefore be threefold:

   (a)   to establish your case or part of it through the evidence elicited from the witness;

   (b)   to present the evidence so that it is clear, memorable and persuasive;

   (c)   to insulate the evidence, in so far as possible, from anticipated attack in cross-examination.

Before turning to look at how these aims can be achieved, let us first consider some preliminary matters.

18.2   Preparation and Planning

18.2.1   ESTABLISHING AN ORDER

While preparing your case (see **Case Preparation Manual**), you will have already identified what you need to prove or disprove at the trial and have determined the facts and legal principles which are relevant to establishing your case. You will have also selected the theory of your case and the key elements of the evidence that support it.

You are now ready for the next step in your preparation. This involves:

   (a)   selecting the order of the witnesses;

   (b)   selecting the order of the evidence to be elicited from each witness.

18.2.1.1   Selecting the order of the witnesses

   (a)   It is preferable to start and finish your case with a witness who makes a strong impression. Avoid calling as your first witness one whose evidence is particularly vulnerable to cross-examination (for example, because it contains many inconsistencies or the witness's recollection is poor).

(b) In a large proportion of cases, it is usual to start with the witness whose evidence is first in time. This may, however, create difficulties where a number of your witnesses deal with matters which are relevant to the whole of your case. It may then be preferable to call as your first witness the one who gives the greatest overview of your case. This is likely to be your client, although not necessarily so.

(c) As a general rule, you do not have to call your client as your first witness. The one exception to this is provided by the Police and Criminal Evidence Act 1984, s. 79. As defence counsel in a criminal trial, you must call the accused (if he or she is giving evidence) before any other witness of fact unless the court directs otherwise.

(d) Avoid calling your client in the middle of your witnesses. It makes a stronger impression if you call him or her either first or last. If you call your client as your final witness it may give him or her an opportunity to settle down and familiarise himself or herself with the atmosphere of the court.

(e) Corroborative witnesses should be called as close as possible to the evidence they are corroborating in order to support and insulate that evidence.

(f) Beware of calling too many cumulative witnesses or of seeking to overprove your case. This may backfire (you may even be penalised in costs on taxation). Calling six witnesses who claim to have seen the same incident may give your opponent the opportunity of highlighting inconsistencies between their various accounts. If you must call a number of cumulative witnesses, particularly where you are prosecuting in a criminal trial, simply tender some of them for cross-examination.

(g) Expert witnesses called at the end of your case will enable you to finish on a strong note and may provide you with an opportunity to recap and/or emphasise the evidence you have already elicited from your previous witnesses. Whilst there is no hard and fast rule, it is preferable to call your expert either first or last and not in the middle of your witnesses. Note, however, that the availability of your expert witness might determine when you call him or her.

18.2.1.2 Selecting the order of the evidence to be elicited from each witness

Your aim should be to organise the key elements of the witness's testimony in a logical order so that the trier of fact, be it judge, jury or tribunal, can understand how each part fits into the overall theory of your case. This will normally result in a strict chronological presentation of the evidence, particularly in the case of a witness to a specific incident. For example, in a claim for damages for personal injuries sustained at work, the claimant might give evidence in this order:

(a) his or her background;

(b) his or her training and experience;

(c) safety instruction in the job;

(d) description of site where the accident occurred or of the machinery being used at the time;

(e) what occurred just before the accident;

(f) how the accident actually occurred;

(g) what happened immediately after the accident;

(h) initial treatment, pain and suffering;

(i) continued treatment, pain, suffering, loss of amenity;

(j)   present disabilities: physical, mental, emotional;

(k)   financial losses to date.

Not every case, however, lends itself to a strict chronological presentation of the witness's evidence. Nor is it always the best way of presenting the evidence. You should structure the evidence so as to emphasise the key elements which establish or support your case rather than simply eliciting the details from the first to last in time. For instance, imagine you are representing a father seeking a residence order in respect of his child. Your aim is to elicit evidence from the family's au pair regarding the mother's financial irresponsibility, alcoholism and physical abuse of the child. Of course you could deal with everything the witness has to say, in a strict chronological order, from the moment she entered the household; but it will be more effective if you elicit the evidence by topic. This does not prevent you from dealing with the subject matter of each topic in a chronological order. However, by eliciting the evidence by topic you will leave the trier of fact with a much stronger impression, a cumulative picture of each aspect of the behaviour.

18.2.2   WRITTEN PREPARATION

Many novices prepare for examination-in-chief by writing out in longhand all the questions they propose to ask each witness. This is usually done as a confidence booster in case they forget to ask the relevant questions or are unable to form their questions spontaneously in an appropriate manner. Some advocates also favour this practice and consider it an essential part of their preparation. Most advocates, however, favour a more selective use of this practice, writing out in full/memorising only those questions which they anticipate will be difficult to formulate 'off the top of their heads' and/or those which involve some complex factual concept/situation, e.g., when dealing with expert testimony. In simple cases, they prefer to examine without using a fully prepared script.

For the beginner, the drawbacks of reading out prepared questions can be manifold. If you have your face in a note-book, you will probably pay scant regard to the witness's answer in your anxiety to find and read the next question. You may lose the vital opportunity of watching the witness, his or her reaction to the question, the manner in which he or she responds and the impression he or she makes upon the court. You may miss what your opponent has seen, the telling gesture, the judge's expression, the jury members' looks of incredulity. You may convey an impression of disinterest in your witness's account. Most important of all, if your preparation is too rigid, you will find it difficult to adapt your questions to suit the witness's answer(s), to cope with an unexpected answer (witnesses do change their stories!) or a piece of evidence which has emerged during the trial.

Therefore, whilst recognising that the practice varies at the Bar, you will be encouraged, during the vocational training course, not to rely upon a prepared script of written questions. If you need to write out some of your questions as a confidence booster, you will be encouraged to restrict these to a couple at the start of the witness's evidence and/or to the most important issues in the case. It is normal practice to use the witness's proof of evidence/statement (containing what the witness ought to say) as the basis of examining him or her in-chief.

This does not mean that you should not prepare for examination-in-chief. On the contrary, preparation and planning are vital. Even at this stage, planning your closing speech will help you to define your goals and prepare your questions with these in mind. (See also **16.5, 16.8(a)**.) However, rather than writing down a string of questions, you will be encouraged to write down a note of the topics you want to deal with, broken down into subheadings or points, where appropriate. Preparing your case in this way, using 'trigger notes' or 'bullet points', will enable you to concentrate on the issues, the key elements of the evidence and allow you greater flexibility. You can then see at a glance where you wish to guide the witness.

18.3   Presenting the Evidence

18.3.1   CALLING THE WITNESS

It is time to call your first witness! You normally do so as follows:

'Sir/Madam, I (now) call Mrs Mary Brown';

or, as a matter of courtesy, just after you have finished your opening speech/statement:

'With your leave Sir/Madam' or 'With your Honour/Your Lordship's leave, I call Mrs Mary Brown'.

While the witness is taking the oath, you must stay both silent and still. Do not shuffle papers!

18.3.2   GETTING STARTED

What you need to do to start the examination-in-chief is to settle the witness. Let the witness introduce himself or herself. This helps the witness to get used to their surroundings, to being the focus of attention, and to the sound of their own voice projected across the courtroom. So you start with easy, short questions to which they know the answers and which allow them to talk a little. For example:

Q: 'What is your full name, please?'
Q: 'Where do you live?'

Then ask the witness some straightforward questions about his or her background.

Q: 'What do you do for a living?'/'Where do you work?'
Q: 'What is your position in that company?'
Q: 'What are your responsibilities?'
Q: 'How long have you worked in that job/capacity/as a . . .?'
Q: 'Are you married?'

Such questions pose no major test for a witness and so they help to take the pressure off. They also introduce the witness as a real person and show the court that he or she is steady, reliable, 'a family person' and so on. The circumstances of the case will dictate the extent to which it is necessary to elicit further personal background information from the witness. Once the witness has relaxed, you can move onto the substance of their evidence.

18.3.3   THE INITIAL HURDLES

You must now guide the witness to the starting point of his or her evidence. This will normally establish his or her connection with the case. Much now depends upon the extent to which the facts are in dispute as this will dictate the extent to which you may or may not lead at this stage. It may be clear from the statements of case/affidavits/witness statements that a matter is non-contentious. If it is not apparent, check with your opponent. If he or she agrees, you may inform the court, where appropriate, that 'my friend has indicated that I may lead on this matter'. Otherwise, you must frame your question(s) so as not to lead on disputed matters.

18.3.3.1   Where there is no dispute
Q: 'Did you let a room at your home to the defendant in July 2001?'
Q: 'Did you examine the claimant in your surgery on 15 May 2002?'
Q: 'Did you meet the defendant in the "Horse and Hounds" public house in Ealing during the evening of 6 October last?'
Q: 'Were you employed by the claimant, Mrs Gray, as a housekeeper during the period from October 1994 to June 2002?'

Q: 'Did you attend at the security office in Harrods store during the afternoon of 3 August 2002?'

18.3.3.2 Where a matter is only partially in dispute

Q: 'Where were you during the morning of 4 September 2002?' (date and time not in dispute)

Q: 'Did you let a room at your premises to the defendant?' (date in dispute)

Q: 'In what capacity were you employed in October 2001?'

Q: 'Did you meet the defendant during the evening of 6 October last?' (place in dispute)

18.3.3.3 Where there is a disputed matter

There are some occasions, however, when it is clear that a matter is entirely in dispute or when your opponent asks you not to lead on a particular point. The way in which you deal with this varies in every case. As a general rule look for some common ground or begin with an uncontentious matter (this may be apparent from the statements of case/witness statements). It may be necessary to generalise or ask the witness about an event which occurred at an earlier time.

Example 1:

Q: 'Where do you work?' (working not in dispute)

A: 'At Lloyds Bank, Charing Cross Road.'

Q: 'How long have you worked there?'

A: 'About two years.'

Q: 'How do you get to work in the mornings?'

A: 'I catch the tube to Charing Cross and then walk down the road to the bank.'

Q: 'During the last two years, has anything exceptional happened in that vicinity on your way to work?'

A: 'Yes. I once saw a car crash.'

Q: 'Where precisely was that?'

Example 2:

Q: 'Do you know Mr Jones?'

A: 'Yes.'

Q: 'When did you first meet him?'

A: 'We met at an office party about a year ago. He came with one of the girls I work with.'

Q: 'How long was your meeting?'

A: 'We were introduced and chatted for about 10 minutes at the party. He and his girlfriend then gave me a lift home.'

Q: 'Did you ever see Mr Jones again?'

A: 'Yes.'

Q: 'When was that?'

A: 'It was 11 September 2002, the night I was burgled.'

Example 3:

Q: 'Do you recall an occasion when you spent a weekend in Manchester?'

A: 'Yes.'

Q: 'When was that?'

A: 'The beginning of May last year.'

Q: 'On what date did you return home?'

A: 'I came back on Tuesday 5 May.'

Q: 'Did you notice anything in particular on your return?'

A: 'As soon as I got to the house, I noticed that the front door had been kicked in and was hanging off its hinges . . .'

18.3.4 SETTING THE SCENE

Having guided the witness to the start of his or her evidence, it will probably be necessary to 'set the scene' further by eliciting details of the surrounding or background circumstances. This is particularly so in the case of a witness to an incident.

Examples:
Q: 'Describe the weather/traffic/road surface conditions.'
Q: 'Where were you standing?'
Q: 'Who else was present at the meeting?'
Q: 'When did you first meet the defendant?'

The nature of the case will determine the extent to which you need to develop a picture of the surrounding/background detail.

18.3.5 WITNESS STATEMENTS

The preparation and exchange of full witness statements, directed to stand as the witness's evidence-in-chief, has increasingly replaced the need for examination-in-chief in civil cases. In such a case, it is unnecessary for the witness to repeat the content of his or her statement. The start of the (civil) examination-in-chief will look something like the following.

Having asked the witness to identify himself or herself, the advocate will ask the court usher to show the witness 'a document'.

Q: 'Do you see a signature on the document?'
A: 'Yes.'
Q: 'Whose signature is it?'

Inviting the witness to then confirm the making and truth of the statement will usually suffice before tendering the witness for cross-examination.

Note that the judge retains a discretion to override a direction that the witness statement stands as the evidence-in-chief. The judge will therefore indicate if there are matters on which he or she would like to hear oral testimony despite the fact that they are dealt with in the witness's statement.

You may only adduce evidence of additional matters in-chief, the substance of which was not contained in the witness's statement if (i) the other party consents, or (ii) such additional evidence relates to new matters which have arisen in the course of the trial, or (iii) you obtain leave of the court.

18.3.6 THE HEART OF THE TESTIMONY: ACHIEVING THE AIMS OF EXAMINATION-IN-CHIEF

We considered briefly at the start of this chapter the three aims of examination-in-chief:

(a) establishing your case;

(b) making the evidence clear, memorable and persuasive;

(c) insulating the evidence, in so far as possible, from anticipated attack in cross-examination.

How can these aims be achieved? Unfortunately, there is no single 'magic' answer to this question but if you observe the following basic principles, you should begin to master the skill of conducting a successful examination-in-chief.

18.3.7 TWENTY BASIC PRINCIPLES

18.3.7.1 Keep it simple
The trier(s) of fact will be listening to the evidence for the first time. It takes longer to absorb new information when hearing it rather than reading it. The main points can be submerged if drowned in too much peripheral detail.

18.3.7.2 Scene first, then action

Before the trier(s) of fact can understand what happened, they will need the backdrop or context against which to understand the action. Set the scene first.

18.3.7.3 Know your objective

Concentrate on the key elements of the witness's testimony and keep them to the forefront of your mind. You should be asking yourself questions such as: What am I seeking to show through this witness's evidence? What part of my case does this witness (help to) establish/support? What is it I want him/her to deal with? In what order do I want to cover these matters?

18.3.7.4 Know the answer before asking the question

Avoid asking questions to which you do not know the answer. This is likely to damage your case and introduce confusion. Examination-in-chief is not a fishing expedition!

18.3.7.5 Do not lead

Avoid questions that suggest or tend to suggest the answer to the witness where the subject matter is in dispute. Do not assume facts are in evidence before they have been elicited from the witness.

18.3.7.6 Keep it clear

Break the evidence down into intelligible pieces. Ask one question at a time. Avoid jargon or legalese. Keep your questions short and simple. Plant a firm question mark at the end of each question and allow the witness time to answer. Cut out unnecessary preamble, e.g., 'Could you please tell the court what the registration number of the car read?'. Ask instead 'What was the car's registration number?'. Use plain English, e.g., 'see' rather than 'perceive', 'car' rather than 'vehicle'.

18.3.7.7 Organise the key elements of the testimony

A logical progression or structure to the order in which the information is introduced will make it easier to follow. You will usually find that, as the witness is telling a story, they will recollect it best (and the trier(s) of fact will remember it better) if you enable the witness to work through their story in a chronological order. The aim here is to enable the trier(s) of fact to understand how each part fits into the overall theory of your case. Do not hop backwards and forwards from one subject to another. Structure the testimony rather than merely presenting it in a haphazard fashion.

It may be that you do not get the necessary amount of detail about a particular matter from the witness when they talk about it for the first time. That can happen because you must not 'lead' your witness but use questions which prompt them to tell the story in their own words. This will mean that, from time to time, you will need to interrupt their narrative in order to go back and cover a topic in more detail. For example, 'You told the court that you arrived at the party at about 10.30 pm — how did you get there? Who did you see when you first arrived? What was he doing at that time?' and so on.

Sometimes, you will decide that the court will have a better understanding of events (or perhaps be more sympathetic to your client) if they learn first what happened to bring the parties to court at all, and then find out what events led up to that conclusion. Having settled the witness with the usual questions, such as, 'Please tell the court your full name' and 'What do you do for a living?', you might then ask the witness, 'Do you know why you are in court today?'. When the witness replies affirmatively, you can then ask, 'Please tell the court what happened.'. The witness is likely to start talking about the conclusion of a sequence of events, for example, 'My car was stolen' or 'I was hit over the head and had to go to hospital' or 'I fell over a broken paving stone and cut my leg'. You can then concentrate on those events with the witness, before turning to more preliminary matters.

18.3.7.8 Get the witness to tell the story

Allow the witness to tell the story in his or her own words. The witness was there — they saw, heard or perceived what happened. It is much more effective and memorable if they relate their experiences to the trier(s) of fact than if they simply answer a series of questions in monosyllables.

18.3.7.9 Let the testimony flow

Try to avoid constant interruption of the witness. A fractured account may leave little impression on the trier(s) of fact. Allowing the witness to tell their story 'in paragraphs' rather than 'sentences' can help to build a picture of the events in the mind of the trier(s) of fact. As indicated below, detail can always be picked up afterwards.

18.3.7.10 Listen to the answers and respond accordingly

Don't however plough on, appearing to others to pay no regard to the answers the witness is giving. You may need to ask a follow-up question to ensure the testimony is clear and complete or that a technical word needs explaining. Or you may need to stop the witness answering your question if, e.g., he or she begins to introduce inadmissible material.

18.3.7.11 Exercise control, keep it relevant

Prune irrelevancies. Control the witness by using transitions, a point of reference or by asking a closed question. If the witness is talking too fast or is dealing with irrelevant matters, interrupt the flow in a firm but polite manner, e.g., 'I'm afraid, Mr Smith that you are going too fast for His Honour to take a full note of what you are saying. Try and watch His Honour's pen ...' or 'pausing there for a moment, Mr Smith, I would like to deal with ...'. Then follow this up with closed questions, keeping them as short as possible.

18.3.7.12 Combine questioning techniques

Vary the types of questions you ask, combining the questioning techniques you have learned, open and closed questions, transitions and points of reference — this should lead to clarity of presentation and enable you to exercise control when required.

Example:
Q: 'Did you see Mr Green again after he left your office that afternoon?'
A: 'Yes, I saw him two days later.'
Q: 'Where was that?'
A: 'He called at my home.'
Q: 'Were you expecting him?'
A: 'No, I was not.'
Q: 'At what time did he call?'
A: 'About 10.30 pm.'
Q: 'Was he with anyone else?'
A: 'No, he was alone.'
Q: 'Who else was at home?'
A: 'No-one. My wife was out visiting her mother.'
Q: 'What happened when Mr Green arrived?'
A: 'As I opened the front door to let him in he pushed past me, knocking me against the wall. He started shouting that he was going to teach me a lesson. Then he pulled a gun out of his coat pocket and threatened me with it.'
Q: 'Pausing there, how would you describe Mr Green's demeanour when he arrived?'
A: 'He was angry, almost mad.'
Q: 'Please describe the gun.'
A: 'Yes, it was a small black pistol.'
Q: 'Where were you when he pulled out this small black pistol?'
A: 'I was still against the wall where he had pushed me.'
Q: 'Approximately, how far away was Mr Green at that time?'
A: 'At first, he was about two feet away but then he came closer.'
Q: 'What happened as he came closer?'

18.3.7.13 Use pace to keep the story vivid

Use pace as an effective means of emphasising important evidence or conveying the speed with which something happened. You and not the witness choose the pace at which the evidence flows from the witness. Keep an eye on your audience — you need them to understand and follow the witness's account.

Example:
Q: 'What happened as he came closer?'
A: 'He came right up to me, mouthing obscenities, pinning me against the wall. He spat on my face. Then he stepped back and whipped me in the face with the pistol. I could feel blood on my cheek.'
Q: 'How did you react?'
A: 'I tried to push him away but he kept coming at me, trying to whip me again with the pistol. I was screaming for him to stop, trying to get the pistol away from him, he was fighting like a maniac . . .'

In the above series of questions, the questioner has let the evidence flow, allowing the witness to tell the important part of the story with little interruption. He or she could have interrupted, for example, to obtain greater detail of the 'obscenities' or 'of how Mr Green had pinned the witness against the wall' but it would have spoilt the effect, 'fractured' the witness's own account of what happened and slowed down the pace. Such detail can be elicited at a later stage, for example:

Q: 'You stated that Mr Green was mouthing obscenities. Do you recall the words he used?'

18.3.7.14 Use frequency for emphasis

A number of specific questions on the same subject emphasises its importance and builds a picture of the event in the mind(s) of the trier(s) of fact.

Example:
A: 'Then the defendant hit me.'
Q: 'With what did he hit you?'
A: 'His fist.'
Q: 'Which fist did he use?'
A: 'His right fist.'
Q: 'Was his fist open or closed?'
A: 'Closed.'
Q: 'Where did he hit you with this closed fist?'
A: 'In my face.'
Q: 'Whereabouts in the face?'
A: 'My right cheek.'
Q: 'How many times did he hit your cheek?'
A: 'Just the once.'

18.3.7.15 Make the connections

Tie the evidence up. Do not leave loose ends or expect the trier of fact to perform mental gymnastics. Do not leave it to your closing speech to make or show the connections between one fact and another or a series of facts and the conclusion they support. Develop the specific facts and then the conclusion which rests upon them or elicit the conclusion and then fill in the supporting facts.

Example 1:
(Supporting facts first; conclusion second.)
A: 'The defendant tried to get out of the car.'
Q: 'How?'
A: 'He opened the car door and put one leg out. He couldn't get any further without my assistance. He could hardly stand up on his own.'
Q: 'Did you have any conversation with the defendant?'
A: 'Well I tried to but he kept slurring his words. He stank of alcohol.'
Q: 'Officer, did you form any opinion as to the defendant's condition?'
A: 'Yes, I did. He was drunk.'

Example 2:
(Conclusion first; supporting facts second.)
A: 'The defendant tried to get out of the car.'
Q: 'Officer, did you form any opinion as to the defendant's condition at that time?'

A: 'Yes, I did. He was drunk.'
Q: 'Upon what did you base that opinion?'
A: 'He stank of alcohol and kept slurring his words. He couldn't get out of the car without my assistance. He put one leg out but could hardly stand up on his own.'

The first example makes a lasting impression. It is persuasive. The second example probably makes less impact although it has the advantage of conveying at an early stage the thrust of the witness's testimony.

18.3.7.16 Fill in the gaps

Do not leave holes in the witness's evidence. Think about what you might ask if you were in your opponent's shoes. For example, in the case of an identification witness, establish (in respect of each occasion he or she has seen the subject) such details as the lighting conditions, distance, angle, length and quality of observation. In this way, you may insulate the evidence from attack in cross-examination to the effect that the witness only got 'a fleeting glance'.

18.3.7.17 Be realistic

For instance, do not expect a witness to repeat verbatim a conversation which took place a long time before or one which is lengthy. The risk with asking 'What did he say to you?' is that you may get an 'I don't remember' response. If this is likely to happen, avoid it in this way:

Q: 'Do you remember exactly what the defendant said?'
A: 'No, it's too long ago.'
Q: 'Do you remember the substance (or gist) of what he said?'
A: 'Oh yes. He said something to the effect that . . .'

18.3.7.18 Illustrate the evidence

Use illustrative aids where they will assist the trier of fact to follow the evidence, for instance, a sketch plan of the scene of the accident, a floor plan of the store, a schedule of figures. See **18.3.8** for the introduction of exhibits.

18.3.7.19 Avoid bad habits

Do not comment on the evidence or proffer your own opinions on the witness's response to your question. Avoid irritating habits such as thanking the witness or stating 'I see' or 'Yes, I see' after every answer. It is equally irritating to keep repeating everything the witness has just said. Do not make a lot of noise or shuffle papers while the witness is giving his or her evidence. It is distracting. It creates an impression of disinterest in the witness's answer or of lack of preparation or both.

18.3.7.20 Establish as much of your case as the witness can testify to

Before you sit down, check that you have elicited from the witness all the relevant evidence that he or she can give to help you establish your case or part of it.

18.3.8 INTRODUCING REAL EVIDENCE

'Real evidence' is evidence in a tangible form such as a weapon, an article of clothing, a document (letter, contract, diagram, lease) or a photograph. There are several matters to consider before introducing such evidence during the examination of a witness.

(a) Location of the exhibit — It may be contained in one party's bundle of documents or exhibits, in an agreed bundle of documents or exhibits, it may be in the possession of a witness or you may have the original in your possession.

(b) Disclosure — ensure that the item/document has been properly disclosed to your opponent and/or that your opponent has had the opportunity to inspect it.

(c) Admissibility — ensure that the item/document is admissible and can be introduced by the witness in question. It may be necessary to lay a proper foundation before it can be admitted in evidence, e.g., by satisfying the requirements of the Civil Evidence Act 1995, s. 9 in respect of business records.

(d) Continuity — ensure that, if necessary, you can show continuity of possession, e.g., in a drugs case, unless the defence concedes the issue, you will need to prove that the substance analysed in the laboratory was the same substance as that found in the defendant's possession. You can do this by eliciting evidence as to the taking of the drugs from the defendant; the packaging of the drugs in a sealed bag and the recording of the seal number; the transmission of the sealed bag to the forensic laboratory; and the analysis of the substance by seal number. (In most drugs cases, however, continuity is admitted. The issue normally relates to whether or not the defendant was 'in possession' of the drugs.)

18.3.8.2 Marking the exhibit

Where the item is not already in an identifiable bundle, it is usual to ask the judge for the exhibit to be marked with an identifying number — this will identify the person or party producing it and enable the exhibit to be distinguished during the trial, e.g., 'Your Honour, may that be marked D.1.' (D for defendant.)

18.3.8.3 Introducing the evidence: no dispute

There are several ways of introducing the evidence. Where there is no dispute, you may lead the exhibit, for example:

Example 1:
A: 'I saw the defendant with a gun in his hand.'
Q: 'Please look at this gun — is that the gun?'
A: 'Yes.'
Q: 'Your Honour, may that be marked P.1?' (Prosecution exhibit 1.)

Example 2:
Q: 'Please look at page 3 of the bundle of documents — did you write that letter?'
A: 'Yes.'

Example 3:
Q: Did you send the defendant a notice to quit the premises?'
A: 'Yes.'
Q: 'Is that a copy of the notice you sent?'
A: 'Yes.'
Q: 'Your Honour, may that be marked C.2?' (Claimant's exhibit 2.)

18.3.8.4 Introducing the evidence: dispute

Where the item is in dispute, do not lead the exhibit. It may be necessary to lay a proper foundation for its admissibility or establish continuity.

Example 1:
A: 'I saw the defendant with a gun in his hand.'
Q: 'Please look at this' (handed to the witness) 'have you ever seen it before?'/'What can you tell us about it?'/'How does that compare with the item you saw in the defendant's hand?'

Example 2:
A: I found two jumpers hidden in the defendant's bag, both still bearing the store's labels and price tags.'
Q: 'Describe the jumpers you found.'
A: One was a size 14 ladies jumper in plain blue; the other was a blue and white striped ladies jumper, size 12.'
Q: 'What is the normal practice in the store when items are purchased?'
A: 'The sales assistant tears off the price tag which is retained for stock purposes, then places the item with a till receipt in a store carrier bag.'
Q: 'What happened to the jumpers after you found them?'

A: 'I took them to the security office and placed them in a plastic bag which I marked with my initials. I then placed them in the security office safe.'
Q: 'Did you see them again?'
A: 'Yes, this morning — I retrieved the bag from the safe.'
Q: 'Will you produce the items to the court?'
A: 'Yes.'
Q: 'Your Honour, may they be marked P.3?'

18.3.9 THE FINAL QUESTION

When you come to your final question, try to make it an important one. Let the witness finish on a strong note. It can be useful to let the court know you are about to finish by starting your last question with the words, 'Finally, Mrs Brown . . .'.

At the end of the witness's answer, a simple 'Thank you, Mrs Brown' will suffice although it is perfectly acceptable to add such words as 'Just wait there, would you?'/'Please wait there'/'You will now be asked some questions by the defendant's counsel.'

18.4 Special Aspects of Examination-in-chief

18.4.1 AFFIDAVIT EVIDENCE

There are occasions where the witness has already sworn an affidavit dealing with the relevant issues. If you call the witness to give evidence it is rarely necessary to examine the witness fully on the contents of his or her affidavit. Unless the judge requests it, he or she will not normally wish to hear a repeat of the matters already set out in the affidavit. It is, however, usual to give the witness the opportunity to explain any change in his or her circumstances since the affidavit was sworn, expand upon any matter which is not comprehensively covered, clarify any ambiguity and/or deal with any matters which have arisen since the affidavit was sworn.

Examples:
Q: 'Did you swear an affidavit in these proceedings on 6 September 2002 (you may add "dealing with . . . e.g., your financial means/your involvement with the defendant company") . . . ?'
Q: 'Has there been any change in your income/position since you swore that affidavit?'
Q: 'In paragraph 4 of your affidavit you refer to a Miss Styles. Who is she?'
Q: 'You deal in paragraph 8 with an incident in which the defendant threatened you. Was anyone else present at the time?'
Q: 'Have you had any further contact with the defendant since you swore your affidavit?'

Two further points about affidavit evidence. The court may have already directed that the affidavit is to stand as the witness's evidence-in-chief. If not, and you are unsure whether or not to take the witness through matters already dealt with in the affidavit, seek an indication from the judge, for example, 'Unless your Lordship/Your Honour considers it would assist, I do not propose to deal (at any length) with the matters already covered in the applicant's affidavit.'. The judge will normally give you the required indication.

You may hear counsel at some stage inviting a witness to verify the contents of his or her affidavit, for example:

Q: 'Did you swear an affidavit in these proceedings on 6 September 2002?'
Q: 'At the time you swore it, were the contents of that affidavit true to the best of your knowledge, information and belief?'

The second question is otiose. The witness has already taken an oath to that effect at the time of swearing the affidavit. It is a bad habit to invite a witness to verify the contents of his or her affidavit — it is best to avoid it.

18.4.2   MEMORY REFRESHING DOCUMENTS

The witness, particularly if it is a police officer, may need to refer to their notebook or statement in order to refresh their memory of the events or part of them. This is permitted provided the notes (or statement) were made at the time of the incident or shortly thereafter, while the events were still fresh in the witness's memory. Often police officers pool their recollections of the events and then only one police officer writes out the notes. The others may be permitted to refresh their memories from the same notebook provided they read and checked the notes at the time and were satisfied that the notes contained an accurate record of what they also saw or heard at the time.

Example:
Q: 'Please give the Court your full name and rank.'
A: 'Police Constable 239X Nigel Smith attached to Paddington Green police station.'
Q: 'Did you attend the scene of a car accident in Charing Cross Road on 4 February 2002?'
A: 'Yes.'
Q: 'What time did you arrive there?'
A: 'I can't recall exactly. May I refer to my notes?'
Q: 'When did you make your notes?'
A: 'About 50 minutes after the incident.'
Q: 'Where did you make the notes?'
A: 'In the canteen at Paddington Green police station.'
Q: 'Did you make your notes on your own or with anyone else?'
A: 'With Officer Bloggs.'
Q: 'How did you make the notes?'
A: 'We discussed what had happened and then I wrote the notes. Officer Bloggs then read them over.'
Q: 'Were the events/was the incident still fresh in your mind/memory at that time?'
A: 'Yes.'
Q: 'Your Honour/Sir, may the witness refresh his memory by referring to his notes?' (Note: the judge/district judge will usually enquire whether your opponent has any objections to this.)

The witness's notes/statement may contain inadmissible evidence. Warn the witness in advance to omit any reference to the offending part. When the witness comes to that part of the evidence, help him or her over it and onto the next admissible part by intervening with a question such as 'Did you then/subsequently . . .?'

Note that when referring to a memory-refreshing document, the witness should use it merely to refresh memory. Some witnesses, particularly police officers, use it as an opportunity to read out their evidence. This is objectionable and it is preferable to remind the witness not to read the evidence *in toto*, for example:

'Officer, refreshing your memory, if necessary, from your notes, what happened upon your arrival at . . . ?'

There are other occasions when you may wish the witness to refresh his or her memory from a statement made at the time.

Example:
Q: 'Can you recall exactly what the other driver said?'
A: 'No. It was too long ago.'
Q: 'Do you recall making a statement to the police after the accident?'
A: 'Yes.'
Q: 'How soon after the accident did you make it?'
A: 'About an hour later down at the police station.'

Q: 'Was the accident still fresh in your mind at that time?'
A: 'Yes.'
Q: 'Were the details of the conversation you had with the other driver fresh in your mind at that time?'
A: 'Yes.'
Q: 'Did you record them in your statement?'
A: 'Yes.'
Q: 'Your Honour, may the witness refresh his or her memory by referring to his or her statement?'

18.4.3   ALIBI EVIDENCE

It is particularly important in the case of an alibi witness not to lead on the date or time. Do not ask an alibi witness 'Where were you on the evening of 7 March 2002?'. Elicit the date from the witness.

Example:
Q: 'Did there come a time when you heard that the defendant had been arrested and charged?'
A: 'Yes.'
Q: 'When was that?'
A: 'The day of his arrest. His brother telephoned and told me.'
Q: 'Do you recall the exact date?'
A: 'Yes. It was a Friday, 10 March 2002.'
Q: 'What did you understand was the nature of the charge?'
A: 'He was supposed to have burgled a house the evening before.'
Q: 'Where were you during that evening?'
A: 'I was at a party with the defendant and two other friends . . .'

18.4.4   EXPERT REPORTS

Where there has been a direction for the disclosure of expert reports, the expert witness's evidence will already be contained in the report. If the report is not agreed it will be necessary to call the expert as a witness at the trial and for him or her to adopt the evidence contained in the report. The fact of prior disclosure is not sufficient for this purpose.

It is necessary to elicit details of the expert's qualifications and experience at the outset (in order to satisfy the court that the witness is an expert) and then proceed in this way:

Example:
Q: 'Did you examine the claimant at your surgery on 14 July 2002?'
A: 'I did.'
Q: 'Are your findings/are the results of that examination/is your evidence of the claimant's medical condition/contained in your report dated 17 July 2002?'
A: 'Yes, they are/it is.'

In civil cases, do not invite the expert witness to repeat what is contained in his or her report save for the purpose of clarification, expansion or updating his evidence. It is then usual to turn to the other expert's report and deal with disputed matters.

Example:
Q: 'Have you read the report prepared by Dr Smith on 14 October 2002?'
A: 'I have.'
Q: 'Dr Smith's measurements of the degree of mobility in the claimant's left ankle are greater than yours. Can you account for that?'
A: 'Yes.' (Note: make sure you know the answer before asking this type of question!)

In criminal cases where the expert report (or part of it) is agreed, it (or the agreed parts) will be admitted. An admission (CJA 1962, s. 10) will be read to the jury, setting out the agreed parts. Where there are disputed matters, the evidence of these must be adduced in the normal way in examination-in-chief.

18.4.5 PREVIOUS CONVICTIONS

If, in a criminal trial, you decide to introduce the defendant's previous convictions in order to take the 'sting' out of the anticipated cross-examination, it is usually preferable to do this at an early stage in your examination-in-chief. Elicit the details of the defendant's past record in a business-like fashion, emphasising any favourable aspects such as the fact that the defendant pleaded guilty on each previous occasion.

18.4.6 TENDERING FOR CROSS-EXAMINATION

If the witness is a cumulative witness in the sense that he or she is giving the same evidence as has already been elicited from the previous witness(es), it is preferable to tender him or her for cross-examination. This often arises where, for example, you are calling several police officers to deal with the same incident. Establish who the witness is and his or her presence at the scene, for example:

Q: 'Officer, please give the court your full name and rank.'
A: 'Police Sergeant Richard Smith attached to Marylebone police station.'
Q: 'Were you on duty at the police station during the evening of 12 January 2002?'
A: 'Yes.'
Q: 'Were you present when the defendant was charged?' (no dispute)
A: 'Yes, I was.'
Q: 'Wait there, the defence may have some questions for you.'

NINETEEN

CROSS-EXAMINATION

19.1   Introduction

Cross-examination is the name given to the process of examining the witness(es) called by your opponent or by another party in the case (e.g. a co-defendant in either civil or criminal proceedings). It is the most challenging and, for the new advocate, the most intimidating of the tasks he or she has to perform. If successful, it provides an advocate with one of the most satisfying moments of his or her work. If unsuccessful, it can cause incalculable anguish.

First of all, forget what you have seen in films — the witness is not likely to break down in the witness box and confess all! You must accept that not all your cross-examinations are going to be successful and you may be knocked about a bit on some occasions. But you must never show it. Show what you want to be seen by your audience and not what you feel. Cultivate a poker face. This is not easy but it can be learned.

Secondly, contrary to popular belief, cross-examination is not, nor should it be, 'cross' in the sense of angry, nor need it be 'cross' in the sense of confrontational or controversial. Apart from applying the cardinal rule set out at **19.3**, cross-examination should be viewed as a constructive art and not necessarily a destructive one. There is no need to shout or adopt an unpleasant, sneering manner in cross-examination. Nor is it necessary to harangue a witness in order to be effective. This will probably only serve to antagonise the jury or the judge. While you must exercise control over the witness, the most effective way is to adopt a polite, courteous approach, use a combination of closed and leading questions and deliver them in the spirit of an inquiry. Appear business-like and quietly confident.

Consider, by way of example, the case of Lizzie Borden:

> Lizzie Borden took an axe,
> Gave her father forty thwacks.
> When she saw what she had done
> She gave her mother forty-one.

The murders occurred when she was alone in the locked house with her parents. Much blood must have been spilt when the axe was used and would have splattered the assailant. The prosecution case was that Lizzie must have taken her clothes off (this was the 1890s) while committing the murders and then washed and dressed again afterwards for there was no blood found on her clothing. Lizzie claimed to have been ironing and to have seen or heard nothing of the crimes until after they were committed. A neighbour was called and cross-examined:

Q: 'We have been told you were the first neighbour into the house.'
A: 'I have been told so.'

Q: 'Did you go into the room where Miss Borden was ironing?'
A: 'I did.'
Q: 'Was there an ironing-board in place?'
A: 'There was.'
Q: 'And an iron on the board?'
A: 'Stood on edge (this was the age of the flat-iron).'
Q: 'And was the ironing completed?'
A: There was a small pile of handkerchiefs which from so nearly as I could see had been ironed.'
Q: And ironing yet to do?'
A: There was a basket of handkerchiefs ready dampened.'
Q: Did you feel the iron?'
A: I did. It was warm.'

Note:

(a) the lack of hostility.

(b) the directness.

(c) the simplicity.

(d) the lack of comment.

(e) the preparation for the closing speech: a woman half-way through ironing, the most domestic of tasks, breaking off to murder her parents?

The objectives for this cross-examination were clearly identified before it began, pursued throughout the cross-examination and achieved. It was conducted in the spirit of a courteous enquiry into the facts rather than in a confrontational manner.

19.2   The Aims of Cross-examination

19.2.1   AIM 1: TO ADVANCE YOUR OWN CASE

This means asking questions which seek to establish facts fitting in with or corroborating your case. For this your manner will not appear hostile. You will, at least in the first instance, be seeking the co-operation of the witness. If the witness proves intransigent or difficult you may eventually need to apply pressure, but don't begin by doing so.

19.2.2   AIM 2: TO UNDERMINE YOUR OPPONENT'S CASE

Of course, these two aims overlap, at least in the sense that anything which advances your case at the same time undermines your opponent's. However, while preparing for cross-examination you should keep the two aims distinct. Your approach to the witness may depend on your aims and this may change during your cross-examination.

Remember too there is a substantial difference between seeking to undermine the witness's evidence and seeking to undermine the witness. In the former case you will probably need to go about your work without letting the witness know what you are about; in which case your manner will be bland and benign. In the latter case it may or may not be so. The choice is yours alone. You will set, maintain or choose to adapt the tone of the cross-examination.

19.3   The Cardinal Rule of Cross-examination

You must put your case. You must challenge all material parts of the evidence given by witnesses called by your opponent which your client (or his or her witnesses) does not accept. If the witness says that your client 'orally agreed to pay him £4,000' and your client denies both the agreement and the fact that the conversation ever took place, you must put these points to the witness. If you fail to do this, the judge will refuse to allow you to challenge your opponent's version in your final speech. He or she will tell you that your failure to challenge that version is the equivalent of accepting it. This can inflict fatal damage to your case.

Also, if you do not challenge the disputed parts and then call evidence which contradicts your opponent's evidence in material particulars, you may find that your client and/or his or her witnesses are accused of inventing their evidence — on the basis that if their version of events was known before the trial began it would be known to you and you would have been obliged to cross-examine and 'put the case'. QED you did not cross-examine, therefore the version now given is a late invention. This is sometimes correct. In which case you can only sit and squirm. If, however, it is your fault because you have failed to comply with the rule, you must immediately stand up and say so — and apologise to the court!

The rule is one which admits of no exceptions. Our adversarial system of trial requires that witnesses be given the opportunity while in the box to answer the case presented contrary to their account of the facts. This does not mean that you have to challenge every unessential detail but you must cross-examine on material particulars.

19.4 Questioning Technique

Cross-examination should not be a re-run of the examination-in-chief. You must avoid giving the witness the opportunity simply to repeat unfavourable testimony which he or she has already given in-chief. (The one exception to this may be where you suspect that the witness has memorised his or her testimony or has planned with another witness to tell an identical story. In that case, you may be able to highlight the fact that the witness is using identical phrases or repeating his or her or another witness's words verbatim.)

Your twofold aim is to use the witness to advance your case and undermine your opponent's. The focus should therefore be on your case rather than allowing the witness the freedom to re-hash theirs.

In the chapter on questioning techniques, **Chapter 6**, we saw that open-ended questions with neutral starts (who, what, how, which, when, where, why, tell and describe) give the witness a chance to give a narrative account, to tell the story in their own words. This is not what you want your opponent's witness to do when you are cross-examining — you want the focus to be on your questions and to retain control over the answers.

In cross-examination, there are therefore two golden rules:

(1)   Tell: don't ask! Include the answer you want in the question.

(2)   Lead, lead, lead — avoid open-ended questions wherever and whenever possible.

Of course, these rules do allow for exceptions and the more experienced the advocate, the more one might risk an open-ended question. But, at this stage, it is best not to do so unless the matter is peripheral or you are clear that the answer is unlikely to damage your case.

A combination of leading and closed questions will best enable you to control the witness. For example, imagine you represent the wife in a disputed maintenance case. Your aim is to show that her estranged husband is profligate with money that ought to be spent on household bills:

Q: 'You go to the pub after work sometimes, don't you?'
A: 'Yes.'
Q: 'Usually with your work colleagues?'

A: 'Yes.'
Q: 'On average, two to three times a week?'
A: 'Yes.'
Q: 'And when there, you drink beer?'
A: 'Yes, usually bitter.'
Q: 'About 6 or 7 pints each time?'
A: 'Well, sometimes but not always.'
Q: 'You normally stay until closing time?'
A: 'Yes.'
Q: 'From about 6.00 pm?'
A: 'Yes'
Q: 'So it would not be unusual to drink 6 or 7 pints during the 5 or so hours you are there?'
A: 'I suppose not.'
Q: 'A pint of beer costs about £2?'
A: 'Yes.'
Q: 'You sometimes grab a bite to eat too while in the pub?'
A: 'Yes although I usually have my main meal at lunch time.'
Q: 'So, it would not be unusual for you to spend £20 during a full evening at the pub?'

During cross-examination, transitions and points of reference can also be used to good effect in moving from one topic to another or referring to the witness's evidence in-chief. (Note that if you are co-defending, although you may use leading questions when cross-examining the co-defendant, it may be wise not to do so where you are using the same defence. A series of leading questions in this situation will give the impression that you do not trust the witness to give favourable evidence without your careful prompting.)

19.5   Achieving the Aims of Cross-examination

19.5.1   ADVANCING YOUR CASE

There are two basic ways of advancing your own case in cross-examination.

19.5.1.1   Eliciting favourable testimony

Frequently you will find that part of a witness's evidence is in fact helpful or potentially helpful to your case. Not everything a witness says is necessarily damaging. For example, a witness to an alleged shoplifting offence may agree that the store was very crowded; a witness to a road traffic accident may agree that the road surface was wet or that the other driver was driving fast; a witness in a child care case may agree that on the occasions when she saw your client and the children together, the children appeared happy and content or that it was usually your client who took the children to their doctor's appointments.

It is therefore important to approach each witness's testimony in the first place with an open mind — avoid dealing with the damaging part(s) of the evidence until you have considered the potentially helpful parts. Ask yourself: Is there any area of consensus between the witness's observation/recollection and my client's? Can the witness say anything which will assist/support my theory of the case? Does the witness say anything that can be expanded upon to assist my case? Is the witness silent on a matter which would have been mentioned if it was detrimental to my case? What must the witness admit if he or she was present at the time of the alleged incident? If having considered the evidence in this way there are positive aspects to the witness's testimony, these are the parts that you want to emphasise.

In some cases your only purpose in cross-examining a witness will be to elicit favourable testimony. However, there are many witnesses whose evidence is both (potentially) helpful in some parts and damaging in others. It is often difficult to achieve a balance when you are seeking assistance from a witness on one aspect of the evidence and yet intend to challenge his or her testimony on another. Nevertheless, it is generally accepted that it is tactically better to elicit any favourable testimony that the witness can provide before attempting to discredit the witness's evidence. This will enable you, at the very least, to obtain some positive help from the witness before he or she reacts in a negative or antagonistic way to the rest of your questions.

19.5.1.2 Developing your case

Both when 'putting your case' (cardinal rule, see **19.3**) and pursuing one or other or both of the aims (see **19.2**) you have the chance to develop your case in the sense that you can begin to show your audience the way you want them to look at all the facts. It is usually better to let the facts speak for themselves depending, obviously, on the nature and quality of the audience. It is much better not to commit oneself too early in case a later surprise turns your early theory on its head. Only commit yourself if you have to or you are sure that it is safe to do so. Until then, keep your comments within your questions to a minimum. In your early days avoid it altogether. It is very tempting to adopt the styles of advocates seen in films or TV who add plenty of running commentary to their questions but you should avoid this.

In putting your case, it is not necessary to use the words 'I put it to you that . . .'. Although you may hear counsel using this expression on occasions, many consider it unnecessarily formal. If you say to a witness 'I put it to you that you have come here to tell the court a pack of lies', the answer will invariably be 'No, I haven't'. How far has that got you? It is equally unimpressive to argue with a witness along childish lines such as 'You did' — 'I didn't' — 'Yes, you did' — 'No, I didn't'.

Be subtler when putting your case. Although in most cases, the witness will not agree with your client's version of events, at the very least you will introduce and develop your theory of the case and prepare the way for your witnesses to give evidence in support of it. Aim to do this without labouring your points or making them in a heavy-handed way. Consider this example:

Q: 'Since Mrs Smith left home, have you taken any steps to encourage the children to keep in contact with her?'
A: 'Well, I tried to but they refused.'
Q: 'Is it right that Mrs Smith used to telephone the household twice a week?'
A: 'Yes'.
Q: 'And on each occasion you put the telephone down on her?'
A: 'I had nothing to say to her and the children wouldn't come to the telephone.'
Q: 'Was that the reason why you changed your telephone number in May?'
A: 'I wanted to stop her bothering me.'
Q: 'Bothering you or the children?'
A: 'Just me.'
Q: 'Was that why you also changed the locks on the front door of the house?'
A: 'Yes. She'd left — she had no right to come back when it suited her.'
Q: 'Not even to see the children?'
A: 'I told you, the children didn't want to see her.'
Q: 'Mrs Smith sent the children several letters and cards, didn't she?'
A: 'A few.'
Q: 'And you returned them unopened?'
A: 'Yes. The children asked me to.'
Q: 'Do you always do everything the children ask you to?'
A: 'No, not always.'
Q: 'Did you consider that it was very rude to return mail unopened without the courtesy of a response?'
A: 'Not really.'
Q: 'Did you consider contacting Mrs Smith and explaining to her that the children were upset by her correspondence?'
A: 'No. It wasn't necessary.'
Q: 'It's right isn't it that you told Mrs Smith when she left you would ensure she never saw the children again?'
A: 'No, I didn't. I told her if she left, I wouldn't have her back.'

Q: 'And, in fact, since she left, despite her attempts, you have ensured she has not seen, spoken to or heard from the children?'

A: 'That was of her own making, not mine.'

Certain types of witness, for example police officers, may give identical, or similar evidence on one or more aspects of the case. It is not usually necessary to put the same challenges to every witness unless:

(a) you consider that in doing so you are likely to achieve a different or inconsistent response; or

(b) you consider that by putting your case more than once it will leave a greater impression upon the mind(s) of the trier(s) of fact.

If you do not wish merely to repeat the same challenges, indicate to the judge that you have already put your case to the previous witness(es) and that you do not propose to put the same challenges again to this witness unless the judge considers it necessary.

19.5.2 UNDERMINING YOUR OPPONENT'S CASE

This is the second aim of cross-examination. In order to undermine your opponent's case, you must successfully meet the unfavourable testimony given by his or her witness(es), This can be achieved in one or more of the following ways.

19.5.2.1 Limiting the testimony

Witnesses frequently observe only part of an incident or overlook the fact that their evidence leaves many unexplained or inconsistent gaps. Try to meet the unfavourable testimony by showing its limitations. Consider such evidence in the wider context of the case. Stress what the witness did not see; highlight the absence of matters that you would ordinarily have expected the witness to see/hear if he or she had witnessed the whole event or those matters that you would have expected to find if the situation was as the witness suggests/believes. For example:

(a) In the case of an alleged assault, a witness gives evidence that he or she saw your client strike the victim. If your case is that the blow was struck in self-defence, you may be able to get the witness to agree that he or she was not present prior to that moment or that his or her view was momentarily obstructed and that he or she was therefore not in a position to see a blow struck first by the alleged victim.

(b) In the case of an alleged burglary, a police officer gives evidence that he or she arrested your client outside the burgled premises. You may be able to limit his or her evidence by establishing that your client's fingerprints were not found at the scene of the crime, yet no gloves/socks were found in the vicinity of the premises or in the defendant's possession at the time of his or her arrest.

(c) In the case of an alleged identification witness, you may limit the evidence by stressing the dissimilarities between the defendant and the description originally given by the witness to the police.

(d) In the case of a contact dispute, the mother gives evidence of the child's apparent distress after Sunday visits to the father. You may undermine her evidence by establishing that there have been no reported problems from the school as to any change in the child's behaviour particularly on Mondays.

19.5.2.2 Discrediting the testimony

The assumption that in every case at least one person is lying to the court is a false one. In many cases, the truth lies somewhere between the witnesses' accounts and/or is obscured by misconception, mistaken/selective recall or simply a different interpretation of the facts. Your purpose in discrediting the evidence is to show or suggest that it is probably less true/reliable than appeared at the end of the examination-in-chief; the emphasis here is not upon seeking to destroy the witness.

Challenging the reliability of the testimony is the most common form of cross-examination. Blatant confrontation however seldom produces agreement. If you put it to the witness that 'the man in the green jacket never had a knife in his hand, did he?', the likely answer you will get is, 'yes, he did'. If you begin by exploring the circumstances in which the observation took place, you may find either that the witness accepts that your proposition is reasonable or the court may well decide it is reasonable and not accept the witness's testimony on the matter. So, you might suggest (if to do so is consistent with your instructions) that the venue was dark, or busy, or the witness's attention was distracted, or something of that sort which might lead on to the witness acknowledging at least the possibility that they might be mistaken, in all the circumstances.

The following are the basic methods for exposing the weaknesses in the evidence:

(a) *Testing the limits of the witness's perception*, i.e., the witness's ability and opportunity to observe the matter in question. It is quite common for a witness to 'fill in' the gaps in his or her observation/memory so as to present a complete picture of events. If a witness hears a car crash and then sees the angle of the cars, he or she may jump to a fairly quick assumption/conclusion as to what in fact happened. He or she replaces the missing gaps in his or her knowledge with what he or she believes to be the best explanation of what must have occurred. He or she then convinces themselves that this is what he or she actually witnessed and the more he or she repeats it, the more he or she believes it. It is not a deliberate attempt to lie or mislead the court. Most of the time this is done subconsciously.

To test the witness's perception, probe what the witness actually perceived/heard, e.g., his or her angle of observation, distance from the events, any factor that may have interrupted, obstructed or distorted his or her view/hearing/powers of observation (e.g., presence of other persons, bad weather conditions, fear, anger); the length and nature of his or her involvement/observation; consider what the witness ought to have seen/heard if he or she had witnessed the whole of the incident; elicit whether there has been any discussion with others since the event occurred which may have influenced the witness's perception.

(b) *Testing the witness's memory*, i.e., the witness's ability to remember the details and his or her efforts to record them. Probe the witness's memory of peripheral matters, those facts which the witness ought to remember if he or she had seen the whole incident or was involved to the extent that he or she suggests. Concentrate on the time lapse since the event, the lack of record of the events, the absence of reference to a particular fact in the record of the events, the number of similar incidents which the witness has experienced that may affect his or her ability to remember (e.g., the number of invoices which a secretary has typed/sent since the one in issue; the number of arrests which a police officer has made since the event in question), the fact of any conversation with others that may have influenced the witness's recollection.

(c) *Testing the witness's powers of communication/appreciation*, i.e., the witness's ability to articulate what he or she observed or heard, and the witness's interpretation of what he or she perceived. Probe the witness's ability to record/assess information especially of a technical nature, to estimate distance, time, etc.

19.5.2.3 Discrediting the witness
On occasion, it may be possible to discredit the witness. The emphasis of this type of cross-examination lies upon destroying the witness's credibility, demonstrating that he or she is unreliable or unworthy of belief. There are three ways to discredit the witness:

(a) *Discrediting the witness's conduct:* Some witnesses give their evidence in a reasonable and persuasive manner which belies the inconsistency of their conduct or behaviour at the time of or after the events in question. For example, a woman seeking an injunction to restrain her husband from using violence against her, gives evidence of an assault she suffered two weeks beforehand and her fear of her husband since that occasion. She fails to mention the fact that she went out for dinner with him the following week. Or a driver, who denies that his or her negligent driving was the cause of a collision, fails to mention that he or she left the scene of the accident in a hurry, refusing to call the police. Look for inconsistencies between the evidence and either the acts or omissions of the witness. Consider what you would have done in the witness's position, how you (and the trier(s) of fact) would have expected the witness to behave as a matter of common sense. You should, however, be prepared for the witness to offer an explanation — either in response to your questions or during re-examination.

(b) *Showing the inconsistencies in the testimony:* The witness's account may contain a fact which is inconsistent with a previous statement of the witness, contradicts other facts, is an exaggeration or is inconsistent with the evidence of another witness.

Many novices approach a prior inconsistent statement like a 'bull in a china shop'. In their anxiety to show that they have caught the witness out they fail to appreciate that the manner in which they show this may well spoil the effect; it may give the witness time to realise his or her error and either correct or explain it away.

The best technique for exposing a previous inconsistent statement is to structure your approach and execute it simply and swiftly. First, commit the witness to the fact that he or she asserts or asserted during examination-in-chief. Secondly, close the door on any possible explanation — consider how you might try to explain it away if you were the witness. Finally, contrast his or her answer with the previous inconsistent statement. For example:

Q: 'Miss White, you say that the man you saw was well over 6 foot tall?'
A: 'Yes.'
Q: 'How tall are you, Miss White?'
A: 'I'm 5 foot 5 inches.'
Q: 'Do you normally wear high-heeled shoes?'
A: 'Most of the time, yes.'
Q: 'Were you wearing them on that evening?'
A: 'Yes.'
Q: 'Approximately how high were the heels?'
A: 'About two inches.'
Q: 'That would have made you about 5 foot 7 inches — wasn't the man you saw about that height?'
A: 'No, he was much taller.'
Q: 'Didn't you tell Detective Constable Myles that the man you saw was about your height?'
A: 'I don't remember saying that.'
Q: 'You remember making a statement to the police a few hours after the incident?'
A: 'Yes.'
Q: 'Is that the statement you made?' (copy handed to witness)
A: 'Yes.'
Q: 'You made it shortly after the incident while everything was fresh in your mind?'
A: 'Yes.'
Q: 'Look at paragraph 2, third line: "the man was about my height . . ." That is what you told the officer at the time?'
A: 'Yes.'

You may also show inconsistencies in the evidence by exposing embellishments/exaggerations in the witness's account, by highlighting any self-serving conclusions or explanations and/or by uncovering differences between the various witnesses' accounts.

(c) *Impeaching the witness:* in some cases, you may be able to show that the witness himself or herself is unworthy of belief or that little weight should be attached to his/her evidence. The ways of limiting/discrediting the evidence in this manner are to establish:

(i)   bias;

(ii)   interest in the outcome of the proceedings;

(iii) motive for testifying in a particular manner;

(iv) previous convictions or bad acts.

This must be done carefully. For example, the fact that a witness is related to a party does not automatically mean that he or she has deliberately come to court to tell lies. Approach it gently. Feel your way in. For example, do not begin a cross-examination of a parent giving alibi evidence for a son by baldly accusing him or her of coming to court to tell lies on behalf of their child. Instead, develop the possible bias of a parent in favour of the child so as to show or at least to give the foundation to suggest that the parent is incapable of being impartial.

Q: 'Mr Reynolds, your son was living with you at the time he was arrested for assaulting Miss Clancy?'
A: 'Yes.'
Q: 'You enjoy a good relationship with your son?'
A: 'Yes.'
Q: 'You were surprised when he was arrested?'
A: 'Yes, I was.'
Q: 'As far as you are concerned, this must all be a dreadful mistake?'
A: 'Yes.'
Q: 'You've discussed it with your son?'
A: 'Yes.'
Q: 'On more than one occasion?'
A: 'Yes.'

Three points emerge from this examination:

(i)   the closeness of the relationship between father and son;

(ii)   the father's inability to believe anything bad of his son; and

(iii) the fact that the father and son have discussed the matter in issue and may have influenced each other.

These points can then be emphasised in your closing speech. But remember that if it is your case that the witness could not be mistaken about the alibi evidence that he has given, and so must be telling lies, it is your duty to put that to him in cross-examination.

The same questions also lay a good foundation for examining the details of the alibi to see how reliable it is. Remembering the cardinal rule (**19.3**) and applying it to a short and simple example like this, it will be necessary before finishing the cross-examination to decide whether you are suggesting simple unreliability in the parent or unvarnished untruthfulness. If the former, you could finish:

Q: Are you sure you are right about the date/time/place?

If the latter, you could finish:

Q: Are you more concerned to help your child escape the charge than help the jury with the truth?

19.6   Preparation for Cross-examination

Provided your questions are relevant and you do not seek to elicit inadmissible evidence, you are generally free to ask whatever questions you consider appropriate. The only restrictions upon your conduct of the cross-examination are the limitations imposed by the Code of Conduct, for example, you must not ask questions which are 'merely scandalous or intended or calculated only to vilify, insult or annoy either a witness or some other person.'

Now that you appreciate the aims of cross-examination and the basic ways of achieving those objectives, you are ready to prepare for cross-examination.

The first step is to ensure that you have the issues clear in your mind. What must you prove or rebut? What is your theory of the case? What are the key elements of the evidence that will support or undermine your case? Make a note of these and keep them to the forefront of your mind at all times.

The next step is to decide whether it is necessary to cross-examine the witness at all. Never cross-examine just because you think the client expects you to or in order to justify your fee or because you think that is what your job as an advocate is all about.

You may already have a good idea of the evidence the witness is likely to give either from the witness statements, reports and/or documents disclosed pre-trial. This is your starting point.

(a)   Look at the potential evidence with a critical eye. Can the witness assist your case in any way? Can he or she give evidence which may undermine/harm your case? Which of the essential elements of your case does the witness support/dispute/contradict? It may help to make a note of this.

(b)   If the witness neither assists nor harms your case (i.e., is neutral), will that be apparent to the trier of fact? Particularly in the case of a jury trial, will the jury appreciate, without a brief cross-examination, that the witness does not take the case against your client any further, e.g., that the witness was not present at the time of an alleged conversation? Does this need emphasising?

(c)   Consider whether you can elicit the favourable testimony or limit/meet the harmful part of the testimony more effectively in any other way, e.g., through another witness/documentary evidence.

(d)   Now apply the test: what is your purpose in cross-examining this witness? What do you hope to achieve? There must be a purpose to your cross-examination, even if it is only to 'put your case' to the witness. If you have no reason to cross-examine, no clear objective or identified purpose, then stay glued to your seat.

(e)   Remember that this is the preparation stage. It will be necessary to reassess the situation, by running through this sequence again, after the witness has given evidence. This is to guard against any unexpected turn in the case or in the witness's testimony. What if, for example, the witness never gave an anticipated and crucial piece of evidence? A large part of your intended cross-examination may just have become redundant. You must be able to respond to the evidence actually given by the witness in-chief. If they haven't hurt your case, and there is no other reason to cross-examine them, leave them well alone.

19.6.1   WRITTEN PREPARATION

Try to get used to jotting down points for cross-examination rather than the whole questions themselves. Although there are times when it may be necessary to write out (some of) your questions in full, for example, when dealing with an expert witness or a particularly difficult or important matter, it is preferable not to cross-examine from a prepared set of questions. To do otherwise may well impair your ability to watch the witness and adapt your questions to suit the manner of the witness's response. If you are restricted by a rigid set of questions, you will probably find it difficult to engage in the 'parry and thrust' of cross-examination.

This does not mean that you should not prepare for your cross-examination. On the contrary, preparation and planning are vital. You should map out the purpose of your cross-examination, the points you wish to deal with and the order in which you propose to deal with them.

19.6.2 STRUCTURE OF CROSS-EXAMINATION

You are not restricted to following the order in which your opponent examined the witness in-chief. Nor are you limited to asking questions which arise out of the examination-in-chief. In cross-examination, you want your questions to be structured in a way that makes them clear and logical to the trier(s) of fact but maybe not so clear to the witness — at least until it is too late for them to do anything about it! The key here may be to have a gentle and patient build-up, through a series of relatively innocuous questions, until you have painted the witness into a corner. Then you ask the key question (probably putting some part of your client's case to the witness), saying something like, '... That must be right, mustn't it, Miss Smith?'. If you have built up the previous questions and answers sensibly and patiently, the court is likely to agree with your proposition even if the witness does not.

Plan your cross-examination using a structure that will best suit what it is you are trying to achieve. As a general rule, elicit the favourable testimony before dealing with the unfavourable. Aim to finish on a strong note.

19.6.3 USEFUL TIPS

Here are some general hints for conducting your cross-examination:

(a) Formulate your questions so that they contain one fact at a time. Use short questions. Do not recite facts at length and then ask the witness 'is that right?'. Be clear and concise.

(b) Do not misquote the witness's evidence in-chief.

(c) Avoid getting bogged down in too much minute detail unless it is really necessary.

(d) Know the probable answers to your questions; if you must risk a question to which you do not know the answer, frame it in a closed manner.

(e) Ensure you listen to the answer before asking the next question.

(f) Keep it relevant — limit the areas of your cross-examination to the aspects of the witness's evidence which concern the key elements of your case. Do not pursue pointless cross-examination or get side-tracked by irrelevancies.

(g) Constantly reassess what questions you need to ask the witness.

(h) Keep a structure. Do not jump backwards and forwards from one topic to another. You may succeed in unbalancing the witness in this way but you will also confuse yourself and the trier of fact at the same time!

(i) Lay the foundations first before putting the conclusion to the witness. If you put to the witness that he was drunk, he may deny it. If you build a picture, step by step, through your questions, showing that the witness had spent all afternoon in the pub, and had drunk several beers and whiskies, had not eaten anthing and had been unable to drive home, the witness may still deny the conclusion you put to him (i.e., that he was drunk) but the court will have formed its own view!

(j) Be a good actor, keep a poker face if the witness's evidence harms you and try not to show your reaction by your face, manner or voice.

(k) Know when to finish and avoid the temptation to ask one question too many. When you have elicited the evidence, leave the concluding argument to your final submission.

19.7 Special Types of Witness

19.7.1 THE EXPERT WITNESS

The cross-examination of an expert witness is often the key to the whole case. Some expert witnesses are extremely difficult to deal with and, on occasions, you may find that you make little headway in cross-examination. All the more reason to ensure that you are fully prepared and have consulted your own expert on the possible weaknesses of your opponent's expert and/or in his or her opinion/reasoning/methods.

In addition to the cross-examination techniques we have already looked at, there are several other techniques which may be used effectively when cross-examining an expert witness. The aim is to cast doubt upon the expert's experience, methods or opinion. This may be achieved by:

(a) limiting the witness's apparent expertise. Narrow the extent of his or her expertise/experience by showing that it is not directly applicable to the case in question or, perhaps, by contrasting it to the experience of your expert;

(b) showing that the witness has had less involvement/contact with the case than your expert, e.g., has only examined a party once; or viewed the machinery long after the accident;

(c) showing off your knowledge of the expert's subject. By showing knowledge of the technical terms involved or the way in which any tests were carried out, the expert will be less inclined to dodge your questions;

(d) inviting the witness to define technical terms and use common language. Some find this difficult;

(e) challenging his or her methods, e.g., showing that there were other tests which the expert could/should have carried out that might have produced a different result.

(f) inviting the witness to agree with the propositions that form the basis of your expert's opinion — he or she is unlikely to disagree with everything your expert says and you should know from your own expert those areas which are in dispute. Remember to 'put your case' to the expert by inviting him or her to deal with your expert's methods/opinion/conclusions;

(g) inviting the witness to agree that, in his or her field, legitimate differences of opinion frequently occur between qualified experts. This shows that the witness is not infallible and that his or her evidence is 'opinion' only;

(h) using hypothetical facts to test the strength of the expert's opinion. Testing whether a different interpretation of the same facts or a slight change in those facts would affect the expert's opinion.

19.7.2 THE EVASIVE WITNESS

You may well find that some witnesses, who gave straightforward responses during examination-in-chief, become evasive during cross-examination. Such evasion can take many forms, for example, the witness may avoid answering the question directly, respond to an entirely different question, ask you to keep repeating your questions, or continually respond with 'I don't know/remember', 'I might', 'I could', 'I would/would not'.

You may deal with this in a number of ways. You can try to pin the witness down by repeating the question. If really necessary, invite the judge to direct the witness to answer the question. Or you can enquire whether the witness is having difficulty understanding or hearing your questions. Or let the witness 'hang himself or herself' by making a terrible impression upon the trier(s) of fact. You can then follow this with a reference to the witness's demeanour in your closing speech, e.g., 'Members of the jury, you may think that Mr Smith was rather evasive . . .'.

19.7.3 THE BELLIGERENT/ARGUMENTATIVE WITNESS

Some witnesses try to 'have their say' at length and either ignore the question or cover matters which you did not ask them; or they answer your question with another question; or become abusive or accuse you of not knowing what you are talking about.

Control the witness by using closed, leading questions. If a witness insists on talking, try to cut him or her off by interrupting the flow with your next question. Make each question short. This will contrast with the witness's response and show the trier of fact what the witness is doing. If the witness asks you a question, e.g., 'What would you know about it?' or is abusive, simply side-step the remarks and/or just repeat your question. You will usually find that the judge admonishes the witness. Never get involved in an argument with the witness.

19.8 A Famous Cross-examination Considered

19.8.1 THE CROSS-EXAMINATION OF DR CRIPPEN

The following is an edited version of the cross-examination of Dr Crippen, who was charged with the murder of his wife, Cora Crippen (also known as Belle Elmore). This extract is taken from *Notable Cross-Examinations* by E. W. Fordham. It illustrates many of the points which we have looked at in this chapter.

19.8.2 THE BACKGROUND

First, the background. Mrs Crippen disappeared from the matrimonial home at 39 Hilldrop Crescent at the end of January 1910. In the course of that month, Dr Crippen had bought (for his practice) five grains of hyoscin hydrobromide, a drug used only in minute proportions by the medical profession. He alleged that his wife had gone to America. Shortly after his wife's disappearance, he pawned jewellery of hers for £195. He gave some of her jewellery to Ethel Le Neve, a girlfriend who came to live with him in March 1910. Shortly afterwards, he announced that he had received a cable informing him of his wife's death.

Suspicion was aroused and Dr Crippen was interviewed by the police. He admitted that he had not, in fact, received any news of his wife's death and had not seen her since February 1910. A description of Mrs Crippen was circulated describing her as 'missing'. Two days later, Dr Crippen and Miss Le Neve sailed for Montreal under the disguise of a father and son named 'Robinson'. A warrant was issued for Dr Crippen's arrest which was effected on board the ship.

Number 39 Hilldrop Crescent was thoroughly searched and human remains were found under the floor of the cellar. Death had resulted from hyoscin poisoning. A scar on part of the remains was one such as would have been caused by an operation which Mrs Crippen had undergone.

Two issues concerned the jury: were the remains those of Mrs Crippen? If so, was she murdered by her husband?

19.8.3   THE CROSS-EXAMINATION

In reading the cross-examination of Dr Crippen by R. D. Muir, you will see that he followed a distinct plan, progressing logically from one subject to another. The underlying purpose of his cross-examination was to show that Dr Crippen knew his wife was dead. He therefore directed his questions to exposing (a) the implausibility of Dr Crippen's assertion that his wife was still alive and (b) the inconsistencies between Dr Crippen's account and his conduct at the time of and subsequent to both his wife's disappearance and his arrest. Note Mr Muir's courteous manner and his use of short questions, each containing only one fact at a time. Note also Dr Crippen's tendency to give evasive answers.

Q: 'On the early morning of the 1st February you were left alone in your house with your wife?'
A: 'Yes.'
Q: 'She was alive?'
A: 'She was.'
Q: 'And well?'
A: 'She was.'
Q: 'Do you know of any person in the world who has seen her alive since?'
A: 'I do not.'
Q: 'Do you know of any person in the world who has ever had a letter from her since?'
A: 'I do not.'
Q: 'Do you know of any person in the world who can prove any fact showing that she ever left that house alive?' (*Note: this is central to the prosecution case.*)
A: 'Absolutely not; I have told Mr Dew exactly all the facts.' (*Mr Dew was the Police Inspector who arrested Dr Crippen.*)
Q: 'At what hour did you last see her on February 1st?'
A: 'I think it would be about between two and three some time that we retired; that would be the last time I saw her.'
Q: 'Did you breakfast at home?'
A: 'I did.'
Q: 'Who prepared your breakfast?'
A: 'I prepared my own breakfast; I nearly always did.'

. . . .

Q: 'We have heard that you were a kind and attentive husband?'
A: 'I was.'
Q: 'Preparing the breakfast in the morning, did you usually take her a cup of tea?'
A: 'Not often; once in a great while I took her a cup of coffee, but very seldom.' (*Note: Line of enquiry unfruitful — Not pursued.*)

. . . .

Q: 'What time did you come home on that night when you say you did not find your wife there?'
A: 'The nearest I should say is, it would be my usual time, about 7.30.'
Q: 'Do you not recollect on that momentous night what time it was you came home?'
A: 'I would not like to say. It was somewhere near 7.30, it might have been 7.25, it might have been 7.35, but it was close to 7.30.'
Q: 'Did you tell Inspector Dew that you got home between 5 and 6?' (*Note: Previous inconsistent statement being put to the witness.*)
A: 'I do not remember telling him that hour.'
Q: 'Listen: "I came back to business the next morning, and when I went home between 5 and 6 pm I found she had gone." Is that right?'
A: 'If I said that to him, that was probably right. I cannot trace it back.'
Q: 'That was a Tuesday?'
A: 'A Tuesday, yes.'
Q: 'The 1st February?'

A: 'Yes.'

Q: 'Where did you think your wife had gone?'

A: 'I supposed, as she had always been talking about Bruce Miller to me, that she had gone there. That was the only thing I could make out.' (*Dr Crippen alleged that his wife had been friendly with this man who, at the time of her disappearance, had returned to America.*)

Q: 'That is to America?'

A: 'To America.'

Q: 'Have you made enquiries?'

A: 'No.'

Q: 'As to what steamers were going to America on or about that date?'

A: 'No, I have not.'

Q: 'At no time?'

A: 'At no time.'

Q: 'Not since your arrest?' (*Note: Counsel showing the inconsistency between Dr Crippen's assertion that his wife was alive and his behaviour, i.e., his lack of effort to substantiate it.*)

A: 'Not at all.'

Q: 'What?'

A: 'Not at any time.'

Q: 'Not to find out whether there was some steamer sailing for America in which there was a woman answering the description of your wife?'

A: 'I have not.'

Q: 'Nobody has made those enquiries?'

A: 'No.'

. . . .

Q: 'Going to America on the 1st February, did your wife take any of her furs with her?' (*Note the use of a point of reference to make a transition to another topic.*)

A: 'That I could not say. She had any quantity of furs — any quantity of dresses.'

Q: 'Did she take any of her boxes with her?'

A: 'I believe there is one missing. There were a lot of trunks and boxes in the house; I do not know how many, because she bought several lately — well, not lately, but early last fall. I believe she bought two or three boxes.'
   Lord Chief Justice:
   You must kindly listen to the question; it is a very important one. You are not asked whether she bought them. Are you able to say whether she took any boxes with her?' (*Note: Judge admonishing the witness for an evasive answer.*)

A: 'I am not able to say definitely.'

Q: 'Is there a cab-stand near your house?'

A: 'There is one round the corner somewhere — round in York Road there is a cab-stand.'

. . . .

Q: 'Did you go to the cab-stand to enquire whether any cabman had come to take away a box for your wife?' (*Note: Counsel asks a series of questions designed to highlight Dr Crippen's failure to seek proof that his wife was alive.*)

A: 'I did not.'

Q: 'At any time?'

A: 'At no time.'

Q: 'Not since your arrest?'

A: 'No.'

Q: 'Had you any neighbours at 39 Hilldrop Crescent on either side?'

A: 'Yes, we had neighbours on either side.'

Q: 'Have enquiries been made of the neighbours to know whether a cab or box was seen to leave your house on the 1st February?'

A: 'I have made none.'

Q: 'And, as far as you know none have been made?'

A: 'Not as far as I know.'

Q: 'You do not suggest that your wife, on a voyage to America in February, would walk away from the house?'

A: 'I am sure I do not know what she would do. She was a very impulsive woman.'

Q: 'But you have made no enquiries?'

A: 'I have made no enquiries.'

. . . .

Q: 'Have you enquired of the milkman whether he saw your wife alive after you had left the house on that morning of the 1st February?'

A: 'I have already said that I made no enquiries.'

. . . .

Q: 'It would be most important for your defence in this case on the charge of murder if any person could be found who saw your wife alive after the Martinettis saw her alive; you realise that?' (*The Martinettis dined with the Crippens on the evening of 31 January.*) (*Note: This is central to the theme of the prosecution case.*)

A: 'I do.'

Q: 'And you have made no enquiries at all?'

A: 'I have not conducted my own defence.'

Q: 'Of tradesmen, or neighbours, or cabmen? You say you have not conducted your own defence?' (*Note: Counsel picking up upon the witness's answer.*)

A: 'I have not.'

Q: 'You have been consulted about it, I suppose.'

A: 'Certainly.'

Q: 'Did you suggest enquiries of that kind?'

A: 'I did not.'

. . . .

(*Note: the following series of questions, designed to show that Dr Crippen knew his wife was dead.*)

Q: 'Have you made any suggestion to Mr Newton or anyone as to enquiries being made anywhere?' (*Mr Newton was Dr Crippen's solicitor.*)

A: 'That is a point that did not occur to me, so I have not made any such suggestions.'

Q: 'Did you know that any such enquiry would be fruitless?' (*Note: Counsel 'putting his case' in a very subtle manner.*)

A: 'I know nothing of the kind.'

Q: 'Supposing that your wife had written for her furs and jewels, what would have happened?'

A: 'I would have kept them. I paid for them, and I should not have given them up — after (her) leaving me.'

Q: 'Did you know that she would not write for them?' (*Note: Again, Counsel 'putting his case'.*)

A: 'I did not.'

. . . .

Q: 'Where do you suppose your wife was going to get the money to pay her passage to America?'

A: 'She always had plenty of money, apparently.'

Q: 'Did you give her any?'

A: 'I did not give her any, no; I asked her if she was provided with money, if she wished any, and she said, "No, she wanted nothing off me".'

Q: 'You asked her if she wanted any money?'

A: 'Yes.'

Q: 'When did you ask her that?'

A: 'I asked her at the time she said she was going to leave me.'

Q: 'How many times had she said she was going to leave you?'

A: 'Numerous times.'

Q: 'Did you always on those occasions ask her if she wanted money to go away with?'

A: 'I never paid any attention because she had never carried it out to such an extent.' (*Note the evasive answer.*)

Q: 'She said she did not want money from you?'

A: 'Yes.'

Q: 'Were you in want of money?' (*Note: Counsel prepares to expose an inconsistency in the witness's conduct.*)

A: 'I was not.'

Q: 'What did you do with the money that you got from pawning your wife's jewels?'

A: 'I used it for advertising a new scheme I was starting — a new preparation I was putting on the market.'

Lord Chief Justice: 'Do you mean the whole £200 — the £80 and the £115?'

A: 'Yes, probably I used most of it.'

Lord Chief Justice: 'You are not asked "probably"; you were asked what you used the money for.' (*Note: Judge again admonishing the witness for an evasive answer.*)

A: 'For paying for the advertising.'

Q: 'Anything else?'

A: 'Well, I also bought some new dental instruments with it.'

. . . .

Q: 'Why were you in such a hurry to pawn your wife's earrings and marquise rings?'

A: 'Because when I contracted for the advertising I would have to pay cash.'

. . . .

Q: 'On the 2nd February you began to raise money (for this scheme) on your wife's jewels.'

A: 'Quite so.'

Q: 'Had you never pawned jewellery of your wife's before?'

A: 'I never pawned my wife's jewellery before.'

Lord Chief Justice: 'Had you ever pawned jewellery before?'

A: 'I had pawned jewellery before, yes.'

Q: 'Of your wife's?'

A: 'No, of my own.'

Q: 'Were February the 2nd and 9th of this year the only two occasions on which you ever pawned jewellery of your wife's?'

A: 'I refuse to accept the idea that it was my wife's.'

. . . .

Q: 'Did you say this to Inspector Dew, "I have never pawned or sold anything belonging to her before or after she left"?' (*Note: Previous inconsistent statement.*)

A: 'I did, but I did not consider it was her property. I considered myself justified in answering in that way.'

Q: 'You told the truth (to Inspector Dew) according to your view about the property?'

A: 'Yes.'

Q: 'Did you account for your wife's jewellery by producing those exhibits which you showed to Inspector Dew at the house?'

A: 'I showed him some she had left.'

Q: 'That she had left behind?'

A: 'Yes.'

Q: 'And did you tell the Inspector that she had other jewellery, and must have taken that with her?'

A: 'She did have some, as I have already said; she had some rings and a watch that belonged to her before she was married.'

Q: 'Did you intend the Inspector to believe that you were accounting for the whole of your wife's jewellery?'

A: 'Certainly.'

. . . .

Q: 'When you found your wife had gone you say you sat down to think how you could cover up the scandal?'

A: 'Yes.'

Q: 'You did your best to cover up the scandal?'

A: 'I did.'

Q: 'Is that your letter written on March 20th at 39 Hilldrop Crescent?' (*Letter handed to Crippen.*)

A: 'It is.'

Q: 'At that time was Ethel Le Neve living with you at that address?'

A: 'I would not be sure whether she came permanently to live with me at that time or not, but she had been on and off there.'

Lord Chief Justice: 'When do you say Miss Le Neve came to live at 39 Hilldrop Crescent.'

A: 'The first time she came there was 2nd February, the Wednesday night. From that time on she was with me probably two or three nights or perhaps more out of the week, but when she came permanently I would not like to say, except that it was shortly before Easter.'

Q: 'On the night of February 2nd did Ethel Le Neve sleep at Hilldrop Crescent?'

A: 'She did.'

(*Counsel now read out Crippen's letter to Mr and Mrs Martinetti of the 20th March:* 'Dear Clara and Paul, Please forgive me for not running in during the week, but I have been so upset by very bad news from Belle that I did not feel equal to talking with anyone. And now I have just had a cable saying she is so dangerously ill with double pleuro-pneumonia that I am considering if I had better not go at once. I don't want to worry you with my troubles, but I felt I must explain why I had not been to see you . . .')

Q: 'Had you, when you wrote that letter, arranged to go to Dieppe with Ethel Le Neve for Easter?'

A: 'Yes, I believe I had.'

Q: 'And did you want to wipe your wife off the slate before you went?'

A: 'It was not a question of that kind. It was that I felt something was necessary to stop all the worry I was having with the enquiries.'

Q: 'Did you want to announce your wife's death before you started for your holiday with Ethel Le Neve on the following Thursday?'

A: 'I do not think that follows a logical sequence.' (*Note the evasive answer.*)

Q: 'That is what you intended to do at the time you wrote that letter?'

A: 'I do not know whether I had at that time fixed the time when I would say that the other cable had arrived or not.'

Q: 'You prepared an advertisement of your wife's death for the Era?'

A: 'Yes.'

Q: 'When did you do that?'

A: 'I cannot tell you.'

Q: 'On the 24th March you sent a telegram to Mrs Martinetti saying that you had had a cable that your wife had died the previous night.'

A: 'Yes.'

Q: 'You sent that from Victoria Station on the eve of your departure with Ethel Le Neve?'

A: 'Yes.'

Q: 'Then you went off and took your holiday with her?'

A: 'Yes.'

Q: 'And you came back?'

A: 'Yes.'

Q: 'And you had to play the role of the bereaved husband?'
A: 'Yes.'
Q: 'Did you do it well'?'
A: 'I am sure I could not tell you that.'

(*A letter from Crippen to a friend on black-edged paper is put to the witness, recording his sorrow for his wife's death.*)

Q: 'Sheer hypocrisy?'
A: 'I am not denying any of this.'
Q: 'Do you ask the jury to believe that, not knowing that your wife might write to those people, you told them she was dead?' (*Note: Counsel showing the implausibility of Dr Crippen's position.*)
A: 'Yes.'
Q: 'Where did you think she was?'
A: 'I thought she had gone to Chicago where Bruce Miller lived.'
Q: 'If she were alive she might call at any moment on her sisters?'
A: 'I did not think she would. If she went off with some other man I did not think she would have the face to go there.'

· · · · · · · ·

Q: 'You had been a tenant of 39 Hilldrop Crescent for five and a half years?'
A: 'Yes.'
Q: 'Had the floor of the cellar of that house been disturbed during the whole of that time?'
A: 'Not to my knowledge.'
Q: 'You were familiar with the cellar; you knew where the place was?'
A: 'I have not said that I was not.'
Q: 'You know, of course, that those remains were found in the cellar?'
A: 'I was told when I returned to England by my solicitor.'
Q: 'So far as you know, they could not have been put there while you were tenants?'
A: 'Not that I know of; of course . . . I would not say it was impossible, because there were times when we were away.'

· · · · · · · ·

Q: 'When did you make up your mind to go away from London?'
A: 'The morning after Inspector Dew was there — the 8th or 9th.'
Q: 'Had you the day before been contemplating the possibility of your going away?'
A: 'I would not like to say that I had made up my mind. When Inspector Dew came to me and laid out all the facts that he told me, I might have thought, well, if there is all this suspicion, and I am likely to have to stay in jail for months and months, perhaps until this woman is found, I had better be out of it.'
Q: 'What crime did you understand you might be kept in jail upon suspicion of.'
A: 'I do not understand the law well enough to say. From what I have read it seems to me I have heard of people being arrested on suspicion of being concerned in the disappearance of other people.' (*Note the evasive answer.*)
Q: 'You thought you were in danger of arrest?' (*Note now the effective use of short, leading, concise questions to highlight Dr Crippen's conduct and its consistency with guilty knowledge.*)
A: 'Yes.'
Q: 'And so you fled the country.'
A: 'Yes.'
Q: 'Under a false name?'
A: 'Yes.'
Q: 'Shaved off your moustache?'
A: 'Yes.'
Q: 'Left off wearing your glasses in public?'
A: 'Yes.'

Q: 'Took Le Neve with you?'
A: 'Yes.'
Q: 'Under a false name?'
A: 'Yes.'
Q: 'Posing as your son?'
A: 'Yes.'
Q: 'Went to Antwerp?'
A: 'Yes.'
Q: 'Stayed in a hotel there?'
A: 'Yes.'
Q: 'Stayed indoors all day?'
A: 'Oh no . . . we went to the Zoological Gardens and walked all over the place.'
Q: 'Enjoying yourselves?'
A: 'Certainly.'
   Lord Chief Justice: 'What name did you give at the Hotel?'
Q: 'If I gave any name anywhere it would be Robinson.'
Q: 'The second description (in the hotel register) is that of Miss Le Neve?'
A: 'Yes.'
Q: 'Disguised as a boy?'
A: 'Yes.'
Q: 'Passing as your son?'
A: 'Yes.'

. . . .

Q: 'When you got to Quebec on board the steamer, or near Quebec, Inspector Dew came on board?'
A: 'Yes.'
Q: 'You were much surprised to see him?'
A: 'I did not expect to see Inspector Dew.'
Q: 'Did you recognise him at once?'
A: 'Yes . . . but not until he came into the cabin.'
Q: 'Did the Inspector say "Good morning, Dr Crippen, I am Inspector Dew"?'
A: 'Yes.'
Q: 'And did you say, "Good morning, Mr Dew"?'
A: 'Good morning, Mr Dew.'
Q: 'Did the Inspector then say, "You will be arrested for the murder and mutilation of your wife, Cora Crippen, in London, on or about February 2nd last"?'
A: 'I would not say that I took that in, because I was so very much surprised and confused that I did not quite have my right senses.'
Q: 'Did a Canadian officer, Mr McCarthy, caution you?'
A: 'He did.'
Q: 'And you realised you were being charged?'
A: 'Yes.'
Q: 'With what?'
A: 'I realised I was being charged.'
Q: 'With what? (*Note: Counsel repeats the question which the witness has evaded.*)
A: 'Well, I realised that I was being arrested for murder; I remember hearing that.'
Q: 'The murder of your wife?'
A: 'Yes.'
Q: 'Up to that time did you believe she was alive?'
A: 'I did.'
Q: 'Did you put any question to Inspector Dew as to whether she had been found?' (*Note: Counsel showing the inconsistency in Dr Crippen's behaviour.*)
A: 'I did not put any question at all.'
Q: 'As to how he knew she was dead?'
A: 'No.'

. . . .

Q: 'As you left the cabin did you say to the Inspector, "I am not sorry, the anxiety has been too much"?' (*Note: Counsel 'putting his case'.*)
A: 'Yes.'

183

Q: 'Anxiety for what?'
A: 'Anxiety thinking I might be pursued from London.'
Q: 'For what?'
A: 'For the same reason that I ran away.'

. . . .

Q: 'Of course you understand that if your wife is alive there is no foundation for this charge at all?' (*Note: Counsel reinforcing his previous examination to show that Dr Crippen knew his wife was dead.*)
A: 'Decidedly not.'
Q: 'And that if she could be found you would at once be acquitted of it?'
A: 'Oh, rather.'
Q: 'What steps have been taken by you to find your wife?'
A: 'I have not taken any steps.'

. . . .

(*Note: Change of subject — Counsel showing that Dr Crippen had the means to kill his wife.*)
Q: 'When did you first think of prescribing hyoscin for your patients?'
A: 'The first I knew of it was in 1885.'
Q: 'Here in London?'
A: 'Yes, it was early in January this year I first prescribed it for patients.'
Q: 'You can give the names and addresses of the persons to whom you sent your remedies?'
A: 'If I went and looked them up.'
Q: 'Were you prescribing hyoscin for any of those patients?'
A: 'Yes.'
Q: 'As a medicine?'
A: 'Yes.'
Q: 'To be administered through the mouth?'
A: 'Decidedly.'
Q: 'For what disease'
A: 'Nervous disease — coughs of a septic character and asthmatic complaints.'
Lord Chief Justice: 'If there is any book in which hyoscin is prescribed for use in this way, you had better produce the book.' (*No such book was ever produced.*)

. . . .

Q: 'Will you answer this question, have you got anywhere left any homeopathic preparation into which you put this hyoscin?'
A: 'They were all sent out as they were made.'
Q: 'You have none left?'
A: 'I have none left.'
Q: 'Have you got any patient to whom you sent such homeopathic preparations?'
A: 'Mr Newton has been looking the matter up; I do not know.'

The skill of Mr Muir's cross-examination was such that he made it appear easy! It is no surprise that the jury found Dr Crippen 'guilty'.

TWENTY

RE-EXAMINATION

20.1 Purpose

As soon as the cross-examination of your witness has been completed, you have the opportunity to re-examine the witness. Re-examination does not mean 'repeat examination'. It is not an opportunity to rehash the evidence given during examination-in-chief. The purpose of re-examination is to clarify, explain or develop matters arising out of cross-examination so as to limit, where possible, any damage to your case. In preparing for re-examination, it is usual to mark your note of the witness's testimony with any potential matters for re-examination as they occur to you. You often have little time to do more than mark your notes with 'Re-X'.

20.2 The Cardinal Rules

The cardinal rules of re-examination should be indelibly printed in your mind. These are:

(a) You have the right to re-examine only on matters that arise out of cross-examination. Re-examination is therefore not an examination-in-chief all over again, nor is it an opportunity to ask questions on some matter which you forgot to ask about in-chief and on which your opponent has not asked questions. If you realise during the cross-examination that you omitted to ask in-chief about some point which could be important and you want to repair your own self-inflicted damage, then you must ask the judge for leave to do so. This will, of course, give your opponent the right to further cross-examination, so you ought to do this before you begin your re-examination. Remember to apologise. It is your mistake, not your client's.

(b) Never re-examine just for the sake of it. Never re-examine unless you are clear about what you can achieve by doing so. Ask yourself 'does the evidence need clarifying or explaining?'; 'can I achieve that by my question(s)?'; 'can I show the evidence in its proper context?'; 'can the matter be developed further so as to shed a different light upon it?'; 'can I clear up an inconsistency?'; 'can I meet the attack on the witness's credit?'. Unless you are satisfied that the answer to one or more of these questions is 'yes', leave well alone. A bungled attempt at re-examination will only damage your case further.

(c) Never use leading questions to elicit evidence from your own witness in re-examination (see the exceptions in **6.6.1**).

(d) Never ask a question in re-examination to which you do not know the answer. This is a dangerous practice at any time: it could destroy your case at this late stage.

20.3 Is it Necessary to Re-examine?

The most common situations where it may be necessary to re-examine arise where:

(a) the cross-examiner has elicited only that part of a conversation or an occurrence which is favourable to his or her case; **or**

(b) he or she has attacked the witness's conduct/character; **or**

(c) he or she has highlighted an inconsistency in the witness's evidence or has impeached the witness with a prior inconsistent statement; **or**

(d) where the witness has become muddled or confused or you think the audience has become muddled or confused. In either event, order and clarity need to be restored.

20.4   Examples of Re-examination

If you must re-examine, make it short and business-like. Beware of the 'just one more question' syndrome.

20.4.1   EXAMPLE 1

A mother, who is opposed to contact between her children and their father, is cross-examined to the effect that she stopped the visits only after the father reduced the maintenance he was paying her. She denies that the money had anything to do with her decision to stop contact between the children and their father.

Re-examination

Q: 'How much is your weekly income?'
A: '£102.'
Q: 'How is that figure made up?'
A: 'I get £20 in child benefit and £50 a week now from my ex-husband. The rest is made up from Income Support.'
Q: 'How much was your ex-husband paying you before he reduced it?'
A: '£82 a week.'
Q: 'What was your total income at that time?'
A: 'With the child benefit, it was the same, £102 per week.'

20.4.2   EXAMPLE 2

The defendant is charged with taking and driving away a motor vehicle without the owner's consent. The owner is cross-examined to the effect that he had loaned his car to the defendant, his neighbour, on a previous occasion and had told the defendant he could take it at any time. The owner admits the former but not the latter allegation.

Re-examination

Q: 'You told the court, in answer to my friend, that you had let the defendant borrow your car on a previous occasion.'
A: 'Yes.'
Q: 'When was that?'
A: 'About six months beforehand.'
Q: 'What were the circumstances?'
A: 'It was the day of the tube strike. He asked me if he could borrow the car or he'd miss an important job interview. He brought it back a few hours later.'
Q: 'What happened to your car keys on that occasion?'
A: 'He returned them to me.'
Q: 'Did you give him your car keys at any other time?'
A: 'No.'
Q: 'Did you give him permission to borrow your car on any other occasion?'
A: 'No, I did not. It was a once-off.'

20.4.3   EXAMPLE 3

The cross-examination of an assault victim has emphasised the fact that she originally told the police she did not know her attacker. It was only two weeks later that she 'pointed the finger' at the accused.

Re-examination

Q: 'Why did you tell the police initially that you did not know your attacker?'
A: 'I was frightened. He told me he knew where I lived and he would come and get me.'
Q: 'Why did you subsequently change your mind.'
A: 'I managed to find another place to live. I felt safer.'

20.5   In Conclusion

If you decide not to re-examine, you can simply say 'I have no further questions (of this witness) Your Honour/Sir/Madam.'.

Whether you decide to re-examine or not, it is proper to give the judge or magistrate the opportunity of asking the witness any question he or she deems necessary.

'Unless your Lordship/Your Honour has any questions?'/'Have you any questions, Sir/Madam?'

If the judge or magistrate does question the witness, he or she must give both you and your opponent the opportunity of asking further questions **arising out of** what he or she has asked.

20.6   Releasing the Witness

Unless the witness is a party to the proceedings or the defendant in a criminal trial, you must ask the court to release the witness from continued attendance at court.

'My Lord/Your Honour/Sir/Madam, may this witness he released?'

The judge or magistrate will ask your opponent whether he or she objects to the witness being released. The answer is usually 'No'. The judge or magistrate will then indicate that the witness is free to go.

It is time to call your next witness or to inform the court: 'That is the case for the prosecution/claimant/defendant.'.

TWENTY ONE

ETHICS, ETIQUETTE AND CROSS-CULTURAL COMMUNICATION IN THE COURTROOM

21.1 Introduction

There are various rules of professional conduct that must be observed by any advocate, breach of which will lead to serious consequences. There are also certain conventions of etiquette to be observed in the courtroom, and guidelines relating to cross-cultural communication of which you should be aware. The following sections cover the main points but are not exhaustive.

21.2 Rules of Professional Conduct

21.2.1 DUTIES TO THE COURT

You must:

- bring to the attention of the court all relevant decisions and legislative provisions of which you are aware, whether or not their effect is favourable to your case;

- assist the court in the fair administration of justice;

- bring any procedural irregularity to the court's attention during the trial itself and not reserve such matter to be raised on appeal;

- take all reasonable and practical steps to avoid unnecessary expense or waste the court's time;

- observe the rules relating to disclosure of documents/information.

You must not:

- deceive or knowingly or recklessly mislead the court. For example, if your client tells you that he or she has committed a similar offence in the past for which he or she was never caught, you cannot tell the court in mitigation that this was the 'only time' your client has done such a thing. Equally, if your client tells you he or she is guilty but insists on pleading not guilty, you may continue to represent him or her and make the prosecution prove their case against him — but the ways in which you can test the prosecution case against him or her will be limited. You can test and probe the view that the witness had of the alleged perpetrator, exposing the fact that the lighting conditions were poor or the witness was quite far away

188

from the scene, but you cannot assert that which you know to be false, e.g., you cannot suggest to a witness that your client was elsewhere at the time;

- misquote the evidence;

- make assertions of fraud without clear instructions to do so and without reasonably credible material which establishes a prima facie case of fraud;

- manufacture or assist your client to manufacture a defence or other explanation for his or her conduct;

- devise facts which will assist in advancing your lay client's case;

- make statements or ask questions which are merely scandalous or intended or calculated only to vilify, insult or annoy either a witness or some other person;

- express your personal opinions, view or belief to the court unless invited by the court to do so;

- by assertion in a speech impugn a witness whom you have had the opportunity to cross-examine unless in cross-examination you have given the witness the opportunity to answer the allegation.

21.3   Conventions of Etiquette

These derive from custom, and can be divided into do's and don'ts.

Do:

- dress and robe appropriately;

- use the correct mode of address for the judge or tribunal;

- stand when the judge enters and leaves the courtroom. He or she will normally bow before being seated and you should return the bow. You should also bow to the judge when leaving court and, if the judge is already in the courtroom, as you sit down;

- sit down if your opponent rises to object. Only one advocate should be on their feet at the same time unless the judge is addressing you both;

- show courtesy and respect to your opponent and the other personnel in the courtroom;

- accept blame when you are at fault and apologise.

Don't:

- leave the judge 'unattended', i.e., if there is no other advocate present in the courtroom, wait for a signal from the judge before leaving;

- speak or shuffle papers while a witness is taking the oath;

- comment on the evidence as it is being given;

- make faces/sigh to show a jury your incredulity of an opponent's witness;

- show your emotions at a verdict or a judge's ruling;

- continue to argue a point after the judge has heard the arguments and ruled upon it: the proper place for this is an appeal.

21.4   Cross-cultural Communication in the Courtroom

It is not suggested that any advocate will intentionally cause offence to any party in the courtroom. However, working in a multi-cultural society often requires sensitivity to the ways in which norms and customs may differ from one community to another. It is important to recognise the influence of your own cultural background on your unconscious perceptions and behaviours and to bear in mind that:

- no matter how well intentioned, use of racial and ethnic terms (such as coloured, oriental or half caste) are liable to give offence;

- cultural differences in body language can contribute to misunderstandings and conflicts between members of ethnic minorities and, for example, police officers;

- on the other hand, stereotyped notions about the body language of particular cultures should be avoided;

- there may be differences in language — jargon, slang and metaphors — which may not be familiar to all witnesses/jury members and so on;

- words may not have the same meaning in all cultures, for example, descriptions of family relationships (e.g., uncle, cousin) and times of the day (afternoon and evening);

- just because someone responds to questions in English in court, that does not mean that person necessarily understands fully what has been said;

- in some cultures, looking away rather than maintaining eye contact is not necessarily a sign of dishonesty or disrespect — it may be the opposite! Equally, raised voices do not necessarily equate with loss of control or aggression.

TWENTY TWO

CONDUCTING A 'TRIAL WITHIN A TRIAL'

22.1   Defence

If you are likely to require a 'trial within a trial' (also known as a 'voir dire') to challenge the admissibility of some part of the prosecution evidence, you will probably have been aware of this before the start of the trial at the Plea and Directions Hearing. The first thing to do is what you are being paid for — think. In particular, think about what you are trying to accomplish by challenging the evidence. The same good tactical reasons exist for not making an unfounded challenge to the evidence — juridical irritation and possible jury confusion — as exist for a submission. There is also the crucial point that if you put prosecution witnesses in the witness box on a trial within a trial, you may simply allow them to rehearse their evidence and so look better in front of the jury. Bear in mind that any witness is likely to be nervous when they give evidence for the first time and that as a general rule it is better that they appear nervous in front of the jury rather than in front of the judge. On the other hand, it may be a good idea to give your defendant a taste of giving evidence. As with a submission, tactics become much easier with experience, so don't be afraid to ask other barristers in your chambers/the robing room or whom you know socially for advice, provided you do so on a counsel to counsel basis.

Mark the witness statements clearly, showing which parts of the evidence you believe are inadmissible. See the prosecutor as soon as possible and tell him or her the parts of the evidence to which you object. This is essential because otherwise he or she may open the evidence to the jury (i.e., refer to it in the opening speech). See if you can agree with the prosecutor that some or all of the evidence is not given — in nine cases out of ten you will be able to agree. For example, no prosecutor will (or should) seek to rely on evidence which is clearly hearsay. Mark clearly those parts which remain in dispute after you have talked to your opponent.

Mark clearly for your own use the sections of the Police and Criminal Evidence Act 1984, *Archbold, Blackstone's Criminal Practice* and any other texts on which you rely. Take two unmarked copies of the authorities with you to court. Give a copy to the prosecution and hand one in to the court clerk in advance.

Explain to your client what you are going to do and why. Take instructions on whether or not you are going to call your client on the trial within a trial, remembering to explain that he or she can only give evidence on admissibility, not on guilt or innocence. Think about what you will do if the evidence is ruled admissible and make the decisions arising in advance. For example, try to decide in advance whether or not your client will give evidence in front of the jury.

Agree with the prosecutor the appropriate moment at which to raise the issue of admissibility. This will usually be when the relevant witness is about to give the disputed evidence. In any event, ask for the jury to retire in the same way as when making a submission, i.e., 'Your Honour, there is a point of law I wish to raise in the absence of the jury', coupled with a sensible time estimate of how long the trial within a trial will last. As with a submission, err on the side of caution with your estimate. You cannot assume that all will go smoothly.

In conducting the trial within a trial remember to stick to the point of the exercise, which is solely the exclusion of the disputed evidence. Direct your questions to that issue only, and do not make 'jury points', such as minor inconsistencies between witnesses, to the judge. Not only will he or she be unimpressed but you will lose the element of surprise. Any appeal to the judge's supposed emotions is wasted — the judge is there only to consider a point of law.

Again, remember that you may not succeed in excluding the evidence and accordingly, try to keep questions in reserve to ask in front of the jury. If you can, plan a different line of cross-examination altogether, so as to retain at least some element of surprise, whether or not the evidence is excluded.

Make a list of the points that you wish to make to the judge. Either put these in reverse order of merit, or deal with your best points first and last. Both methods are acceptable and it is often a question of style which one you choose. Always remember that you are only concerned at this stage with admissibility. As much as possible, cross-reference your points to the authorities on which you rely. Do not be afraid to modify your list according to the evidence — for example, the absence of a caution being given may look like a fine point on the papers, but if the police say that they gave one and forgot to write it down, be prepared to embarrass them in front of the jury rather than bang on about it before the judge — be flexible and think tactically.

A judge will usually make it plain whether or not he or she has taken your point. If he or she has, do not belabour it but move on to the next point.

When you have run out of things to say, stop talking.

If at any stage you need time to take instructions or simply to think about your next move, then request it.

22.2 Prosecution

It is always a good plan to put yourself in the position of the defence and accordingly try to anticipate likely challenges to admissibility. If you see a likely trial within a trial on the papers, then plan your response in the same way — set out your arguments, mark the statements, flag and photocopy authorities.

Always ask the defence before a trial whether they object to your opening any part of the evidence. Try and agree with the defence what parts of the evidence are inadmissible. Make sure that you do not open those parts or allow your witnesses to refer to them.

There may be cases where you cannot open the facts to the jury without the disputed evidence — for example where the only evidence is a confession which the defence says is inadmissible. If so, ask for the jury to retire as soon as they are empanelled and tell the judge why. Give the best time estimate you can as soon as you can.

Remember, in conducting the trial within a trial, you may not cross-examine the defendant on the truth of the evidence — do not ask if the disputed confession was true! As with the defence, keep your questions and submissions brief and to the point, and if you cannot think of anything more to say, sit down.

22.3   Check List

For the **defence**:

- Think about tactics and what you are trying to achieve by challenging the admissibility of the evidence. Plan your attack accordingly. Mark those parts of the evidence you object to.

- Mark all authorities and take photocopies where required.

- Discuss your plan with your client. Decide what you will do if the evidence is ruled admissible.

- Tell the prosecutor which parts of the evidence you object to and disclose any authorities to him or her.

- When the prosecution are about to put in the disputed evidence, ask for the jury to retire.

- In conducting the trial within a trial, be brief and keep to the point. Remember that you may fail and so try to keep something in reserve.

For the **prosecution**:

- Think about likely questions of admissibility and mark the statements accordingly.

- If you have the chance, mark all authorities and take photocopies.

- Ask your opponent if he or she objects to any part of the evidence being opened. If you need to, ask for the jury to retire after being empanelled.

- In conducting the trial within a trial, concentrate solely on admissibility and be as concise as possible.

- If evidence is ruled inadmissible and you need time to consider your next move, request it.

22.4   The Trial within a Trial

The most common example of a trial within a trial is where the defence considers, or
the judge questions whether, a confession upon which the prosecution seeks to rely is
inadmissible. The procedure in such cases is as follows:

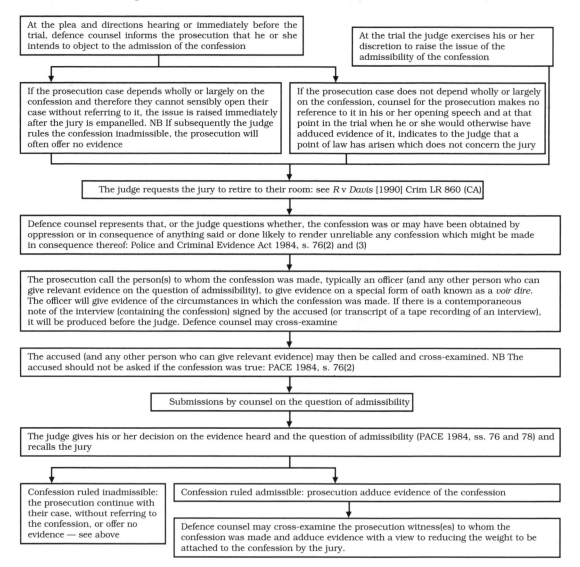

22.5   Example of a Trial within a Trial in *R* v *Lewis and Others*

IN THE CROWN COURT SITTING AT LEWES

R v *Lewis and others*

Instructions to Counsel for the Prosecution

Counsel has herewith:

1. Bundle of depositions and witness statements
2. Antecedent history of the accused

Counsel is instructed

    (i)   to prosecute in this matter and

    (ii)   to settle the appropriate indictment.

The four accused were committed to stand trial on a single charge of robbery, contrary to the Theft Act 1968, s. 8, by Brighton Magistrates' Court on 3.6.02.

Case Summary
On 12.4.02 a branch of the South Downs Building Society was held up at gunpoint by two masked men. One kept watch by the door, observing both the people inside the branch and passers-by. The other demanded money from a cashier. On obtaining a holdall containing £15,967, the two men fled on foot. They were pursued by a passer-by and one of the men stopped and shot the pursuer, a Mr Goodbody. They then made good their escape, using a car parked nearby.

The prosecution case at committal was that three of the accused, namely Lewis, Duke and Ella, were involved in the actual robbery with Ella as the driver of the escape vehicle, a stolen Ford Escort XR3i. The fourth accused, Peterson, stored the vehicle in his garage for several days prior to the robbery.

Committal charge
Against Finlay LEWIS, Arthur DUKE, Gerald ELLA and Leonard PETERSON

You are charged that, on the 12th day of April 2002, you did rob Mary Penny of £15,967, contrary to the Theft Act 1968, s. 8(1).

<u>STATEMENT OF WITNESS</u>

Statement of: Mary Penny

<u>Age</u>:   Over 18

<u>Occupation</u>:   Building society cashier

[Usual declaration omitted]

<u>Dated</u>: 29th May 2002

<u>Signed by</u>: *M. Penny*   <u>Signature witnessed by</u>: *D. Law DS 494P*

My name is Mary Penny. I live at 44 Racecourse Road, Kemptown, Brighton.

I am a cashier for the South Downs Building Society. I work in the Churchill Square Branch. I have been there for about 4 years.

I remember the 12th of April 2002. I was at work that morning. At about 10 am two men entered the branch. Both were wearing dark-coloured donkey jackets which had orange fluorescent material on the top half. They had on dark balaclava helmets with 'Porky Pig' masks. They were both carrying what looked like sawn-off shotguns.

One of the men shouted for everyone to get on the floor. There was some screaming and the same man shouted to shut up.

He came to my window and said 'fill this with money and nobody will get hurt'.

He produced a nylon holdall and passed it through the window. I looked at the manager who indicated that I should do as the man asked.

I emptied the contents of the tills into the bag. This was both cash and cheques. Then I gave it back to the man at the counter.

All this time the other man had just stood by the entrance door, pointing his gun at the staff and customers.

The man with the holdall joined the other one by the door. One of them shouted 'Nobody move and you won't get hurt' and they both ran out. I think it was the man with the holdall who shouted.

I had pressed the silent alarm as the man approached my window and about two minutes after the men left, several police officers arrived.

I would describe the man with the holdall as about 6 feet tall and medium build. His voice was unusual. He had an accent. Irish is how I would describe it.

I saw his hands when he gave me the bag — they were white.

On the 13th of May I attended an identification parade at Brighton Police Station where I saw a number of men. They all looked about the same height and build as the man with the holdall.

They each said the words 'fill this with money and nobody will get hurt'. I picked out the 5th man. I am sure he was the man with the holdall.

I did not get a good look at the second man. I think he was about 2 inches shorter than the other one, again medium build. I would not recognise him again.

The whole incident lasted for about 5 minutes.

I did not see the face of either man. I did not see their hair, they were both wearing balaclava helmets. I saw no distinctive features on either man. The voice was distinctive. I would call it Irish.

Signed by: *M. Penny*   Signature witnessed by: *D. Law DS*

<u>STATEMENT OF WITNESS</u>

<u>Statement of:</u>   Reginald Goodbody

<u>Age:</u>   Over 18

<u>Occupation:</u>   Retired grocer

[Usual declaration omitted]

<u>Dated:</u> 29th May 2002

<u>Signed by:</u> *R. Goodbody*   <u>Signature witnessed by:</u> *D. Law DS 494P*

On the 12.4.02 I was in Brighton, to do some shopping, my wife was with me.

We started looking around the shops in Churchill Square. Just after 10 o'clock we were going past a small parade of shops when two men ran out of the South Downs Building Society premises there. I was about 20 yards away from them. They ran towards me and my wife. They had a bag and guns. They were wearing balaclava helmets. They had workmen's jackets on — black I think, with orange patches.

I realised they had robbed the Building Society and I put up my arms to try and stop them. One got past me but I caught hold of the bag that the other one was carrying.

We got into a bit of a struggle over the bag. I think people were coming out of the Building Society by now.

The other man ran back and shouted at me to let go. When I said No, he deliberately took aim and fired. He shot me in the leg with his gun. I fell over and let go of the bag. Both of them ran off.

The one I was struggling with was about my height and build. I am 6 feet tall and weigh about 13 stone. The other one was about the same. I can't recall him clearly. I would not recognise either of them again. Their features were quite obscured by their helmets.

I went to hospital in an ambulance with my wife. It was the Royal Sussex Hospital in Brighton. I was there for 8 days. My leg was badly damaged by the shot from the gun. I lost some blood and quite a bit of muscle and flesh in my calf.

I now have to walk with a stick. I find my mobility is very restricted. I attend the hospital physiotherapy department every week to build my leg up.

The one with the bag shot me. The gun did not go off in the struggle — I am quite sure.

<u>Signed by:</u> *R. Goodbody*   <u>Signature witnessed by:</u> *D. Law DS*

STATEMENT OF WITNESS

Statement of: Brenda BROWSE

Age: Over 18

Occupation: Housekeeper

[Usual declaration omitted]

Dated: 1st May 2002

Signed by: *B. Browse*   Signature witnessed by: *D. Law DS 494P*

On the 12th of April 2002 I left my home to meet a friend in Brighton. We had arranged to meet by the Oxfam shop, just along the road from Churchill Square. I got there early, at about 9.30 am. There were several cars parked around the area but I did not take any notice of them. I went to a cafe over the road for a cup of tea.

While I was in the cafe, I could see the road ahead — Mountfort Road. There was a dark blue Ford Escort parked there with a man sitting behind the wheel. The car was there the whole time I was in the cafe. At about 10 o'clock, as I was about to leave, two men came running along the road, shouting something. The man in the car started the engine and the two men leaped into the car. It tore off down the road, towards the junction by the cafe and straight over without waiting to see if anyone was crossing the road.

I was astonished by this behaviour and made a note of the car registration number. It was E838 JPO.

I would not recognise the two men who jumped into the car again but both were wearing workmen's jackets with orange fluorescent patches like Council workmen wear. I think they both had dark hair.

The man in the car was quite slim with dark wavy hair, fair-skinned and in his early twenties. I would recognise him again.

I am willing to attend court to give evidence.

Signed by: *B. Browse*   Signature witnessed by: *D. Law DS*

<u>STATEMENT OF WITNESS</u>

Statement of: Brenda BROWSE

Age: Over 18

Occupation: Housekeeper

<u>Dated</u>: 11th May 2002

Further to my statement of 1st May 2002, on the 11th of May 2002 I was asked to attend Brighton Police Station. I was met by Inspector Charger who explained that there was going to be a parade where the man I saw in the Ford Escort might be. He explained that the man might not be there and I was to look at all of the men very carefully. He said only if I was sure I saw the same man, I should stop and touch him on the shoulder.

I was escorted into a waiting room by a WPC and eventually taken to a larger room with several men lined up against one wall. I went to one end of the line and walked along it. The seventh man was the one I had seen driving the Ford Escort on the 13th of April. I was quite sure and I touched him on the shoulder. He did not do anything. The Inspector asked me to leave the room as the parade was now over.

I was then brought to a room where I wrote this statement.

Signed by: *B. Browse*   Signature witnessed by: *D. Law DS*

STATEMENT OF WITNESS

Statement of: David LAW

Age: Over 18

Occupation: Detective Sergeant 494P, Brighton CID

[Usual declaration omitted]

Dated: 18th May 2002

Signed by: *D. Law*   Signature witnessed by: *A. Libby, DC 675P*

On 12th April 2002 at 12.10 pm, as a result of information received, I went to 33 Dials Lane in Brighton where I found a navy blue Ford Escort XR3i which appeared to have been abandoned in a hurry. The doors were wide open. Under the driver's seat were some shotgun cartridges. The registration number of the vehicle was E838 JPO.

I had reason to believe that this vehicle had been used in an armed robbery which had occurred earlier that day in Brighton and I requested that a Scenes of Crime Officer attend the location in Dials Lane.

On 11th May 2002, I went to a private house at 72 Power Station Row, Southwick. The door was opened by a woman who identified herself as Sharon Ella. I asked her if I could speak to Gerald Ella — she replied that he was not in. Subsequently, I attended the rear of the house where colleagues had apprehended Gerald ELLA, while he was climbing over a fence in the garden of number 72.

I said to him, 'Are you Gerald Ella?' He replied, 'What if I am?' I said to him, 'I have reason to believe you were involved in an armed robbery on the South Downs Building Society in Brighton on the 12th of April, specifically as the driver of the getaway vehicle.' He replied, 'You've got a very good imagination for a copper'.

I then told him that his fingerprints had been identified on the getaway vehicle, the navy blue Ford Escort. He seemed to be about to fall down so I grabbed him and said, 'I am arresting you for your part in the South Downs robbery on the 12th of April 2002. You do not have to say anything. But it may harm your defence if you do not mention when questioned something which you later rely on in court. Anything you do say may be given in evidence.' He made no reply and was taken to Brighton Central Police Station under escort.

He was later seen by myself and DC Libby in an interview room at Brighton Central at 10.25 pm on the 11th. He was reminded of the caution and I then asked him if he was prepared to talk to us about the robbery. He indicated that he did not wish to talk to us and he was returned to his cell at 10.28 pm.

I was present at 7.35 am on the 12th of May 2002 when ELLA was charged with robbery, the charge was read over to him, he was cautioned and made no reply.

At 2.40 pm on the 12th of May I interviewed Arthur DUKE at Brighton Central Police Station where he was in custody. DC Libby took a contemporaneous note of what was said. At the end of the interview, DC Libby read the record to DUKE who signed each page as a correct record. The interview concluded at 3.02 pm.

At 6.00 am on the 13th of May 2002 I went to 22 Bramber Street, Brighton. There I saw a man I now know to be Finlay LEWIS. I said to him, 'Are you Finlay Lewis?' He said, 'Yes, why?' I told him that he had been implicated in the robbery of the South Downs Building Society in Brighton and he replied, 'Someone's a grass. I'm saying nothing till I see my solicitor.'

After a brief search of the premises, I told LEWIS that he was under arrest for robbery and cautioned him. He replied 'I'll be wanting a word with my solicitor.' He was then taken to Brighton Central Police Station and booked into a cell.

I saw LEWIS again at 2.10 pm that day in the interview room, together with DC Libby. The interview was recorded by DC Libby and ended at 2.25 pm. DC Libby read his contemporaneous notes over to LEWIS who then signed each page as correct.

At 4.45 pm on the 13th of May 2002 LEWIS was charged with robbery, the charge was read over to him, he was cautioned and made no reply.

Signed by: *D. Law*   Signature witnessed by: *A. Libby*

STATEMENT OF WITNESS

Statement of: Alan LIBBY

Age: Over 18

Occupation: Detective Constable 675P, Brighton CID

[Usual declaration omitted]

Dated: 18th May 2002

Signed by: *A. Libby*   Signature witnessed by: *V. Worthy PS 111P*

At 6.00 am on the 12th of May 2002, I went to a private flat at 344 Lewes Road, Brighton, together with several other officers. The door was answered by a man I now know as Arthur DUKE. I said to DUKE, 'I have reason to believe that you were involved in an armed robbery last month on a Brighton building society. Have you got anything to say?' He replied, 'You've got the wrong man this time.' I asked if we could look round his flat and he said 'Yes'.

On the floor of a wardrobe in the bedroom I found a balaclava helmet. A shoebox in the same wardrobe contained six shotgun cartridges. Hanging in the wardrobe was a navy blue donkey jacket with an orange fluorescent upper half. I said to DUKE, 'Where did you get this jacket?' He said, 'I've had it for a while now. I wear it if I get any building site work.' I then showed him the balaclava and cartridges and said, 'How do you explain these then?' He did not reply.

I said, 'I am arresting you for robbing the South Downs Building Society in Brighton on the 12th of April this year.' I cautioned him and he made no reply. He was taken to Brighton Central Police Station.

At 2.40 pm on the same day, I was present when DS Law interviewed DUKE at Brighton Central Police Station. I recorded the interview contemporaneously. At its conclusion I read the record over to DUKE who then signed each page as a correct record. The interview was terminated at 3.02 pm. I produce the record of interview, AL/1.

At 5.25 pm on the 12th May 2002 DUKE was charged with robbery, the charge was read over, he was cautioned and made no reply.

On the 12th of May at 10.50 pm, I went to 65 Brighthelmstone Street where I saw a man I now know to be Leonard PETERSON. I said to him, 'Are you Lennie Peterson?' He said, 'That's right. Who are you?' I showed him my warrant card and explained that I was investigating the robbery of the South Downs Building Society.

I said, 'I have reason to believe that you garaged the car for the gang before the robbery. What have you got to say?' He said, 'I know nothing about it.' I said, 'It's right that you've got a lock-up garage at the back of the house, isn't it. That's where the car was kept.' He replied, 'Who's been talking out of turn?'

I said, 'The car was stolen on the 5th of April — that's a week before the robbery. It had to be kept somewhere, out of sight. I think you warehoused it for the gang. For all I know, you stole it, too.' He said, 'Look, I'm no car thief. Gerry ELLA asked me to keep it safe for him until he needed it. He brought it round on the 6th and took it away on the 12th. That's all I know.'

I told him he was being arrested for the robbery and cautioned him. He made no reply and was then taken to Brighton Central Police Station.

At 7.30 pm on the 13th of May 2002 at Brighton Central Police Station PETERSON was charged with robbery, the charge was read over to him, he was cautioned and replied, 'I've been very silly and it's all for nothing. What can I say'.

On the 13th of May at 2.10 pm, I attended an interview of Finlay LEWIS by DS Law in an interrogation room at Brighton Central Police Station. I recorded the interview contemporaneously and produce the record, AL/2.

Signed by: *A. Libby*   Signature witnessed by: *V. Worthy*

Extracts from interview of Arthur Duke and DS LAW, recorded by DC Libby (AL/1):—

Q. Do you want us to wait for your lawyer?
A. No, let's get it over.
Q. As I mentioned on the way here, we've found some fingerprints on the Escort and it looks like they are yours.
A. Oh yeah.
Q. I'm serious. Those prints place you in the car. Take them together with what we found in your home ...
A. All right. It was never meant to end up the way it did.
Q. What do you mean?
A. The old man. Finlay's always been stupid but that tops the lot.
Q. So it was Finlay that shot Mr Goodbody?
A. Yes.
Q. Is that Finlay LEWIS?
A. Yes. I should never have agreed to take part in it. Finlay had it all set up before I got invited. His original partner had to drop out — he's on remand in Brixton at the moment.
. . .
A. Finlay had Gerry ELLA and Len PETERSON lined up. He knew Gerry from Wandsworth and Len was a friend of Gerry's.
. . .
A. I kept watch while Finlay played the hard man with the cashier. Everything went smooth as silk until the old man grabbed Finlay's bag. I couldn't believe what they were doing. Just as I went back to help, Finlay's gun went off and the old boy went down. I don't know whether it was an accident or not.

Extracts from interview of LEWIS by DS Law, recorded by DC Libby (AL/2):—

Q. I am refusing to delay this interview so that you can have your solicitor present because I believe that delay may prevent recovery of the stolen money.
A. No reply.
. . .
Q. ... remind you that you are under caution ...
Q. This was a very serious offence. I tell you now — I'm more worried about the guy that got shot than the money. Have you got anything you want to say?
A. No reply.
Q. Look I'll be straight with you. We've got a confession from Arthur and he's dropped you right in it.
A. I don't believe it.
Q. Have a look at this. (Hands piece of paper to Lewis)
A. Well, it seems like you know it all. Why bother talking to me?
Q. We need to get your side of things, to see how everything fits together.
A. There's no point in holding back now — so much for honour amongst thieves. It was Arthur's idea — he's planned it for weeks before he spoke to me. We decided that we needed a driver and I knew Gerry from our time in Wandsworth.
Q. You mean Gerry ELLA and HMP Wandsworth in South London?
A. That's right.

. . .
Q. Who got the car?
A. That's down to Gerry. I don't know where it came from — he just got it for the day. The first time I saw it was when I got in it after the job.
Q. Who did what in the shop?
A. I asked for the cash while Arthur kept everyone calm.
Q. With a sawn-off?
A. You don't want heroes in a situation like that.
Q. Like Reg Goodbody?
A. Is he the old boy? He never should have interfered. He got what was coming to him.
Q. From you?
A. No way. That was Arthur. I could have got the bag away from the old man but Arthur got impatient with him.
. . .
Q. So where's the money now?
A. Money? That's rich. Lots of it was cheques. The rest, well, I'll need a nest egg for when I get out, eh?
Q. So you won't tell me where it is?
A. No reply;
. . .

Summaries of the antecedent histories of the accused men:—

Finlay LEWIS (Age 40) Born Stornaway, Outer Hebrides.
18 previous convictions including 2 for wounding (s. 18 OAPA) and 3 for armed robbery. Last conviction was at Portsmouth Crown Court for robbery in May 1994. Sentenced to 10 years' imprisonment. Released June 2000.

Arthur DUKE (Age 43) Born Catford, London.
8 previous convictions, mainly for offences of dishonesty, 1 recorded for robbery. Last conviction was at Winchester Crown Court in February 1995 for a fraud on the Department of Health and Social Security. Sentenced to 6 years' imprisonment. Released April 1998.

Gerald ELLA (Age 26) Born Worthing, West Sussex.
6 previous convictions, all for theft of cars, except the last one. In 1996 a 3-year term of imprisonment was imposed by Inner London Crown Court. In September last year, Brighton Magistrates' Court fined him £250 and banned him from driving for 1 year for driving whilst unfit through drink or drugs.

Leonard PETERSON (Age 55) Born Brighton.
16 previous convictions, all for petty offences of dishonesty. Imprisonment has been ordered in the past, but the last conviction was in 1984 and resulted in a conditional discharge.

At the trial of Lewis and Duke on charges of robbery and wounding with intent, Miss Vaughan, counsel for the prosecution, addresses the judge:

Miss Vaughan: Your Honour, at this stage there has arisen a matter of law which need not trouble the jury.
His Honour: Members of the jury, counsel and I will be spending some time discussing matters of law and I would therefore ask you to retire to your room while these discussions take place.

The jury then retire.

Trial within a trial (on Duke's interview):

DS Law is called and gives evidence-in-chief that he interviewed Duke and that a record was made.

Miss Vaughan: What did you actually say to Mr Duke regarding the fingerprints?
DS Law: I told Duke that we had his fingerprints from the Ford Escort.
Miss Vaughan: What reason did you have for telling him this?
DA Law: At that time I thought that there was a strong possibility that some of the prints we found might belong to Duke.
Miss Vaughan: Can you assist by stating at what stage you became aware of the result of any checks made regarding the fingerprints?
DS Law: Some time after that interview occurred, I was informed by our forensic laboratory that none of the prints taken from the car matched Duke's fingerprints.
Miss Vaughan: Please wait there, officer, there may be some questions from Counsel for the defence.

Cross-examination of DS Law by Mr Good, counsel for defence.

Mr Good: At the time when you told Duke you had his fingerprints, you knew very well that that was not true, didn't you?
DS Law: When I told Duke we had his prints, I genuinely thought that was the case.
Mr Good: It was in fact a deliberate lie which you had told, wasn't it?
DS Law: It was not a deliberate lie.
Mr Good: You needed to lie because you had no evidence against Mr Duke, had you?
DS Law: I didn't need to lie, he knew what we'd found at his place.
Mr Good: Would you not agree that your conduct could be described as a deliberate deceit of my client?
DS Law: I would describe it as unfortunate, that's all.

Summary of defence submissions.

Mr Good submits that DS Law obtained the confession by deceit, as he had deliberately lied to Duke about the fingerprints, knowing full well that they were not Duke's; that the officer needed to lie to obtain a confession, as there was no direct evidence against the defendant; that the evidence ought to be excluded under s. 76(2)(b) of the Police and Criminal Evidence Act 1984 (PACE) as the prosecution had not proved beyond reasonable doubt that the confession was not obtained in consequence of anything said or done which was likely to render unreliable the confession obtained; that alternatively, the confession should be excluded under s. 78 of PACE as the admission of the evidence would have such an adverse effect on the fairness of the proceedings that the court ought not to admit it.

Summary of the prosecution submissions.

Miss Vaughan submits that DS Law did not lie to the defendant; that he genuinely, albeit mistakenly, believed that the fingerprints were Duke's; that the prosecution had proved beyond reasonable doubt that the confession was not obtained in consequence of anything said or done which was likely to render it unreliable; and that alternatively, the confession should not be excluded under s. 78 of PACE, as the admission of the evidence would not have an adverse effect on the fairness of the proceedings.

The defence then replies and the judge delivers a reasoned ruling.

TWENTY THREE

MAKING A SUBMISSION OF NO CASE TO ANSWER

23.1 Defence

Whether in the magistrates' court or the Crown Court, you should have some idea in advance as to whether or not you will be making a submission of no case to answer for the defence. This will be based on the papers rather than the evidence. The following guide is written on the premise that you have some time to prepare the submission. On occasion you may wish to make a submission at short or no notice because, for example, the prosecution witnesses have not come up to proof. Usually, you will find that you can deal with the matter on your feet (without authorities or extensive preparation), but if you need time to prepare, request it. Most judges, district judges or magistrates will be sympathetic if you have been taken by surprise, and there is no point in making a muddled or flustered effort which will do neither you nor your client justice. The court will probably give you up to about 15 minutes.

Always think about whether or not you should make a submission. As a general rule, in case of doubt — have a go, but bear in mind that there are good reasons **not** to make an ill-founded submission, especially in the Crown Court. It is never wise to irritate the judge unnecessarily, and if your submission is hopeless (known in the trade as a 'try-on') he or she will assuredly be irritated. Also, jurors who have already sat on at least one trial may guess why they are asked to leave court, and there is a danger that they will draw an adverse conclusion if the submission fails. In other words, 'Well, if the judge thinks there's such a good case against them . . .'.

All that having been said, if in doubt, make the submission. The decision is a question of judgment that will become much easier with experience.

23.2 Prosecution

In responding to a submission, remember what you are there for — you are not there to obtain a conviction at all costs, but to put the case for the Crown fairly. If the submission is a good one in your opinion, then be prepared to say so, or indeed to save the defence the trouble by saying to the court that you cannot ask for a conviction on the evidence. For example, if your only identification witness describes the perpetrator as a four foot six inch red-headed man and the defendant is a six foot tall and bald man, then do not tell the judge that this is a question of fact for the jury to decide — give in gracefully.

23.3 Organising the Case

Whether prosecuting or defending in whatever court, organisation of your case is crucial. If you can, have all authorities flagged and marked for your own benefit. It is a good idea to have *Turnbull* [1977] QB 224, *Galbraith* [1981] 1 WLR 1039, *R* v *Shippey*

[1988] Crim LR 767 and the criteria in *Archbold* and *Blackstone's Criminal Practice*, flagged, whatever the case. Obtaining copies of *Galbraith* and *Turnbull* in full is also a good investment. If you have prior notice and intend to rely on case authority and/or texts then, in the magistrates' court, if the authorities are in anything other than *Archbold, Blackstone's Criminal Practice*, or *Stone's Justices' Manual*, take at least two photocopies — one for your opponent and one for the clerk to the justices or court legal adviser. It is a good idea to provide the bench with copies as well. Do not mark these copies. Hand them in when you make the point arising from the authorities and read from the authorities yourself.

In the Crown Court there may be a more extensive library for the judges with at least the *All England Law Reports* and *Criminal Appeal Reports*, but it is still a good idea to come armed with your own photocopies. Certainly, if the report or texts that you intend to rely on are at all obscure, you should try to get copies for the judge and your opponent; failing which, take photocopies. In any event, take your authorities with you. Hand the copies in to the court clerk as soon as you can, flagged at the appropriate points. All of this will save time and is likely to make the court more disposed to listen to what you have to say.

You may well decide to make a submission of no case upon reading the papers in advance of trial or committal. In such cases a skeleton argument should be prepared, served on the prosecution and filed at court in advance of the hearing.

23.3.1   STRUCTURING YOUR SUBMISSION

If you have time, write down the points you intend to make for your own benefit either in reverse order of merit or by listing your best points first and last. Always try to end your submission with a strong point so that it sticks in the minds of the tribunal. Conversely, if you are responding to a submission, deal with your opponent's best points first and his worst point last, for the same reason. Sometimes this may not be possible because of the need to go through the evidence chronologically, but always bear in mind that you should try to end on an up-beat note, with a point in which you have confidence.

In the Crown Court, submissions are to be made in the absence of the jury, so you will ask for the jury to go out. An acceptable form of words is 'Your Honour, there is a matter of law arising which would be more conveniently dealt with in the absence of the jury'. A less pompous way of putting it can be 'Your Honour, there is a matter of law I wish to raise; perhaps this would be a good time for the jury to have a break for refreshments'. This may also help to ingratiate you with the jury, if you can carry it off.

It will help all concerned if you can give a realistic time estimate at this stage, such as, 'The matter will probably take five minutes/hours/days'. Err on the side of caution, as submissions have a habit of expanding themselves no matter how brief you intend to be.

23.3.2   THE CLIENT

Apply your mind in advance to what you are going to do if the submission fails in whole or in part. If it does fail, you are likely to be faced with what I think is the most difficult decision you have to make as an advocate: whether or not to call your client to give evidence. Remember that a submission you are certain will succeed may still fail. Calling your client will depend on the circumstances of the case, but you do not want to make the decision on your feet if you can possibly avoid it. At the end of the day, if you are completely confident that you have made a good submission and there genuinely is no case to answer, then it may be that the proper course is not to call the defendant. This is, of course, subject to clear and informed instructions from the defendant.

Note: you must explain all this in advance in plain English to your client and get his or her instructions on giving evidence. In the end, it is the client's decision as to whether or not he or she will give evidence. You can only advise him or her — the client is not obliged to take your advice. In a marginal case (e.g., your instructions say the client will testify and he or she then decides not to), have the client sign your brief with a note saying, 'I have had the advantages and disadvantages of giving evidence explained to me and I do/do not wish to give evidence'.

23.3.3   THE TRIBUNAL

Adapt your submission or response to a submission to the tribunal you are addressing. Lecturing a Crown Court judge or a district judge on the burden or standard of proof will lessen his or her respect for your judgment and may affect his or her view of your best points. It is also likely to irritate. On the other hand, you may be faced with lay justices who feel that they 'want to hear more'. As a general rule, in the Crown Court or before a district judge, be as brief as you can. Before lay justices in the magistrates' court, start from first principles and build your submission up stage by stage.

23.3.4   RESPONDING TO A SUBMISSION

On the prosecution side, you are likely to have less time to prepare your response to a submission. If your opponent tells you that he or she is making a submission, ask him or her if he or she has any authorities on which he or she wants to rely and if he or she has copies. If so, ask to read them. Again, keeping *Galbraith* and *Turnbull* with you is a good investment. Prepare a skeleton argument and serve and file it in response to your opponent's skeleton.

23.4   Check List

For the **defence**:

- Think about whether or not to make a submission.

- After doing any necessary research, write a rough list of your points in one of the ways suggested above.

- Where appropriate, prepare, serve and file a skeleton argument in advance of the hearing.

- Think about what you intend to do if the submission fails.

- Take instructions from your client — explain clearly what you are going to do and discuss whether or not he or she will give evidence.

- If possible, have all texts and authorities on which you intend to rely marked clearly.

- Take photocopies of all such texts ready to hand in to the court. You will need at least two of each — one for the court, one for your opponent.

- Modify your list of points based on the evidence.

- In the Crown Court, ask for the jury to go out while you make the submission. Give a realistic time estimate.

- If you need time to prepare, **request it**.

- Provide your opponent with copies of your own authorities and references and hand the other copies in to the court.

- Make your submission — remember, no jury speeches at this stage and modify your submission according to the court. Refer clearly to any authorities on which you rely.

- If your submission succeeds, good. If not, then if you need time to consider your next step, **request it**.

For the **prosecution** if you think there is likely to be a submission of no case:

- Consider whether you should oppose it.

- If you decide to oppose it, write a list of your points in one of the ways suggested above.

- Prepare a skeleton argument in response, serve and file.

- Mark all the authorities on which you intend to rely and take photocopies.

- Revise your list of points according to the evidence.

- If you need time to consider your response, **request it**.

- Disclose all authorities to your opponent and give him or her copies. Hand in your other copies to the court.

23.5 Procedure on Submission of No Case to Answer (Jury Trial)

(a) Defence counsel indicates that there is a matter of law to be decided in the absence of the jury.

(b) The judge asks the jury to retire.

(c) Defence counsel outlines the submission, citing appropriate authorities. It is usually argued that the case should not proceed as there is either no evidence of an essential element of the case, or the evidence is so tenuous that a jury properly directed could not convict on it: *R* v *Galbraith* [1981] 1 WLR 1039.

(d) Prosecuting counsel responds to the submission.

(e) Defence counsel replies.

(f) The judge delivers a reasoned ruling.

PART 7
APPLICATIONS TO THE COURT

TWENTY FOUR

APPLICATIONS TO THE COURT

The chapters in this Part are all about making your life easier. They are a set of how-to-do-it guides which cover some of the most common types of applications that you may face as an advocate at the start of your career. Usually they are written by practising barristers with considerable practical experience of the matters they are writing about. The matters range from the sort of hearing where your application is the sole purpose for the hearing (for example, an application for summary judgment) to those applications which have to be made as and when the need arises, in the context of other proceedings in the case (for example, applying for bail when a criminal case is remanded). Some of these guides are necessarily more extensive than others.

The aim of these chapters is not to render you competent to make such an application overnight. You should read them in conjunction with the **Case Preparation Manual**, the **Evidence Manual** and either the **Civil Litigation** and **Drafting Manuals** or the **Criminal Litigation and Sentencing Manual** (or similar works), whichever is appropriate for the application. The aim is to give you some advance notice of what happens in court when a particular application is made: who starts, what documents are needed, how many copies must be provided and so forth.

After reading this material, you should have a basic idea of how to plan for a particular application, rather than making your first one in a state of '**un**blissful' ignorance! Never neglect the other resources at your disposal, though. You should always feel able to ask other, more experienced barristers for advice or hints when you are in chambers. If possible, try to get to court early so that you can watch how similar applications are being made, note the judge's likes and dislikes.

The chapters start with some guides for work in the civil courts and tribunals. It is hoped that these are of particular assistance as civil interlocutory matters so often take place in private, with only the parties and their advocates present, so there is limited opportunity simply to observe them. These are followed by some guides to work in the criminal courts; do remember that **Chapters 22** and **23** in this Manual may also be used for this purpose.

TWENTY FIVE

DEFAULT JUDGMENTS

25.1 Setting aside Default Judgments — an Introduction

A very common type of interim application is that made to set aside a judgment which a claimant has obtained against a defendant in default. Applications to set aside default judgments are so common that the correct procedure is often overlooked. Applications will be either to set aside an irregular judgment or to set aside a regular judgment. An irregular judgment is one which has been obtained in breach of one or more of the relevant rules of court (CPR, r. 13.2 or 'old' rules) and is known as a judgment wrongly entered. A regular judgment is one which is obtained in strict compliance with the relevant rules of court. In many applications to set aside an irregular judgment, an alternative application is made at the same time out of an abundance of caution, to set aside even if the judgment is regular.

A default judgment is simply a judgment obtained by the claimant as an administrative act (i.e., by presenting the necessary forms to the court staff ordinarily with no consideration of the application by a judge, Master or district judge) because the defendant has failed to take some step which is required by the rules.

The label 'default judgment' is sometimes applied to a judgment obtained as a result of breach of a peremptory order of the court. A peremptory order is a specific order addressed to one or more parties specifying that in default of taking a certain step in the action within a specified time, judgment may be entered against that party. Peremptory orders are commonly referred to as 'unless' orders. Applications to set aside a judgment in default of an 'unless' order are considered separately at **25.7**.

The effect of a decision on an application to set aside a default judgment was clarified by the Court of Appeal in *Mullen* v *Conoco Ltd* [1997] 3 WLR 1032 which held that a decision on an application to set aside a default judgment would give rise to a final determination (subject to any appeal) on whether a judgment was regular or not, but it would not be a final decision on any discretionary element. A discretionary refusal to set aside a default judgment because the proposed defence of set-off of a counterclaim was thought too weak did not give rise to a plea of *res judicata* or issue estoppel. A fresh action based on the proposed counterclaim was not an abuse of the process of the court and could not be struck out on that ground. This decision is one which ought to be followed despite the introduction of the Civil Procedure Rules.

25.2 Old Law

There will still be cases in which the default judgment was obtained under the Rules of the Supreme Court or the County Court Rules. The main categories of default judgment under those old rules may need to be considered.

25.2.1 HIGH COURT

In the High Court default judgments will normally be obtained:

(a) where a defendant failed to give notice of intention to defend in a case to which RSC O. 13, rr. 1–5, applied; or

(b) where having given notice of intention to defend, the defendant failed to serve a defence in accordance with RSC O. 18, r. 2, whereupon judgment would be entered under RSC O. 19, r. 2;

(c) where a claimant failed to serve a defence to a counterclaim whereupon judgment would be entered under RSC O. 19, r. 8.

25.2.2 COUNTY COURT

In the County Court default judgments were normally obtained:

(a) in a fixed date action to which CCR O. 17, r. 11, applied, under CCR O. 9, r. 4A;

(b) in a default action for liquidated claims where no payment, admission, defence or 'reply to the summons' has been delivered, default judgment may be entered under CCR O. 9, r. 6(1);

(c) in a default action for unliquidated claims where no admission of liability or defence was delivered, judgment would be entered under CCR O. 9, r. 6(2).

25.2.3 THE OLD APPROACH

When it came to setting aside judgment, there were a number of important differences between a regular judgment and an irregular judgment. The irregular judgment would be set aside by the court as of right — *ex debito justitiae* — usually with the party entering the irregular judgment bearing the costs. The regular judgment will only be set aside as a matter of discretion, usually with the party against whom judgment was entered bearing the costs.

25.2.4 COMMON IRREGULARITIES

The main irregularities which were encountered in practice were:

(a) judgments which were entered too soon;

(b) judgments for a liquidated claim when the claim is unliquidated; and

(c) judgments which are entered for too much.

For a detailed examination of the law in this area you should consult a pre-CPR White Book or Green Book.

25.3 Civil Procedure Rules

The distinction between irregular and regular judgments is maintained by the CPR. Irregular judgments are now known as wrongly entered judgments. Wrongly entered judgments are those falling within CPR, r. 13.2, and the court must set them aside. In all other cases the Court has discretion whether to set aside or vary the default judgment (CPR, r. 13.3(1)). The wording of the discretion mirrors the existing approach (*Alpine Bulk Transport Co. Inc.* v *Saudi Eagle Shipping Co. Inc.* [1986] 2 Lloyd's Rep 221). The defence must have a prospect of success which is better than merely arguable (*International Finance Corporation* v *Utexafrica nrl* [2001] CLC 1361). Delay remains relevant to the exercise of the discretion (CPR, r. 13.3(2)). The court can still attach conditions to an order setting aside a default judgment (CPR, r. 3.1(3)). Historically the most common condition was requiring the defendant to pay some or all of the money into court. That is likely to remain the most common condition.

A wholly new obligation has been introduced on the claimant who discovers that his or her judgment was wrongly entered. The claimant is now obliged to apply to set aside his or her own judgment and should not enforce it in the meantime (CPR, r. 13.5).

25.4 Making the Application

You should familiarise yourself with the requirements of CPR, Part 23 for all interim applications, for evidence and for selecting the court in which the application should be made. These are set out in your *Civil Procedure Manual*.

25.5 Documents Required to Set Aside a Default Judgment

The documents required to set aside a default judgment are:

(a) an application (complying with CPR, Part 23) which should as a matter of good practice state the irregularity where it is alleged that the judgment was wrongly entered;

(b) evidence in support of the application, unless the application to set aside is only based on the judgment being wrongly entered.

25.6 The Hearing of the Application

At the hearing of the application it is for the party applying to set aside judgment to open the application. In the Queen's Bench Division the Master will probably not have seen any of the papers in advance of the hearing, so the party applying must hand in to the Master the original application and evidence in support and take the Master through the evidence in support. The party opposing the application should then take the Master through any evidence in answer. If the party applying has further evidence the Master should be taken through that additional evidence. When the evidence stage is completed it is for the party applying to make submissions (if required to do so), then for the party opposing to make submissions (if required to do so) and finally for the party applying to respond (if required to do so).

In the Chancery Division and in the County Court there will be a court file which should contain the application and the evidence (provided it has been filed by the parties). Where there is a court file it is appropriate to ask the Master or district judge whether he or she has had an opportunity of reading any of the papers, before the parties go through the stages set out in the preceding paragraph.

It is sometimes convenient to deal with any question of wrongly entered judgment before considering any alternative application to set aside as a matter of discretion. This is particularly useful where the argument that the judgment is wrongly entered is strong. If the hearing is divided in this way it may save court time as, if the judgment is set aside as being wrongly entered, it is not normally necessary to consider the merits at all. If the judgment is set aside the party applying should seek its costs and directions. If the judgment is not set aside as being wrongly entered, the Master will have to dismiss that application and go on to consider any alternative application on the merits.

A chronology is often required to show the Court the sequence of events and any period of delay in making the application to set aside the default judgment. The only delay which is relevant is delay after issue of proceedings (*Thorn plc v MacDonald* [1999] CPLR 660). Usually some evidence explaining the delay is required but if the period of delay is short, the absence of an explanation is not now fatal to the exercise of the discretion to set aside.

At the end of the submissions the Master or district judge should give a reasoned judgment.

After judgment, if the application to set aside is dismissed, the only issues are likely to be the costs (which should follow the event), and any application by the party applying for a stay of execution pending any appeal. Permission to appeal will also be required.

If the application is successful and the judgment is set aside, there may be discussion about the directions to be given (e.g., when the defence is to be filed by and other directions); about the conditions (e.g., how long should be given for any money to be brought into court as a condition of the judgment being set aside); and costs. If the judgment was irregular, the party applying will be awarded his or her costs unless there is an exceptional feature such as substantial delay. If the judgment was regular, the party applying will normally have to pay all the costs of the entry of judgment, or any execution, and of the application and will usually be ordered to pay those summarily assessed costs forthwith rather than in any event.

25.7   Peremptory or 'Unless' Orders

A judgment entered upon a failure to comply with a peremptory order is sometimes referred to as a default judgment. The judgment can consist of a dismissal of the whole or any part of the claim, judgment for a specified sum, judgment for damages to be assessed or some other judgment.

Judgment obtained for breach of an 'unless' order is quite different from other types of default judgment. Although the actual entry of the judgment is an administrative act, it almost always flows from consideration of the case by the court when the 'unless' order was made (the main exception being where a party consents to the order being made). Since the order is a specific one directed at a party, any failure to comply with the order is extremely serious.

Immediately prior to the CPR there were an ever increasing number of reported cases in which a party tried to avoid the consequences of an 'unless' order. Some of those cases are not easy to reconcile. For example, there is authority for the proposition that where a party's solicitor was solely at fault non-compliance should be excused (*Pereira v Beanlands* [1996] 3 All ER 528) and there is also authority for the proposition that a party is bound by the default of his lawyers (*Hytec Ltd* v *Coventry City Council* [1997] 1 WLR 1666). This is one area in which it is to be hoped that the approach in most of the old cases will be abandoned.

25.7.1   MAKING THE 'UNLESS' ORDER

In the past it was not normal practice to make an 'unless' order for a first default. That approach is likely to end, particularly with fast-track cases where the timetable is tight. As the court exercises greater case management control 'unless' orders may become more common.

One old rule which may survive the introduction of the CPR is that a party consenting to an 'unless' order cannot thereafter challenge the validity or extent of the order (*Fearis* v *Davies* [1989] 1 FSR 555).

The 'unless' order should be absolutely clear in describing the action required to be taken by the party, the date and time by which it is to be taken and the sanction to be imposed if that order is not complied with. The sanction should be proportionate to the potential default and can consist of striking out part or all of the claim or defence (CPR, r. 3.5, PD 40B para. 8.2).

25.7.2 CHALLENGING THE 'UNLESS' ORDER

Once the 'unless' order has been made it should be treated in the same way as any other interim direction of the court: it should be complied with or appealed. It is unlikely that the courts will now, save in exceptional cases, allow a party to ignore an 'unless' order or escape the sanction merely because the order is not in proper form. The parties cannot agree to extension of time (CPR, r. 3.8(3)).

25.7.3 NON-COMPLIANCE WITH THE ORDER

Subject to the right to seek an extension of time for compliance (either before or after the deadline), the sanction set out in the order will take effect (CPR, r. 3.8).

25.7.4 EXTENSION OF TIME FOR COMPLIANCE

The court has power to extend time. Application should be made on notice supported by evidence. The Court will then have regard to all the circumstances and the factors set out in CPR, r. 3.9.

25.7.5 THE HEARING OF AN APPLICATION FOR AN EXTENSION OF TIME

The evidence from the defaulting party should explain the default (where that is possible) and address the factors set out in CPR, r. 3.9, and the overriding objectives. There may be evidence in reply which should address those same issues. It is the stated intention of the courts to take a far more stringent approach to default than hitherto.

At this type of hearing a carefully prepared chronology is probably the most useful weapon. If you are applying for the extension of time a chronology which shows that there have been delays by the other party, or 'unless' orders against the other party, may assist as part of the background before turning to the reasons for your particular application for extra time. If you are resisting an application for an extension, particularly if the delays have been largely or exclusively on the part of the party applying for the extension, or there have been previous 'unless' orders against that party, a chronology can be a devastating weapon in resisting a further extension of time or limiting the extent of the extension.

The party seeking the extension of time will almost always have to pay all the costs of the application which will usually be assessed immediately.

TWENTY SIX

SUMMARY JUDGMENT

26.1 Introduction

The Civil Procedure Rules 1998, Part 24, sets out a procedure whereby the Court may decide a claim or a particular issue without a trial. Applications can be made by a claimant or by a defendant or of the Court's own motion.

26.2 Before Attending Court

Check that the procedural requirements have been complied with, for example:

(a) when acting for a claimant ensure that the defendant has filed an acknowledgement of service or a defence;

(b) when acting for a claimant ensure the claim is one to which summary judgment is available, i.e., not proceedings for possession of residential premises against a tenant, a mortgagor, or person holding over after the end of his tenancy, not proceedings for an admiralty claim *in rem*, not Crown proceedings, not proceedings against the Crown;

(c) has the respondent been given at least 14 days' notice of the date fixed for hearing and of the issues which it is proposed that the Court will decide at the hearing?

(d) The contents of the application notice:

    (i) the application notice must include a statement that it is an application for summary judgment made under Part 24 of the Civil Procedure Rules 1998;

    (ii) it must state what order the applicant is seeking and why the applicant is seeking the order;

    (iii) it must identify the written evidence on which the applicant relies unless no evidence is relied on or the application notice itself contains all the evidence relied on;

    (iv) it must draw the respondent's attention to the time limit for filing and serving its own written evidence (at least seven days before the summary judgment hearing).

(e) Written evidence:

    (i) an applicant may rely on written evidence set out in his claim form, statement of case, application notice, or in a witness statement. Each item of written evidence relied on must contain a statement of truth. Affidavit evidence is also permissible but is subject to cost implications;

(ii)   the applicant's written evidence must be served at the same time as the application notice;

(iii) the respondent must file and serve his written evidence at least seven days before the summary judgment hearing;

(iv)   if the applicant wishes to rely on written evidence in reply this must be filed and served at least three days before the summary judgment hearing;

(v)   the application notice or the supporting evidence must identify concisely any point of law or provision in a document on which the applicant relies and/or state that it is made because the applicant believes that on the evidence the respondent has no real prospect of succeeding on the claim or issue or of successfully defending the claim or issue to which the application relates, and in either case state that the applicant knows of no other reason why the disposal of the claim or issue should await trial.

(f) Check that any directions given by the Master or district judge in relation to the hearing have been complied with.

Note: if a procedural requirement has not been complied with, consider whether the defect could be cured, e.g., by an application to the Court under CPR, r. 3.10 for an order to remedy the error.

Familiarise yourself with the contents of the statements of case and the written evidence in support so that you are able to refer the Court to specific passages and points quickly and smoothly even though this may not follow the set order you planned for your submissions. It is unlikely that the court will allow you to develop all your submissions without interruption — the court will strive to get to the heart of the issues as quickly as possible.

Take with you spare copies of the statement of case, the application notice and the written evidence. Although these should have all been filed, occasionally documents go missing from Court files.

26.3   At Court

The hearing will be either before a Master in the High Court at the Royal Courts of Justice or before a district judge, if in a High Court District Registry or in the County Court. If however a summary judgment application includes a claim for an injunction the hearing should take place before a High Court or a County Court judge as Masters and district judges have limited jurisdiction in relation to injunctions. The hearings are likely to be in public but no robes are required.

26.3.1   BEFORE A MASTER

Fill in a case slip outside Court to enable the Master to have a note of the advocates' names. Don't forget to introduce yourself and your opponent to the Court notwithstanding having completed a slip. Address the Master simply as 'Master'.

If you have a short appointment you are likely to have to address the Master from a standing position. Stand close to the Master's desk and use the shelf or ledge for your papers. Longer appointments are taken with the advocates sitting. As a rule of thumb, if there are no chairs in position facing the Master's desk, be prepared to make your submissions standing. The Master will indicate that you can bring chairs forward from the back of the room if she or he is minded to permit counsel to be seated.

26.3.2   BEFORE A DISTRICT JUDGE

A member of the Court staff is likely to be on hand to take your name and/or to ask you to fill out an advocate's name slip. Address the district judge as 'Sir' or 'Madam' as appropriate. The advocates will make their submissions seated however long or short the application is.

26.3.3 THE HEARING

Unless or until the Court invites argument on a specific point or issues, the claimant's counsel should be prepared to give a brief outline of the application by referring to the particulars of claim and the terms of the application notice. She or he should ask whether the Master or district judge has had the opportunity to read the written evidence and if not whether the Court would like them read now. Usually a Master or district judge will prefer to read such material themselves but it is courteous to enquire whether they wish to do this or to have the written evidence read aloud. If the written evidence is to be read aloud, the respondent's counsel should read the respondent's written evidence. Once the written evidence has been read the claimant's counsel will make his or her submission. In reply the respondent's counsel will make his or her submissions and the claimant's counsel will usually be given an opportunity to make further submissions after that. Do not be surprised if the Court selects only certain points from your submissions or if the Master or district judge departs from the usual order of submissions. Do not be afraid to emphasise or reiterate what you consider to be your best point (or points) if the Court seems to have ignored it or misunderstood it. When preparing your submissions or indeed making them remember how difficult it will be for a Master or district judge to pick up the issues in all the cases listed before him or her each day if advocates are overelaborate or verbose. Clear succinct submissions will be welcomed.

26.3.4 THE COURT'S APPROACH

Where a claimant applies for judgment on his claim the Court will give that judgment if:

(a) the defendant has no real prospect of successfully defending the claim or issue; and

(b) there is no other compelling reason why the claim should be dealt with at trial.

Where a defendant applies for judgment in his or her favour on the claimant's claim, the Court will give the judgment if it considers that:

(a) the claimant has no real prospect of succeeding on the claim or issue; and

(b) there is no other compelling reason why the claim should be dealt with at trial.

Where it appears to the Court possible that a claim or defence may succeed but improbable that it will do so, the Court may make a conditional order.

26.3.5 THE ORDER

The Court will give judgment orally, setting out reasons for the order and declaring the terms of the order. Make a verbatim note of both aspects. The Court may order:

(a) judgment on the claim or on any issue therein;

(b) the striking out or dismissal of the claim or of an issue therein;

(c) the dismissal of the application;

(d) a conditional order which requires a party to pay a sum of money into court or to take a specified step in relation to his or her claim or defence and provides that the party's claim will be dismissed or his or her statement of case struck out if he or she does not comply;

(e) an order relating to costs.

After judgment is given the question of costs has to be decided. Costs are very important. Be prepared to make submissions on the appropriate order as to what the costs should be and why.

The Court is empowered to give further directions about the management of the case when it determines a summary judgment application (CPR, r. 24.6; PD 24, para. 10). Be prepared.

26.4   Appeals

In order to appeal a summary judgment order it is necessary to obtain permission to appeal either from the Court which made the order or the Court to which the appeal is to be made. You need either to apply at the summary judgment hearing or make an application for permission in an appeal notice within 14 days from the initial hearing.

The appeal notice must be filed at the appeal court within such period as directed by the lower court or, in the absence of a direction, within 14 days of the date of the decision to be appealed. Copies have to be served on the respondents to the appeal not later than seven days after the appeal notice is filed. If you do wish to appeal, consider whether you need a stay pending appeal.

Note that permission is granted only where:

(a)   the Court considers that the appeal would have a real prospect of success; or

(b)   there is some other compelling reason why the appeal should be heard.

See generally CPR, Part 52.

TWENTY SEVEN

INTERIM PAYMENTS

27.1 Introduction

An interim payment application seeks a payment on account of any damages, debt or other sum (excluding costs) which the respondent may be held liable to pay to or for the benefit of the applicant.

An order for interim payment can be obtained in all proceedings where the claim includes a claim for some form of money save for cases proceeding on the small claims track (CPR, r. 27.2(1)(a)).

27.2 Procedural Requirements

(a) An application must be made by filing and serving an application notice at any time after the time limit to acknowledge service has expired.

(b) A copy of the application notice must be served at least 14 days before the hearing of the application and must be supported by evidence.

(c) The written evidence must deal with the following:

    (i) the sum of money sought by way of interim payment;

    (ii) the items or matters in respect of which the interim payment is sought;

    (iii) the sum of money for which final judgment is likely to be given;

    (iv) the reasons for believing that the conditions set out in CPR, r. 25.7, have been satisfied;

    (v) any other relevant matters;

    (vi) exhibit any documentary evidence relied on in support of the application, including in personal injuries claims the medical reports.

(d) In a Fatal Accidents Act 1976 claim the written evidence must give details of the persons on whose behalf the claim is made and the nature of the claim.

27.3 The Basis of the Application

27.3.1 LIABILITY

The Court may make an order for interim payment only if:

(a) the defendant against whom the order is sought has admitted liability to pay damages or some other sum of money to the claimant; or

(b) the claimant has obtained judgment against that defendant for damages to be assessed or for a sum of money (other than costs) to be assessed; or

(c) the Court is satisfied that if the claim went to trial the claimant would obtain judgment for a substantial amount of money (other than costs) against the defendant from whom he is seeking an order for interim payment; or

(d) in a claim for personal injuries where there are two or more defendants, the Court is satisfied that if the claim went to trial the claimant would obtain judgment for substantial damages against at least one of the defendants (even if the Court has not yet determined which of them is liable); or

(e) in a claim for possession of land, the Court is satisfied that if the case went to trial the defendant would be held liable (even if the claim for possession fails) to pay the claimant a sum of money for the defendant's occupation and use of the land while the claim for possession was pending.

27.3.2   CLAIMS FOR PERSONAL INJURIES

Additional conditions apply. The Court may only make an order for an interim payment if:

(a) the defendant is insured in respect of the claim; or

(b) the defendant's liability will be met by an insurer under section 151 of the Road Traffic Act 1988, or an insurer acting under the Motor Insurers Bureau Agreement or the Motor Insurers Bureau where it is acting for itself; or

(c) the defendant is a public body.

27.3.3   QUANTUM

Once satisfied regarding liability, and the insurance status of the defendant in a personal injury claim, the Court has a discretion whether to make an interim payment and if so of what amount:

- CPR, r. 25.7(1): 'The Court *may* make an order for an interim payment ...'.

- CPR, r. 25.7(4): 'The Court must not order an interim payment of more than a reasonable proportion of the likely amount of the final judgment.'

- CPR, r. 25.7(5): 'The Court must take into account (a) contributory negligence; and (b) any relevant set-off or counterclaim.'

27.4   The Hearing

In the High Court the appointment will be before a Master but prima facie in public. Address the Master simply as 'Master'. No robes will be required in whatever Court the application is proceeding.

Outside London if the action is proceeding in the High Court the interim payment application will be directed to a district judge sitting in the District Registry of the High Court. The hearing will prima facie be in public. A district judge will be addressed as 'Sir' or 'Madam'.

In the County Court the application will be made to a district judge sitting prima facie in public who should be referred to as 'Sir' or 'Madam' as appropriate.

Your basic tools in an interim payment application will be the statement of case and the witness statements or other written evidence in support. Any evidence that is not included in the filed and served written evidence will be inadmissible and will require an adjournment, if you can get it, so that a supplemental statement can be provided.

The first step, if it is your application, is to introduce yourself and your opponent to the Court. Then introduce the case by declaring what the application is for and briefly mentioning the claim in the main action and how it arises. The next step is to place the evidence before the Court. Enquire whether the Master or district judge has had an opportunity to read the written evidence. The likelihood is that he or she will have read such material in advance. If not, direct him or her to the passages that he or she should read. Usually the Master or district judge will find it easier to read to himself or herself but if in doubt ask.

Prepare your submissions by dealing with liability first. In some cases this will require only a sentence or two if interim judgment has already been obtained or there is a clear admission in the statement of case. However, in other cases, liability will be a much greater problem. The standard of proof required is to the civil standard, but compare 'would succeed' with 'would be likely to succeed' (*British & Commonwealth Holdings plc v Quadrex Holdings Inc.* [1989] QB 842; *Andrews v Schooling* [1991] 3 All ER 723). It is often useful when dealing with quantum to outline the overall size of the claimant's claim and then to deal with any heads of damage where the claimant is either bound to succeed or where the possibility of failure is remote. In personal injury actions the Court may be assisted by a valuation of the damages for pain, suffering and loss of amenities. Take the *Judicial Studies Guidelines* or *Kemp on Quantum of Damages etc.* to Court plus photocopies of what is relevant.

It is a requirement that the written evidence sets our the amount you are asking for. You will need to justify the sum as a fraction or percentage of the overall claim. The Courts are sometimes wary of giving an interim payment when no specific need for the money has been dealt with in the written evidence or when the interim payment may be a payment on account of general damages in a personal injury action.

There was clear authority that there was nothing under the old Rules requiring the claimant to show a specific need (*Stringman v McArdle* [1994] 1 WLR 1653). You may need to be prepared to argue this not so much as a requirement but as an aspect that the Court can take into account when considering its discretion. Also bear in mind that, with the expected improved speed of getting cases to trial, you may have to argue why the claimant should be awarded some money now rather than have matters disposed of in one go at trial.

It is easier if you can justify your interim payment against special damages, but there is no reason why a payment in respect of general damages cannot be obtained. Remember, the Court is primarily concerned to see that there is no risk of overpayment at the interim stage, since return of the money if the claimant has spent it can often be problematic.

27.4.1   THE INTERIM PAYMENT ORDER

The Court will give judgment orally setting out reasons for the order and declaring the terms of the order. Make a verbatim note of both aspects.

In a personal injury case where there are repayments to be made to the Compensation Recovery unit, the order should set out the amount of the relevant deduction. Payment of the net amount only will be made to the claimant.

As the fact of an interim payment should be kept from the trial judge if another application is made at the same time which results in an order, there should be two separate orders drawn up, not one. Don't forget you will have to deal with costs at the end of the application.

27.5   Appeals

In order to appeal an interim payment order it is necessary to obtain permission to appeal from the Court which made the order or the Court to which the appeal is to be made. You need either to apply at the interim payment hearing or make an application for permission in an appeal notice within 14 days from the initial hearing.

The appeal notice must be filed at the appeal court within such period as directed by the lower court or, in the absence of a direction, within 14 days of the date of the decision to be appealed. Copies have to be served on the respondents to the appeal not later than seven days after the appeal notice is filed. If you do wish to appeal, consider whether you need a stay pending appeal.

Note that permission is granted only where:

(a)   the Court considers that the appeal would have a real prospect of success; or

(b)   there is some other compelling reason why the appeal should be heard.

See generally CPR, Part 52.

It is therefore usually easier to obtain the order you seek on the first hearing than it is to correct it on appeal.

TWENTY EIGHT

APPLYING FOR AN INJUNCTION

28.1 Introduction

This chapter considers the procedure at the hearing of an application for an interim injunction in civil proceedings (other than matrimonial proceedings).

Whether you are in practice or merely a regular visitor to a County Court you will soon notice that a very large number of applications for injunctions are made in matrimonial cases. Whilst interim injunctions are less common in other civil litigation, they are by no means rare. It is important to be familiar with the basic procedure for applying for an interim injunction in non-matrimonial cases as injunctions are, by their very nature, often required quickly, and in the case of without notice (formerly *ex parte*) applications extremely quickly.

28.2 Some Expressions Explained

A number of expressions are used in connection with injunction applications with which you ought to be familiar. The main expressions are:

ancillary orders	refers to any order which is connected with the main injunction or injunctions (e.g., an order to disclose the whereabouts of an object or asset);
Angel Bell	an order within a freezing injunction permitting the payment of certain (usually specified) business debts or commitments or living expenses. The order is named after *Iraqi Ministry of Defence v Arcepey Shipping Company SA (The 'Angel Bell')* [1981] QB 65;
Anton Piller	the old name for a search order (see below);
freezing injunction	the new name for a *Mareva* injunction which freezes the use of some or all of the assets of a person, firm or company;
interim	a temporary injunction or order granted for a specified period of time 'until the ... day of ...' or 'until trial or further order'. Formerly known as an interlocutory injunction;
Mareva injunction	the old name for a freezing injunction (see above);
ne exeat regno	an ancient prerogative writ which prevents a debtor leaving the realm which fell into disuse in 1893, was applied for (unsuccessfully) in August 1968 and has been used on only a handful of occasions since then;
ouster order	common expression for an order removing (ousting) a person from property (usually a home) most commonly made in matrimonial proceedings but can also be obtained in other disputes;
quia timet	(because he apprehends) an expression used in relation to a threatened wrong which has not yet taken place;
radius order	an order prohibiting someone from entering a specified area near a building or home, commonly used in matrimonial proceedings but can be obtained in other proceedings, see *Burris* v *Azadani* at **26.3**;

return date	the date fixed for further consideration of the injunction (usually the with notice hearing fixed after a without notice injunction has been granted);
search order	the new name of an *Anton Piller* order, an order which requires the giving of access to premises and of immediate delivery up of documents or property. Order originally named after *Anton Piller KG* v *Manufacturing Processes Limited* [1976] Ch 55;
short service	an order obtained (usually without notice which permits an application to be considered when the other party has not been given the full notice required by the Rules);
penal notice	a notice on the court order which warns the person injuncted of the consequences of a breach of the order.

28.3   The Nature of the Order

An injunction is an order of the court requiring a person or company to do a specific act or acts (a mandatory injunction) or to refrain from doing some act or acts (a prohibitory injunction). The distinction between a mandatory injunction and a prohibitory injunction depends not upon the wording of the order but upon its substance. Do not waste time trying to make a mandatory order look as if it is prohibitory merely because the latter are more likely to be granted at an interim stage. Individual injunctions will be either mandatory or prohibitory (although both may appear in the same order).

Quite separately, injunctions can also be divided into final and interim (historically known as interlocutory injunctions). This distinction is often based upon when they are obtained in the proceedings. An interim injunction is usually obtained before any trial and a final injunction is obtained at the end of the case (usually, but not always at a trial).

The statutory power for the High Court to grant an injunction is contained in s. 37, Supreme Court Act 1981 and gives the power 'in all cases in which it appears to the court to be just and convenient to do so'. In the County Court the statutory power is now to be found in s. 38, County Courts Act 1984 which gives the County Court power to make any order which the High Court could have made.

The traditional view is that injunctions are not a cause of action in themselves but a relief granted in support of an existing legal or equitable right (*The Siskina* [1979] AC 210).

In many cases the 'right' to be enforced by a proposed injunction will be obvious. However, the courts seem prepared to extend the concept of 'rights' where necessary. The House of Lords has qualified the strict approach to be found in *The Siskina* on more than one occasion. More recently the House of Lords has doubted whether the strict approach to 'rights' in *The Siskina* is correct; see, for example, the speech of Lord Browne-Wilkinson (with whom Lords Keith and Goff agreed on this point) in *Channel Tunnel Group Limited* v *Balfour Beatty Construction Limited* [1993] AC 334. To make matters more complex the Privy Council refused to uphold a wholesale challenge to *The Siskina* in *Mercedes-Benz AG* v *Leiduck* [1995] 3 WLR 718. However, it seems that the approach in *The Siskina* may now be limited to cases involving private law rights, and not the wider interests of the public, in cases such as those brought between a trustee in bankruptcy and the bankrupt (*Morris* v *Murjani* [1996] 2 All ER 384).

Thus, whilst *The Siskina* may be a good starting point, take care to consider the statutory power to grant an injunction 'in all cases in which it appears to the court to be just and convenient to do so' before deciding that there is no power in the court to make the particular order sought.

In the light of attacks being made on the traditional view in *The Siskina* it is becoming more and more difficult to decide the exact circumstances in which the court may grant an injunction. Seven recent examples may assist in demonstrating the way in which the traditional view of 'rights' has been extended by the courts.

Re Oriental Credit Limited [1988] 2 WLR 172   In this case the court granted an injunction restraining a former director of a company from leaving the jurisdiction until after completion of his examination under orders made pursuant to s. 561, Companies Act 1985. The court held that power existed to make the order even though it was not to enforce a legal or equitable right as it was an order in aid of the existing Companies Act order.

TSB Private Bank International SA v *Chabra* [1992] 1 WLR 231   In this case the court granted a *Mareva* (now freezing) injunction in a claim under a guarantee which covered, *inter alia*, assets being sold by a UK company of which the defendant was the majority shareholder. The court, of its own motion, joined the company in the action as a necessary party under RSC O. 15, r. 6(2)(b)(ii). The court then held that where a claimant has a right against one defendant, it had power to grant an injunction against a co-defendant against whom no cause of action lay.

Aiglon Limited v *Gau Shan Co. Limited* [1993] BCLC 1321   In this case the court found that the claimant's evidence disclosed a strong *prima facie* case under s. 423, Insolvency Act 1986 which gave the claimant a direct cause of action under s. 425(1)(d) of that Act, but also held that the court had jurisdiction under s. 238 of that Act to grant the worldwide *Mareva* (now freezing) injunction even though that section gave no direct cause of action or claim.

Khorasandjian v *Bush* [1993] QB 727   In this case the majority of the Court of Appeal granted a *quia timet* injunction restraining persistent unwanted telephone calls as the inconvenience to the recipient constituted an actionable interference with the ordinary and reasonable use of property which could be restrained without proof of damage.

The Mercantile Group (Europe) Ag v *Aiyela* [1994] 3 WLR 1116   In this case the Court of Appeal continued a *Mareva* (now freezing) injunction against a person who was not a judgment debtor, and against whom the claimant had no surviving cause of action, as the order was ancillary to the order against the judgment debtor and was properly made in the interests of justice.

Burris v *Azadani* [1995] 1 WLR 1372   In this case the Court of Appeal upheld the making of an injunction restraining the defendant from approaching within 250 yards of the claimant's home distinguishing (on grounds which are somewhat tenuous) the well-known earlier decision of the Court of Appeal in *Patel* v *Patel* [1988] 2 FLR 202.

Morris v *Murjani* [1996] 2 All ER 384   In this case the Court of Appeal limited the requirement that there be an existing cause of action as the basis for granting an interlocutory (now interim) injunction, to cases involving a violation of private rights. Thus an injunction restraining a bankrupt from leaving the country before the hearing of an application for his committal for breach of s. 333, Insolvency Act 1986 could properly be made.

The courts seem prepared to extend the concepts of 'rights'. The exact limits of the concept of 'rights' is unclear and may now be different for cases involving private rights from those involving public duties. It should be noted that this extension does not mean that the court will simply grant any order which is sought, as two further examples will illustrate.

Law Debenture Trust Corporation v *Ural Caspian Oil Corporation Limited* [1993] 1 WLR 138   In this case the Court of Appeal accepted that a purchaser of property who acquired it in the knowledge of some contractual covenant binding the vendor might be restrained by negative injunction from breaching that covenant, but refused to extend that approach so as to grant a mandatory injunction against the purchaser to perform the covenant.

Zucker & others v *Tyndall Holdings plc* [1992] 1 WLR 1127   In this case the Court of Appeal refused to grant a *Mareva* (now freezing) injunction when there was only the threat of breach of a term of a contract which was itself not presently enforceable or performable.

Frequently an injunction will be sought to prevent repetition of a wrong which has already taken place, or the undoing of the wrong (e.g., removal of a trespass or obstruction). However, it is not necessary to wait until the proposed defendant has committed the wrong before applying to the court. A *quia timet* injunction can be obtained if a wrong is merely threatened, see, for example, *Redland Bricks Limited* v *Morris* [1970] AC 652. Two criteria normally have to be satisfied: first that there is a threatened wrong; secondly that the wrong infringes some right which the claimant already has (although this second criterion may now have to be reconsidered in cases involving some public duty).

It must be remembered that an injunction remains a discretionary remedy of the court to which equitable principles are still applied. Even if a clear right has been infringed, an injunction will not necessarily be granted at trial or at the interim stage. An injunction (like the remedy of specific performance) will be refused where it serves no useful purpose, but the mere fear that the defendant will not obey is not sufficient to justify the refusal to grant an injunction (*Castanho* v *Brown and Root (UK) Limited* [1981] AC 552). An injunction may be refused: where there is only a trivial infringement or threatened infringement of a right; where there would be undue hardship to the party being restrained; where the party seeking the injunction has been guilty of some equitable fraud or has unclean hands; or where there has been undue delay or acquiescence on the part of the person seeking the injunction.

The Civil Procedure Rules have not changed the discretionary nature of the injunction remedy. The general criteria for the grant of an interim remedy is now that it will give effect to the overriding object (CPR, r. 1.2). Detailed provisions appear in CPR, Part 25 and PD 25 (Interim Injunctions).

28.4   Enforcement of the Order

As an injunction is an order of the court, breach of its terms constitutes a contempt of court punishable by imprisonment, sequestration of assets or a fine. It is beyond the scope of this chapter to set out the detailed procedure for applying to commit a person for breach of an injunction. However, it should be noted that as the defendant's liberty may be in jeopardy, a technical approach is always adopted by the court both on the procedural aspects of the application and in interpreting the wording of the order. Although most injunctions are complied with, without any applications to commit being made, it is extremely important that the wording of the order is crystal clear and that the order which is served has a 'penal notice' included (see **28.11**). Finally, in some cases it is essential that the order has been properly served upon the defendant.

28.5   Jurisdiction

When applying for any interim injunction it is important to consider both the jurisdiction of the court in which you intend to make the application and the jurisdiction of the person hearing the application to grant the order.

28.6   The Undertaking as to Damages

If a party wishes to obtain an interim injunction it is normally necessary to give an undertaking in damages. The undertaking is a promise to the court to pay damages to the party restrained by the order if the court subsequently finds that (a) they have suffered any damage by reason of the order and that (b) the party obtaining the order ought to pay for that damage.

The courts do not require such an undertaking in every case. The main exceptions being:

(a) matrimonial injunctions involving conduct rather than money or property (such as those restraining assaults);

(b) applications by public bodies charged with enforcement of some area of law (*Kirklees Metropolitan Borough Council* v *Wickes Buildings Supplies Limited* [1993] AC 227).

In most cases the undertaking is only invoked by an inquiry as to damages either upon discharge of the order shortly after it is granted (e.g., on discharge of an order without notice) or at the trial of the action when the parties' true rights are established. Upon discharge of an injunction prior to the trial the court will have to decide whether to order an immediate inquiry or leave the decision until the conclusion of the case. The practice to be followed has been considered by the Court of Appeal in *Cheltenham & Gloucester Building Society* v *Ricketts* [1993] 1 WLR 1545.

Five practical points need to be noted:

(a) Although it may not be absolutely essential that the court be given information about the financial status of the party seeking the injunction, it is good practice to do so in the evidence in support of the application.

(b) If you are aware of any factor which makes the undertaking in damages of doubtful value or worthless, that fact should be made known to the court. In *Schmitten* v *Faulkes* [1893] WN 64, a solicitor who failed to disclose to the court that the undertaking was worthless because he had commenced bankruptcy proceedings against his own client was ordered to pay the costs and damages personally.

(c) The fact that the undertaking is of limited value is not an absolute bar to obtaining an injunction; see the unusual case of *Allen* v *Jambo Holdings Limited* [1980] 1 WLR 1252 in which the Court of Appeal reinstated a *Mareva* (now freezing) injunction although the undertaking in damages was virtually worthless.

(d) In some cases the court may require an undertaking to be fortified by a guarantee or deposit of money or by an undertaking from someone else (e.g., a parent company of a newly formed or impecunious subsidiary). Obviously you should ensure that you have actual authority to give an undertaking from someone else before doing so. In *Udall* v *Capri Lighting Limited (In Liquidation)* [1988] QB 907, the Court of Appeal ordered an inquiry into the conduct of the solicitor for the defendant and any losses occasioned by that conduct. The solicitor had given an undertaking that the defendant's directors would provide security for its liabilities towards the claimant by creating second charges in the claimant's favour on their personal properties but, when the judge subsequently ordered the solicitor to carry out his undertaking, the evidence showed that the directors were unable to fulfill the commitment. If the solicitor's failure to implement the undertaking was inexcusable and merited reproof, the judge could make a compensatory order of a disciplinary nature. A requirement for security may be imposed either at the without notice stage or at any later stage prior to discharge of the order as a condition of continuing the order. When a deposit or security is sought by the party restrained, the court would require evidence in support of the application to show that there is a risk of substantial loss being caused by the order and some sound basis for the belief that the undertaking given may be insufficient (*Bhimji* v *Chatwani* [1992] 1 WLR 1158).

(e) Although there is no question of a party buying an injunction merely by being wealthy enough to give a valuable undertaking in damages, if the person or company applying for the injunction has assets it will not harm them to say so.

In the case of a company filed accounts can be exhibited. In the case of an individual some estimate or statement of net worth can be made.

If undertakings are given to the court and accepted in lieu of an injunction take care that you note the difference in practice over the undertaking as to damages between (i) the Chancery Division and (ii) the Queen's Bench Division and the County Court set out at **28.12**. It is vital that it is clearly understood whether an undertaking as to damages has been given or not.

28.7   A Without Notice Application

A without notice application can only be made in cases of urgency, for example where there is some imminent danger which the court is being asked to prevent. This element of urgency should be clearly set out in the evidence in support of the application, which should also state when the facts which are the foundation of the application became known to the party applying or to his or her advisers. (It is particularly important to state when those facts became known if they occurred some time before or if you cannot state exactly when they occurred.)

There is a duty of full and frank disclosure in applications made without notice and failure to make proper disclosure may lead to any order being set aside without consideration of the merits of the case. The duty extends to factors affecting the value of the undertaking in damages (see **28.6**). In *Intergraph Corporation & another v Solid Systems CAD Services Limited* [1993] FSR 617, the court stressed that merely exhibiting a large number of documents to the evidence does not constitute disclosure. Unless the judge reads the document on a without notice application it has not been disclosed.

28.7.1   ARRANGING THE HEARING

Your solicitor or your clerk may make the arrangements for the hearing of an application without notice. However, you should be familiar with the procedure, particularly for out of hours applications.

In cases of the utmost urgency it is possible to arrange for application to be made to the duty judge at any time outside court hours by telephoning the officer on duty at the Royal Courts of Justice on (020) 7936 6260. There is always a duty judge who will hear the application. The practice in the Chancery Division is to be found in the *Chancery Guide*, the practice in the Commercial Court is to be found in the *Commercial Court Guide*. In all divisions a hearing can be arranged at the High Court, at the judge's home or in extreme cases application can be made by telephone; see, for example, *Allen v Jambo Holdings Limited* [1980] 1 WLR 1252. If you seek a prohibitory injunction it is effective and binding on the person restrained as soon as he or she is notified of it (even before personal service of the order).

In cases which do not require an application to be made outside normal court hours, the hearing is arranged by contacting security at the Royal Courts of Justice and leaving details for a return call from the judge's clerk.

In the Chancery Division the papers should be lodged on the day before the hearing of the motion or in cases of extreme urgency immediately before the hearing of the without notice motion which will be at 10.30 am or at 2.00 pm. The arrangements for hearings are set out in the *Guide to the Administration of Chancery Chambers and Companies and Bankruptcy Courts*. The documents required will be the claim form; particulars of claim, if any; the evidence in support (or approved drafts thereof) and the draft order which is being sought.

In the Queen's Bench Division the papers should have been lodged by your solicitors at 3.00 pm on the day before the application is listed at 10.00 am; or in cases of extreme urgency by 9.50 am for a 10.00 am hearing or by 12.30 pm for a 2.00 pm hearing. The documents required will be as in the Chancery Division.

In the Commercial Court the papers should be lodged in advance, save in exceptional circumstances, in accordance with the *Commercial Court Guide.*

In the County Court the papers should be lodged prior to the hearing. If time permits they can be lodged the day before the without notice application, but more commonly they will be lodged only when the Court Office opens on the day of the application. Take care if you are told that your application will be heard by the judge at 10.00 am as most County Court Offices do not open until that time and it will be difficult to lodge the papers at the Court Office and be heard by the judge at the same time (particularly if the judge is not sitting in the same building as the Court Office). Obviously appearing before the judge is likely to be more important than issuing the proceedings, as an undertaking to issue forthwith can be given to the judge if an injunction is granted. The documents required will be as in the Chancery Division.

28.7.2   PROCEDURE AT THE HEARING

In the Chancery Division the hearing will normally be in open court with counsel wearing their robes and the procedure will be the same as for other applications (see **Chapter 30**). The applications judge normally goes through the applications in the order in the Daily List for that day to ascertain which are 'effective' (i.e., agreement has not been reached between the parties on all the matters in dispute) and which are 'ineffective' and in each case the time estimate for the application. The judge is likely to indicate the order in which he or she will dispose of the applications when he or she has gone through the list that first time.

In the Queen's Bench Division and the Commercial Court the hearing will be in private with counsel not wearing their robes. The judge will normally allow you to address him or her seated.

In the County Court applications are usually heard in private but the practice varies from court to court so you should ensure that you have your robes with you in case they are needed.

You should open your application by briefly describing the injunction you seek such as, 'My Lord [or 'My Lady'], this is an application for an injunction without notice restraining a trespass to the claimant's land . . .'. The judge should be taken to:

(a)   the statements of case or draft statements of case to show the cause of action;

(b)   to the evidence or draft evidence in support of the application and to any exhibits; and

(c)   to the draft order which is sought indicating, if necessary, that only certain parts of the order are being sought at the without notice stage. The formal parts (e.g., any undertaking to issue and the undertaking as to damages) can usually be dealt with very briefly.

If the judge has read the papers in advance (do not be afraid to ask whether that is the situation) you may not be required to go through the statement of case or evidence.

It should not be necessary to explain to the judge the test to be applied if you are relying upon *American Cynamid* v *Ethicon* [1975] AC 396. You should be familiar with the recent decision of *Series 5 Software Limited* v *Philip Clarke & others* [1996] FSR 273 which reconsiders or explains the factors to be taken into account in granting an injunction. If your case falls within an exception to the test in those cases, you may have to explain why it is exceptional and the test which is then to be applied.

You should end your submissions by asking the judge to make an order in the terms of the draft. There is almost always discussion about the draft order before the judge announces what order, if any, he or she is prepared to make. If you are seeking several different orders you should be able to link each part of the order sought to the evidence justifying the part of the order. For example, if you are seeking a freezing injunction and want an order that evidence be sworn setting out the defendant's assets, you may have to explain why the order requires that a particular officer of the company is to swear the evidence.

There will often be discussion about the duration of the without notice order. Liberty to apply to the court on specified notice to your solicitors to vary or discharge the order is almost always given. You should remember to put the name, address, telephone and facsimile numbers of your solicitors in the draft order when dealing with liberty to apply (in a freezing injunction or search order an out of hours contact number is frequently required to be given). Even where liberty to apply is given, the court may still wish to fix a date for further consideration of the order which will then appear in the order itself (a return date). In the Chancery Division and in the County Court it is still common practice to fix a date for further consideration of the order. In the Queen's Bench Division and in the Commercial Court it is less common to fix a date for further consideration, the liberty to apply provision being thought adequate for most cases.

The judge will then announce the terms of the order which he or she is making. It is rare for anything approaching a formal judgment to be given for a without notice application. The judge will normally merely state that an order is being made in the terms of the draft order, as amended in some stated respects.

If you are refused any form of without notice relief you can still properly ask for permission to serve an application on short notice. If such an order is given the judge will normally specify that there be a with notice hearing on a particular day provided that you serve the defendant quickly, often by a stated time later that day.

If you obtain any injunction or an order for short service you must deal with costs. Normally at this stage costs should be reserved to the return date (if any) or to the trial. If you are refused both the injunction and permission to serve on short notice there will be little point seeking any with notice costs order.

Your solicitors will have to arrange for the order to be drawn up and sealed by the court (except in the Chancery Division and County Court where the orders are drawn up by the court itself). In every case your solicitors will have to arrange for service of the order, normally personal service of an order indorsed with a penal notice.

28.7.3 PROCEDURE AT THE HEARING FOR FREEZING INJUNCTIONS AND SEARCH ORDERS

Freezing injunctions and search orders are, by their very nature, orders which are almost invariably required without giving any notice to the defendant. The procedure when applying for a freezing injunction and/or search order will be similar to that for any other without notice injunctions.

The procedure has been made much more straightforward as a result of the adoption of standard form orders for both types of injunction (CPR, PD 25 (Interim Injunctions)). The following additional points should be noted:

(a) if a defendant is outside the jurisdiction you will have to satisfy the requirements of Council Regulation (EC) No. 44/2001, so that service outside the jurisdiction can be effected without permission or you must obtain permission when you obtain the injunction;

(b) great care should be taken in giving full and frank disclosure as most of the applications to discharge for breach of this duty arise in freezing injunction and search order cases and the court seems to take an even more stringent view of the duty than it does with less Draconian orders;

(c) there is normally a requirement to inform third parties of a freezing injunction order which affects them and to pay any costs of the third party in complying (such as the costs of a bank inquiring whether the defendant holds any accounts and whether those accounts are in credit);

(d) a freezing injunction order should normally have a maximum sum to which the injunction applies (calculated by reference to the proper value of the claimant's claim);

(e) a freezing injunction order should allow the defendant to draw reasonable living expenses and legal costs up to a stated sum, often with a proviso that the sum can be increased by written agreement between the parties' solicitors to save the time and expense of applying to the court for every variation of that amount;

(f) in both freezing injunction and search order cases the variety of ancillary orders is extremely wide and needs to be considered with great care particularly if a writ *ne exeat regno* is sought (see **28.7.4**).

Although the adoption of standard form orders has made the task of preparing the draft order simpler, the standard wording may not always be appropriate. It seems that the judges of the Queen's Bench Division are more prepared to vary the standard wording than other judges and some commonly accepted variations can be found in the editorial notes in the *White Book*. In error the standard forms make no provision for costs.

28.7.4 PROCEDURE AT THE HEARING FOR A WRIT *NE EXEAT REGNO*

The prerogative writ *ne exeat regno* is not strictly available merely as an ancillary order to another injunction such as a freezing injunction. It is for this reason that the court has used the general s. 37 power in cases such as *Re Oriental Credit* (see **28.3**). The requirements for the writ are:

(a) that the defendant would have been liable to arrest prior to the Debtors Act 1869;

(b) that a good cause of action exists for at least £50;

(c) that there is probable cause for believing that the defendant is about to leave England unless arrested; and, crucially,

(d) that the defendant's absence will materially prejudice the claimant in the prosecution of his action.

Now that an established a freezing jurisdiction exists which can, in appropriate cases, be extended worldwide, it will be exceptionally difficult to establish that each of the four criteria is established. The final criterion has been interpreted as restricting the use of the writ to the period before any judgment as thereafter it is judgment and not the action which is being prosecuted.

The application is made without notice and, if the above criteria are fulfilled, the writ will be issued addressed to the Tipstaff of the High Court requiring him or her to bring the defendant before the court as soon as possible so that any appropriate further order can then be made by the court.

28.8 The Opposed Without Notice Application

As it is now possible to send documents considerable distances very quickly by facsimile there is an increasing tendency (particularly in the Chancery Division) to notify a defendant or proposed defendant that application is being made for an order without notice. This practice is not used where giving the defendant prior notice of the order will enable him or her to defeat it (e.g., in most freezing injunction and search order cases).

At an opposed without notice application the role of the defendant will be either to sit silently and take no active part in the proceedings, or to treat the hearing as a hearing with notice even if there has been no time in which to prepare evidence in answer. A defendant given notice of a hearing faces a considerable dilemma. If the defendant takes an active part in the hearing he or she may encourage the court to make an order at that stage by, for example, being wholly unable to offer any explanation for some apparently obvious wrongful or unlawful act. If the defendant fails to attend or takes no part it may appear to the court that the defendant has little interest in the outcome of the application. Finally, by attending, there may be additional pressure on the defendant to offer some undertakings rather than face the prospect of an injunction being granted.

The main disadvantage to the claimant in giving notice is that if the application is dismissed the claimant is likely to be ordered to pay the defendant's costs whereas, if the application were made without giving notice the claimant would only be responsible for his or her own costs.

28.9   Applications to Vary or Discharge

An order may be made (whether with or without notice) giving liberty to the defendant and to third parties to apply to vary or discharge the order. If there is to be a hearing with notice shortly after the without notice hearing you are less likely to find an express power to apply to discharge.

In some circumstances application may be made without notice to vary or discharge an injunction but the power will only be used in cases which are exceptionally urgent.

If there is an application to vary or discharge the injunction or some parts of the order, it should be supported by evidence setting out the reasons for the variation or discharge. The application can be made simply by giving notice but the usual course is to issue an application. The other documents required will be those used at the initial hearing, save that the draft order will be an actual order of the court. If time permits there may be further evidence from the claimant. There are three main reasons for seeking an early variation or discharge:

(a)   that there has been some non-disclosure by the claimant which entitles the defendant to have the order set aside;

(b)   that the injunction should be varied or discharged because of some facts not known to the court or the claimant at the time of the grant of the order; and

(c)   that the defendant wishes the court to impose conditions upon the continuation of the injunction (such as security for the undertaking as to damages).

Applications for discharge are sometimes made at a much later stage (e.g., if the claimant having obtained the injunction does not proceed diligently with the action or because of a change in circumstances).

At the hearing of the application to vary, the defendant should have the right to open and close his application. The judge may be prepared to treat the hearing as if it were any return date already set and then dispense with a further with notice hearing making the injunction (whether or not varied) continue to trial or further order. The judge will consider all the evidence and determine whether the injunction should be set aside or varied using the same approach as on any return date.

28.10 Applications With Notice

The procedure will differ according to whether there is an order without notice in place and whether the same judge deals with the with notice hearing. If there was an order without notice and it is the same judge hearing the with notice application, it may be possible to introduce the evidence leading to the grant of the order without notice very briefly leaving it to the defendant to explain why the order should not be continued until trial or further order. If you have a different judge, or if there was no without notice hearing or order, it will be necessary for the claimant to deal with the case more fully.

The hearing of the with notice application will have been fixed when the application was issued.

Once counsel for the claimant has introduced counsel for the other parties, the nature of the application should be explained briefly. The statements of case should be explained to show the causes of action relied upon. Unless the judge indicates that it is unnecessary, the next stage is to explain the evidence before the court. Counsel for the claimant should take the judge through the evidence in support without comment (which may mean reading it out to the judge), the evidence in opposition should be gone through by counsel for the defendant(s) without comment, finally any evidence in reply should be gone through by counsel for the claimant. When the evidence stage has been completed counsel should make their submissions. Counsel for the claimant should address the court in support of the orders sought, going through the proposed order in detail. Counsel for the defendant(s) will then answer (if called upon to do so). Finally (if called upon to do so), counsel for the claimant can reply. The reply should not be merely a repetition of the opening submission but should address the points made by counsel for the defendant(s).

It may be possible for counsel to agree before the hearing what test should be applied by the court. It should not be necessary to explain to the judge the test to be applied if you are relying upon *American Cynamid* v *Ethicon* [1975] AC 396. You should be familiar with the decision of *Series 5 Software Limited* v *Philip Clarke & others* [1996] FSR 273 which reconsiders or explains the factors to be taken into account in granting an injunction. If your case falls within an exception to the test in those cases, you may have to explain why it is exceptional and the test which is then to be applied.

In many cases there will be discussion between counsel over the possibility of the application being disposed of by the parties giving undertakings (see **28.12**). If undertakings are offered in lieu of an injunction it should be made clear whether the offer is an open one (i.e., one which can be mentioned to the judge) or is made 'without prejudice' (i.e., may only be used on any questions of costs).

In many cases that strict sequence of events for a with notice hearing will be varied at the behest of the judge who will have particular questions or issues which he or she wishes counsel to deal with as they arise. The result may be that the evidence stage becomes muddled with the submissions stage. If the judge announces that he or she is going to grant an injunction there may be further discussion about the wording at that stage, even though it may already have been dealt with in submissions. In a complex case counsel may be asked to prepare a form of wording which reflects what the judge ordered.

Finally, the judge will need to deal with the costs of the injunction. See **Chapter 34**. If costs were reserved to this hearing it is important that they are mentioned to the court.

28.11 The Order

It is extremely important that the order is clearly worded so that the defendant will know exactly what he or she can or cannot do. In the County Court the wording of orders has been changed after the experimental work carried out on the North Eastern Circuit. The word 'forbidden' is now used instead of 'restrained' and 'servants or agents' has disappeared when the defendant is an individual rather than a firm or company.

The order should also contain a penal notice. The penal notice is the warning which tells the defendant that he or she must obey the order or be guilty of contempt of court for which he or she may be sent to prison. In the County Court the wording now appears in bold immediately after the name and address of the defendant to whom the order is addressed.

28.12 Undertakings

At any hearing attended by the party against whom the injunction is sought, an offer may be made of an undertaking in lieu of an injunction. Such an offer is almost invariably given without any admission of liability. An undertaking is a promise to the court to do or refrain from doing some stated act or acts. It is enforceable in the same way as an injunction.

When undertakings are given in lieu of an injunction there is sometimes a dispute as to whether the party seeking the order has to give the undertaking as to damages. The practice in the Chancery Division is that a cross-undertaking as to damages will be given unless the contrary is expressly agreed at the time. No similar presumption applies in the Queen's Bench Division or the County Court so any cross-undertaking must be recorded in any order.

Just as a party may apply to vary or discharge an injunction, application may be made to be released from an undertaking given. The application should be made in the usual way, with evidence in support, explaining the basis for the application (e.g., that there has been a change in circumstances or that there has been unnecessary delay by the claimant in prosecuting the action).

TWENTY NINE

APPLICATIONS TO STRIKE OUT FOR WANT OF PROSECUTION

29.1 Introduction

The court has the power to strike out an action for want of prosecution where there has been delay in progressing the action to trial. This chapter deals with High Court applications to strike out for want of prosecution. The procedural timetable previously imposed by CCR O. 17, r. 11, in the County Court together with the provision for automatic striking out in the event that a hearing date was not requested within 15 months of the commencement of the timetable, means that such applications are rarely made in the County Court. If you are instructed in such an application the same principles and approach should be adopted as in the High Court. The logistics in terms of reporting to the usher, filling in slips and the documents available to the district judge from the court file will be different. The introduction of the Civil Procedure Rules 1998 with greater control and case management powers vested in the Court and tougher sanctions for failure to comply with procedural steps timeously, should lead to the demise of these applications.

29.2 In the High Court

In the High Court the application is made by application notice (CPR, Part 23) to the Master. In the Queen's Bench Division the application will initially be given a date in the general list. These applications should be dealt with in less than 20 minutes. It is highly unlikely that a contested application to strike out for want of prosecution can be dealt with in that time. Your solicitors should have arranged a private room appointment. If they have not done so you should advise them to do so unless you think that it can be dealt with in 20 minutes. There is no point in you turning up and running up the costs in the process if the application should be adjourned to a private room appointment. If it is in the general list you should check that it is in counsel's list. If the application is in the solicitor's list and objection is taken to your presence the application will be adjourned with your side paying the other side's costs of the adjournment. These points should be checked as soon as the brief arrives on your desk. Do not assume that your solicitor has made all the necessary arrangements. In the Chancery Division the principles canvassed below still apply but the venue is different.

29.3 The Test

Before the Civil Procedure Rules, the court would ordinarily only strike out an action for want of prosecution if:

(a) there has been inordinate and inexcusable delay on the part of the claimant or his or her lawyers; and

(b) that delay:

   (i) will give rise to a substantial risk that it is not possible to have a fair trial of the issues in the action; or

   (ii) is likely to have caused serious prejudice to the defendant.

It is not the purpose of this chapter to set out and explain the principles of law applicable to such applications. You will find a useful summary of the relevant principles in *Trill* v *Sacher* [1993] 1 WLR 1379 at p. 1398 onwards, but note, however, that principle (7) is no longer correct in the light of the House of Lords decision, *Roebuck* v *Mungovin* [1994] 2 WLR 290. You should also read and be familiar with the notes that appear at paragraphs 25/L/1 to 25/L/22 in the *White Book* (1999 edition).

The extent to which the Civil Procedure Rules 1998 and the ethos underlying them will alter the court's approach has yet to be determined. There is nothing in the Civil Procedure rules of direct application to striking out for want of prosecution which remains an exercise of the court's inherent jurisdiction to control its own proceedings. Nevertheless claimants can probably expect to receive less sympathy than prior to the introduction of the Civil Procedure Rules, see, for example, *Shikari* v *Malik*, *The Times*, 20 May 1999.

In *Biguzzi* v *Rank Leisure plc* [1999] 1 WLR 1926, Lord Woolf gave some guidance on how the Civil Procedure Rules would apply to applications to strike out for want of prosecution. The test set out above will no longer be rigorously applied and the previous authorities are of little value as an indicator of when an action ought to be struck out. The test was reduced to the 'simple' question 'Is there anything unfair in letting the case proceed to trial?'. That question has to be answered with an eye on the overriding objectives and the list of factors set out in CPR, r. 3.9. It is likely that a case which would not have satisfied the 'old' test will be struck out under the new test. Equally, the broader range of sanctions and controls over proceedings now given to the court may mean a lesser sanction than strike out might be applied. Each case will turn on its own facts. Although the Civil Procedure Rules will apply to the hearing of the application and result in a decision taken against a CPR background, the conduct of the litigation before the introduction of the Civil Procedure Rules falls to be judged against the rules, practices and procedures applicable at that time.

It will be apparent from the statement set out at the beginning of this section that there were two distinct inquiries that the court had to conduct before striking out an action for want of prosecution. The first relates to delay and the second to the consequences of the delay. These two factors set the structure for the application. You must first ascertain whether there has been delay and, if so, whether it is excusable, when the period(s) of delay occurred and how long the period(s) of delay lasted. It is only after those issues are dealt with that you can look at the effect of the delay that is inordinate and inexcusable to see whether **that delay** gives rise to a substantial risk that a fair trial will not be possible or a serious risk of prejudice to the defendant. Under the Civil Procedure rules the rigid approach is no longer required and any delay giving rise to prejudice may result in a strike out if that is the only way to do justice between the parties.

Where the delay is substantial it may amount to an abuse of the process of the court with the result that the action may be struck out even if the requirements set out in (b)(i) and (ii) above are not satisfied and the limitation period has not yet expired (see *Grovit* v *Doctor* [1997] 1 WLR 640 and *Arbuthnot Latham Bank* v *Trafalgar Holdings* [1998] 1 WLR 1426.

29.3.1 DELAY AND THE LIMITATION PERIOD

When your brief arrives on your desk in chambers you need to look at it straightaway. You should check whether or not the limitation period has expired. If it has not it is unlikely that the court will strike out the action, as there will be nothing to stop the claimant starting a fresh action with the result that the final trial and resolution of the dispute will be even further in the future than would otherwise be the case. The position may be otherwise if the delay can be characterised as an abuse of process. You should check that the evidence before the court includes a suitable chronology from your point of view. You should check whether there is adequate evidence relating to the consequences of the delay alleged by the defendant and whether the evidence can or should be bolstered in any way by a further witness statement. There is no point in sitting down to prepare the brief the day before the hearing only to discover that some further enquiries could have been made or some further evidence could have been put before the court which would have strengthened your position. The majority of applications that fail do so because there is inadequate evidence of the consequences of the delay, or the court is not persuaded that the consequences are so serious that the action should be dismissed. It is difficult to do anything, beyond the power of your own advocacy, to avoid the latter but it is often easy to do something to remedy the former.

29.3.2 A CHRONOLOGY AND SKELETON ARGUMENT

If your brief does not contain a suitable chronology you must prepare one yourself and be ready to give it to the Master at the beginning of the hearing. If you can do so, as a matter of professional courtesy you should send a copy to your opponent before the hearing so that he or she has a chance to consider and agree it. Treat your opponent as you would wish him or her to treat you. A **suitable chronology** means one that presents the history of the action in the best possible light from your client's point of view but without misleading the court. From the defendant's point of view the chronology should ideally show lengthy periods of time between the various stages of the proceedings with not a lot happening in between. Such steps as the claimant takes which are inadequate in terms of progressing the action should be identified. The defendant's chronology is likely to concentrate on the various procedural stages of the litigation process. It should also help the Master to focus on the consequences of the delay that the defendant relies on; so, for instance, if an important witness dies, the date of his death should appear in the chronology, and if allegations raised in the action are only raised for the first time long after the cause of action accrued, the date and nature of the allegations raised should appear in the chronology. On the other hand if the important witness died before the onset of delays in the prosecution of the action, it is difficult to attribute any prejudice arising from death of the witness to the claimant's delay.

From the claimant's point of view the chronology should give the impression that the claimant has been busy getting on with the action albeit the defendant may not have been aware of the industry involved. The chronology should also highlight those factors which might excuse the claimant's delay. For example, a chronology prepared by the defendant may show that there has been a substantial delay in giving disclosure of documents relating to a claimant's loss of earnings in a personal injury action. The claimant's chronology may well show that this period has been taken up with writing numerous letters to the claimant's employers to obtain the relevant documentary evidence and that the employers are responsible for the delay rather than the claimant or his legal advisers. It is important to retain a sense of proportion; a chronology that refers to each and every letter written by the claimant's solicitors may lose its impact if it is so detailed that the Master cannot quickly achieve an overall grasp of how the action has been progressing.

Any chronology must include the date upon which the cause of action accrued, the date upon which the proceedings were issued and the date upon which they were served. The latter two dates are not the same and may be months apart. From the defendant's point of view the first he or she knows of the commencement of the proceedings will be when the claim form is served upon him or her.

In all but the most straightforward applications you will need to prepare a skeleton argument.

29.4   Before the Hearing

Before entering the Master's room, counsel for the defendant should make sure that the application notice and the defendant's witness statements and exhibits are readily available to be handed to the Master at the outset. Counsel for the claimant should also ensure that the claimant's witness statements and exhibits are readily to hand to give to the Master when required. Counsel should also ensure that there is a bundle comprising the writ (issued before the introduction of the Civil Procedure Rules) or the claim form (post CPR) and any statements of case in the action which can also be handed to the Master. In the High Court none of the statements of case are filed at court and unless you give them to the Master he or she will not be able to see what the issues in the action are. Counsel for the parties should ensure that they have completed the slip identifying the protagonists. The slip is usually to be found in a little box on the outside of the Master's door and should be handed to the Master when the parties enter the room. If the application is in the general list there will be an usher who will collect the relevant details and hand out a slip to be filled in and returned.

29.5   The Hearing

29.5.1   INTRODUCTIONS

Counsel for the defendant who issued the application notice should begin by introducing those who appear before the Master for the various parties. There is no need to introduce your solicitors, just yourself and other counsel present. If one of the parties is represented by a solicitor only, you should introduce him or her too. By convention other counsel are introduced as 'my learned friend' whereas solicitors are simply 'my friend'. You could instead introduce the solicitor as 'Mr Speed of Messrs Wright, Sloe and Stops the solicitors for the second defendant'.

29.5.2   THE OPENING

Having advised the Master from whom he or she can expect to hear, you should then move on to explain what you are there for. You simply tell the Master what the application is about, e.g., 'Master, as you will see from the application notice, this is an application by the defendant to strike out the claimant's claim for want of prosecution'.

You are now embarking on opening the application to the Master. The opening should be neutral and should inform the Master what the case is about and outline the nature of the issues which the application involves. It is often the defendant's first opportunity to lay the foundations for the submissions that he or she will make after the evidence has been dealt with. It also gives counsel for the defendant an opportunity to undermine the claimant's arguments before they are heard by the Master. You should already have a good understanding of what the claimant is likely to say based on his or her evidence. You should not strive to do so to the extent that your opening becomes overtly partisan. If you are representing the claimant and your opponent is making a lot of comments relating to submissions of the parties, you might whisper to him or her in a voice sufficiently loud for the Master to hear that he or she should save their submissions for closing speeches and get on with opening the case.

By the time the opening has finished the Master should be able to embark on reading the evidence with a real understanding of the case and the questions that he or she will have to decide. A good opening should set out in a logical order the information that needs to be fed to the Master to help him or her understand the case, hopefully from your point of view. The following sets out the sort of logical progression that is helpful. It is only an example and not a definitive or complete model to be followed come what may.

After finding out who is appearing before him or her and what the application relates to, the Master will want to know what sort of action he or she is being asked to strike out. You should try and work out a way of formulating a short introduction which tells the Master the nuts and bolts of the claim and how it arises, e.g.:

In the action the claimant claims damages for personal injury. The claimant was formerly employed by the defendant at his factory in Toytown as a press operator. The defendant is a manufacturer of car body panels. The claimant was injured on 4 March 1990 when he caught his arm in the press he was supposed to be operating. As a result of the accident his arm was amputated at the elbow. He did not return to work after his accident and on 24 December 1990 he was dismissed from his employment with the defendant.

Whilst dealing with the accident you can expand the information available by outlining the parties' allegations and contentions. It is important to establish what these are because the risk that it is not possible to have a fair trial, or the existence of serious prejudice to the defendant will usually relate to the issues that are thrown up in the action and how they will be proved or established at the trial. At this point you might give the Master the particulars of claim and defence so that he or she can see what the pleaded issues are. Again you should be able to set out the issues very shortly, e.g.:

The claimant alleges that the accident was caused by the defendant's failure to maintain properly the guards and safety cutout switches on the pressing machine so that it was capable of being operated when the claimant's arm was still in it. Latterly the claimant has alleged that he and another employee, Mr Cotton, were both trying to remove an extra sheet of metal from the machine when the guards were down and it was ready for action and Mr Cotton inadvertently pressed the button to start the machine. The defendant contends that the machine was in perfect working order at the time of the accident and that the accident was caused by the claimant attempting to retrieve a sandwich from the machine after it had already started its action. Mr Cotton had, as something of a prank, thrown the claimant's sandwiches into the machine. The defendant's health and safety regulations specifically direct employees not to take food on to the factory floor and to keep it in their lockers adjacent to the canteen and rest rooms.

At this point one might begin to set up the points which prejudice the defendant so that the Master can see where the argument is likely to go. As an example the opening might carry on with the following:

The press was inspected the next day by an expert engineer, Mr Flat. His inspection disclosed no fault with the machine at all and he concluded that it was in perfect working order. Regrettably Mr Flat died in a road traffic accident in December 1997. The machinery accident was also witnessed by the defendant's foreman, Mr Snoop, who saw Mr Cotton throw the claimant's sandwiches into the machine. Mr Snoop suffered a stroke in April 2000 and it appears unlikely that he will live for more than another six months.

The Master will need to know how the claim has been conducted and what steps have been taken in the action. At this stage the chronology comes into its own. You should be able to take the Master to it and use it as a skeleton for this part of your opening. You should mark your own copy with the various dates by which things should have been done so that you can, in opening the case, explain to the Master what should have happened and when it should have happened, in contrast with what did in fact happen and when it did in fact happen. Your opening might carry on along the following lines:

Master, if I can take you to the chronology you will see that the accident occurred on 4 March 1990. The claimant's trade union instructed solicitors who wrote to the defendant's insurers on 19 March 1991 intimating a claim for negligence and breach of statutory duty and alleging that the machine and in particular its guards and safety switches were not maintained in proper working order. **Not much happened thereafter until** the claimant issued the writ on 3 September 1992 **some six**

months before the expiry of the limitation period. The writ was served on 2 January 1993 **shortly before its validity lapsed**. The defendant gave a notice of intention to defend on 12 January 1993. **Pursuant to Order 18 Rule 1 of the Rules of the Supreme Court the claimant should have served his statement of claim within 14 days i.e., by 26 January 1993. In fact** the statement of claim was not served until 28 November 1993 when **for the first time** references were made by the claimant to Mr Cotton assisting him to remove a sheet of metal from the press and alleging that Mr Cotton started the machine when it was unsafe to do so as the claimant's arm was still within it.

In a perfectly neutral opening the emphasised words might well be omitted. By making those points in opening, counsel for the defendant can begin to create a prima facie impression that the claimant has been laggardly in his conduct of the action to the prejudice of the defendant, without going so far as to give an unduly partisan opening or making submissions which should be saved for closing speeches.

The opening should conclude with a short résumé identifying the period of delay relied on by the defendant and the prejudice that makes it unjust to allow the claim to continue. You should be stating the conclusion you want the Master to reach and not all the arguments that lead to the conclusion. It may help you to arrive at a good formulation if you try to write down in two short sentences the substance of your argument on prejudice. In the present opening you might well conclude with, e.g.:

There has been four years of delay in the prosecution of the claim. In that time the defendant's expert witness has died and therefore can no longer be called to give evidence at the trial and an important witness of fact, Mr Snoop, has suffered a stroke which has impaired his memory. Given the rate of progress to date it is likely that Mr Snoop will die before the trial of the claim. Had this claim progressed with proper speed the trial should have been over and done with five years ago in 1995.

29.5.3 THE EVIDENCE

It is then time to move on to the evidence. The defendant's evidence should be read first. Counsel should enquire whether the Master wishes to hear it read out aloud or merely to read it for himself or herself. You will often see the Master skimming through the evidence leaving you with the impression that he or she has not read it as carefully as you did in preparing your brief and that he or she may not have appreciated the nuances that appear in it. As part of your preparation you must be thoroughly familiar with the evidence and where the important points are made. You may well be asked simply to take the Master to the meat of the witness statement or to deal simply with the question of prejudice or risk that a fair trial is not possible. Counsel should then give way to counsel for the claimant who should take the Master through the claimant's evidence. Counsel for the defendant can then take the Master through any evidence in reply.

If the Master indicates that he or she wishes to hear you read the witness statements (highly unlikely), you can start by saying, 'Mr Smith says at paragraph . . . as follows' and just read on with the evidence. You should avoid reading aloud as fast as possible in monotone speech. The likely effect is that the Master will not be reading with you and may well doze off. You should modulate the pitch and tone of your voice by placing emphasis where it is required, i.e., on the strong points which you wish to push home. You might also slow down a little when you reach a particularly important passage to make sure the Master follows it with you. You should read aloud clearly and distinctly at a speed which allows a half informed listener to take in what you are saying. The common error is to go too fast: it can be avoided by adopting the approach of telling a story rather than simply reading aloud.

You should not add comments or explanations as you go through your evidence nor should you interject with too many comments about your opponent's evidence. You should sit quietly and patiently awaiting your turn to speak. You might interject if both the Master and your opponent seem to be getting it horrendously wrong but any interjection should be helpful rather than adversarial. That does not mean you switch off. You should be listening to what is being said by your opponent and the Master. You should be watching to see how much of the evidence the Master appears to be absorbing and be alert to points which seem to sway him or her either for or against your opponent.

29.5.4 CLOSING SPEECHES

Counsel for the defendant goes first followed by counsel for the claimant and then counsel for the defendant in reply. Closing submissions should be structured. You should not just ramble through the evidence without saying what conclusions should be drawn nor why they should be drawn. The structure for your submissions is the structure canvassed above, i.e., (1) delay and (2) consequences. The same structure should be followed by both sides.

Counsel for the defendant should be seeking to maximise the periods of delay and undermine the excuses put forward by the claimant. For example, in the disclosure example considered above in dealing with chronologies, the defendant's riposte is that writing letters to the claimant's employer clearly was not achieving the desired end, that a summons for third party disclosure should have been issued and had the claimant done so the action could have moved on with no undue delay. A measure of the pace at which the action should have progressed can be taken from the interim timetable provided by the various old Rules of the Supreme Court governing the interim stages of the action. RSC O. 25, r. 8, contained automatic directions applicable to personal injury actions. Failure to follow the timetable amounts to delay which becomes inordinate once it becomes longer than one can reasonably allow. This part of the closing submission should conclude with a realistic appraisal of the period of time which amounts to inordinate and inexcusable delay. There is no point in putting forward an unrealistic suggestion as it may be taken to indicate that the rest of your arguments are similarly misconceived. You should then move on to deal with the prejudice that flows from that delay. This involves identifying the prejudice and then establishing a causal connection between the prejudice and the delay. Using the example opening, counsel for the defendant would argue that prejudice arises from the death of Mr Flat as he is no longer available to give evidence. You would need to acknowledge that there are likely to be reports and notes relating to his inspection that would be admissible under the Civil Evidence Act and go on to point out that the admissibility of those documents as evidence does not help at all with questions which arise outside the scope of the documents, nor does it help with the detail of what Mr Flat saw at the time or adequately deal with points which would otherwise have arisen in cross-examination. The defendant may well be unfairly handicapped at the trial if the claimant has a live, contemporaneous, expert witness and the defendant does not. Having established the nature of the prejudice the causal link can be established by pointing out that the trial should have taken place in 1995 and Mr Flat did not die until 1997, i.e., after the trial should have taken place in the ordinary course of events.

It is of the utmost importance to keep in mind that there are two things to establish: (i) prejudice or risk of an unfair trial; and (ii) caused by the delay. A good opening accompanied by a well drafted witness statement raising the right points, which has been well read and digested by the Master, may leave you with little to do beyond recapping the main points where delay has occurred, the adequacy of any excuse put forward and the prejudice that flows from it. If your application is based on serious prejudice within the limitation period accompanied by more than just minimal prejudice arising thereafter as a result of the delay, you must make sure that your closing submissions adequately canvass the serious prejudice that your side has suffered together with the prejudice suffered later.

Counsel for the claimant will probably have little to say on the delay as the facts tend to speak for themselves so far as what was done and when it was done. You may well find that the best way forward is to look at individual stages in the litigation with a view to arguing that the time taken for each stage was not unduly long or, if it was, the time taken was excusable. The best sort of excuse is that it was beyond the claimant's control or it was the defendant's fault. Again you should not simply assert that a particular period of delay was excusable, you must go on to refer to the evidence giving rise to the excuse so that your submissions explain why the delay was excusable. Having dealt with the delay, if there is some delay for which the claimant has to accept responsibility, counsel should deal with the questions of prejudice, risk to a fair trial and whether those factors were caused by the delay. You will need to look at the length of delay which you accept as relevant and also the periods of delay which the defendant contends is relevant. Just because the Master accepts the defendant's submissions as to the relevant period of delay does not mean that the defendant will establish the requisite degree of prejudice arising from that delay. In dealing with these substantive issues you must not lose sight of the fact that there must be **evidence** of the prejudice and evidence that it is caused by the delay. An assurance by the defendant's solicitor that the defendant has been prejudiced by the delay is not likely to be sufficient. In our example the witness statement should deal with the evidence that Mr Flat could have given and explain how the lack of that evidence damages the defendant's case. The claimant's submissions will generally follow this pattern depending on the contents of the witness statements:

(a) there is no inordinate delay;

(b) if there is, it is excusable;

(c) if it is not, there is no sufficient evidence of prejudice;

(d) if there is evidence of prejudice, there is no sufficient evidence that the prejudice is attributable to the delay;

(e) on the evidence of prejudice put forward by the defendant there is not in fact any prejudice caused to the defendant;

(f) on the evidence of causation the prejudice was not in fact caused by the delay;

(g) any prejudice is not sufficiently serious to warrant the striking out of the action;

(h) some lesser sanction such as payment of costs or limitation of interest recoverable is proportionate and just.

Questions of prejudice are rather like peeling the layers of an onion; e.g., the defendant says that Mr Flat is no longer available to give evidence; the claimant says that there is no serious prejudice as his report and notes are admissible in evidence, i.e., this is not a case where death deprives the defendant of admissible evidence; the defendant says that Mr Flat made no report and took no notes; the claimant says that prejudice is caused by Mr Flat's failure to make proper notes and compile a proper report, therefore there is no prejudice attributable to the delay; the claimant might well say 'instruct another expert' but that may be of no assistance if the machine does not still exist in the same form as at the time of the accident. Under the Civil Procedure Rules the court will take an overview rather than deal with details in this way.

Counsel for the claimant should be alert to look behind the prejudice alleged by the defendant to see whether it exists and what the real cause of it is. If the defendant has had an early opportunity to investigate the circumstances surrounding the accident and has good, contemporaneous witness statements available, it may be difficult to establish that he will be prejudiced by the delay: the witnesses will have plenty of material to refresh their minds about what did or did not happen. Industrial accidents are often well recorded and documented in compliance with the relevant Health and Safety at Work Regulations, rendering the quality of witness recollections at the trial of less significance. On the other hand if no proper investigations were undertaken by the defendant, the cause of any prejudice to the defendant may be his own failings rather than any delay on the claimant's part.

If the Master has been skimming through the evidence you should make sure that you cover all the evidence fully in your closing submissions by taking him or her to the important passages: instead of simply saying, '... as you will have seen from the claimant's witness statement ...', you should be more direct, 'Mr Speed states in paragraph 7 of his first affidavit that ...', then deal with what he says and then apply what he says to the submissions that you are making. You must take the evidence and use it to support the point you are trying to make.

29.5.5   JUDGMENT

After hearing your submissions the Master will, in the vast majority of cases, give a reasoned judgment there and then. You should take as full a note as possible of the judgment as it is delivered. You may not want to appeal whatever the outcome, however, your opponent may wish to do so. You can hardly agree a proper note of judgment if you did not take one yourself. You should also be listening carefully to the way in which the Master expresses himself or herself in dealing with the various issues in the application. By doing so you increase your prospects of working out what sort of point appeals to that particular Master or does not appeal to the particular Master and the sort of language to use in putting the point across. If you speak the same language as the Master the point is more likely to strike home. An important quality of a good barrister is knowing what sort of argument the court will swallow. As no two judges are the same you need to build up a store of knowledge about individual judges before whom you are likely to appear. It may not help you to win this application but it may help you next time you appear before the same Master.

29.5.6   COSTS

Please refer to **Chapter 34**.

29.5.7   THE ORDER

The Master will endorse the order he or she makes on the application notice. You should be clear about precisely what has been endorsed on it before you leave the room. If you think you might wish to appeal, you must ask for permission.

If the application fails, the Master will wish to review what needs to be done to get the case to trial as directed in the Civil Procedure Rules. Both sides need to be fully prepared to argue about how the claim should proceed and fully briefed about the time scale required to complete the procedural steps required to get the claim to a trial.

29.5.8   LEAVING THE ROOM

Before you leave you should ensure that the Master has handed back all the documents handed in, except the witness statements. The witness statements are filed with the court but the exhibits are returned to the custody of the solicitor to whom they belong. Courtesy costs nothing: make sure you thank the Master for dealing with your case, even if you think he or she has got it completely wrong. You should also consider whether an apology is merited from all concerned if the hearing has substantially overrun the allotted time. If it has, you should make a mental note to ensure that next time you give a more accurate time estimate.

29.6   Law and Lore

The vast majority of applications turn on their own facts as to delay and prejudice. It is most unlikely that a legal point will arise which requires any great explanation of the law in opening the case to the Master. You may well need to refer to authorities in your closing submissions to underline the points that you are making as to how the legal propositions should be applied. It is prudent to prepare your brief on the basis that the Master will be unfamiliar with the law: it will enhance your understanding of the area and your advocacy. You may draw a deputy Master on his or her first day in court in which case you may have to go back to basics and improve his or her understanding of the law.

There is one area of fertile debate which is partly a matter of law and partly a matter of fact. It relates to the adequacy of the evidence of prejudice and the extent to which the court can infer or rationalise the existence of prejudice from the existence of the delay. The principal reported authorities are *Hornagold* v *Fairclough Building Ltd* [1993] PIQR 400, *Rowe* v *Glenister & Sons* [1995] TLR 463, *Slade* v *Adco Ltd* [1995] TLR 650 and *Shtun* v *Zaljejska* [1996] 1 WLR 1270. Lore has it that substantial delay, more or less as night follows day, leads to diminution in witness recollections. The law tends to require some evidence of it. Under the Civil Procedure Rules it is likely that lore will prevail. In a perfect world one would hope to adduce evidence of what a witness could say when first proofed and what that witness could say at about the time the application to strike out is made. It leads to an unreal exercise in trying to extract from a witness what it is that they have forgotten and when they managed to forget it. The more balanced approach seems to be to put before the court sufficient material for the court to judge the importance of the 'lost' evidence and the likelihood that it will prejudice the defendant or create a risk of an unfair trial. Whether the evidence is sufficient or not is down to the power of your advocacy.

THIRTY

APPLICATIONS IN THE CHANCERY DIVISION

30.1 Chancery Division Proceedings

Claims involving Chancery business may be dealt with either in the High Court or in a County Court. CPR, PD 7, para. 2.5, defines 'Chancery business' as including any of the matters specified in the Supreme Court Act 1981, sch. 1, para. 1. The classes of claim specified in sch. 1, para. 1 are those relating to:

(a) the sale, exchange or partition of land, or the raising of charges on land;

(b) the redemption or foreclosure of mortgages;

(c) the execution of trusts;

(d) the administration of the estates of deceased persons;

(e) bankruptcy;

(f) the dissolution of partnerships and the taking of partnership or other accounts;

(g) the rectification, setting aside or cancellation of deeds or other instruments in writing;

(h) probate business, other than non-contentious or common form business;

(i) patents, trade marks, registered designs, copyright and design right;

(j) the appointment of a guardian of a child's estate; and

(k) the exercise of the High Court's jurisdiction under the companies legislation.

The Civil Procedure Rules and Practice Directions supplementing them contain information on Chancery Practice. Additional practical information may be found in the *Chancery Guide* (see the Chancery Division Website (www.courtservice.gov.uk)) and in practitioners' books.

30.1.1 APPLICATIONS

Any procedural application (e.g., for directions) should be made to a Master unless there is some special reason for making it to a judge. Otherwise the application may be dismissed with costs. CPR, Part 23, contains rules as to how an application may be made and it is worth noting that in some cases it can be dealt with without a hearing, or by a telephone hearing. Further details can be found in the **Civil Litigation Manual**, **Chapter 10**. An application is usually for interim relief although orders may be made which finally dispose of a question or issue in a proceeding (e.g., the vacation of a caution on a register of title, or the grant of a declaration). Only applications which need to be heard by a judge (e.g., most applications for an injunction) should be made to a judge and in such case, the application notice should state that it is a 'judge's application'.

30.2 Procedural Aspects

Unless an application is to be made without notice, or the court gives permission to the contrary, the documents which must be filed with the Listing Office are the Application Notice (minimum four copies where the proceedings involve one defendant and additional copies for further defendants), two copies of the proceedings and the Judges' Application Information Form (containing details of solicitors, counsel and parties etc.). The Application Notice must be served a minimum of three clear working days before the hearing (not including Saturday, Sunday or recognised holidays) and must not include either the day of service or the day of the hearing. If service is effected after 4 pm (fax service) or 5 pm (personal service), it is deemed to have taken place on the following working day.

Applications are generally heard in open court. Where it may be unjust for the application to be heard in public, the judge may exercise a discretion to sit otherwise than in open court.

30.2.1 SKELETON ARGUMENTS

The general rule is that for the purpose of all hearings before a judge skeleton arguments should be prepared. The exceptions are where the application does not warrant one, for example, because it is likely to be short, or where the application is so urgent that preparation of a skeleton argument is impracticable.

On judge's applications without notice, the skeleton argument should be filed with the papers which the judge is asked to read on the application. In more substantial matters, such as applications by order, they should be filed not less than two days before the hearing. In all other applications to a judge, including interim applications, they must be filed no later than 10 am on the day before the hearing. The arguments should be filed with the judge's clerk, if the name of the judge is known; otherwise filing is done at the listing office.

The *Chancery Guide* (Appendix 3) contains guidelines on the content of a skeleton argument. See also the **Civil Litigation Manual, 33.8**. Failure to lodge this document in accordance with the Guide may result in the matter not being heard on the scheduled date and/or disallowance of the costs of preparation and/or an adverse costs order (see the *Chancery Guide*, para. 7.30).

30.2.2 BUNDLES, TIME ESTIMATES AND READING LISTS

Bundles of documents for use in court will generally be required for all hearings if more than 25 pages are involved (and may be appropriate even if fewer pages are involved). The efficient preparation of bundles of documents is very important. Where bundles have been properly prepared, the case will be easier to understand and present, and time and costs are likely to be saved (*Chancery Guide*, para. 7.9). The representatives for all parties involved must co-operate in agreeing bundles for use in court. The court and the advocates should all have exactly the same bundles (para. 7.12). When parties agree a bundle of documents, they should also make clear whether they are simply agreeing the contents of the bundle or whether in addition they are agreeing that the documents may be treated as evidence of the facts stated (even if a Civil Evidence Act 1995 notice has not been given) and/or that the documents in the bundle are authentic (para. 7.13). Detailed guidelines on the preparation of bundles are set out in the *Chancery Guide*, Appendix 2. These should always be followed unless there is good reason not to do so.

The general rule is that the claimant/applicant must ensure that one copy of a properly prepared bundle is delivered at the Listing Office at least two clear days before the hearing of an application and at least seven days before a trial. However, the court may direct the delivery of bundles earlier than this. Where oral evidence is to be given, a second copy of the bundle must be available in court for the use of the witnesses. In the case of bundles to be used on Judge's Applications (other than applications by order), the bundles must be delivered to the Clerk to the Interim Applications Judge by 10 am on the morning preceding the day of the hearing unless the court directs otherwise (para. 7.16). When lodging the agreed bundles there should also be lodged a further agreed time estimate, together with an agreed reading list and an agreed time estimate in respect of that reading list. The time estimates and reading list must be signed by the advocates for the parties. Failing agreement as to the time estimates or reading list, then separate reading lists and time estimates must be submitted signed by the appropriate advocate (para. 7.17).

Where documents are copied unnecessarily or bundled incompetently, the cost may be disallowed. Where the provisions of the *Chancery Guide* as to the preparation or delivery of bundles are not followed, the bundle may be rejected by the court or be made the subject of a special costs order (para. 7.10).

If the case is one which does not require the preparation of a bundle, the advocate should check before the hearing starts that all the documents to which he or she wishes to refer and which ought to have been filed have been filed, and, if possible, indicate to the associate which they are (para. 7.18).

30.3 Conduct of Applications before the Judge

30.3.1 GENERAL

The interim applications judge is available to hear applications each day in term and an application notice can be served for any day in term except the last. If the volume of applications requires it, any other judge who is available to assist with interim applications will hear such applications as the interim applications judge may direct. Special arrangements are made for hearing applications out of hours and in vacation.

Counsel appearing on an application will be robed. Where the circumstances of a case require a 'short notice' period, permission to abridge time may be obtained on an application without notice, usually made after the mid-day adjournment.

The usual practice is that the judge will ascertain at the sitting of the court which of the listed applications will be 'effective', that is, disputed, and if so, what counsel's estimate of length is, or 'ineffective', that is, disposed of by agreement or which the parties wish to be adjourned. It is a matter of courtesy both to the court and to other counsel and litigants:

(a) to be present in court when the judge takes his or her seat;

(b) to be ready to say whether the application is 'effective' or 'ineffective';

(c) to have carefully considered the estimate of length (if the application is to be effective) and to have agreed that estimate with one's opponent;

(d) not to waste the time of the court when the judge is going through the list 'first time round' by explaining the substance of the application instead of simply indicating whether it is effective or ineffective.

Although the judge has a discretion as to the order of hearing applications, he or she will normally deal with ineffective applications first, e.g., matters which are to be adjourned or have been settled. Applications likely to take two hours or more will usually be given an order that they are given a subsequent fixed date for hearing (they are then called 'interim applications by order'). In these cases the judge will, at the first hearing, hear argument for any application for a court order to last until the application is heard fully. The hearing where the main application will be fully argued will be fixed through the solicitors or the clerks to counsel for all parties with the Clerk of the Lists. All other listed, unlisted and applications without notice will be heard in the order determined by the judge. Those affecting the liberty of a subject (e.g., for release from committal to prison for contempt, or for *habeas corpus*) are always accorded priority.

Counsel with effective applications may be asked to wait, in case another judge becomes free to hear the matter. The judge may transfer any application as deemed appropriate, irrespective of priority. Counsel should not leave the precincts of the court unless released by the judge until a particular time. Counsel should also ensure that the court staff can easily locate them if a judge becomes free. Any application which at the end of the day is part heard (i.e., unfinished), will normally head the list for the next court day.

30.3.2   TIME ESTIMATES

Time estimates are critical. The applications judge will determine only applications which are estimated to last less than two hours. Counsel will be required to lodge with the Chancery Listing Officer a written time estimate signed by the advocates for all the parties as soon as possible after the application notice has been lodged. An indication may be given that an application by order is to be treated as urgent. If it is apparent that it will be likely to last more than two hours, the only proper course is to inform the court that it is ineffective, and 'second time round' to inform the judge, 'This application is likely to occupy the court for two days, and I therefore ask your Lordship to stand it over as an interim application by order. Subject to your Lordship's approval, the defendant is to give certain undertakings in the meantime'.

30.3.3   UNLISTED AND EMERGENCY APPLICATIONS

Frequently, counsel is instructed to apply to the court urgently without notice so that the application has not been listed. It also happens that instructing solicitors sometimes forget to lodge the papers for applications on notice in accordance with the directions mentioned above. Counsel may in these circumstances ask the judge to hear the matter although unlisted. The judge's clerk should be notified (usually through counsel's clerk) as early in the day as possible, that an application is to be made, and two copies of the proceedings (showing the title of the action), and the draft of the order to be sought should be made available. If the proceedings have not yet been issued, every effort should be made to issue the claim form before the application is made. If this is not practical, the party making the application gives an undertaking to the court to issue the claim form forthwith. The usual practice is to rise in counsel's place after the judge has worked through the list for the first time, and to say, 'I have an unlisted application in the claim of Smith and Jones [giving the claim number]'. Such an application will only rarely be ineffective, and counsel should go on to indicate the time estimate. Unless the application affects the liberty of the subject or is of exceptional urgency and importance, listed applications will be given priority.

30.3.4   INEFFECTIVE APPLICATIONS

An application can only genuinely be described as 'ineffective' if there is *no point of disagreement between the parties which requires the decision of the judge*. Counsel must ensure that all such points have been dealt with, and not attempt to be heard first under the guise of an ineffective application. The degree of information which the judge will require to have on the substance of an application depends on the nature of the order which the court is to be asked to make. It is usual to indicate in very general terms the nature of the claim (e.g., 'This is an application for an injunction to restrain the defendant from dealing with certain land which is alleged to be subject to an option agreement'). Counsel will then usually inform the judge orally of the terms of the order which the judge is invited to make. If the order involves undertakings to the court or submission to an order (other than a purely procedural order) by one of the parties, the judge is likely to wish to know the exact terms of the undertakings. It is therefore not merely a formality to say 'The parties have agreed *subject to your Lordship's approval* that the application should stand over for 14 days on the defendant's undertaking not to dispose of the land known as [describing it]': the terms of the undertaking or an order in the same terms are subject to the approval of the judge.

30.3.5 EFFECTIVE APPLICATIONS

The order in which effective, i.e., disputed, listed applications are dealt with is in the discretion of the judge. Normally the judge will direct that the shorter applications be heard first. Naturally, this must not be abused by underestimating the time which the matter will take. The procedure will then follow this outline:

(a) Counsel presenting the application will open by giving a short account of the facts giving rise to the application.

(b) Counsel for the applicant then makes his or her submissions on the evidence as presented.

(c) Counsel for the respondent makes his or her submissions.

(d) Counsel for the applicant is entitled to reply to the submissions of the opposing party.

30.3.6 AGREED ADJOURNMENTS

If all parties to an application agree to do so, an application can be adjourned for not more than 14 days by attending the Chancery Listing Officer in Room W94 with signed consents from all parties before 4.00 pm on the day before the listed hearing. A litigant in person who is a party must attend before the Clerk as well as sign a consent. Not more than three successive adjournments may be made and no adjournments are to be made to the last two days of any sitting (*Chancery Guide*, para. 5.13). Undertakings previously given to the court may be continued unchanged over the duration of any adjournment. If an existing undertaking is to be varied or a new undertaking given, the adjournment must be dealt with by the judge.

An application may be adjourned to be heard as an application by order without attendance before the judge where the parties are agreed that the application will take two hours or more. The consents signed by all parties should also contain an agreed timetable for the filing of evidence or confirmation that no further evidence is to be filed. Any application arising from the failure of a party to abide by the timetable and any application to extend the timetable must be made to the judge. Interim Applications by Order will, initially at least, enter the Interim Hearings warned list on the first Monday after the close of evidence. See the *Chancery Guide*, para. 5.14.

30.3.7 DRAFTING OF ORDERS

It may often be possible for the court to prepare and seal an order more quickly if a draft of the order is handed in. Speed may be particularly important where the order involves the grant of an interim injunction or the appointment of a receiver without notice. In all but the most simple cases a draft order should be prepared and brought to the hearing.

The court may in any case direct the parties to agree and sign a statement of the terms of the order made by the court. Where a draft or an agreed statement of the terms of an order exists in electronic form, it is often helpful if the draft or agreed statement is provided to the court on disk as well as in hard copy, particularly if the order needs to be drawn quickly. Any disk supplied for this purpose must be new and newly-formatted before writing the material on it so as to minimise the risk of transferring a computer virus. The current word processing system used by the Chancery Associates is WordPerfect 5.1 for DOS. Where a judge directs that a statement of the terms of an order be agreed and signed, the agreed statement should be lodged in Room TM 3.07. Agreed statements will normally be adopted as the order of the court.

Orders will be drawn up by the court, unless the judge or Master directs that no order be drawn. Unless a contrary order is made, or the party concerned has asked to serve the order, a sealed order will be sent to each party.

30.3.8   USE OF INFORMATION TECHNOLOGY

The Civil Procedure Rules 1998 contain provisions about the use of information technology in the conduct of cases. No standard practice for its use in Chancery cases has yet evolved although this is likely to change over the next few years. In any case where the solicitors for one or more parties take the view that some form of IT will assist the presentation or management of a case, the solicitor should obtain at an early stage, directions from the judge who is to try the case. Where no nomination of a specific judge has yet been made, solicitors who wish to use any form of IT should invite the Vice-Chancellor (by request to his or her clerk) to nominate a judge to hear the case including all interim applications. The solicitors for all parties should try to agree a common protocol for the electronic exchange and management of information.

When skeleton arguments or chronologies exist in electronic form, inquiries should be made of the judge (via his or her clerk) as to whether the provision of these documents on disk as well as in hard copy would be welcome. Any disk supplied to a judge should be new and newly formatted to minimise the risk of transferring a computer virus.

The *Chancery Guide* contains specific provisions relating to transcripts, the use of fax and evidence by video-link. See Chapter 14, Use of Information Technology.

THIRTY ONE

THE COMPANIES COURT

31.1 Insolvency Proceedings: Winding-up Petitions

31.1.1 INTRODUCTION

A petition for the compulsory winding up of a company incorporated by registration under the Companies Acts may be presented by the company, or its directors, or by any creditor or creditors (including any contingent or prospective creditor or creditors), or by a contributory (i.e., shareholder) or contributories, various officials (e.g., Secretary of State for Trade and Industry and the Attorney General), administrators and administrative receivers, or by all or any of those parties, separately or together (Insolvency Act 1986, s. 124(1)). The matter most frequently encountered in the Companies Court is a creditor's petition for a compulsory winding-up order in respect of a company (see the **Company Law in Practice Manual**). An inexperienced advocate should beware of believing that such petitions present no difficulties simply because they are very numerous and usually undisputed. Before appearing on the hearing of such a petition, the advocate should study carefully the relevant provisions of the Insolvency Act 1986 and the Insolvency Rules 1986 (SI No. 1925) which will be referred to in this chapter as 'the Act' and 'IR 1986'. References to forms, by number, are references to the forms prescribed by the Rules. The Rules prescribe the form which a petition should take (see sch. 4, Form 4.2). Where written evidence is required, it may take the form of affidavits or witness statements verified by statements of truth (r. 7.57(5)). Generally the High Court and County Courts have concurrent jurisdiction and a petitioner may choose in which court to proceed.

31.1.2 EVIDENCE VERIFYING PETITION

The petitioner or someone with knowledge of the matters giving rise to the petition must file written evidence (in a witness statement or affidavit) verifying the petition (see Form 4.3, the Rules). The written evidence must state various facts and comply with IR 1986, r. 4.12. It must state that the allegations in the petition are true or are true to the best of the deponent's knowledge, information and belief.

31.2 The Court

High Court winding-up petitions are listed for hearing before the Registrar of the Companies Court sitting in open court on Wednesday mornings at 10.30 am. Petitions are listed in 30 minute batches, so that a number of matters will be found in the list marked 'not before 11.00' and so on. The Registrar is addressed as 'Sir'. In addition to counsel, solicitors and legal executives, properly robed, have a right of audience before the Registrar.

31.3 Petitions by Creditors

While petitions may be presented by a variety of parties mentioned above, the most common category of petitioners are creditors. To qualify as a creditor within the meaning of the Insolvency Act 1986, the petitioner must establish that a debt is due from the company to him or her which is not bona fide disputed on substantial grounds. Some creditors may be described as 'trade' creditors (meaning that their debts have been incurred in the course of the company's business). Others may be 'judgment' creditors where the company has failed to satisfy a judgment order made against it.

31.3.1 RESTRAINING PRESENTATION OF THE PETITION

If the company disputes the *locus standi* of the petitioner as a creditor, on the ground that the debt upon which a petition is to be or has been presented is disputed, the company may make an application to restrain the presentation or advertisement of the petition (which occurs after the petition has been served on the company). Such application must be made to the judge by the issue of an originating application (Form 7.1). See ***Company Law in Practice Manual***, **9.6**.

If the company fails to take such preventive steps, it may still dispute the petitioner's entitlement to a winding-up order on the ground that the debt is disputed by giving notice to the solicitors for the petitioner. Because of the danger of spurious disputes being used to defeat creditors, the Companies Court judges have introduced a practice of requiring the company in doubtful cases to make a payment into court of (or otherwise securing the amount of) the debt, pending an application for summary judgment by the petitioner.

31.4 Before the Hearing

The following is a checklist of the matters which must have been attended to by the instructing solicitors before the hearing. Counsel should ensure that he or she has copies of these documents in preparing the file for the hearing and that any defects which are found in them, e.g., inconsistent dates or sums owed, erroneous title of company in the advertisement, etc. are discussed with the solicitor before the hearing. If there has been non-compliance with the rules, remedial action will be required, as indicated after each point.

31.4.1 PETITION AND VERIFYING EVIDENCE

Counsel should have a copy of both of these documents.

31.4.2 EVIDENCE OF SERVICE

Service must be proved by written evidence in the form set out in Form 4.4 or 4.5. The text of the witness statement or affidavit should state the date on which the petition was served. It is a strict requirement that it must also specify the method of service used. Service of the petition and verifying written evidence must generally be effected at the company's registered office: IR 1986, r. 4.8(2). Permissible methods of service are set out in r. 4.8(3), which provides:

> Service of the petition at the registered office may be effected in any of the following ways—
> (a) it may be handed to a person who there and then acknowledges himself to be, or to the best of the server's knowledge, information and belief is, a director or other officer, or employee, of the company; or
> (b) it may be handed to a person who there and then acknowledges himself to be authorised to accept service of documents on the company's behalf; or
> (c) in the absence of any such person as is mentioned in sub-paragraph (a) or (b), it may be deposited at or about the registered office in such a way that it is likely to come to the notice of a person attending at the office.

If service by any of the above methods is not practicable, the petitioner may instead either:

(a) effect service at the company's last known principal place of business, under r. 4.8(4); or

(b) apply without notice by witness statement or affidavit for an order for substituted service under r. 4.8(6), (7);

The Court Manager of the Companies Court is authorised to deal with applications for substituted service.

The witness statement or affidavit of service should exhibit the petition and any order for substituted service (r. 4.9).

31.4.2.1 Remedies
If the written evidence of service is defective the court will have to be asked for an adjournment of the petition either:

(a) to file a fresh witness statement or reswear the affidavit, if the petition was properly served but the written evidence does not correctly state the facts or failed to specify the manner of service; or

(b) to effect reservice, if the petition has not been properly served.

If the company appears on the hearing, it may seek dismissal of the petition on the ground that it has been advertised after defective service. If the company has been properly served and appears at the hearing, a defect in the written evidence will cease to be relevant.

31.4.3 ADVERTISEMENT

Unless the court directs otherwise, each petition must be advertised once in the *Gazette* and contain certain required information as set out in IR 1986, r. 4.11. There is a prescribed form of advertisement (Form 4.6):

The advertisement of the petition must state—
(a) The name of the company and the address of its registered office, or
    (i) in the case of an unregistered company the address of its principal place of business;
    (ii) in the case of an oversea company, the address at which service of the petition was effected;
(b) the name and address of the petitioner;
(c) where the petitioner is the company itself, the address of its registered office or, in the case of an unregistered company, of its principal place of business;
(d) the date on which the petition was presented;
(e) the venue fixed for the hearing of the petition;
(f) the name and address of the petitioner's solicitor (if any); and
(g) that any person intending to appear at the hearing (whether to support or oppose the petition) must give notice of his intention in accordance with r. 4.16.

A copy of the advertisement should be included in the brief for counsel for the petitioner. Unless it is the company's own petition, the advertisement must have appeared not less than seven business days after service of the petition, nor less than seven business days (which do not include Saturdays, Sundays or bank holidays) before the hearing date (see IR 1986, r. 4.11(2)(b)). This is a most important requirement, as it enables the company to prevent the highly damaging consequences of advertisement by applying for an injunction if the petitioner's debt is disputed. Counsel should ensure that the advertisement complied with r. 4.11, that there are no printing errors in the advertisement, and the time requirements have been met.

31.4.3.1 Remedies
If the advertisement rules have not been complied with, the court may dismiss the petition. In the case of premature publication, if the publication is a day early, e.g., because of an innocent failure to count a bank holiday, the court may waive the defect.

Counsel should point out the premature advertisement, state the reason shortly, and ask that the defect be waived. There is always a serious risk that the petition will be dismissed on this ground.

If a court orders that a petition be re-served due to defective service, counsel should ask whether a second advertisement will also be required. If this is required, counsel may request that the required time periods be abated although this is at the discretion of the court.

31.4.4   CERTIFICATE OF COMPLIANCE

In order to assist High Court practitioners, the time laid down by IR 1986, r. 4.14 for filing a certificate of compliance and a copy of the advertisement has been extended to no later than 4.30 pm on the Friday before the hearing (PD Insolvency Proceedings, para. 3.1). A certificate of due compliance shows the dates of presentation, service, advertisement and hearing (Form 4.7), together with a copy of the advertisement. The present practice is to stand petitions out for 14 days to allow time to file the certificate where this has not been done in time. The Registrar will normally mention this matter as soon as the petition is called on.

31.4.5   LIST OF APPEARANCES

Every person including creditors or the company itself intending to appear on the hearing to support or oppose the making of a winding-up order must give notice to the solicitors for the petitioner not later than 4.00 pm on the business day before the hearing (IR 1986, r. 4.16). Failure to comply means that person cannot appear without the permission of the court. If the company intends to oppose the petition, its witness statement or affidavit must be filed in court not less than seven days before the hearing (IR 1986, r. 4.18). It is the duty of the petitioner's solicitors to prepare a list of the persons who have given such notice (Form 4.10, known formally as the 'list of appearances', informally in court as 'the list', and colloquially from its colour as 'the blue form'). The list must be handed in **before the hearing** (IR 1986, r. 4.17(3)). If it is not handed in, the Registrar will usually simply say when the petition is called on 'There is no list', and decline to proceed further.

31.4.5.1   Remedy

The only help for this is to make sure that the solicitors' representative is seen well before the time for which the petition is listed, and told to hand in the list when the current half-hour's petitions are over. If the list has not been handed in, ask the Registrar to 'take this matter second time round'.

31.5   Substitution

If the original petition is not proceeded with (because the petitioner withdraws), or is not advertised, or in other similar circumstances (see IR 1986, r. 4.19(1)), the court may, on such terms as it thinks just, substitute as petitioner any creditor or contributory who in the court's opinion would have a right to present a petition, and who is desirous of prosecuting it. The 'new' petitioner asks for a substitution order (see **31.7**, 'The Hearing', Counsel C below).

31.6   Noting the Back Sheet

It is helpful to compile the relevant information and the dates on which the required steps were taken for use as a quick guide during the hearing to avoid having to search through a file during the presentation. One example would be as follows:

Re: [name of company]
Trade creditors' petition based on a statutory demand in the sum of £_____
List: [enter any creditors, contributories, or others supporting/opposing the petition and the nature of their interest]
Co: [note whether the company will make an appearance]

Relevant dates:

Presented:	[e.g.,	27/4/02]
Verified:	[	28/4/02]
Served:	[	4/5/02]
Affidavit:	[	5/5/02]
Advert:	[	24/5/02]
Cert. Comp:	[	28/5/02]

UCO (Asking for the usual compulsory order)

31.7   The Hearing

The following applications may be heard in unopposed petition situations:

(1) Associate: 'Petition number 546, Tyro Advisers Limited.'
Counsel A
(for Petitioner):'This is a trade creditor's petition based on a statutory demand for the sum of £3,459- odd. The company is not represented, and the list is clear (or 'negative'). I ask for the usual compulsory order.'
Registrar: 'Usual compulsory order.'

(2) Associate: 'Petition number 547, D-I-Y Services Limited.'
Counsel B: 'This is a petition based on a statutory demand for unpaid solicitors' fees.'
Registrar: 'This petition was advertised only five business days after service, and r. 4.11 has not been complied with.'
Counsel B: 'Sir, I am instructed that my instructing solicitors unfortunately overlooked the fact that seven business days must elapse between service and advertisement, and therefore did not omit from their calculation of the time two weekends and a bank holiday. In those circumstances, I ask that the defect be waived.'
Registrar: 'No. These errors are capable of causing severe damage to a company which may wish to dispute the debt. There has been no effort in this case by the solicitors to cure the error, or to communicate with the court office in lieu of complying with r. 4.11. In the circumstances I propose to dismiss the petition.'
Counsel C: 'I appear for Suppliers Limited, a supporting creditor which has not given notice to the petitioner's solicitors prior to this hearing. My client has a trade debt amounting to £78,968 odd, and my application is for leave to be added to the list out of time and for an order substituting my client as petitioner.'
Registrar: 'I will give you leave to be added to the list out of time on the usual terms. I will also make an order substituting Miss C's client as the petitioner, and adjourn the matter for 28 days for amendment of the petition, re-service and re-advertisement.'

31.8   Notes on the Hearing

(a) It is usual to describe the basis of the petition and to show what is alleged to prove the inability of the company to pay its debts (in this case failure to comply with a statutory demand, but other evidence may also be adduced).

(b) The court is told whether the company is represented.

(c) The court should be informed whether there are any supporting or opposing creditors or contributories on the list of appearances, and if so, how many of each and whether any of them have in fact appeared at the hearing. If there are none, the court is told that the list is clear or 'negative'.

(d) The usual compulsory order is set out in Form 4.11. (See **Figure 9.3, *Company Law in Practice Manual*.**)

(e) The 'usual terms' on which a creditor is added to the list of appearances out of time are that the applicant's solicitor undertakes not to seek any costs of giving notice or of the application to be added to the list in the event of a compulsory winding up being made. (A substituted petitioner will normally obtain an order for the subsequent costs of amendment, re-service, re-advertisement, and hearing.)

31.9   Opposed Petitions

If it becomes apparent that the petition is opposed the Registrar will adjourn the matter for hearing before the judge.

31.10   Adjournments

If an order is made, the winding up commences with the presentation of the petition (s. 129(2) of the Act). Section 127 avoids dispositions of property of a company made after the commencement of the winding-up, unless the court has otherwise ordered (see ***Company Law in Practice Manual*, 9.7.**). For this reason, the court will not permit a petition to remain outstanding for protracted periods (except in the case of petitions by contributories, where a winding up is sought, the company is solvent, and the judge has made appropriate orders under s. 127). Even if the petitioner and the company have agreed that the company should have time to attempt to pay the petition debt, the court may refuse an adjournment if the petition has been current for a long period, and require the petitioner either to seek a winding-up order or withdraw his or her petition.

31.11   Rescission of a Winding-up Order

An application for the rescission of an order must be made within seven days after the date the order was made (IR 1986, r. 7.47(4)). Applications can only be made by a creditor, a contributory, or by a company jointly with a creditor or with a contributory. The application must be supported by written evidence of the company's assets and liabilities. If the petition is unsuccessful, the costs will normally be ordered to be paid by the petitioner.

THIRTY TWO

A GUIDE TO POSSESSION ACTIONS

32.1   Introduction

The recovery of land by court proceedings often forms an important element in the practice of junior counsel. Even those of you in predominantly criminal chambers may well be sent off to the local County Court to obtain an order for possession at some time. Possession actions are often regarded as intrinsically different from other civil claims. Save in a limited number of situations, where special provisions are made by statute and/or by the rules of the court, this is not the case. Possession actions should be dealt with in the same manner in terms of evidence and procedure as any other civil claim.

This guide deals with the main issues which will concern you when faced with a brief in some of the more common types of possession action. It is not a guide to the substantive law, although substantive matters are referred to. Nor does it deal with every type of possession action you might be faced with. Although limited in this way, this guide is extensive in order to cover the various elements that you will have to consider in even the simplest possession action, for example, questions of status, title, and security of tenure.

There is no avoiding the need for a solid understanding of substantive land law generally, and landlord and tenant law in particular. The four statutes you are most likely to encounter are the Landlord and Tenant Act 1954 ('the 1954 Act'), the Rent Act 1977 ('the 1977 Act'), the Housing Act 1985 ('the 1985 Act') and the Housing Act 1988 ('the 1988 Act'). You must be familiar with these statutes and how they relate to each other. For example, the 1977 Act has not been abolished by the 1988 Act although there are now only limited circumstances in which new protected tenancies can be created. Statutory provisions also limit the power of the court to suspend the operation of orders for possession and it is important that you are aware of the powers of the court in this respect in the case in which you are appearing. For details of the relevant substantive law see the ***Landlord and Tenant in Practice Manual***.

Mention must be made of the Woolf reforms, and the fundamental procedural changes brought about by the Civil Procedure Rules (CPR). The CPR purport to provide a complete and self-contained procedural code for both the High Court and the County Court, supplemented by numerous Practice Directions. Unfortunately a number of anomalies exist, and a number of the old rules are preserved as stop-gap measures. Generally the CPR apply to all proceedings commenced on or after 26 April 1999.

One immediate consequence of the CPR is that the person who commences proceedings is now called 'the claimant', and this title will be used in this guide to describe the person claiming possession. The person against whom the claim for possession is made is referred to herein as 'the defendant', a title preserved by the CPR. Remember: no more legal Latin!

32.2   Jurisdiction

Possession proceedings issued after 15 October 2001 are governed by Civil Procedure Rules, Part 55, and PD 55. Most proceedings will be in the County Court, as claims may be started only in the High Court if there are exceptional circumstances (CPR, r. 55.3(1) and (2)). PD 55, para. 3.1(3), sets out the circumstances which may justify starting a claim in the High Court:

(a)   there are complicated disputes of fact;

(b)   there are points of law of general importance; or

(c)   the claim is against trespassers and there is a substantial risk of public disturbance or of serious harm to persons or property which properly require immediate determination.

The value of the property and amount of the financial claim may be relevant circumstances but will not alone normally justify starting the claim in the High Court (PD 55, para. 3.1(4)).

Proceedings must be issued in the County Court for the district in which the land is situated (CPR, r. 55.3(1)).

32.3   Status of the Occupier

The next step, whether you are instructed for the claimant or defendant, is to establish the status of the defendant. This is relevant to the statutory provisions which apply to his or her occupancy and which may provide the defendant with some degree of security of tenure, that is, the right to remain in occupation of the premises notwithstanding that the claimant has taken the necessary steps at common law to regain possession. The types of occupiers you are most likely to encounter are those who entered into occupation as tenants, licensees or trespassers.

It is not enough to be satisfied that the defendant is simply a tenant or licensee. You must establish the precise nature of the tenancy or licence. For example, the period of notice required to determine a yearly periodic term at common law is different from that required to determine a weekly tenancy. Therefore you can only be sure sufficient notice has been given by first establishing the nature of the periodic tenancy. Occupiers other than tenants are not always without rights. For example, some periodic licensees of dwelling-houses are entitled to not less than four weeks notice in writing, which notice must contain certain prescribed information. Note, a 'lodger' is a licensee who receives board or attendance.

It is important not to be blinded by the formality or informality of the circumstances under which the defendant was permitted to occupy the premises. A written agreement drafted in the grand style may only have been intended, or effective, to grant a licence to occupy. On the other hand, a brief exchange of words may have been sufficient to grant a periodic tenancy which has lasted for tens of years, or a fixed term tenancy for a term of not more than three years. Indeed, in cases concerning short term occupancy of residential accommodation, written agreements tend to be the exception rather than the rule.

Do not take the terms of a written agreement at face value. As in other areas, the court is concerned with the substance not the form, so the fact that the written agreement says the defendant has been granted a licence does not necessarily mean that is the case as a matter of law.

32.4   The Premises Occupied and User

Consider the type of premises which the defendant is occupying. This is relevant to the question of which statutory provisions, if any, apply, and can be relevant to the type of notice to quit to which the occupier is entitled. For example, the 1977 Act only applies to dwelling-houses. Although Part II of the 1954 Act is concerned with business tenancies, it may apply to a dwelling-house provided it is lawfully occupied by the tenant for the purposes of a business carried on by him or her, or for those and other purposes. Mortgagors of dwelling-houses are given extra protection against claims for possession by mortgagees.

It may also be necessary to consider the defendant's use of the premises. The agreement between the parties frequently provides the use to which the occupier can put the premises. If there is such a provision, this is the important factor, not the nature of the premises demised or the actual user. If there is no express provision, the court will look at the circumstances of the letting and will infer a purpose for which the premises were let, if able to do so. If a dwelling-house is let without anything being said about user, the court is likely to find the dwelling-house was let as a dwelling, not as business premises. Where the circumstances are neutral, the court will look at the actual user. The user permitted under the planning legislation is usually irrelevant as between a landlord and tenant unless, for example, user in contravention of the planning legislation amounts to a breach of covenant.

32.5   Determination of the Right to Occupy

You must ensure that the right to occupy has come to an end, otherwise the claimant cannot recover possession. The right to occupy can be ended by the act of the claimant, the defendant or by operation of law. In most cases it is the claimant who takes some step to remove the defendant from the premises. Of course if the defendant had no right to occupy the premises in the first place, for example if he or she entered as a trespasser, no question of determining the right to remain in possession arises, as the defendant has no right to remain in possession. The correct approach is to consider what is necessary to determine the right to occupy at common law, if anything, and then consider how the position has been modified, if at all, by statute.

In the case of tenancies, ensure that the claim reveals how the tenancy came to an end before the proceedings were commenced. In a possession action in the County Court against a tenant holding over, you are most likely to find the tenancy has been determined by notice to quit or has expired by effluxion of time. Claims based upon determination of the tenancy under a proviso for re-entry (that is, forfeiture proceedings) are also very common.

As to notices to quit, you should ensure the form and the period of notice are correct for the tenancy in question. You should also check that the notice has been properly served. Some of the common law rules concerning the date upon which a notice to quit should expire are quite complex, and often those who serve them fall into error. For example, one full period of the tenancy, to expire at the end of a complete period of the tenancy, is the usual period of notice required at common law; yearly tenants being a notable exception. A monthly periodic tenancy which commenced on the first day of the month must therefore be determined by a month's notice to expire at the end of a month. Again, be aware of the statutory provisions: a weekly tenancy of a dwelling-house cannot be determined by a week's notice even if the notice expires at the end of a week.

The most common possession action in which you will appear will involve the determination of a periodic tenancy of a dwelling-house. Where the premises consist of a dwelling-house, the notice must be in writing, the period of notice must be not less than four weeks, and it must contain prescribed information.

Whether or not a tenancy has expired by effluxion of time usually does not cause any problems. If the claimant has commenced his action directly after the tenancy has apparently come to an end, you should ensure the tenancy has in fact ended. The date the term commenced is the important factor, and this depends upon the words used in the agreement between the parties.

It is the service of forfeiture proceedings which brings the tenancy to an end; there is no notice to quit to serve. Save where the lease is being forfeited for non-payment of rent, a notice under s. 146 of the Law of Property Act 1925 must be served; such a notice is effectively a statutory letter before action. You should ensure the content of the s. 146 notice is correct as errors are not infrequent. If you are representing the defendant, always consider whether the claimant has waived the right to forfeit the lease.

The position under the 1985 and 1988 Acts is slightly different from that described above. Under the 1985 and 1988 Acts, statutory notices must be served on the tenant before the court will entertain proceedings. The notices must be in a prescribed form and contain certain information. These provisions apply instead of the common law and therefore no steps to determine the tenancy at common law need be taken, or if they are taken, they have no effect on the application of the statutory provisions. The simple point is that the court will not have jurisdiction to deal with the case unless the notice of proceedings has been served. Under the 1985 and 1988 Acts it is the order of the court which brings the tenancy to an end.

A tenancy to which Part II of the 1954 Act applies cannot be brought to an end otherwise than in accordance with the provisions of the Act. Again special statutory notices with prescribed periods of notice are set out in the Act. In most cases, until one of these notices has been served, the tenancy continues. Accordingly, if a business tenancy comes to an end at common law by effluxion of time, the provisions of the 1954 Act will continue the tenancy until the statutory procedures are followed.

32.6 Title

32.6.1 THE IMPORTANCE OF PROVING TITLE

It is only those with superior title to the land occupied by the defendant who may be entitled to possession. It is therefore important to ensure the claimant has such title and that you are in a position to prove it. Frequently, there will be no issue between the parties on the question of title; for example, the defendant tenant will admit the claimant is his or her landlord or be estopped from denying it. Almost as frequently, the occupier fails to attend at trial, and you, as counsel for the claimant, will be asked by the judge to 'prove your case'. Unless title can be shown the action is bound to fail before it gets going. Generally on the question of proof, you should approach a brief for the claimant in a possession action on the basis that it is entirely possible the defendant will not attend, and each and every part of the claimant's case will have to be strictly proved.

32.6.2 REGISTERED LAND

If the claimant is the owner of the freehold interest in registered land, or a lease of registered land granted for a term of more than 21 years, title can be proved by producing office copy Land Registry entries. The proprietorship register will contain the claimant's name. In the case of a claimant who owns a registerable leasehold title, it is not strictly necessary to produce the headlease unless of course it is relevant to some other issue in the action. Office copy land registry entries are admissible in evidence in all actions and matters to the same extent as the originals would be, so the originals, which are often locked away in the vaults of a bank or building society, need not be produced at trial.

It sometimes happens that the claimant who says he or she 'owns' registered land is not registered as proprietor. This often happens where, for example, the claimant has recently purchased the premises and wishes to resell it immediately after gaining vacant possession. The claimant may not have applied to be registered as proprietor (it is not necessary to be so registered to effect a valid disposition of registered land), or the land registry may simply not have registered him or her as proprietor by the time the action comes on for trial. In such cases, it is sufficient if title from the last registered proprietor can be deduced. In the example given, you would need to produce office copy land registry entries showing the claimant's vendor as registered proprietor, and an executed transfer by that person to the claimant.

The leasehold owner under a lease not capable of substantive registration proves his or her title by producing his or her lease or tenancy agreement. The original should be produced. In theory the court will only accept secondary evidence of the lease if there are grounds for so doing, for example if the original is lost or destroyed.

32.6.3 UNREGISTERED LAND

If the land is unregistered, the claimant must deduce title, but it is not necessary to provide an epitome of title as a vendor would do on a conveyance of unregistered land. If the claimant's interest is freehold, the conveyance to him or her is sufficient. If leasehold, the headlease is sufficient, or if the claimant is an assignee of the term, the headlease and the assignment. Again, originals of such documents should be available for the trial.

32.6.4 ELIMINATING CONFUSION

The title to a piece of land can sometimes become confusing. If a number of derivative leasehold interests have been carved out of the freehold over the years, and there have been assignments of the various terms, assignments of the reversion, and the odd concurrent lease granted from time to time, it is sometimes difficult to know how the claimant comes to be the claimant. It is essential that you understand precisely how your client comes to be the claimant, and are in a position to explain it to the judge. A simple line diagram will often assist you.

32.6.5 IN PRACTICE

In practice you will more often than not find you do not have the title documentation referred to above. You might only have a copy of the claimant's lease, or your solicitors may not have taken the trouble to obtain office copy entries and have formed the view it will be enough if the claimant simply tells the judge he or she 'owns' the premises in question. It is often possible to get by with such evidence of title, especially in a simple case in the County Court, but there is no guarantee a particular judge will accept secondary evidence of title, particularly if the defendant does not attend, You should therefore insist, if it is not too late when you receive the brief, that proper evidence of title be available at court.

32.7 Parties to the Action

By the time the brief is delivered to you, counsel for the claimant, it will probably be too late to do very much about joining additional defendants and still go ahead on the hearing date. It is important, however, to ensure all those in occupation of the premises, or at least all adults, are joined as defendants. The husband might be the former tenant but is living in the premises with his wife; the wife should be a defendant. The same applies to grown up children living at home.

Although the bailiffs can remove anyone they find on the premises when they attend to execute the warrant, it is clearly wise to have all the occupiers before the court. Joining all occupiers in the first instance reduces the risk of a dispossessed occupier making an application without notice to be allowed back into the premises, thereby delaying matters and increasing costs.

If you arrive at court and the named defendant says his or her wife or husband and/or child is living in the premises also, provided the other occupier is not alleging a right to remain in occupation other than that based upon the named defendant's alleged right to occupy, the judge will probably allow you to amend the claim to join the additional occupiers and order that service of the claim on them be dispensed with.

32.8 Statements of Case

It is important to check the content of your statements of case; the new name for pleadings. As stated, the CPR have sought to introduce uniformity between the pleadings in the High Court and the County Court, and there are detailed rules which seek to achieve this and which must be complied with. In respect of residential possession proceedings, the procedure is now closer to that which applied in the County Court under the old rules. As a result, substantially more information is now needed in proceedings issued in the High Court. For example, proceedings seeking possession of residential premises on the ground of non-payment of rent must now contain a significant amount of information concerning rent arrears history and the defendant's financial circumstances. Remember also the requirement for a statement of case to contain a statement of truth.

32.9 Evidence Generally

32.9.1 PROVING THE CASE

If counsel for the claimant, you must ensure there will be someone at court who can prove the case. Most obviously, this means there must be someone at court who can prove the claimant 'owns' the premises and the terms on which the defendant occupies the same. If the claimant is the assignee of the reversion, it is not necessary to call the person who granted the lease, provided the claimant can give evidence to the effect that he or she acquired the freehold or headlease subject to the tenancy granted to the defendant. All the other elements of the claimant's case must be proved. For example, service of the notice to quit, the grounds upon which possession is sought, if grounds need be shown. Problems often arise concerning rent arrears, as the person who can prove title is not always the same person who was concerned with the collection of rent. You must avoid the trap of being left with nothing but hearsay evidence. In this respect, take care with expert valuation evidence. Such evidence might be called to prove the level of mesne profits claimed, and experts are often keen to give hearsay evidence of the details of transactions in which they were not involved.

A defendant can often defeat a claim simply by not admitting anything and sitting back as the claimant is unable to prove his or her case. If counsel for the defendant, make the claimant prove his or her case; as indicated above, claimants often find themselves in difficulty proving the level of rent arrears. An inability to prove termination of the relevant tenancy is also a common problem for claimants.

32.9.2 EVIDENCE

The normal rules about evidence in CPR, Part 32, will apply in cases allocated to the fast track or multi-track or where the court so orders. Thus witness statements will be used and will stand as the evidence-in-chief of witnesses unless the court gives permission for the witness to amplify or give evidence of additional matters. The normal rules on cross-examination will also apply. If the claimant or his or her agents have served the proceedings themselves, you should be prepared to prove this in case the defendant fails to attend.

32.9.3   FAILURE OF WITNESS TO ATTEND HEARING

It not infrequently happens that you arrive at court to discover one of your vital witnesses has failed to attend. If there is no prospect of the witness being brought to court that day, you should ask for the hearing to be adjourned. If the claimant or one of his or her witnesses does not attend, the court will probably agree to this course, although it might strike out the claim. If the defendant attends and is represented, it is likely that an application will be resisted. If there is some good reason for the failure of your witness to attend, for example, a sudden illness or transport strike, the court is likely to adjourn the hearing, but the claimant will have to pay the costs in any event.

If there is no good reason for the witness's failure to attend, you may be in some difficulty if the court refuses to adjourn the hearing. To have the claim struck out is an expensive nuisance only; fresh proceedings can be issued the same day. What you must avoid is having the case dealt with on its merits, as this would prevent the claimant commencing a fresh action based upon the same cause of action.

Under the CPR it is possible to use at trial a witness statement which has been served notwithstanding that the witness does not attend. A witness statement can be so used if the court so orders, or the party who wishes to rely upon the witness statement puts the witness statment in as hearsay evidence. Of course the weight to be attached to such evidence is much reduced and this should be avoided if possible.

32.10   Compromise

Frequently agreement is reached between the parties. Often the defendant agrees to leave the premises in return for a monetary payment, or because the claimant agrees to waive a money claim. Sometimes the claimant will agree not to proceed with his or her claim for possession if the defendant does not pursue his or her counterclaim for damages for breach of repairing covenant. Very frequently, the defendant merely wants an order for possession made against him or her in order that it can be presented to the local housing authority.

As counsel for the claimant, you should always take a realistic view of your case. Even if the case can be proved, the net result is often that the occupier remains in possession. To prove a regulated tenant is in arrear with his or her rent is unlikely to result in an immediate order for possession being made; at best the court will suspend the order provided the tenant pays the arrears plus the current rent. The position is now somewhat different under the provisions of the 1988 Act.

32.10.1   REGULATED TENANCIES

It frequently happens that agreement is reached between a landlord and a regulated tenant under which the tenant agrees to vacate the premises in return for a capital sum. As counsel for the claimant, you should take great care; the basic rule is that one cannot contract out of the Rent Acts. Accordingly, an agreement by a tenant to vacate premises which are subject to a regulated tenancy cannot be enforced by the landlord, even if the tenant has accepted the money. The fact that the agreement may be supported by an order for possession made by the court may make no difference.

The court cannot make an order for possession against a regulated tenant otherwise than under s. 98 of the 1977 Act. Accordingly, if it is desired to reach an effective agreement under which the defendant will vacate the premises, the court must be given jurisdiction under this section. This is done by the tenant admitting, which admission should be recorded in the body of the order, the elements of the claimant's claim which will give the court jurisdiction. For example, the defendant should admit the rent is in arrear and that it is reasonable to make an order for possession (although that is, strictly speaking, a matter for the court); or admit that suitable alternative accommodation is available. Similar care should be taken in cases under the 1988 Act. Such a form of compromise will not arise in cases to which the 1985 Act applies.

32.10.2 CONSEQUENCES FOR THE DEFENDANT

If you are counsel for the defendant, you should take care that the defendant is fully aware of the consequences of any agreement made. It is too simple to say that if an order for possession is made, the local housing authority has a duty to rehouse the defendant. Local housing authorities have a duty to house the homeless who have a priority need. A single man in good health will not fall within this class. Even where the defendant is likely to have a priority need, for example a young, unmarried mother, you should explain that the type of accommodation made available to the homeless is often very uncomfortable, especially for a family. Further, there is always the risk that if a claim for possession is not contested where there is an arguable defence, the local housing authority may take the view the defendant has become intentionally homeless, and in such circumstances, the local housing authority is under no duty to rehouse the defendant even if he or she does have a priority need.

If you are representing a legally-aided defendant who agrees to compromise the action on terms which involve the payment of a sum of money to him or her, you should ensure your client is fully aware of the consequences of the legal aid board's charge.

32.11 Costs

The usual rules concerning costs apply equally to possession actions as they do to other types of civil action. A successful party will usually be awarded his or her costs.

Under the CPR costs are assessed by the court. There may be a 'summary assessment' of costs, or a 'detailed assessment'. A summary assessment is an assessment made by the court at the end of the trial or other hearing. A detailed assessment is, in general terms, the modern equivalent of the old taxation procedure.

Generally, summary assessments of costs will take place on interim hearings and in cases which last less than one day. PD 44, para. 4.5, requires a written statement of costs to be prepared in Form 1 of the schedule of costs forms. This is the starting point for the judge's assessment of costs. You should have a copy of the schedule and understand the basis of the figures contained in it. The court can call on evidence in deciding the figure, for example looking at counsel's brief to see the brief fee. Ensure your brief is marked!

Detailed assessment of costs is a more complicated process done by a costs officer at a separate assessment hearing some time after the hearing. Generally the paper work and representation at such hearings is done by the solicitors.

Inevitably the amount of costs awarded on a summary assessment is less than the amount that would have been awarded on a detailed assessment, but the procedure avoids the time and expense of having the costs determined on a detailed assessment. It is not an exact science.

Possession actions in the County Court are often heard on a particular day. It is often useful to sit in the court room before your case is called on to see how the judge is dealing with the cases before him or her. You will be able to see how generous the judge is when asked to assess costs. However, the opportunities to do this have been reduced since the introduction of the CPR, as the bulk of possession hearings now take place in private.

In mortgagee possession actions, it is usual nowadays for the terms of the mortgage to provide that any costs incurred by the mortgagee are to be 'added to the security', i.e., to the total indebtedness of the mortgagor, and then recovered from the proceeds of sale of the premises. The district judge usually notes on the order that the costs are to be added to the security.

In actions against trespassers there is no reason why the successful claimant should not obtain his or her costs against a named defendant. Where, however, the proceedings have been commenced against unidentified occupiers, the court will not award the successful claimant his or her costs.

32.12   A Rent Act Possession Action

32.12.1   PRELIMINARY MATTERS

Such a claim will be in the County Court and, like most claims in the County Court, the proceedings are usually served by the court. This will be marked in the case file, so there is no need to prove service. If the claimant has served the proceedings, service must be proved. Ensure the tenancy has been determined, all pre-proceedings notices have been served, the statements of case are in order, title and any grounds for possession can be proved and your witnesses will be at court. If there is no defence in the papers, it is likely the defendant has not bothered to respond and therefore the hearing will be uncontested. It is still possible, however, that the defendant and his or her lawyers will attend at court, and if the claim is to be contested, the court may give case management directions. If you are counsel for the claimant and this happens, you should consider asking for the costs of the hearing in any event, or at least for the costs of counsel attending.

32.12.2   HEARING

Although the general rule is that hearings are in public, a claim by a landlord against one or more tenants, or former tenants, for possession of a dwelling-house based upon non–payment of rent (the most common type of possession action) are now listed in private. If the hearing is in open court, wig and gown must be worn.

If the defendant attends but there is no real defence available to him or her, the court will deal with the matter there and then. If the papers do contain a 'pro-forma' defence completed by the defendant in person, the case is still listed in a general possession list. If there may be some merit in the defence and the case is before the court for the first time, again, the hearing is likely to be treated as a case conference, unless there is no need for further statements of case or disclosure, the parties are able to proceed (that is, they have their witnesses at court) and the court has time, in which case the action can be dealt with on its merits.

Be alert to PD Costs, para. 8.7(3), which provides that the court should consider recording whether the hearing was fit for counsel, in particular where the paying party asks for the court to express a view or where the judge thinks the hearing was not fit for counsel.

32.12.3   CASE 1 CASES

Case 1 cases (rent arrears or breach of other obligations, usually repairing) rarely raise many difficulties for the claimant. Sometimes when you attend at court on a case 1 rent arrears case, you will be met by a counterclaim that the claimant is in breach of a repairing covenant which is usually sufficient to get the action adjourned. If you are representing the defendant in a case 1 action do not forget that the court must consider it reasonable to make an order, even if the arrears or breach of obligation are proved. As a general rule, the arrears or breach of agreement must be substantial, or the defendant's record on such matters very poor, before an immediate order for possession will be made.

A landlord frequently increases the contractual rent of his or her regulated tenant during the term. Tenants frequently agree to such increases as they consider it fair that the rent should be increased from time to time. Unless the parties reach agreement in a form prescribed by the 1977 Act, any such increase is irrecoverable from the tenant. This provision is often ignored because landlords and tenants are not aware of it. As counsel for the defendant in a case where the rent, other than a registered rent, has been increased over the years, you should ensure a proper rent agreement has been made between the parties on each occasion that the rent was increased. If it has not, the level of rent arrears pleaded by the claimant may be inflated.

As counsel for the defendant, consider your client's entitlement, if any, to assistance with payment of rent given by the local housing authority and/or the Department of Social Security. If the judge is persuaded future arrears are unlikely because of support from local or central government agencies, he or she may be inclined to give your client another chance in circumstances where he or she would not otherwise have done so.

However, as a matter of strict law the fact that a defendant is entitled to such assistance, but has not received the same, is not a defence to a claim for possession on the ground of non-payment of rent. The non receipt of the rent from the public authority is of no concern to the claimant. Having said that, where the defendant can show he or she is entitled to such money, and there has been some mix-up by the public authority, the court may adjourn the hearing to allow the defendant to chase the authority for payment.

If the case 1 claim is based upon non-payment of rent, the CPR now provide that the hearing will, in the first instance, be listed for hearing in private.

32.12.4 CASE 9 CASES

If you are representing the defendant in an action based upon case 9 (premises reasonably required for occupation by the landlord or his or her family), you should question the claimant very closely on the circumstances under which it has become necessary for him or her, or his or her family, to occupy the premises, as the claim may not be entirely genuine. Disclosure of the claimant's financial position is relevant in such cases, so do not agree to proceed with such a claim unless and until there has been full disclosure. Remember also the greater hardship test, and that it must be reasonable for the court to make an order.

32.12.5 CASE 11 CASES

Provided the claimant can prove each element contained in a case 11 claim (premises required by an owner-occupier) there is usually no difficulty. Sometimes the defendant can only make the claimant prove his or her case. As counsel for the defendant you should ensure the relevant notice has been served, and be satisfied the claimant did in fact live in the premises at some time before the tenancy was granted. If the claimant persuades the court to dispense with the notice requirements, you should insist the court gives its reasons why it has decided so to do.

32.12.6 CASE 19 CASES

Case 19 (mandatory ground for possession against a protected shorthold tenant) frequently causes the claimant problems in respect of the service of the 'appropriate notice' as the provisions are somewhat complex. Errors frequently arise where the claimant is seeking to determine the tenancy by relying upon a proviso for re-entry. Always check the notice has been served at the correct time and gives the correct period of notice.

32.13 A Housing Act 1988 Possession Action

The technical nature of many of the relevant statutory provisions, and the need for strict compliance with the same, means that claims under the 1988 Act contain rather more potential pitfalls than claims under the 1977 Act. Having said that, the amendments made to the 1988 Act by the Housing Act 1996 have eliminated some of the more dangerous pitfalls. Care is needed whether you are acting for the claimant or the defendant.

Assured shorthold tenancies are very common, as they were intended to be, and it is more likely than not that this is the type of 1988 Act possession action you will be briefed in. As counsel for either the claimant or the defendant, you must ensure that the pre-tenancy notice provisions have been complied with. If the judge exercises his or her discretion to dispense with the pre-tenancy notice requirement, you should ask him or her to state his or her reasons. A pre-action notice by the landlord that possession is required is also necessary. Ensure it was served at the correct time, as the relevant provisions in the 1988 Act are not entirely clear at first glance and errors are made by claimants.

Authority has established that the prescribed form of notices to be served under the 1988 Act must comply precisely with the statutory requirements. If there are any deviations from that required, or a precis of the statutory words, in any notice served under the 1988 Act, counsel for the defendant may well be able to contend successfully that the notice is ineffective.

The failure to comply with pre-tenancy notice provisions often resulted in the inadvertent creation of assured tenancies. It was thought to be such a problem that since the day on which s. 98 of the Housing Act 1996 came into force, namely 28 February 1997, the service of a pre-tenancy notice is not required to create an assured shorthold tenancy.

Remember an assured tenancy does not come to an end until an order for possession is obtained from the court. Accordingly, a landlord is entitled to rent up until the date the order takes effect.

32.14 Possession Proceedings Against a Business Tenant

Simple possession actions against business tenants arise where it is alleged that the provisions of the 1954 Act do not apply to the tenancy in the first instance, or where the tenancy has been determined in accordance with the provisions of the 1954 Act and the tenant has failed to take the steps required under that Act to ensure his or her tenancy continues until the court grants a new tenancy. In either case, if you represent the claimant, all you need to show is that the tenancy has come to an end. You do not need to show any grounds for possession.

Business tenants sometimes lose the protection of the 1954 Act when they start to operate their business through a company. The tenancy is still vested in the individual, but it is the company that is carrying on the business. In such circumstances the 1954 Act does not apply. This is often not appreciated.

32.15 Possession Proceedings Against a Secure Tenant

Local authorities and housing association landlords usually get the procedure right, as they are involved in a great many possession actions. Nevertheless, if you are instructed for the defendant, ensure the correct procedure has been followed. Speak to the representative of the local authority or housing association (often not a lawyer) and try to reach agreement for the discharge of any rent arrears. Such landlords are frequently sympathetic save where it is alleged the defendant has been causing a nuisance to other tenants. If the claim is based upon rent arrears, the hearing will be in private.

32.16 Mortgagee Possession Claims

These claims are governed by CPR, Part 55. Ensure that the charge certificate is available at the hearing and a recent land registry search or, in the case of unregistered land, a search of the land charges register. This is necessary to prove to the Master/district judge that no entry has been made to protect rights under the Matrimonial Homes Act 1983 since the claim was settled and filed. The standard form of mortgage or charge used by the institutional lenders frequently incorporates terms and conditions by reference to a separate document. Ensure that a copy of this document is in evidence.

As counsel for the mortgagee, it is important that you understand how the arrears figure stated in the affidavit in support is made up. Matters can sometimes be rather complicated because of the nature of the mortgage; there seems to be no end to the varieties. Mortgagors in arrear often take issue with the level of arrears; they cannot believe they owe so much. It is very useful to have an up-to-date computer print-out of the state of the account between the parties.

It appears the attitude taken by district judges around the county to claims for possession by mortgagees varies from reluctant accommodation to outright hostility! Any error or omission in the claimant's case is likely therefore to result in an adjournment or even to a striking out. It is vital that the claimant's case is in order.

If you are instructed on behalf of the mortgagor, consider the powers of the court under the Administration of Justice Acts 1970 and 1973. Recent Court of Appeal authority has clarified how the court's powers under these sections should be exercised in a usual case. For the reason stated in the preceding paragraph, you should not feel uncomfortable about taking technical points. More time in the property may provide your client with an opportunity to put his or her finances in order.

32.17 Possession Proceedings Against Trespassers

CPR, Part 55, contains specific provisions for obtaining possession of land against trespassers, squatters and licensees whose licences have been determined. The provision enables possession to be obtained quickly and on the basis of the claim form, particulars of claim and witness statements. Frequently the owner will not know the names of some or all of the occupants. In such a case, the claim must be brought against 'persons unknown' in addition to any named defendants (CPR, r. 55.3(4)).

In many cases, no defendants will appear at the hearing. However, the court is astute to ensure that the requirements of the CPR have been fulfilled. Matters to check are:

(a) the claim form and particulars of claim contain all the relevant information. A new form of particulars of claim (N121) relates specifically to trespassers. Ensure that the matters required by PD 55, para. 2.6, are included;

(b)   service has been properly effected. Although the normal rules of service apply to named defendants, 'persons unknown' must be served by the method set out in CPR, r. 55.6. This involves attaching copies of the documents to the main door or some other part of the land so they are clearly visible and inserting another set through the letter slot in a sealed transparent envelope addressed to the 'occupiers'.

These procedures are to be used in straightforward cases only. If there are serious issues as to title, the summary procedure is inappropriate. Where a defendant raises a triable issue on such an application, the court can deal with it, although it is often reluctant to do so.

The court does have the power, frequently used, to adjourn the application to be dealt with as if the proceedings were commenced as ordinary possession proceedings. On such occasions, the court gives directions for the future conduct of the case.

32.18   Possible Counterclaim

If you are instructed on behalf of the defendant, consider whether there are any breaches of agreement by the landlord. Landlords are frequently in breach of their implied obligations to repair and maintain the structure and exterior of the demised premises. Any such breach may form the basis of a set-off and counterclaim. A set-off is a defence of course, and accordingly even a modest set-off and counterclaim can effectively eliminate a ground for possession.

32.19   The Hearing

Actions in the County Court in which possession of residential accommodation is claimed last for, on average, 90 seconds. An ideal first court appearance perhaps. On the other hand this reflects the fact that judges wish to deal with such actions quickly, and therefore it is important that you are able to match the pace set by the judge.

It is an unlucky beginner who, attending on his or her first possession action, finds his or her case listed first in a long possession list. If you are not so unlucky, it is a great help to spend a short period in court watching how others, perhaps more experienced, are doing it. As, if not more, important is the benefit you receive from seeing how the judge is dealing with his or her list. However, as stated above, the opportunities to do this are much reduced by the rule changes which provide for the bulk of possession actions to be listed in private.

In general, however, you should proceed as follows. Once your case is called on, introduce yourself and your opponent (or the defendant in person) and briefly indicate the nature of the claim. Refer the judge to the statements of case (he or she may indicate this is unnecessary) and then proceed to call your evidence. The witness statements should contain evidence which establishes the claimant's title, the terms of the letting, the determination of the tenancy and the other elements (for example, the amount of rent arrears) needed to prove the claimant's claim. Ask the witness(es) to produce any relevant documents. Witness statements are to stand as evidence-in-chief, although the court may allow a witness to amplify his or her witness statement, or add to it if new matters have arisen since it was made.

As in any other civil claim, the defendant will then have the opportunity to cross-examine the witness(es) and call evidence at the close of the claimant's case. Even if the defendant in person has no defence, the judge inevitably asks him or her what he or she has to say. If the defendant admits the claim, explain this to the judge, and he or she will proceed to make an order provided the defendant has confirmed this is the case.

It is usually unnecessary to refer the judge to the substantive law in simple possession actions as he or she will be very familiar with it. You should, however, be prepared to refer the judge to the relevant statutory provisions if necessary. The defendant has the opportunity to make any submissions to the court at the end of the defence case. The claimant then has the final opportunity to address the court if this is necessary.

As counsel for a successful claimant, you must be able to inform the judge of the order you seek. In particular, if your claim involves a claim for rent or other money, ensure you have the correct figure to give to the judge. If you are claiming interest, make sure you have calculated the amount you claim in order that you can make an immediate response when the judge asks for the figure.

Although this is the usual course of events, do not be surprised if the judge invites you, counsel for the claimant, to proceed in a different manner. Under the post Woolf regime judges will be more interventionist. Some judges will have read the papers and will simply want to hear the evidence. Some will not only allow you, but encourage you, to lead your witness in order to maintain the 90-second average! There is a great deal of variation between judges. Whatever the judge says, do not panic. Provided you know the elements of your client's case, you should be able to adapt to whatever approach the judge adopts without too much trouble.

It is fair to say that some solicitors do not prepare a brief for what they consider to be a simple possession action with the care and attention which it requires. Frequently, by the morning of the hearing, you will still not be entirely clear how you are going to prove your case, or resist the claim made against your client, as the case may be. You will not understand, because your papers will contain no explanation, how a rent arrears figure has been calculated. Even as a beginner, it is likely you will have some criticisms to make of the statements of case.

Do not assume you are the first to have received such a brief, and keep calm. Speak to your solicitor the night before or in the morning before the hearing; you may catch him or her in the office before he or she leaves for court. In any event, be at court in good time in order to take further instructions. Your team may not arrive until 10.28 am. If you need more time, and your case is near the top of the list, inform the usher that you are not quite ready, and invite him or her to drop you a little way down the list. If the usher feels unable to do this, ask the judge for more time. It is vital that you fully understand your case before you stand up before the judge, so do not feel embarrassed to ask for time.

The oral process in the County Court of a claim against an unrepresented assured shorthold tenant with no defence will often be as follows:

Court clerk:	Martin Kelly against Anastasia Lynch.
Judge:	Yes, Miss Daly. [*Counsel for the claimant.*]
Counsel:	May it please Your Honour, I appear for the claimant in this action. Miss Lynch, the defendant, is not represented, but appears in person. Your Honour, this is Miss Lynch. [*Counsel points out the defendant to the judge.*]
Judge:	Will you please step forward Miss Lynch [*who does*]. Yes, Miss Daly.
Counsel:	Your Honour will see from the short Particulars of Claim that the claimant claims possession of the flat premises known as 25A Dunmore House, Tuam Road, Kilburn, London NW6, which flat was let to Miss Lynch on 28 August 1998 for a term of six months from that date at the rent of £300 a month. Your Honour, the tenancy granted to Miss Lynch is an assured shorthold tenancy within the meaning of s. 20 of the Housing Act 1988.
Judge:	Yes, Miss Daly, call your evidence.
Counsel:	I'm obliged, Your Honour. I call Mr Kelly. [*The claimant enters the witness box and takes the oath or affirms.*]
Counsel:	Mr Kelly, would you give your full name and address to the court please.

Mr Kelly:	I will. My name is Martin Kelly and I live at The Dunmore Inn, Ballindine Way, Kilburn, London NW6.
Counsel:	Will you look at the witness statement in front of you. Please turn to the last page of the statement. Can you confirm that your signature appears on the statement, and that it is a true copy of a statement made by you on 19 June 2002?
Mr Kelly:	That is my signature and this is a copy of the statement I made on 19 June 2002.
Counsel:	Mr Kelly, is the content of the witness statement true to the best of your knowledge and belief?
Mr Kelly:	It is.
Counsel:	Your Honour, thre are one or two points I would wish Mr Kelly to amplify, which I submit will assist the court. Do I have Your Honour's permission?
Judge:	You do Miss Daly, but please take it quickly.
Counsel:	I'm obliged Your Honour. Mr Kelly, although the tenancy you granted to Miss Lynch was for a fixed term of only six months, it is right, is it not, that she remained in possession of the flat long after the expiration of that term?
Mr Kelly:	That's right. We got on really well. Miss Lynch was a really good tenant: she paid the rent and caused me no trouble at all so I was happy for her to stay. I checked it with my solicitor and he told me it was alright for her to stay.
Counsel:	I see, but there came a time when you wished to regain possession of the flat?
Mr Kelly:	That's right. I feel a bit guilty about it, she having been such a good tenant and all, but I have a cousin who is new in the country and I want the flat for him; he plans to work with me in the pub.
Counsel:	That being the case, did you take any steps to remove Miss Lynch from the flat?
Mr Kelly:	Well I don't know anything about taking steps, but I went to see my solicitor and he gave me another form to give to Miss Lynch and that I did on 28 March 2002.
Counsel:	Mr Kelly, is this a copy of the form you gave to Miss Lynch on 28 March 2002?
	[*Counsel hands a copy of the s. 21 notice to the witness via the usher or court clerk which is immediately handed on to the judge.*]
Mr Kelly:	It is.
Counsel:	Finally Mr Kelly, can you confirm that Miss Lynch remains in the flat and that there are no rent arrears or other sums due to you.
Mr Kelly:	She is still in the flat alright, but she doesn't owe me anything; she is well up to date when it comes to the money.
Counsel:	Thank you, Mr Kelly. Does Your Honour have any questions?
Judge:	No.
	[*Witness starts to leave the witness box.*]
Counsel:	Would you wait there a moment, Mr Kelly.
Judge:	Thank you, Miss Daly. Miss Lynch, do you want to ask Mr Kelly any questions? Please just ask questions, I'll give you an opportunity to have your say in a minute.
Miss Lynch:	I don't want to ask any questions.
Judge:	You can step down, Mr Kelly. Is that your case, Miss Daly?
Counsel:	It is, Your Honour.
Judge:	Now, Miss Lynch, what do you have to say about all this? Look at this agreement with your name at the top of the first page. Is that your signature at the bottom of the last page?
Miss Lynch:	It's my signature alright.
Judge:	You accept therefore that you are the tenant of the flat and the rent is £300 a month.
Miss Lynch:	I've never disputed that.
Judge:	Please look at this notice [*handing the witness the s. 20 notice*]. Do you remember receiving this? It appears to have your signature on the bottom saying you received it on 27 August 1998.

Miss Lynch:	I got the notice alright. It was the day before I signed the agreement and moved in. I didn't know there would be so much paper.
Judge:	Yes. Did Mr Kelly give you this notice on 28 March 2002? [*Hands the witness the s. 21 notice.*]
Miss Lynch:	He came around with that the other night. I got a bit of a shock because I thought we were all set, but he says he wants the flat for his cousin. It's a bit unfair, I'm bound to say.
Judge:	Thank you, Miss Lynch. Miss Daly, do you have any questions?
Counsel:	No, Your Honour.
Judge:	Now, Miss Lynch, is there anything you wish to say to me?
Miss Lynch:	Only that it's a bit unfair as I said. I have done nothing wrong yet he wants me out.
Judge:	I follow that, Miss Lynch, but the position is that the tenancy Mr Kelly granted you allows him to remove you from the premises even if you have been a good tenant. That is what all those notices were about.
Miss Lynch:	I didn't really read them.
Judge:	Well there it is. Miss Lynch, do you have somewhere else to go?
Miss Lynch:	My brother has a place up in Cricklewood where I can stay until I can find somewhere else. It's not as nice as the flat I have but it will have to do.
Judge:	Thank you, Miss Lynch you can sit down now. Miss Daly, is there anything you wish to say?
Counsel:	Not unless I can assist Your Honour.
Judge:	Well there is just one thing. Miss Lynch's fixed term tenancy came to an end in February 1999, but she has remained in possession paying the rent long after that date. Does that affect the position under the 1988 Act?
Counsel:	In my submission no, Your Honour. The position under the 1988 Act is as follows. When the fixed term of six months came to an end and Miss Lynch held over, she did so as a statutory periodic tenant within the meaning of s. 5(3) of the 1988 Act. Your Honour will recall that it is s. 5 of the 1988 Act which essentially provides assured tenants with security of tenure.
Judge:	Yes.
Counsel:	As the grant to Miss Lynch was undoubtedly an assured shorthold tenancy, and as the statutory periodic tenancy was of the same premises and between the same parties as the original assured shorthold tenancy, Miss Lynch's tenancy remained, in effect, an assured shorthold tenancy. That is the effect, I submit, of s. 20(4) of the 1988 Act.
Judge:	I see.
Counsel:	That being the case, provided Mr Kelly served a notice in accordance with s. 21(4) of the 1988 Act, which he did, he is entitled to possession of the flat as of right.
Judge:	Yes, I see. Thank you, Miss Daly. Miss Lynch, I have now clarified one or two points with counsel for Mr Kelly and I am left in no doubt that Mr Kelly is entitled to possession of the flat. I am sorry about that but that is the law and I have no say in the matter. Miss Daly, what do you say about when the order for possession should take effect?
Counsel:	Your Honour cannot suspend the order for more than two weeks unless your Honour is convinced Miss Lynch will suffer exceptional hardship. I submit there may be hardship but it is not exceptional.
Judge:	That must be right. What do you say about costs?
Counsel:	Your Honour, in my submission the claimant should have his costs, and I invite Your Honour to assess them.
Judge:	Again, that must be right. I assess the claimant's costs at £150. Miss Lynch, please listen carefully. I have made an order for possession against you, suspended for two weeks. That means you must be out of the flat by 15 July 2002. You must continue to pay your rent to Mr Kelly until you go. Mr Kelly also wants his costs against you which I have said are £150. Do you want to say anything to me about costs. I know it is

hard, but it was your failure to leave the flat that forced him to come to court.

Miss Lynch: Nothing I could say would make any difference, I suppose.

Judge: There it is then. I make an order in those terms. Thank you, Miss Daly, for your assistance. You can go now, Miss Lynch.

[Claimant leaves the court triumphant. Defendant leaves the court feeling a little uncomfortable. Counsel bows, struggles to fight her way out of the crowded front bench with her arms full of papers and the Civil Court Practice 2002, red tape hanging from her jacket pocket.]

THIRTY THREE

APPLICATION FOR A PRELIMINARY REFERENCE TO THE EUROPEAN COURT OF JUSTICE

33.1 References to the European Court of Justice: Article 234 EC

When a matter of European Community law arises before any court or tribunal, it may be possible to have the proceedings stayed in order that the particular matter be referred to the European Court of Justice (ECJ) for a determination of the relevant point of European law. Article 234 (ex 177) of the EC Treaty establishes the jurisdiction of the ECJ in these matters. In particular, it provides that the ECJ has jurisdiction to give a preliminary ruling concerning the interpretation of the EC Treaty and the validity and interpretation of EC legislation.

Note that jurisdiction is limited to examining EC law and that there is no provision for the ECJ to determine the validity or interpretation of English law (or any other national law). It is common, however, for questions to be referred in which the ECJ is asked whether a particular piece of national legislation is compatible with the EC Treaty or with EC legislation. In such case, the ECJ usually answers the question by reference to the meaning to be attributed to the relevant EC law. Technically, it is then for the referring national court to apply that meaning to its own national law. The delimitation of jurisdictions in these cases is therefore relatively clear: it is for the ECJ to determine the true meaning and effect of EC law, while it is for the national court to apply that meaning in the context of the proceedings before it. Accordingly, the ECJ is not, in this context, a court of appeal. Rather, Article 234 EC provides a means of co-operation between the national court and the ECJ to ensure that EC law is properly and effectively applied.

The mere fact that a question of EC law arises does not, of course, mean that the issue should be referred to the ECJ. Every national court is required to interpret and apply EC law in the normal course of events. Generally speaking, it is only where a particular difficulty arises which cannot confidently be solved by the judge that a reference should be considered.

33.2 Which Courts can make a Reference?

Article 234(2) EC provides that where a question of EC law is raised before any court or tribunal of a Member State, that court or tribunal may, if it considers that a decision on the point is necessary to enable it to give judgment, request the ECJ for a ruling thereon.

The definition of court or tribunal is a question of Community law, so that the classification of the body for the purposes of English law is not directly relevant. The court or tribunal must be a public body exercising official authority and it must have a judicial function. References have been made from the House of Lords, Court of Appeal (Criminal and Civil Divisions), High Court, Crown Court, County Court, magistrates' courts, VAT tribunals, Employment Appeal Tribunal, employment tribunals, Social Security Commissioners and the Special Commissioners for Income Tax. It is arguable that certain professional bodies exercising disciplinary powers may be considered as tribunals. Arbitration tribunals are not competent to make a reference to the ECJ since they are not public bodies and have no connection with the exercise of official authority.

Under the Brussels Convention on jurisdiction and the enforcement of judgments in civil and commercial matters, a reference may only be made from appellate courts. This is therefore in the United Kingdom limited to the House of Lords, the Court of Appeal and the High Court sitting in an appellate capacity.

The Rome Convention on the law applicable to contractual obligations has been in force in the United Kingdom since 1991. However, a protocol attached to the Convention which provides for the possibility of making a reference to the ECJ (and which limits references to appellate courts) has not yet entered into force.

The application of Article 234 EC was modified by the Amsterdam Treaty in relation to Title IV matters. Title IV governs visas, asylum, immigration and other policies relating to the free movement of persons and the Council is required to adopt various legislative measures governing these matters. However, Title IV also covers other measures concerning judicial cooperation in civil matters, administrative cooperation, and measures in the field of police and judicial cooperation. Measures in the field of judicial cooperation in civil matters having cross-border implications will include improving and simplifying the system for service of judicial documents, cooperation in the taking of evidence and the recognition and enforcement of decisions in civil and commercial cases. Article 68 (ex 73p) EC provides that Article 234 will apply to Title IV such that, where a question on the interpretation of Title IV or on the validity of Community legislation based on Title IV is raised in a national court against whose decisions there is no judicial remedy under national law, that court must, if it considers that a decision is necessary to enable it to give judgment, request the ECJ to give a preliminary ruling. The ECJ will have no jurisdiction to rule on any measure or decision taken pursuant to Article 62(1) (ex 73j) EC relating to the maintenance of law and order and the safeguarding of internal security.

33.3 Which Courts must make a Reference?

Article 234(3) EC provides that where a question of EC law is raised in a case pending before a court or tribunal against whose decisions there is no judicial remedy under national law, that court or tribunal must refer the matter to the ECJ.

In the United Kingdom, this is generally limited to the House of Lords. Although it is necessary to obtain leave to appeal to the House of Lords, the Divisional Court and the Court of Appeal have specifically stated that in the absence of such leave being granted those courts may not be considered as falling within Article 234(3) EC. Thus, even though the clear intention of Article 234 EC seems to be that a party has the right to seek a reference at some stage in the appeal procedure even though the relevant court may not deem it necessary to enable it to decide the matter, the appeals procedure involving the House of Lords may frustrate that. It is not possible to go back to the Court of Appeal after the House of Lords has refused permission and then argue that the Court of Appeal has become the court to which Article 234(3) EC refers. See further **33.5**.

Where the question at issue involves the validity of EC legislation (such as a regulation or directive) it is not possible for the national court to decide that the legislation is indeed invalid, no matter how strong the arguments to that effect. The court has two possibilities open to it. It may decide, having regard to the arguments, that the legislation is valid and continue the proceedings on that basis. Alternatively, if it is of the opinion that the legislation is invalid (or that there is a strong argument to that effect), it must refer the matter to the ECJ, since only the ECJ has competence to declare EC legislation invalid.

33.4 In what Circumstances is a Reference to be made?

Generally, a reference is only to be made if an answer is necessary to enable the court to give judgment. Accordingly, it is common practice for English courts to seek to decide the action on the basis of English law issues which do not raise questions of EC law.

The Court of Appeal has laid down guidelines for the exercise of the discretion to refer (contained in Article 234(2)) in rather general terms. If the facts have been found and the EC law issue is critical to the court's final decision, the appropriate course is ordinarily to refer the issue to the ECJ unless the national court can with complete confidence resolve the issue itself. In considering whether it can with complete confidence resolve the issue itself the national court must be fully mindful of the differences between national and EC legislation, of the pitfalls which face a national court venturing into what may be an unfamiliar field, of the need for uniform interpretation throughout the EC and the great advantages enjoyed by the ECJ in construing EC legislation. Other factors which might be considered are the delay and costs involved, the difficulty of the point of law and the presence of similar actions before the ECJ.

A lower court might also be mindful of the fact that its decision may be appealed with a reference being sought at the appeal stage. However, if the parties have made clear that they will seek a reference at each stage, it might be more sensible to impress on the judge in the lowest court that it would save time and costs if he or she were to refer the matter immediately.

33.5 Exceptions to the Requirement to Refer under Article 234(3)

There are three exceptions to the general requirement to make a reference under Article 234(3) EC for a court from whose decisions there is no judicial remedy. First, no reference is necessary if the question raised is materially identical to a previous question already referred to the ECJ. Secondly, a decision for interim measures which depends on a question of EC law need not be the subject of a reference even if it is final, as long as this does not bind the court which hears the substantive action and provided that either party can ensure that proceedings in the main action are actually instituted.

Thirdly, the national court need not make a reference if the matter is *acte clair*. The extent of this exception is not wholly clear and there has been some suggestion in recent years that it should be relaxed. However, in general it means that a reference is unnecessary where the answer is so obvious as to leave no scope for any reasonable doubt as to the manner in which the question raised is to be resolved. Before it comes to that conclusion, the court must be convinced that the matter is equally obvious to the courts of the other Member States and to the ECJ. This must involve consideration of the different language versions of the particular EC legislation. Even where the different language versions are entirely in accord with one another, it must be borne in mind that EC law uses terminology which is peculiar to it and that legal concepts do not necessarily have the same meaning in EC law and in the laws of the various Member States. Finally, every provision of EC law must be placed in its context and interpreted in the light of the provisions of EC law as a whole, regard being had to the objectives of EC law and to its state of evolution at the date on which the provision in question had to be applied.

33.6 It is the Court (not the Parties) which makes the Reference

The decision of whether or not to make a reference is solely for the court. If the parties suggest that a reference is desirable, it is likely that the judge will agree. However, it is quite common for one party to oppose the reference and for the other to be in favour. In those circumstances, the party seeking the reference must make representations to the judge seeking to convince him or her to take this action. It is, however, not unknown for a judge to decide of his or her own motion (and even against the wishes of the parties) that a reference should be made. In those circumstances, this is solely a matter for the discretion of the judge and the parties (subject to a right of appeal) cannot resist the decision to refer.

33.7 At what Stage in the Proceedings should the Reference be made?

A party which is seeking to have a matter referred to the ECJ should make this plain to the judge at the earliest opportunity. Apart from courtesy, it means that the judge can possibly cut the time in the national court considerably.

Before the reference is made, it is necessary for the facts to be established although the relevant facts may, of course, be agreed between the parties. In most civil matters this should not pose too much of a problem. A statement of agreed facts can then be drawn up and handed to the judge.

Criminal cases pose special problems, since once the jury is sworn in it is difficult, from a practical point of view, to make a reference to the ECJ with the consequential delay of up to two years before the jury is called on to decide the factual issue. On the one hand, the defendant may wish to argue that, even if the facts alleged against him or her are proven, there will still be no offence committed since EC law precludes a prosecution in those circumstances. This may be either on the basis that the relevant English law conflicts with EC law or that, for instance, an EC Regulation which is central to the prosecution is invalid. In that case, the facts may be deemed to be agreed solely for the purpose of the reference. It is preferable for the question of EC law to be determined at that stage, with a reference if necessary, before the issue is put to a jury. Accordingly, the issue of EC law should be raised by means of a motion to quash the indictment before the jury is chosen. This approach has the added advantage that defendant, particularly if he or she is of previous good character, does not suffer the ignominy of being found guilty at first instance only to be vindicated on appeal. On the other hand, once the trial has started and the jury is in place, the House of Lords has said that it can scarcely be a proper exercise of the court's discretion to make a reference. Instead the trial must proceed, leaving the possibility of a reference for the appellate court.

There are no hard and fast rules about making submissions on the point of EC law in the national court prior to the reference being made. Clearly, if the parties have agreed that a reference is desirable, counsel should immediately suggest this course of action to the judge. However, since the reference is solely at the discretion of the judge (except in the case of courts of last instance) it may well be that the judge will require argument on the point before he or she is satisfied that a reference is appropriate. From the point of view of the parties, this may well also be desirable since it gives an idea to each side as to the submission which will be made before the ECJ. (Having said that, the parties are not limited to repeating in the ECJ only those arguments put to the national court.)

33.8 Procedure for Making the Reference

Much of the procedure for making the reference to the ECJ is carried on behind the scenes rather than in open court. RSC O. 114 (preserved in CPR, sch. 1) governs references from the High Court and the Court of Appeal. Similar rules apply to the Crown Court in accordance with r. 29 of the Crown Court Rules. There are no specific rules laid down for references from magistrates' courts and other tribunals which, therefore, take their power to refer solely from Article 234 EC as incorporated by s. 2(1) of the European Communities Act 1972.

The form of the Order for Reference from the High Court or the Court of Appeal was set out in form 109 of the *White Book*. Although there are no specific rules regarding forms from other courts or tribunals, it is generally thought that a similar form of order should be used.

The prescribed form is as follows:

[*Heading as in cause or matter*]

It is ordered that the question[s] set out in the Schedule hereto concerning the interpretation [*or* validity] of [*specific Treaty provision or Community instrument or act concerned*] be referred to the Court of Justice of the European Communities for a preliminary ruling in accordance with Article 234 of the Treaty establishing the European Community.

And it is ordered that all further proceedings in the above-named cause [*or* matter] be stayed until the said Court of Justice has given its ruling on the said question[s] or until further order.

SCHEDULE

REQUEST FOR A PRELIMINARY RULING OF THE COURT OF JUSTICE OF THE EUROPEAN COMMUNITIES

(Here set out a clear and succinct statement of the case giving rise to the request for the ruling of the European Court of Justice in order to enable the European Court of Justice to consider and understand the issues of Community law raised and to enable the Government of Member States and other interested parties to submit observations. The statement of the case should include:
  (a) particulars of the parties;
  (b) the history of the dispute between the parties;
  (c) the history of the proceedings;
  (d) the relevant facts as agreed by the parties or as found by the Court or, failing such agreement or finding the contentions of the parties on such facts;
  (e) the nature of the issues of law and fact between the parties;
  (f) the (English) law so far as is relevant;
  (g) the Treaty provisions or other acts, instruments or rules of Community law concerned.)

The preliminary ruling of the Court of Justice of the European Communities is accordingly requested on the following questions:
1., 2., etc *(Here set out the questions on which the ruling is sought, identifying the Treaty provisions or other acts, instruments or rules of Community law concerned.)*

Dated the   day of   19

See also: *Practice Direction (ECJ References: Procedure)* [1999] 1 WLR 260.

33.9   Costs and Legal Aid

Costs will usually be reserved until the reference has returned from the ECJ. Usually costs will follow the event.

Legal aid is generally extended to cover the proceedings before the ECJ.

33.10 Proceedings before the European Court of Justice

The proceedings before the ECJ fall into separate parts only two of which involve the lawyers for the parties. First, the parties submit their written observations. Secondly, the parties subsequently make an oral presentation at the ECJ in Luxembourg. Thirdly, the Advocate General gives his Opinion and, finally, the ECJ gives its decision. Lawyers are directly involved only in the first two stages. There is no need for lawyers or the parties to be present at the ECJ either when the Advocate General's Opinion is given or when the judgment is handed down.

Written observations are the most important part of the proceedings. These should be clear and concise. There is, however, no prescribed format for written observations and each counsel has his or her own style. Unlike English court proceedings, it is inadvisable to recite large chunks of case law. Rather, the precise dictum relied upon should be set out, with other references to the cases being made in footnotes. It is quite permissible for reference to be made to academic articles or books in order to substantiate arguments. As a general rule, written observations should not be overly long, although this depends on the complexity of the case. Twenty pages of argument should usually be quite enough! Another unusual aspect of the written stage is that all parties submit their observations at the same time rather than one after the other. Accordingly, there is no opportunity at this stage to know precisely what is being argued by the other side. Needless to say, this may call for some ingenuity since counsel then have to put themselves in the position of second guessing the other side. It is also possible for Member States to intervene in the proceedings; they need not show any direct interest.

Guidance notes are given by the ECJ to all counsel prior to the oral hearing. This is a short hearing with counsel for each side having a maximum of thirty minutes. It is not an opportunity to put the entire case. Instead, the essence of the argument should be quickly put, concentrating on the strongest points. It is also the only opportunity counsel has for rebutting the arguments put by the other parties. Questions may be asked by the judges, although sometimes no questions are asked.

Some months later the Opinion will be given followed some months after that by the judgment. In all, the delay between reference and judgment is usually about 18 months.

THIRTY FOUR

APPLYING FOR COSTS IN A CIVIL CASE

34.1 Orders for Costs

This chapter deals with making an application for an order for costs. The following are the principal costs orders:

(a) Claimant's costs.

(b) Defendant's costs.

(c) Claimant's costs in the case/application.

(d) Defendant's costs in the case/application.

(e) Costs in the case.

(f) Costs reserved.

(g) *Bullock* order.

(h) *Sanderson* order.

(i) Each party to bear their own costs, i.e., no order for costs.

For an explanation of the various orders see the **Civil Litigation Manual**, **Chapter 36** and CPR, PD 44, para. 2.4 dealing with costs orders. The Civil Procedure Rules (CPR) have made substantial changes to the costs regime with the objective of relating the level of costs payable to the value of the dispute between the parties and providing a more balanced approach in defining the 'winner' and 'loser' to avoid the situation where a party who has been largely unsuccessful but still recovers something recovers all of his or her costs. The CPR also introduced summary assessments of costs to avoid the situation where the litigation is fought again in the assessment of the amount of costs payable to the receiving party. This has resulted in an increase in the scope of counsel's duties as counsel now need to be aware of the way in which costs will be assessed and argue for and against summary costs estimates provided by the parties' solicitors. At the end of the trial or application the court must consider whether to make a summary assessment of the costs payable or to order a detailed assessment. In most interim applications and in most simple trials a summary assessment of costs will be made. To facilitate summary assessment of costs each party who intends to claim costs has to prepare a written statement of the costs incurred, in compliance with CPR, PD 44, para. 4.5. You must, before arriving at court, obtain instructions from your solicitors as to what if any of the costs set out in the written estimates can be agreed and what if any arguments can be raised against an opponent's written statement of costs. Some will be obvious as, for example, in a simple case both parties' solicitors ought to have spent the same amount of time in dealing with it. If a detailed assessment is ordered the court can order a payment on account pending the outcome of the detailed assessment. See, for example, *Mars UK v Teknowledge Ltd (No. 2)*, *The Times*, 8 July 1999.

The court exercises an absolute and unfettered discretion in awarding costs. There are no rules of law applicable. There are guidelines that govern the exercise of the judge's discretion; the most important being that costs generally follow the event. The principles to be applied are set out in CPR, r. 44.3. Those principles together with the overriding objectives and achieving proportionality provide an agenda for points to make in an application for costs.

Ordinarily a successful party can expect an order for costs to be made in his or her favour but the court can award costs against a successful party. Given that the court has a complete discretion, anything is possible provided the judge can be persuaded that the order suggested is just and fair in the circumstances of the case in question. The court may award a proportion of a party's costs or costs before or after a specified date. No two cases are the same; this chapter provides a guide to what you can expect to encounter. The arguments on costs that can be raised in any given case are dependent on how the case has been conducted from the outset, the conduct of the hearing or trial and the practical result achieved. A judge will be unwilling to order costs in favour of a party whose conduct has caused the costs to be incurred. A failure to comply with the Rules of the Court will generally result in an order for costs against the defaulting party. Unreasonable conduct by a party, e.g., failing to accept a reasonable offer of settlement or failing to agree an obvious order, will almost certainly persuade a judge either to award costs against that party or deprive that party of costs she or he would otherwise have obtained.

Note: reference cannot be made to 'without prejudice' correspondence to demonstrate unreasonable conduct unless the correspondence states it is without prejudice save as to costs.

34.2   When Should the Application be Made?

After the pronouncement of the judgment or order that the court proposes to make. An application for costs should not form part of your closing submission or final speech.

34.3   Who Should Address the Court First?

As costs generally follow the event the successful party should address the court first. He or she should tell the court what order he or she wants the court to make. He or she should also set out the reasons why the court should make the order requested. If the order required is unusual it may be better to lay the foundations of the application by setting out the reasons first and then inviting the court, in the light of the submissions, to make an order for costs in the desired form. The order requested should be the most favourable that the party can *realistically* invite the court to make.

For example,

> 'I invite your Lordship to order the defendant to pay the claimant's costs of this action. The claimant has been successful in this court. The defendant's defence has been shown to be wholly without merit. . . . (*include any other reasons justifying an order for costs in the claimant's favour*).'

Where neither party has won, submissions as to the appropriate order for costs should be made first by the claimant or the party whose application was before the court.

In many cases the judge will invite counsel for the successful party to tell him or her what order for costs he or she seeks and then ask counsel for the unsuccessful party if he or she has any objections to an order in that form. In cases where there is likely to be little dispute about the order, the judge may tell both parties what order he or she proposes to make and ask if there are any objections. If the successful party desires an order other than that indicated by the judge he or she should say what order he or she requires and why. Counsel should be ready and prepared to state the order he or she requires the judge to make, word for word, as judges often look to counsel for assistance on the phrasing of orders.

After the successful party has made his or her submissions the unsuccessful party has an opportunity to address the court. He or she should deal with each of the reasons put forward by the successful party that can be answered. If there is no realistic answer to any of the submissions made he or she should not seek to refute those submissions. The only result will be an irritated judge. He or she should then tell the judge what order he or she considers ought to be made and make further submissions giving any reasons for making that order which have not been canvassed.

The successful party then replies to the submissions made by the unsuccessful party. It is **not** an opportunity to restate all the submissions previously made by him or her. He or she should deal **only** with new matters raised by the unsuccessful party. Before sitting down he or she should ask the judge if there are any other points on which the judge requires assistance. Be prepared to suggest a less favourable order if your opponent's submissions have weighed heavily on the judge's mind.

Example — interim application:

(a) Claimant seeks order for claimant's costs.

(b) Defendant contends no order for costs.

(c) Claimant submits 'revised order', e.g., claimant's costs in the case.

34.4   Costs on Interim Applications

The same procedure applies. At this stage there is no determination as to which party is successful in the action and which is not. This enables the court to put off the moment of decision as to which party is entitled to costs by reserving the costs of the application to the trial judge or ordering costs in the case, i.e., that the successful party at trial will be entitled to the costs of the application. In the vast majority of interim applications the 'event' will be the outcome of the application and the court will proceed to make an order against one or other of the parties to it rather than reserving the costs to the trial judge.

If any party in an interim application intends to ask the court to make an order for costs in any event, a statement of the costs incurred in the application must be served on the other parties and filed with the court as soon as possible and in any event not less than 24 hours before the hearing. Unless there is a good reason not to do so, a summary assessment will be made. You need to have a list of the points to attack in your opponent's statement and points of defence for your own. The paying party will have to pay the assessed sum within 14 days unless some other period is ordered at the time of the assessment is made. You need to make sure that your client will be able to pay within 14 days and, if not, to have ready the explanation and arguments you will need to make to obtain a longer period for payment. Alternatively, you will need to have ready an explanation and argument for there being a good reason not to have a summary assessment at all. An impecunious party may avoid the consequences of 'pay as you go' litigation if the effect would work a gross injustice, e.g., where he or she has a good claim which would otherwise be stifled and in which enough will be recovered in damages to meet the costs order.

34.4.1   APPLICATIONS FOR AN INJUNCTION

Costs will usually be reserved to the trial judge. If it is an obvious case for the grant of an injunction, the successful party may obtain an order for costs in his or her favour by arguing that the unsuccessful party has wasted both time and money by resisting an application that was bound to succeed. If the application lasted one day or less a summary assessment will be the order of the day.

Similarly if the successful party was forced to apply for the injunction by reason of the unsuccessful party's failure to comply with previous written requests asking him or her to act as the court subsequently ordered, an order for costs will probably be made. If the application was hopelessly misconceived, the party successfully resisting the application can use that as an argument for an order for costs in his or her favour.

34.4.2 APPLICATIONS FOR PERMISSION TO AMEND AND EXTENSIONS OF TIME

In these cases the applicant is seeking the indulgence of the court, in consequence he or she will usually be ordered to pay the costs.

For example — where a Master grants permission to amend a statement of case.

> Defendant: 'Master, this application is the result of the claimant's failure to set out his case properly at the outset. There is no reason why this should not have been done. In consequence the defendant will now have to amend his defence to meet the new allegations raised by the claimant. In the circumstances I would invite you to order that the claimant pay the costs of this application and any costs occasioned by the amendment to the defendant.'

The claimant might avoid such an order if he or she can show that the amendments are due to circumstances arising after service of the particulars of claim, e.g., the defendant alleges in his or her defence that another person is liable instead of the defendant in respect of the claimant's claim. The claimant might also argue that it was an obvious case for the grant of permission to amend so that the defendant should have consented to the application. In an obvious case the defendant might have to pay the costs of the hearing, e.g., where the claimant has sought the defendant's consent to leave to amend with the claimant paying the costs thrown away and the defendant has refused to consent.

34.4.3 APPLICATION TO SET ASIDE JUDGMENT OR WHERE A PARTY IS IN DEFAULT OF AN ORDER

The applicant or the defaulting party will almost invariably be ordered to pay the other party's costs unless there is a good reason to explain why that party was in default. Unless the explanation involves fault on the part of the other party, the defaulting party will have to pay the costs of the application in question. For example: the claimant applies successfully for an order for the defendant to answer a request for further information of his or her defence; the defendant fails to serve his or her replies; the claimant applies for an 'unless' order. The defendant is in default. He or she will almost invariably be ordered to pay the costs of the application for an 'unless' order.

34.4.4 APPLICATIONS FOR SUMMARY JUDGMENT

If the party responding to the application can show that the application is misconceived, e.g., the claimant knew there was a defence at the outset, he or she can argue that the claimant ought to pay his or her costs. If the Master can be persuaded that the application probably ought not to have been made, or that it has been wrongly pursued by the claimant or that the claimant has conducted the application in a dilatory or deficient manner, he or she may order defendant's costs. If the claimant seeks to rely on affidavits or witness statements that are defective and only admitted in evidence with the leave of the court, it should be possible to persuade the Master that no costs ought to be recovered in connection with their preparation. If the claimant pursues an application where there is clearly a real prospect of success he or she may be ordered to pay the defendant's costs. It is not unusual for the claimant to be ordered to pay the defendant's costs incurred after service of his or her affidavit in any event if the affidavit discloses a clear issue, with the balance of the costs, i.e., before that time, to be costs in the case.

34.4.5   APPLICATIONS TO ADJOURN TRIAL

Usually the application is made by the party who is not ready for trial. Unless he or she can show that he or she is not ready because of something outside his or her control, he or she will be ordered to pay the costs of and occasioned by the adjournment to the other party. It can be argued that the other party should pay the costs if the party is not ready for trial because of some default on the part of the other party, e.g., failure to serve an expert's report timeously or a late amendment to the statements of case.

Where an application to amend is made at or shortly before the trial the other party may require an adjournment to consider his or her position and obtain further evidence. In those circumstances the other party ought to receive the costs thrown away both by the amendment and the adjournment.

34.4.6   APPEALS

Counsel must ensure that the costs of the appeal and the costs of the decision appealed are dealt with in the order made on the appeal. The costs below do not necessarily follow the same course as the costs of the appeal, e.g., if the claimant applied for permission to amend the particulars of claim and the application was dismissed by the district judge but allowed on appeal by the County Court judge, it would, prima facie, be wrong for the claimant to recover the costs of the first hearing if, had permission been given by the district judge, the claimant would have been ordered to pay the defendant's costs of the application. In those circumstances it is likely the County Court judge would order the defendant to pay the costs of the appeal as the claimant's appeal succeeded and order the claimant to pay the costs below, i.e., the costs of the application up to and including the hearing before the district judge.

34.5   County Courts

34.5.1   SMALL TRACK CLAIMS

Rule 27.14 of the CPR restricts the costs that can be ordered in small claims hearings. Costs over and above the items referred to in r. 27(14) may only be awarded where a party has been guilty of unreasonable conduct. The following are examples of arguments that might justify an award of additional costs:

(a)   A defence was filed where the defendant knew he or she had no reasonable defence.

(b)   The defendant has offered to pay the full amount of the claim — if he or she intended to pay the claimant's claim he or she ought not to have filed a defence.

(c)   Failure to appear at the hearing.

(d)   Pursuing a hopeless claim.

34.5.2   FAST TRACK COSTS

Cases allocated to the fast track have their own costs regime set out in CPR, Part 46. Summary assessment will be the order of the day in the absence of a good reason for a detailed assessment. The fee recoverable for the advocate at trial is a prescribed amount (see CPR, r. 46.2) which can be increased or decreased in the circumstances set out in r. 46.3. The 'punishment' provisions set out in r. 46.3(7) and (8) are new. What will be considered to be unreasonable or improper behaviour will be worked out with the passage of time. From counsel's point of view the interesting issue is whether 'the party' includes the party's legal representatives or refers only to the lay client. It is probably the latter, so that the lay client who proves to be an obstreperous witness can be punished for his temerity and counsel who asks too many contentious but irrelevant questions cannot. Counsel appearing in fast track cases need to consider how the costs provisions will apply and prepare arguments about their application to the case in which he or she is instructed. The provisions of r. 46.2(2), which allow apportionment of costs to reflect respective degrees of success on the issues at trial, leave plenty of scope for argument in any case in which one party does not win hands down on every single issue (a rare event).

34.5.3 BASIS OF ASSESSMENT

Costs recoverable on assessment are governed by the basis of taxation. If the court so orders the costs may be taxed on an indemnity basis. Such an order is rarely made but will never be made if (i) you do not ask for it and (ii) you do not justify it. There is no express guidance in the CPR as to when an order for assessment on an indemnity basis might be made. It would appear that the considerations set out in CPR, r. 44.3(4) and (5) are relevant. Pursuit of an issue which was bound to be decided against that party may well justify indemnity costs.

34.6 The High Court

CPR, Parts 43 to 48, apply to both the High Court and the County Court.

34.7 Part 36: Payments into Court and Offers to Settle

Payments into court (now known as a Part 36 payment) can turn a successful claimant into the unsuccessful party so far as costs orders are concerned. If the claimant fails to recover more than the sum paid into court by the defendant he or she will be liable to pay the defendant's costs from the last date for acceptance of the money paid into court. He or she will be entitled to an order for his or her costs prior to that date. In this situation the defendant is the successful party and makes the application for costs.

For example,

> On 1 January 1998 the defendant paid £15,000 into court. Your Lordship awarded damages to the claimant in the sum of £12,000. The claimant ought to have accepted the payment into court. She did not do so. In consequence the defendants have incurred the costs, expense and burden of preparing for and conducting this trial. In the circumstances I invite your Lordship to order the claimant to pay the defendant's costs from 1 January 1998 to be assessed if not agreed on the standard basis by detailed assessment.

The claimant should then make any submissions against such an order and ask for an order for costs up to the date of payment into court on the basis that liability on the part of the defendant has been established and until that stage no acceptable proposals were forthcoming from the defendant. Given the increased flexibility that the Civil Procedure Rules have introduced, it may be possible to avoid this consequence if, for example, the defendant had information or evidence undisclosed to the claimant which would have influenced the claimant's assessment of the acceptability of the payment in.

Where the claimant recovers more than the sum paid into court he or she is the successful party and should ask for his or her costs. Part 36 allows claimants to make offers to settle. Where the claimant does better than proposed in his or her Part 36 offer, r. 36.21 imposes sanctions on the defendant for failing to accept the claimant's offer. In that event the defendant may be liable to pay (1) costs on an indemnity basis from the last date for acceptance of the claimant's Part 36 offer, (2) interest at up to 10 per cent a year on the whole or part of the claim and the costs assessed on an indemnity basis. Rule 36.21(4) requires the court to make those orders unless it would be unjust to do so. The principles upon which the court will act are yet to be worked out, with the consequence that the defendant will in every case argue that it is unjust. The case of *Little* v *George Little Sebire & Co., The Times*, 17 November 1999, indicates that the starting point is to consider making an order at ten per cent above the base rate and then consider what if anything justifies making a different order. That would seem to be wrong given the general discretion to select any rate between zero and ten per cent above the base rate. Some guidance as to the relevant criteria to consider is given in r. 36.21(5).

Where a payment into court has been made but not accepted in time, the money cannot be paid out again without an order from the judge. Whilst the money has been in court interest will have accrued. It is usual to order payment of the sum in court, or such part thereof as the claimant has recovered, to the claimant and the balance, if any, and accrued interest to the defendant.

A payment into court can only be made where the claimant has a monetary claim. If the claim is not of a monetary nature the parties can put forward Part 36 offers of settlement in correspondence. In the event that the court decides the offer of settlement was one that should have been accepted, the party making the offer will usually recover his or her costs from the other party from the last date for acceptance of the offer onwards. If the terms of the offer are as good as or better than the relief granted at the trial the court will consider that it should have been accepted. The court is not to take such an offer into account if the party making the offer could have protected his or her position by making a payment into court.

Do not forget to ask the court to make an order for payment out of any moneys in court.

34.8　Publicly Funded Costs

In all cases in which a party is publicly funded at the end of the case, counsel for that party **must** obtain an order for detailed assessment of his or her client's publicly funded costs. If he or she fails to do so payment will not be obtained from the Legal Services Commission. It is prudent to ask for such an order at the end of any interim application that is likely to put an end to the case, e.g., interim injunction where the case is unlikely to come back to court.

Where costs are awarded against a publicly-funded person the court can only order that person to pay such amount as it is reasonable for him or her to pay in all the circumstances of the case (Access to Justice Act 1999, s. 11). This restriction only applies to costs incurred during the period that the party was legally aided. In consequence a losing party who obtains public funding in the course of the proceedings should ordinarily be ordered to pay the winner's costs incurred prior to the date upon which the certificate was granted. Note: this is not necessarily the same date as the date upon which the publicly-funded party gave notice to the winner of the grant of funding — solicitors often overlook giving such notice until some time after a certificate is granted to their client. If you represent a publicly-funded person against whom an order for costs would ordinarily be made, you **must** ensure that either the court makes an order for costs not to be enforced without the permission of the court, or that the court directs an assessment of the amount it is reasonable for the litigant to pay. See the Community Legal Service (Costs) Regulations 2000 (SI 2000 No. 441), regs 9 to 13.

The judge may conduct an assessment of the publicly-funded party's means there and then.

In ascertaining what is a reasonable amount for the assisted person to pay, the court will have regard to the amount of his or her contribution towards that person's own costs as shown on his or her certificate. The costs order will usually contain a limitation along the following lines:

Costs not to be enforced in so far as the same exceed £ [amount of contribution].

The court will also have regard to any damages the legally-aided party may have recovered in the action, e.g., where a publicly-funded claimant is awarded a substantial sum in damages but fails to beat a payment into court, he or she will be ordered to pay the defendant's cost from the date of the payment into court. As they will include the trial costs they are likely to be substantial. The judge may take into account the damages the defendant will pay the claimant as part of the claimant's means for the purpose of determining the amount of the costs that it is reasonable for the claimant to pay to the defendant.

In certain circumstances a successful litigant may be entitled to recover his or her costs from the Community Legal Services Fund. Section 11 of the Access to Justice Act 1999 contains the provisions which may apply. (See the *Civil Litigation Manual*, **Chapter 35**.) The Community Legal Service (Costs) Regulations 2000 and the Community Legal Service (Cost Protection) Regulations 2000 (SI 2000 No. 824) prescribe the procedure to be followed.

In interim applications where the assisted party is unsuccessful, it may be appropriate to invite the court to order 'costs to be enforced by set off against costs or damages now or in the future awarded in this action' (see *Lockley* v *National Blood Transfusion Service* [1992] 1 WLR 492).

Where the publicly-funded party is the receiving party the court cannot make a summary assessment of the costs payable to him or her. It can, however, make a summary assessment against a publicly-funded party but it is not enforceable without the permission of the court (see PD 44, para. 4.7).

34.9 Certificate for Counsel

Where the court orders a detailed assessment of the costs of an interim hearing at which counsel appeared, it is prudent to ask the court to certify that it was fit for counsel to represent the client at that hearing. The costs officer will have regard to the costs opinion so expressed at the detailed assessment of the costs. It would appear that the costs officer may reject that opinion in due course. If you have not asked for such a certificate it is more likely that the costs officer will refuse to allow anything for your attendance at the hearing. Some courts have issued practice guides indicating that counsel's fees will be allowed unless the court has indicated otherwise.

34.10 Reserved Costs

Reserved costs are dealt with by the trial judge. If your client has a good claim to an order for costs the judge must be asked to deal with the costs of the particular application that were reserved. If nothing is said at the conclusion of the trial about costs which were reserved on a previous occasion the costs will, by default, go to the party who is awarded the costs of the action or proceedings. This does not apply in family proceedings.

For example, the claimant applies for and is granted permission to amend a statement of case with costs reserved. At trial the amendments play no significant part in the hearing. The claimant wins and will obtain an order for costs against the defendant. The defendant should specifically raise reserved costs — he or she should not have to pay costs for an amendment sought by the claimant that was of no significance to the conduct of the trial.

Judges show a marked dislike to consider what order for costs to make where the application in question was determined long ago. The view is often expressed, 'If you wanted your costs you should have asked for them then' or 'The judge/Master/Registrar who heard the application did not consider it right to make an order in your favour then and I am not prepared to do so now'. In practical terms once an order for reserved costs has been made, unless the judge is invited to deal with that order specifically, the order will operate in effect as costs in the case.

34.11 Costs Against Solicitors and Counsel

The court has power under s. 51 of the Supreme Court Act 1981 to order costs against a solicitor or counsel personally. The court will only do so if costs have been wasted. Wasted costs are those incurred as a result of any improper, unreasonable or negligent conduct or those incurred prior to such conduct which the court considers it unreasonable for the party to pay. An example of the latter might be where the defendant prepares for an interim application made by the claimant and at the hearing the claimant's solicitors and counsel fail to appear through some negligent oversight on their part. The costs incurred by the defendant in preparing for the application may be wasted costs. Examples of relevant conduct are where a hearing is adjourned because the solicitor has not sent a brief to counsel in sufficient time for counsel to deal with the hearing or where counsel fails to devote adequate time to preparing for the hearing. If the party in default is legally aided, an order for costs against his or her solicitors or counsel is the only order that will, in practical terms, benefit the other party. Before such an order can be made the court must be persuaded that the solicitor has failed to conduct the proceedings with reasonable competence and expedition. Rule 48.7 of the CPR sets out the procedure to be followed and which you will need to ask the court to consider. Applications should only be made if there is a real prospect of success and not just for the sake of it; the application is based on alleging professional negligence against a solicitor or counsel. Further guidance as to when such an application should be made can be found in *Ridehalgh* v *Horsfield* [1994] 3 WLR 462, *Filmlab Systems International Ltd* v *Pennington* [1995] 1 WLR 673 and *R* v *Horsham District Council, ex parte Wenman* [1995] 1 WLR 680. You must not on any account threaten an application for a wasted costs order in order to intimidate the other side. It is a contempt of court and likely to attract a highly unfavourable reaction from the judge should he or she get to hear of it. As a matter of professional courtesy you might alert your opponent that such an application will be made if it is your intention to do so. You must avoid the impression that you are seeking to dissuade a party's legal advisers from fulfilling their duties to their client for fear that you might make such an application against them. The courts have expressed dismay at the extent to which these applications have fostered satellite litigation between the parties. Unless the application is going to be simple, straightforward and short, the court should refuse to entertain it.

THIRTY FIVE

EMPLOYMENT TRIBUNALS

35.1 Introduction

This chapter considers some basic points of advocacy for a hearing before an employment tribunal. Industrial tribunals were renamed employment tribunals on 1 August 1998 by s. 1, Employment Rights (Dispute Resolution) Act 1998. This is not intended to be an exposition of the principles of employment law for which you should use the *Employment Law in Practice Manual*.

You should familiarise yourself with the rules which govern the constitution and powers of the employment tribunal in England and Wales. The current rules are to be found in the Employment Tribunals (Constitution and Rules of Procedure) Regulations 2001, SI No. 1171; see sch. 1. A large number of statutes give jurisdiction to the employment tribunal to determine questions. This chapter is concerned with the most common claims numerically, namely unfair dismissal claims, redundancy claims and contract claims.

You should note that almost 25 years after the statutory power was enacted so that employment tribunals can hear contractual disputes arising out of a contract of employment, on 12 July 1994 the necessary statutory instrument was passed. The Employment Tribunals Extension of Jurisdiction (England and Wales) Order 1994, SI No. 1623 enables most contractual employment disputes with a value of less than £25,000 to be heard and determined by the employment tribunals.

35.2 Some Expressions Explained

You may encounter a number of expressions with which you may not be familiar. The main ones are:

ET1	The number given to the form used as the Applicant's Originating Application (claim)
ET3	The number given to the form used as the Respondent's Notice of Appearance (defence)
Compromise agreement	A binding agreement settling a complaint complying with the statutory requirements of s. 77(4A), Sex Discrimination Act 1975; s. 72(4A), Race Relations Act 1976; s. 288(2B)(c), Trade Union and Labour Relations (Consolidation) Act 1992; s. 9(3)(a), Disability Discrimination Act 1996; or s. 203(3)(c), Employment Rights Act 1996.
Constructive dismissal	A resignation by the employee which amounts in law to a dismissal (as being the acceptance of a serious breach of contract by the employer)
COT3	An ACAS settlement form
ACAS	The Advisory, Conciliation and Arbitration Service which receives a copy of every claim for unfair dismissal and has a statutory responsibility to attempt to achieve a settlement of the claim

Preliminary hearing	An initial jurisdictional hearing
Pre-hearing assessment	An obsolete type of hearing designed to sift out weak cases (replaced by the pre-hearing review)
Pre-hearing review	The current sifting process designed to eliminate weak cases
Recoupment	The system by which certain state benefits may be reclaimed from part of the compensatory award in an unfair dismissal claim

35.3 Steps Prior to any Hearing

The Employment Tribunals have a number of case management powers which you should consider using prior to any hearing; in particular:

(a) the power to order further particulars of the pleadings — r. 4(3);

(b) the power to order discovery — r. 4(4);

(c) the power to order attendance of any person and/or production by that person of documents — r. 4(5)(b);

(d) the power to order written answers to questions — r. 4(3).

These case management powers are now to be exercised by reference to the overriding objective (r. 10).

If you are instructed before any proceedings are issued you should consider whether a binding compromise agreement can be negotiated which avoids the need for a claim to be made. The criteria for such an agreement are set out in the statutory provisions listed under the explanation of the term 'Compromise Agreement' (see **35.2**).

35.4 Listing of Hearings

Except where a shorter period of time has been agreed with the parties, every party must receive at least 14 days' notice of the date fixed for hearing (r. 5(2)).

The notice of hearing is accompanied by information about the documents required for the hearing, the facilities available at the particular employment tribunal and a map showing the location of the tribunal.

35.5 Addressing the Employment Tribunal

The employment tribunal can consist of a chairman sitting alone or, more normally, a panel of three persons. Tribunals will occasionally sit with two persons (provided one is a chairman) if the parties consent, in which case the chairman has the casting vote. The chairman (who is legally qualified) tends to deal with most points which arise during the hearing (after consulting the other members where necessary).

The parties normally sit at tables facing the tribunal, with the witnesses using a smaller table nearer the tribunal or in the centre between the representatives. In most tribunals the applicant will sit on the right (looking towards the employment tribunal) and the respondent will sit on the left.

In London the members of the employment tribunal are normally present in the room used for the hearing when the parties are brought in by the clerk. In some tribunals outside London the parties and public are shown in first, in which case you should stand when the tribunal members arrive.

Although witnesses stand to take the oath or to affirm at the beginning of their evidence, all other steps take place with everyone seated, incuding counsel addressing the tribunal. The chairman and members if addressed individually are 'Sir' or 'Madam';

they can conveniently be referred to collectively as 'the tribunal' or 'this tribunal' or through the chairman as 'you and your colleagues'. When your witnesses have finished their evidence, at the point at which you would normally ask the judge whether he or she has any questions, you should ask 'Do you Sir/Madam, or your colleagues have any questions for this witness?'. The chairman will normally ask each member in turn whether they have any questions (often they do have questions) and will then ask any questions of his or her own.

35.6   Adjournments

The employment tribunal has a general power to adjourn any hearing. The power must be exercised in the interests of justice in the individual case and the CPR overriding objective has been introduced into tribunals. There is no power to impose conditions upon an adjournment (such as one party paying costs) although an order for costs may be made in the normal way; see **35.10.9**.

Two particular situations involving adjournments require special mention. First where there are also other proceedings between the same parties (e.g., a wrongful dismissal claim). Secondly, where there are criminal proceedings pending.

35.6.1   OTHER CLAIMS

In unfair dismissal cases the compensation powers of the employment tribunals are severely limited by statute. An employee may therefore wish to bring a wrongful dismissal claim as well as a claim for compensation for unfair dismissal. A very long line of cases exists which considers when the employment tribunal claim should be adjourned pending the determination of the wrongful dismissal claim; see, for example, *O'Laire* v *Jackal* [1991] ICR 718 and *Bowater plc* v *Charlwood* [1991] ICR 798 which identify some of the factors which ought to be considered.

Two changes in the law may affect the way in which employment tribunals exercise this discretion in the future. First, the changes in employment tribunal jurisdiction to include contractual claims have yet to be considered in this context. Secondly, the effect of the Civil Evidence Act 1995 has yet to be considered.

Since July 1994 the employment tribunals have had power to determine contractual claims under the Employment Tribunals Extension of Jurisdiction (England and Wales) Order 1994. You should look at the text of the order for its full terms. The most important qualifications are that the claim must be made within three months of the effective date of termination or the last day worked (although there is a limited power to extend time) and there is a limit on damages of £25,000. Although there are as yet no reported cases on this aspect it seems that employment tribunals might now refuse to adjourn an unfair dismissal claim pending wrongful dismissal proceedings, if the wrongful dismissal proceedings could also have been brought before an employment tribunal. This might be particularly appropriate where a tactical decision had been made to have two sets of proceedings, for example, in order to obtain legal aid for the wrongful dismissal claim.

One reason why employment tribunal claims are adjourned is that employment tribunals are not bound by the strict rules of evidence (r. 11(1) of the 2001 Rules). Since a decision reached by an employment tribunal will give rise to an estoppel *per rem judicata* in a subsequent court hearing, the preference was to have the court hearing first. In *O'Laire* v *Jackal* a decision by the employment tribunal was described by Browne-Wilkinson LJ, a former President of the Employment Appeal Tribunal, as 'plainly wrong', yet the High Court and Court of Appeal were bound by it. The difference which used to exist over admissibility of evidence has been considerably reduced now that the Civil Evidence Act 1995 has been brought into force. It may be that applications to adjourn employment tribunal proceedings will be made less often or with less success.

35.6.2 CRIMINAL PROCEEDINGS

Employment tribunals often have to decide whether to adjourn proceedings for compensation for unfair dismissal pending criminal proceedings against the employee. The fact that the employee has been charged with a criminal offence certainly does not mean that his or her dismissal will always be fair (even if the offence arises out of or at his or her work). However, a conviction will often affect an award of compensation for unfair dismissal. The employment tribunals have a wide discretion to adjourn pending criminal proceedings and frequently do so despite the decision in *Bastick* v *James Lane (Turf Accountants) Ltd* [1979] ICR 778 in which the decision not to adjourn was upheld on appeal. Perhaps the crucial words in the decision of the Employment Appeal Tribunal in that case are (at p. 784) that:

> we are bound to conclude that, although it would have been perfectly reasonable to come to the opposite conclusion, nevertheless the conclusion which this chairman reached is not so unreasonable a conclusion as to lead us to a finding of perversity.

Truly a case of being damned by faint praise.

The common decision to adjourn also avoids the difficulty highlighted in *Ladup Ltd* v *Barnes* [1982] ICR 107. In that case the employment tribunal found a dismissal unfair when the employer dismissed on learning that the employee had been arrested and charged with growing and possession of cannabis plants. The employment tribunal awarded compensation. Later the employee was convicted of possession of cannabis. The employment tribunal refused to review its decision (see **35.12.1** for an explanation of review). The Employment Appeal Tribunal allowed the appeal against the refusal to review the decision and found that the employee had contributed towards his dismissal 100%, thus extinguishing his compensation.

35.7 Preliminary Hearing

Unfortunately a preliminary hearing is often confused with a pre-hearing review or pre-hearing assessment. They are quite different procedural creatures. A preliminary hearing is normally ordered where there is a legal or jurisdictional issue to be determined before any consideration of the merits of the claims. A pre-hearing review (formerly known as a pre-hearing assessment) is an initial consideration of the merits of the claim (see **35.8**).

A preliminary hearing can be ordered at any stage prior to the hearing of the Originating Application (at the request of one or more parties or by a chairman). Slightly more unusually a preliminary issue may be directed to be considered at the beginning of the main hearing under an employment tribunal's general power to regulate its own procedure. It is imperative that the legal or jurisdictional issue is carefully defined so that all relevant evidence is given and submissions are made. So, for example, if the jurisdictional issue is whether a claim for compensation for unfair dismissal is made within time, it should be decided if the subsidiary question, i.e., to grant an extension of time, if necessary, is to be heard at the same time (as would be normal), or only after a decision has been made as to whether the claim was in fact in time.

The most common examples of preliminary hearings are:

(a) A hearing to determine whether the claim has been brought within the relevant statutory time limit and, if not, whether time should be extended under the relevant power.

(b) A hearing to determine whether the applicant is an employee within the meaning of s. 230(1), Employment Rights Act 1996 (unfair dismissal and redundancy claims).

(c) A hearing to determine whether the applicant has the necessary length of service to qualify to bring the claim.

If the disputes of fact which have to be resolved at the preliminary hearing are inextricably linked to the merits of the case, an employment tribunal may refuse a separate preliminary hearing. A common example would be where there is confusion as to the exact date of dismissal which is relevant to determine whether the claim is brought within time and whether any extension of time should be given. In such a case it is easier to hear all the evidence and determine all the issues together.

A preliminary hearing can be heard by an employment tribunal chairman sitting alone.

The practice of holding preliminary hearings has existed for more than 20 years. It was first recognised by the Rules in 1993. The Rules suggest that written representations and oral argument can be used but make no express reference to oral evidence being heard. In practice oral evidence is required at most preliminary hearings before the legal or jurisdictional issue can be properly decided and a number of decisions have criticised attempts to short-circuit the need to make proper findings of fact; see, for example, *BL Cars Limited* v *Brown* [1983] ICR 143. An unusual example of a case where oral evidence was not taken can be found in *Janstorp International (UK) Limited* v *Allen* [1990] IRLR 417 where the employment tribunal decided whether wages in lieu of notice fell within the statutory definition of 'wages' in the Wages Act 1986 without hearing evidence and the Employment Appeal Tribunal gave guidance on situations where a case might be decided without hearing evidence. It is occasionally possible to agree facts for the purposes of a preliminary issue but the employment tribunals are not strictly bound by that agreement and Mummery J has warned of the dangers which exist if the facts are agreed hurriedly at the door of the hearing or during the hearing. Errors can have most unfortunate consequences: *Waters* v *Metropolitan Police Commissioner* [1995] IRLR 531.

The procedure at a preliminary hearing is similar to that at a main hearing. The party upon whom the burden of proof lies will normally go first. The burden is usually upon the applicant employee to show that the employment tribunal has jurisdiction to hear and determine the claim. The applicant's representative will briefly outline the basic facts indicating the extent of the preliminary issue. The applicant's evidence will then be given, cross-examination will take place and, if necessary, any re-examination or questions from the employment tribunal. Any witnesses for the applicant will then be heard. Thereafter any witnesses for the respondent will be heard. The respondent's counsel will address the employment tribunal and finally the applicant's counsel will have the last word.

The employment tribunal will often give a brief decision very quickly to be followed by written reasons in short or extended form (see **35.10.6**).

35.8 Pre-hearing Review

In 1980 pre-hearing assessments were first introduced in the hope that hopeless cases would be weeded out. The procedure never worked as intended and it fell into disuse.

In 1993 the current weeding-out process known as a pre-hearing review was introduced (r. 7).

A pre-hearing review may be ordered by the employment tribunal of its own motion or at the request of a party. It may be conducted by a full employment tribunal or a chairman sitting alone.

If the employment tribunal decides that a party's contentions have no reasonable prospect of success, then a party may be ordered to pay a deposit of up to £500 as a condition of the case proceeding to a full hearing. Account must be taken of the means of the party being ordered to pay the deposit. The decision is recorded in a summary form and sent to the parties with a warning that if the claim continues, costs may be awarded against the party ignoring the warning. If the deposit condition is not complied with, the Originating Application or Notice of Appearance (or certain specified parts of it) may be struck out.

If the claim continues to a full hearing after a pre-hearing review, no member of the employment tribunal may sit on the employment tribunal which hears the substantive claim. If the person against whom the order is made pays the deposit it will then be returned if the claim is withdrawn before the main hearing, in the unlikely event of the claim succeeding, or if the claim continues but an award of costs is not made against the party paying the deposit.

This sifting process seems to be used against more applicants than respondents.

At a pre-hearing review the employment tribunal considers the pleadings and the contentions of the parties, but does not make detailed findings of fact and rarely hears any oral evidence. If you represent the party against whom the hearing has been convened you should be prepared to explain the basis of your case clearly and succinctly. Since the employment tribunal does not make a detailed inquiry into disputed facts at this stage, it should be asked to accept the facts asserted as correct at that stage. Although it is not often necessary to cite authority, if the contention which you rely upon is not well known, citing the relevant authority may be essential.

35.9   Directions Hearings

The employment tribunals now make much more frequent use of directions hearings, particularly in complex cases involving difficult issues. Directions hearings are heard before a chairman who will seek to determine the real issues in dispute. Those issues will usually be recorded in writing, will be sent to the parties in a letter and will be placed on the file so that the employment tribunal hearing the case can see the issues. For example, in a case in which an employee alleges that it is unfair to dismiss him or her because others have not been dismissed for similar activities, a directions hearing might be convened to see which activities of which other employees are relied upon. If concessions or statements which are sought are not made, the chairman can order further particulars, discovery or questions to be answered within a specified further period.

As it is common practice for the employment tribunal to make orders for discovery and further particulars *ex parte* in response to a letter from one side requesting an order, if the recipient wishes to set aside the order or part of it a directions hearing can be arranged as the most convenient forum for an *inter partes* hearing.

If you attend a directions hearing you should be ready to explain the chronology of events, the basis of your case and identify which issues are not in dispute and which are in dispute. You should also be in a position to identify any further steps which you believe are required (such as discovery or written questions which ought to be answered).

35.10   The Substantive Hearing

The preparation for the hearing should include attempting to agree a bundle of documents for the hearing. If agreement cannot be reached, each side should prepare at least six copies of its paginated bundle (three for the members of the employment tribunal, one for the witness and one for each party). An agreed bundle means that the parties accept that the documents are to be placed before the employment tribunal, not that the contents of each document are admitted to be accurate.

If there is a claim for reinstatement or re-engagement the respondent should be in a position to give any evidence opposing the making of such an order at the main hearing.

It is becoming increasingly common to prepare written witness statements for each witness. This is not compulsory but saves considerable time, particularly if they are exchanged in advance of the hearing. The witness can then read the witness statement as his or her evidence-in-chief. If this practice is adopted the employment tribunal generally limits supplementary questions to matters arising on exchange of witness statements and more recent events.

There is a power for the employment tribunal to receive written representations or submissions provided that they are given not less than seven days before the hearing (r. 10(5)). This is not the same as admitting written evidence.

The hearings are held in public. There is a limited power to hear part or all of the claim in private under rr. 8 and 10. There is also a very limited power to impose reporting restrictions and to prevent the identification of a person affected by a sexual harassment allegation under r. 16. In England and Wales the witnesses normally remain in the tribunal room throughout the case and hear the evidence of earlier and later witnesses.

35.10.1   NON-ATTENDANCE

If one party does not attend the clerk normally tries to contact the party to see if there is any reason for the non-attendance (such as not receiving the notice of hearing). You should also ask if any written submissions have been submitted by the absent party.

If the party absent is the one with the burden of proof, then the other party may ask for a finding in its favour without hearing evidence. If the employment tribunal adopts the approach and the finding is in favour of the employee, the employment tribunal will still have to calculate the redundancy payment or determine the remedy for an unfair dismissal. If, for example, the employer admits dismissal but does not attend to establish an acceptable reason for dismissal, the applicant may seek a finding of unfair dismissal. The statutory presumption that a dismissal was for redundancy in s. 163(2), Employment Rights Act 1996 applies only to a claim for a redundancy payment and not to claims for unfair dismissal and so would not assist the absent employer.

35.10.2   OPENING

At the substantive hearing the first issue is which side opens the case. In unfair dismissal or redundancy claims, if dismissal is admitted, the respondent employer will go first. The respondent must still establish the reason for dismissal even though there is no longer any burden of proof in relation to fairness. If dismissal is not admitted then the applicant employee will go first and must show that there was an actual or constructive dismissal. In contract claims the applicant will go first.

It is important that it is established whether the entire case is to be heard at once or whether the question of liability is to be separated from the question of remedy. Many employment tribunals prefer to consider remedy separately after deciding liability, even if both aspects are dealt with on the same day. If the remedy of reinstatement or re-engagement is sought by the applicant, separate subsequent consideration of remedy is usually directed as detailed evidence may have to be heard on the availability of other jobs. If no indication is given by the employment tribunal on this point a ruling should be sought well before the applicant begins giving evidence about his or her losses resulting from dismissal. When this aspect is being considered you should ensure that it is clear whether or not liability includes any finding of contribution towards dismissal and/or any deduction for the risks of a fair dismissal at some future point.

The opening can often be extremely brief. Employment tribunals are regularly critical of overlong openings by counsel. It is useful to indicate the correct basic facts or the extent of the dispute about those basic facts such as dates of employment, rates of pay, job description, place of work. Any amendments to the ET1 (the Originating Application) or the ET3 (the Respondent's Notice of Appearance) should be made at this stage. If the respondent's business is not obvious from its name, or well known, a brief explanation of the business may assist the tribunal. Finally it is often helpful to give some indication of the size and administrative resources of the respondent in opening, mentioning the size of the business and/or the number of staff employed at the applicant's place of work and generally. Finally it is often much quicker to take the employment tribunal through the bundles of documents in opening rather than ask each witness to 'produce' documents which it has been agreed should be placed before them.

35.10.3　THE TAKING OF EVIDENCE

Evidence is usually taken on oath or affirmation (r. 9). Before the hearing the clerk will normally check who is giving evidence and how they wish to take the oath so that the necessary form of oath and appropriate holy book will be ready. As in court a separate oath will be taken by any interpreter. As in court the oath should be taken standing and whilst everyone else is silent (never use this time to take last-minute, spoken instructions).

Witnesses are normally released once their evidence has been taken. However you should ask the employment tribunal to release a witness before allowing a witness to leave.

If more than one claim is being heard at the same time, the evidence which is relevant and admissible on each claim may require careful consideration. The most common problem is where claims for wrongful dismissal and claims for unfair dismissal are heard together.

(a)　At the liability stage of a claim for unfair dismissal the employment tribunal is focusing on the knowledge and actions of the employer up to and at the time of dismissal. No account should be taken of subsequently discovered facts (until remedy is considered): *Devis (W) & Sons* v *Atkins* [1977] AC 931. Thus, for example, evidence coming to light after dismissal supporting an allegation of misconduct is not admissible in the unfair dismissal claim.

(b)　In a wrongful dismissal claim, as in most contract claims, the tribunal is concerned to determine whether the employee was justifiably dismissed summarily. Subsequently discovered misconduct and subsequently discovered evidence can be relied upon by the employer to justify the dismissal: *Boston Deep Sea Fishing & Ice Co.* v *Ansell* (1888) 39 Ch D 399.

35.10.4　SUBMISSIONS OF NO CASE TO ANSWER

Although it is possible to make a submission of no case to answer at the end of the evidence from the party with the burden of proof, such a practice should only be used in exceptionally plain and obvious cases. Before making a submission take care to determine whether the employment tribunal will regard you as having elected to call no evidence if you make a submission (as would be the case in a civil trial but not in a criminal trial).

35.10.5　CLOSING SUBMISSIONS

Employment tribunals often criticise lengthy closing speeches and excessive reference to authority. The party with the burden of proof should have the final say. You can usually assume that the employment tribunal will be familiar with the leading cases. If the law in your case is more complex, then you may need to cite authority, in which case you may find a written skeleton argument extremely useful. If you are citing authorities let the clerk to the tribunal know in the morning so that copies can be obtained for the employment tribunal.

35.10.6 THE LIABILITY DECISION

If time permits, the employment tribunal will give a decision on liability very shortly after hearing closing submissions. A written decision will then be sent to the parties at a later date signed by the chairman. The written decision can be in summary form or in extended form. In certain cases (such as discrimination claims) reasons in extended form must be given. In other cases the employment tribunal must give extended reasons if asked for at the hearing, or if a written request is made before the summary reasons are sent out, or if a written request is made within 21 days after the summary reasons are sent out.

35.10.7 THE REMEDIES ISSUE

If the claim is for a redundancy payment, the calculation of the correct payment should be a matter of simple mathematics, applying the formula in s. 162, Employment Rights Act 1996.

If the claim is for unfair dismissal employment tribunals are obliged to consider an order for reinstatement or re-engagement and only thereafter to award compensation. In practice orders for reinstatement or re-engagement are extremely rarely sought and even more rarely made by a tribunal. If re-engagement or reinstatement is sought, employment tribunals will normally hear evidence from both parties. If only compensation is sought the tribunal will normally only hear evidence from the applicant about efforts to find a new job and any temporary or permanent position found.

If employment tribunals announce that a dismissal is unfair, it is quite common for the parties to be recommended to attempt to reach a settlement because the financial benefits of settlement can be considerable (see **35.11**).

35.10.8 INTEREST

In awards of a redundancy payment or compensation for unfair dismissal no interest is included in the award. However interest will run in repect of an unpaid award from 42 days after the date of the decision — the period allowed for lodging an appeal (see **35.12.2**).

35.10.9 COSTS

Costs are rarely awarded by an employment tribunal. The power to award costs is set out in r. 14. The power is used where a party has acted frivolously, vexatiously, abusively, disruptively or otherwise unreasonably. However note that an employment tribunal must award costs if the respondent asks for an adjournment to oppose the making of an order of reinstatement or re-engagement, provided that the wish to make such a claim was communicated to the respondent at least seven days before the hearing (as would be the case if it is sought in the IT1).

If costs are awarded they may be a specific sum of up to £10,000 fixed by the employment tribunal, any sum agreed between the parties, or assessed costs on the appropriate County Court scale.

If, on a pre-hearing review: (i) a party was ordered to pay a deposit as a condition of continuing to participate in the proceedings; (ii) the party paying the deposit has lost; and (iii) no award of costs has been made under the general power, an employment tribunal must consider whether to award costs on the grounds that the party continued the proceedings unreasonably in persisting with the case. However an employment tribunal must not make an award unless the document recording the decision at the pre-hearing review and the eventual decision are substantially the same.

The application for costs is normally made at the end of the hearing. If no decision is announced at the end of the hearing, the question of costs would have to be considered at a further hearing (involving additional expense) or by written representations. The Employment Appeal Tribunal has suggested that to avoid a further hearing a party could indicate that, if successful, he or she wished to apply for an order for costs. In practice that is rarely a sensible approach as: (i) it is not until the basis of the decision is known that the application for costs can properly be formulated by labelling the conduct frivolous, vexatious or merely unreasonable; and (ii) the employment tribunal could not be informed of the decision at any pre-hearing review before they have arrived at their own decision.

35.11 Settlement

Employment tribunals frequently encourage parties to settle claims 'at the door of the court'. If a liability decision is announced, a further opportunity is often given for settlement before the employment tribunal rules on the remedy. In addition to the usual benefits of settlement, there is one factor peculiar to claims before employment tribunals which you should bear in mind. The factor is the effect of recoupment of state benefits received by the employee after termination.

The position is governed by the Employment Protection (Recoupment of Jobseekers' Allowance and Income Support) Regulations 1996. In short if an applicant is awarded compensation for unfair dismissal, an employment tribunal has to calculate the period covered by past loss and the net award made for that period (known as the prescribed element). The Secretary of State is then informed of the decision and will reclaim any benefits paid in that period up to the amount awarded. Thus the applicant actually receives less than the sum awarded to him but the respondent pays out the amount awarded, diverting some part to the Government.

If a settlement is reached there is no recoupment of benefit. In this respect the approach in employment tribunals is quite different from the approach in personal injury actions. In many unfair dismissal cases the sum which will be recouped will be a substantial part of the compensatory element of the award.

An example may assist. If the employee has been unemployed for, say, six months prior to the hearing and has received £4,000 in recoupable benefit, the position is as follows:

(a) If the employment tribunal awards compensation of £5,000 for the six month period of loss, and further compensation (including a basic award) of, say, £5,000, the respondent will have to pay out £10,000 but the applicant will only receive £6,000 of that sum.

(b) If the case is settled there is no recoupment of the benefits of £4,000 received. Thus an agreed settlement of £8,000 payable to the applicant will mean that both parties are better off by £2,000.

If you reach a settlement at the hearing you should ensure that it is binding and enforceable. There are a number of ways of making the settlement binding. Many chairmen have their own preferred way and some will seek to impose their preferred approach on the parties. The most common methods are a consent order or a type of 'Tomlin' order.

(a) A simple consent order for payment can be made by an employment tribunal. There will be no recoupment because there is no prescribed element to which a recoupment notice can be applied.

(b) Employment tribunals do not favour the normal 'Tomlin' form — where the proceedings are stayed indefinitely — as they are anxious to close their files. A common practice is therefore to order that the claim is dismissed on withdrawal by the applicant at some future date, unless either party notifies the employment tribunal that the claim should be released. If, for example, the settlement payment is to be paid in 21 days, it might be convenient for the case to be dismissed on withdrawal by the applicant in 42 days' time if a request for a further hearing has not been made within 35 days. If the payment is received, no request is made and the claim ends in 56 days. If the payment is not made in 21 days (or even shortly thereafter) the applicant would request a further hearing well within the 35 days allowed.

35.12 Further Steps

There are two ways of challenging a decision of an employment tribunal: by review and by appeal.

35.12.1 REVIEW

A review is a reconsideration of the decision by an employment tribunal. The power to grant a review is found in r. 13. It is rarely exercised. An application by a party for a review must be in writing made within 14 days of the date the decision was sent to the parties. The employment tribunal has power to review its own decision of its own motion without time limit. The grounds for a review are very limited and are that:

(a) the decision was wrongly made as a result of an error on the part of the tribunal staff;

(b) a party did not receive notice of the proceedings leading to the decision;

(c) the decision was made in the absence of a party;

(d) new evidence has become available since the conclusion of the hearing to which the decision relates, provided that its existence could not have been reasonably known of or foreseen at the time of the hearing; or

(e) the interests of justice require such a review.

35.12.2 APPEAL

An appeal against the decision of an employment tribunal lies on a point of law to the Employment Appeal Tribunal: Part II, Employment Tribunals Act 1996. The procedure is governed by the Employment Appeals Tribunal Rules 1993 (SI 1993 No. 2854). The Notice of Appeal normally has to be lodged within 42 days of the date on which the written decision of the employment tribunal was sent to the parties.

THIRTY SIX

BAIL APPLICATION

The following is a check list for the preparation and conduct of a bail application. Reference should be made to the *Criminal Litigation and Sentencing Manual* for the procedure.

36.1   Preparation

The first and most important step is to discover what the objections to bail are. These may be fairly obvious, e.g., your client may have allegedly committed the offence whilst on bail for another offence; or may have a history of absconding; he or she may be charged with a serious offence such as supplying drugs or a series of offences such as burglary.

If not apparent, then ask the prosecuting counsel/solicitor what the objections to bail are. Get to court early enough to have the opportunity to speak to him or her; in the magistrates' court, he or she is likely to be dealing with a considerable case load.

Ensure you have an up-to-date copy of the defendant's antecedents; if you don't, ask the prosecution for a copy. Never rely solely on a client's description of his or her past record.

Consider with your client whether he or she wants you to make a bail application and advise on the prospects of success. Some clients are realistic and appreciate when their prospects of obtaining bail are hopeless; others anticipate a custodial sentence and prefer to serve part of their eventual sentence on remand (see Crime (Sentences) Act 1997, s. 9). Consider whether it is the right time to make a bail application or whether it is appropriate to wait, e.g., until you have been served with advance disclosure of the prosecution case, have fuller instructions or there is a surety at court.

Consider the strength of the prosecution evidence. If advance information has not yet been served on the defence, consider the nature and extent of the charge(s), the amount of any money involved, the gravity of any alleged injury; ask the prosecutor for basic information such as whether there are any eye witness accounts, whether the evidence is circumstantial, whether the defendant is alleged to have confessed.

Take as full instructions from the client as time permits upon the circumstances of the alleged offence(s), and his or her tentative plea.

Go through the client's previous record in detail, establishing the circumstances of any serious or similar offences to the present charge(s), whether he or she pleaded guilty in respect of any past offences, the reasons for any previous failure to appear, whether he or she has ever been convicted of committing an offence whilst on bail.

Find out the client's present circumstances; job, home ties, responsibilities, the potential/probable effects of a continued loss of liberty.

Look at whether there has been any change in the client's circumstances since the time of the alleged offence, e.g., has he or she moved from the area, changed his or her crowd of friends? Is any change likely in the future?

Discuss any possible conditions that can be put forward to meet the objections to bail and whether your client is prepared to abide by them. Consider practical solutions to the objections, e.g., if the defendant has no fixed abode, is a place in a bail hostel a possibility? Speak to the probation officer at court about this; if necessary ask for your case to be put back in the list for this purpose. Note that bail hostels will not normally consider a defendant with a drug habit or convictions for violence. If possible, discuss any proposed conditions with the prosecutor in advance to determine whether such conditions would meet the objections. (If so, the bail application will become effectively 'unopposed' and offering the 'agreed' conditions to the court will be likely to succeed.)

Consider whether any surety is (or is likely to be) available, the amount any surety is/would be prepared to offer; if the proposed surety is at court, ensure he or she understands the meaning of standing as a surety and the likely consequences in the event of the defendant absconding. Consider whether a proposal to lodge security at court is a practical option (normally more appropriate in the case of a foreign defendant or where a risk of leaving the country is involved).

36.2   Making the Application

In making your application for bail, keep it as brief as possible and to the point. Do not repeat yourself, wander off on a tangent or lecture the court upon your client's rights to bail. Deal with your points in a logical sequence, making your strongest points first and last. Do not make weak points which will detract from the strength of your other submissions.

Deal with the objections in two ways. *Step 1*: undermine/cast doubt on their validity. *Step 2*: propose how such objections (if still of concern) could sensibly be met.

For example, if the objection is that the defendant is likely to commit offences whilst on bail, draw the court's attention to such matters as the weaknesses in the prosecution case, your client's intention to plead 'not guilty'; the fact that he or she has always pleaded guilty in the past, or has no history of committing offences whilst on bail; the dissimilarity between the present charge(s) and his or her previous offences; the amount of time that has elapsed since his or her last conviction; the fact that he or she has an address to stay at away from previous associates or has moved since the time of the alleged offence(s). Suggest possible conditions such as: a condition of residence, a curfew, restriction to/from a particular location.

Or, if the objection is that he or she is likely to interfere with witnesses: draw the court's attention to the fact that there is no suggestion the defendant has ever done so before; and/or that no threats or pressure are alleged to have been made/applied in this case; point to the lack of any close connection between the defendant and the witness (e.g., family relationship, neighbour) that would enable him or her to influence the alleged victim/witness if he or she were released on bail. Suggest possible conditions such as: prohibiting the defendant from contacting or interfering with any witness; restricting his or her entry into the areas where the alleged victim/witness lives.

Or, if the objection is that the defendant is likely to abscond: highlight such matters as the fact that the defendant has never done so before; or explain the circumstances of any failure to appear in the past (e.g., dates mixed up; went to the police/court as soon as he or she realised); and/or point to the fact that he or she has in the past attended court even where he or she has pleaded guilty or anticipated a custodial sentence; address the court upon the weaknesses in the prosecution case and/or the unlikelihood of a custodial sentence even if the defendant were to plead guilty/be convicted; emphasise the defendant's community ties, employment, secure home, family responsibilities as indicators of the unlikelihood of his or her absconding. Suggest possible conditions such as: (daily) reporting to the nearest police station; condition of residence; residence at a bail hostel; surrendering his or her passport; providing a surety; lodging security.

There are some cases where it is simply not possible to undermine the objections. If the defendant has a history of absconding, it is useless to argue that 'she has learned her lesson and has asked me to assure the court that she will not abscond again'. That will get you nowhere! If you cannot deal with the objection(s) in this way, be realistic about it. Concentrate your efforts upon persuading the court that there are (stringent) conditions which could be imposed to ensure the defendant's good behaviour and attendance at court.

Having dealt with the objections to bail, it may assist to point out the likely consequences of a continuing loss of liberty upon the defendant, e.g., losing his or her job; mortgagee possession proceedings in respect of his or her home; children will be taken into care.

If you call any proposed surety, establish his or her relationship to the defendant; then ask questions designed to elicit that he or she understands the meaning of what he or she is proposing and the consequences if the defendant fails to attend the trial (e.g., 'Do you understand that you will be liable to forfeit such a sum if the defendant absconds?'); establish the amount of money he or she is proposing to pledge and the manner in which he or she would raise that sum in the event of the defendant absconding (it should be otherwise than by selling/mortgaging his or her home, such as from savings in the building society), e.g., 'Are you worth £x after all your debts are paid?'; 'How would you raise that sum if ordered to do so?'; confirm that he or she is still prepared to stand as a surety to ensure the defendant's surrender to bail (e.g., 'Are you still prepared to stand surety in the sum of £x?').

If bail is granted, ensure your client understands the nature and extent of any conditions imposed and the likely consequences if he or she breaches them.

If bail is refused by the magistrates, obtain a copy of the magistrates' certificate recording their reasons for the refusal (see the Bail Act 1976, s. 5(6A)). Consider with your client whether he or she wishes you to renew the application before the magistrates on the next or a subsequent court appearance or whether he or she wishes to appeal to a Crown Court/High Court judge for bail. You must know the procedure on the application itself and also that relating to appeal. Advise your client realistically of the prospects of such an appeal.

36.3   Procedure

Bail applications

The following table charts the procedure in a magistrates' court when the magistrates, having asked the defence whether there is an application for bail, receive an answer in the affirmative.

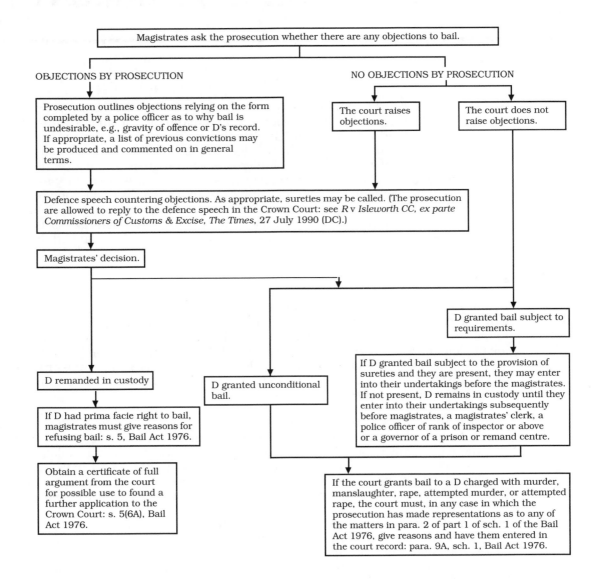

THIRTY SEVEN

REMANDS/ADJOURNMENTS

Among the first court appearances you are likely to undertake during your second six months' pupillage, are an application for a remand in the magistrates' court, an application to stand a case out of the list in the Crown Court, or an application to adjourn a hearing in the County Court/High Court. Often the case will not actually be your case but that of a member of chambers. As you progress in practice, however, you will continue to find that there are many occasions when it is necessary to apply for a remand or adjournment in cases of your own and often you will consider such an application appropriate even where your instructing solicitor has not briefed you specifically for that purpose. Sometimes, unforeseen circumstances arise at court which make it necessary to make or respond to such an application with little notice.

37.1   Preparation

Before you make an application for a remand or adjournment, investigate the reasons why the case is not ready to proceed. The most common grounds for applying for a remand/adjournment are insufficient time to prepare the case (e.g., investigations incomplete; client only recently instructed solicitors; public funding just granted; late service of affidavit or witness statement, late disclosure of documents); or the court or one of the parties is not in a position to proceed (e.g., witness unavailable; pre-sentence report required; lack of court time).

Consider the history of the case; if it is not your case, try to speak to counsel whose case it is. Have there been any previous adjournments in the case? For what reason? Has there been any delay on your client's/solicitor's part? Can you explain the delay? Always ensure you have clear instructions on these matters and have advised your solicitors where it may be necessary to lay the blame for undue delay at their door. Ensure you have a chronology of the progress of the case clear in your mind.

Advise your client of the reasons why an application to adjourn is appropriate and the consequences this may have for him or her, e.g., on the question of costs. In some cases, the client may instruct you to proceed even if you are not fully prepared, e.g., he or she may prefer to proceed with the witnesses that are at court rather than risk the costs of an adjournment or the agony of further delay simply to secure the attendance of another witness. (It is sensible to invite your client to endorse this instruction on your brief.)

Consider the steps, if any, that have been taken to notify the other party and the court of the application to adjourn the case. Be in a position to explain the absence of any notice. Inform your opponent at the earliest opportunity of your intention to apply for an adjournment. Discover whether your application is likely to be/will be opposed.

Look at the merits of your application. Will your opponent be prejudiced by an adjournment or can any prejudice be compensated, e.g., by an order for costs? Will you be prejudiced by a refusal to adjourn? How vital is it to your case? If you have time, make a note of the main points of your argument.

Consider how long you realistically need to be ready to proceed with the case.

Apply your mind to any orders or directions you want the court to make pending the adjourned hearing (whether you are making or responding to the application), e.g., permission to amend a statement of case; permission to file further witness statement(s); specific disclosure of documents; an interim injunction to maintain the status quo or to protect your client; continuation of any existing order(s) such as an interim injunction; an interim order to provide for your client, e.g., order for maintenance or contact with his or her children; the grant of bail or the continuation of an existing surety. Where appropriate, try to agree any orders/directions with your opponent.

Ask yourself what order for costs you want the court to impose in the event of your/your opponent's application for an adjournment being successful, e.g., an order for the costs thrown away; costs reserved. Advise your client of any risk that he or she will be ordered to pay the costs (or your solicitors if the fault lies with them).

Never assume that the court will accede to your request for an adjournment. Be prepared to proceed if your application is refused **but** never assume an obligation to do a case in such circumstances when you do not feel professionally qualified to do so. If you face such a possibility when the brief is one delivered to another member of the Bar and you are simply making the application because he or she cannot be at court you must discuss the matter with them beforehand and make your position clear to them. If the brief is one which has been delivered to you then you should not hesitate to discuss your position with your former pupil-master or a senior member of chambers. It may be necessary later to speak directly to your instructing solicitor. Always remember, the interests of the client come first.

37.2   Making the Application

When your case is called on for hearing, inform the court at the outset that you have an application to make for a remand/adjournment/the case to be stood out of the list (as appropriate) and indicate if your application is opposed/unopposed.

Set out the reasons for your application in a succinct manner. If appropriate, refer the court to any affidavit or document which is relevant to the application for an adjournment. Explain any delays — be honest. Deal with the merits of your application and the manner in which any possible prejudice to the other party can be met, e.g., an order for interim relief, an order for costs.

Be as brief as possible and do not repeat your arguments! Do not try to argue the merits of your substantive case, remember that at this stage you are applying for an adjournment.

Tell the court how long you will need before you are in a position to proceed with the hearing of the case.

It will then be your opponent's turn to address the court. If resisting such an application, he or she will emphasise any delay on the part of the applicant and the inconvenience and/or prejudice his or her client will suffer as a result of the delay which cannot be met in any other way, e.g., by an interim order or an order for costs.

You may then have a further opportunity to address the court in response to your opponent's submissions. Do not use this as an opportunity to repeat your arguments.

If the application to adjourn is either unopposed or succeeds, indicate to the court the orders or directions which you seek in the interim and whether any or all of them are agreed subject to the court's approval.

Make or respond to the application for costs. Make any appropriate application for legal aid assessment (this is often not granted until the final hearing).

THIRTY EIGHT

TRIABLE EITHER WAY OFFENCES — DETERMINING THE MODE OF TRIAL (ss. 17A–23, MCA 1980)

38.1 The Usual Procedure (ss. 17A–21 and 23, MCA 1980)

If someone aged 18 or over appears or is brought before a magistrates' court on an information charging him or her with an offence triable either way, the magistrate (or magistrates) must determine the mode of trial: s. 17A(1) and s. 18(5). (A single lay justice may do this but it is unusual for this to happen.) The procedure is as follows:

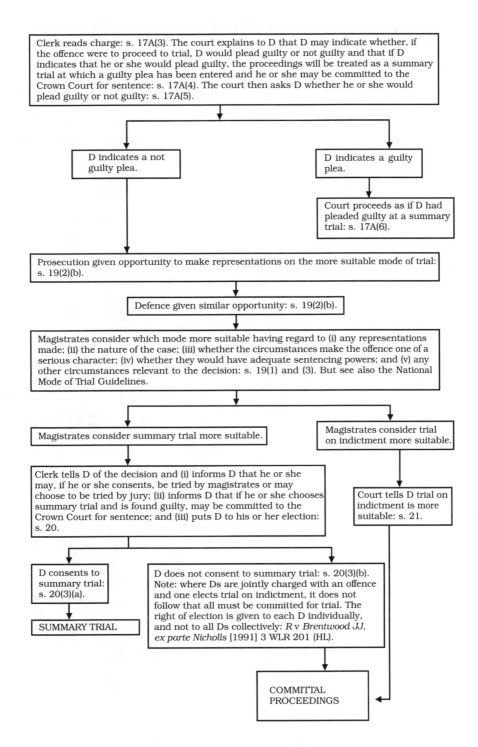

Cross-refer to the ***Criminal Litigation and Sentencing Manual***, **Chapter 4** (Mode of Trial), where offences which are triable either way are considered in more detail.

For charges involving allegations of criminal damage, there is a preliminary procedure which must be followed: MCA 1980, s. 22.

38.2 Preliminary Procedure for Charges of Criminal Damage (s. 22, MCA 1980)

For offences under the Criminal Damage Act 1971, s. 1 (i.e., destroying or damaging property), other than those involving arson, the following preliminary procedure must be used. This applies also to charges alleging that the accused attempted to commit such offence, or incited, aided, abetted, counselled or procured its commission (MCA 1980, s. 22, sch. 2).

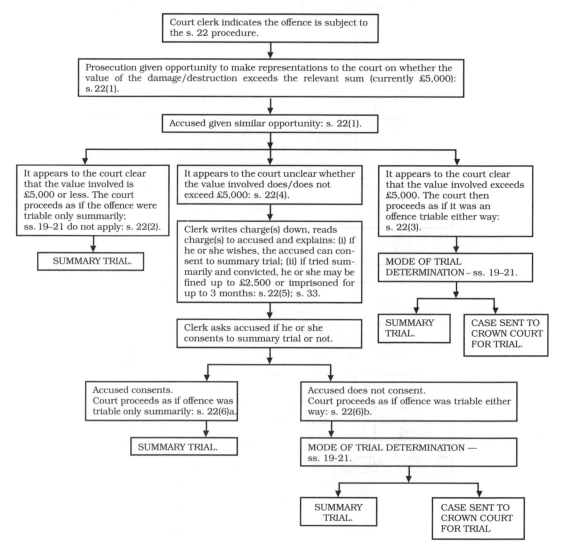

Note that:

(a) The value involved is measured in accordance with MCA 1980, sch. 2. Simply, it is the cost of repair (if possible) or replacement, whichever is the less, at the time the offence was committed.

(b) Where two or more criminal damage offences are alleged against the accused on the same occasion **and** they form a series (or part-series) of offences of the same or a similar character, then the value of the damage/destruction which is used by the court is the aggregate for all the offences: s. 22(11).

(c) The court must treat the offence initially as triable either way, and work through the 'plea before venue' procedure (see MCA 1980, s. 17A; *Criminal Litigation and Sentencing Manual*, **Chapter 4**) with the accused. If the accused either indicates a plea of *not guilty*, or makes no indication as to plea, the procedure set out above will be followed in order to determine where the accused will be tried.

If the accused indicates a plea of *guilty*, there is currently some doubt as to whether he or she may then be committed to the Crown Court for sentence if the value of the criminal damage is £5,000 or less (see, for example, *Blackstones' Criminal Practice 2002*, D3.12). The offence is, of course, triable either way for purposes other than determining the mode of trial. It seems likely, though, that the procedure set out above will be followed up to the point where the value of the criminal damage is established. If the value of the criminal damage is found to be £5,000 or less, then the offence will continue to be regarded as summary only and there can be no committal for sentence under MCA 1980, s. 38. Conversely, if the value clearly exceeds £5,000, then the defendant may be committed for sentence and appropriate representations should be made to the magistrates on that topic. One suggestion is that the magistrates' court should determine the value of a criminal damage charge before it does anything else. If the value is £5,000 or less, then mode of trial procedure would not apply, neither would committal for sentence nor plea before venue. See Inigo Bing, *Criminal Procedure and Sentencing in the Magistrates' Court*, Sweet & Maxwell, 5th edn, 1999, 4–14/6.

THIRTY NINE

THE COURSE OF A TRIAL ON INDICTMENT: FROM ARRAIGNMENT TO VERDICT

39.1 Explanation

The following numbered sequence charts the course of a trial on indictment involving two co-accused, D1 and D2 (named in the indictment in that order), and two offences, Offence X and Offence Y. D1 and D2 are jointly charged with Offence X. There is a separate count charging D2 alone with Offence Y.

The arraignment, as is now normally the case, took place at the Plea and Directions Hearing. The counts in the indictment were put to D1 and D2 to plead guilty or not guilty. In the case of D2, a plea was taken on each count separately. D1 and D2 pleaded not guilty to Offence X. D2 pleaded not guilty to Offence Y.

Square brackets indicate stages which may or may not be taken depending upon the precise facts and circumstances of the particular case.

39.2 Course of the Trial

(1) Jury empanelled by clerk calling at random 12 names from the panel summoned to attend.

(2) [Subject to challenges for cause, the prosecution exercising their 'right' of standby and the judge's power to exclude jurors] each juror takes the juror's oath/affirmation.

(3) Clerk asks the jurors if they are all sworn and puts D1 and D2 in their charge, i.e., '. . . D2 also stands charged with the following . . . (Offence Y). To this charge he [or she] has also pleaded not guilty. It is your charge to say, having heard the evidence whether he [or she] is guilty or not guilty.'

(4) Prosecution opening speech (which should exclude any references to evidence which is either clearly inadmissible or to which counsel for the accused, or either of them, have indicated that they will object).

(5) Prosecution evidence including, as appropriate, real evidence, documentary hearsay and formal admissions.

(6) [Each prosecution witness may be cross-examined by D1 and D2, in that order, and may then be re-examined by the prosecution.] Prosecution declares that that is all of its evidence — i.e., 'closes' its case.

(7)   [Submission of no case to answer by D1 and/or D2. Note: the jury are asked to leave the court before any such submission is made. Defence counsel makes his or her/their submission(s) and prosecuting counsel is given an opportunity to reply. The judge announces his or her decision and the jury return to court. If the submission is upheld in relation to all counts on the indictment, the judge explains this to the jury and asks them to appoint a foreman, and the clerk takes from the foreman on each count a verdict of not guilty on the direction of the judge. If the judge decides that there is no case to answer on one count — e.g., the count containing Offence Y — but that there is a case to answer on the other, the judge will direct the jury that (a) he or she will direct them, at the end of the trial, to return a verdict of not guilty on D2 in relation to Offence Y and (b) during the remainder of the trial they should ignore the count containing Offence Y. If the judge rejects the submission of no case on all counts, the jury are told nothing and the case continues.]

(8)   Counsel for D1 (and D2) either (a) informs the court that D1 (D2) will give evidence or (b) does not so inform the court, or informs the court that D1 (D2) does not intend to give evidence. In the latter case, i.e., (b), the judge should then inquire of counsel whether he or she has advised his or her client about the fact that the jury may draw inferences from a failure to testify. If counsel replies in the affirmative, the case proceeds. If counsel replies in the negative, then the judge must direct the representative to advise his or her client on the matter, and should adjourn briefly for this purpose. See Criminal Justice and Public Order Act 1994, s. 35 and *Practice Direction (Crown Court: Defendant's Evidence)* [1995] 1 WLR 657.

(9)   D1 presents his or her case: co-accused must present their cases in the order in which their names appear in the indictment.

(10)   [D1's opening speech.] Note: if the only defence evidence is to be given by D1 or by D1 and witnesses speaking only as to his or her good character, D1 has no right to an opening speech.

(11)   [D1 called to give evidence.] Note: Police and Criminal Evidence Act 1984, s. 79: if an accused (D) intends to call two or more witnesses to the facts of a case and those witnesses include D, D must be called before the other witness(es) unless the court in its discretion otherwise directs.

(12)   [If D1 does testify, after examination-in-chief he or she can be cross-examined by counsel for D2. Then the prosecution may cross-examine and counsel for D1 may re-examine.]

(13)   [D1's other evidence, including, as appropriate, real evidence, documentary hearsay and formal admissions. Witnesses called by D1 will be examined-in-chief and then may be cross-examined by counsel for D2, then cross-examined by the prosecution and then re-examined by counsel for D1.]

(14)   D2 presents his or her case: see (9)–(13) above, reversing 'D1' and 'D2' throughout.

(15)   [Prosecution closing speech.] Note: the prosecution have no right to a closing speech if an accused (a) is unrepresented and (b) had no right to an opening speech — see (10) above.

(16)   D1's closing speech.

(17)   D2's closing speech.

(18)   Judge's summing-up: functions of judge and jury; burden and standard of proof; definition of offences charged; direction to treat D1 and D2 separately and to treat the separate counts separately; summary of evidence; directions on evidence as appropriate [e.g., effect of character evidence, effect of silence, etc.]; advise appointment of foreman and retirement with a view to reaching a unanimous verdict.

(19)   [If the jury return to court or are sent for by the judge after 2 hours and 10 minutes or such longer period as the judge thinks reasonable, and the foreman, upon being asked whether they have reached a unanimous verdict, answers 'no', the judge may give a majority verdict direction: see *Practice Directions* [1970] 1 WLR 916, [1967] 1 WLR 1198 and the Juries Act 1974, s. 17.]

(20)   Jury's verdict on each count:

  (a)   guilty (unanimous); or

  (b)   guilty (majority); or

  (c)   not guilty (unanimous); or

  (d)   not guilty (majority); or

  (e)   failure to agree upon any verdict.

Concerning (b) and (d), the procedure, following a majority direction and on the jury's return to court, is to ask if at least 10 out of 12 are agreed; if yes, to ask whether guilty or not guilty; if guilty, to ask how many were in favour, how many against; if not guilty, simply to accept the verdict.

If the verdict is either (a) or (b), the court may adjourn for reports prior to sentence, in which event there is still a prima facie right to bail: see Bail Act 1976, s. 4. If no reports are sought, there is usually no right to bail although an application for bail may be made pending appeal against conviction and/or sentence. The Crown Court judge will only be able to grant bail if he or she certifies the case is fit for appeal (rare).

If the verdict is either (c) or (d), the judge will direct the accused that he or she is free to leave the dock (provided, of course, he or she has not been found guilty on some other count and is not in custody on other matters).

Concerning (e), the judge may ask the jury to retire again [with or without a majority direction] or discharge the jury. Discharge of a jury in such circumstances is not an acquittal — there may be a retrial.

Mitigation should be prepared in advance: preparation during the jury's retirement may be interrupted by their early return to court!

FORTY

PROSECUTING A PLEA OF GUILTY IN THE CROWN COURT

40.1   Preparatory Steps

(a)   Ensure you have a copy of the indictment. This is often settled after the brief has been sent to counsel and can therefore be missing from the brief.

(b)   If the defendant is in breach of any sentence, such as a suspended sentence of imprisonment, conditional discharge or probation order imposed on an earlier occasion, ensure you have details of the original offence(s) in respect of which such sentence was imposed.

(c)   If there are other offences to be taken into consideration (TICs), ensure the appropriate form has been prepared (this is normally done by the officer in charge of the case) and signed by the defendant. A copy of this form should be handed to the clerk of the court before the case is called on for hearing.

(d)   Ensure you have an up-to-date copy of the defendant's antecedents. The court and defence counsel should also have copies in advance of the trial/listed plea. You will be required to give the antecedent information to the court (see below).

(e)   Obtain instructions from the CPS representative at court as to the amount of any costs order you should seek.

40.2   The Hearing

(a)   The defendant will be arraigned and plead guilty to some or all of the counts on the indictment. If you are instructed to proceed with the other counts, it will be necessary to empanel a jury to try those matters. If the plea to some of the counts is acceptable, introduce yourself and your opponent to the court and inform the judge either that you are instructed to offer no evidence on the other matters or invite the judge to leave such matters 'on the court file'. Then proceed to stage (b) below. If the defendant pleads guilty to all the counts on the indictment, start by introducing yourself and your opponent.

(b)   Briefly outline the facts of the offences. The judge is likely to have read the committal papers in any event. There is no need to go into great detail, simply deal with the salient facts either in a chronological or the most convenient order. This usually involves a summary of the way in which each offence was committed, any aggravating or mitigating features, the amount of any money or the nature of any injury involved, brief details of the arrest, the defendant's response to the arrest/charge, any important replies during an interview and acknowledging, where appropriate, that the defendant frankly admitted his or her guilt or co-operated with the police.

(c) If there are any TICs, it is normal to mention this to the judge either before or when dealing with the brief facts. The judge will have or be given a copy of them by the clerk. Either the judge or the clerk (at his or her direction) will read out the offences and ask the defendant if he or she admits each of the offences and wants them taken into consideration when sentence is passed. As soon as the defendant confirms that this is the case, deal **briefly** with these other offences. It is usual to deal with them together, for example, by mentioning the fact that they are all similar offences committed over X period and involving £ Y.

(d) You will then have to take the judge through the antecedents — a copy is annexed to this chapter. Check that the judge has a copy.

Q: 'Does Your Honour have the antecedents of Jane Forrester dated 10 June 2002?'

In dealing with the antecedents, it is usual to read out each part of the relevant information. The order in which you deal with the defendant's history is as follows:

(i) Date of birth/birthplace, etc.

Example:

'The defendant was born on 21 December 1977 in London and is now aged 24 years.'

(ii) Previous convictions.

Example:

'There are a number of matters recorded against the defendant including offences of dishonesty.'

Q: 'Where would Your Honour like me to start?' (This is to enable the judge to determine which of the previous convictions are relevant.)
A: 'Deal with the last three matters — from June 1998.'

'On 2 June 1998, at the West London Magistrates' Court, for an offence of theft, the defendant was fined £400 and ordered to pay costs of £75.'

'On 9 September 1999, at the same court, for two offences of obtaining property by deception, the defendant was also fined £300 in respect of each matter and ordered to pay costs of £80.'

'Finally, on 5 January 2002, at this court, for three offences of theft, the defendant was sentenced to a period of one month's imprisonment on each count concurrent, such sentence being suspended for a period of one year.'

At this point, ask for the breach of the suspended sentence to be put to the defendant. Upon the judge's direction, the clerk will then put the fact of the conviction and sentence to the defendant and ask the defendant whether they agree with it. If the defendant does not (this is rare) it will be necessary to put the case back in the list in order to produce strict proof of the conviction, i.e., a certificate of the conviction (see the Police and Criminal Evidence Act 1984, s. 73). If the defendant admits the details, the clerk will inform the defendant that, as the current offences were committed during the period of the suspension, the defendant may now be dealt with again in respect of the original offences.

(iii) Give the court brief details of the facts of the original offences. If your information is sparse, and an officer is present, he or she may be able to assist the court with more detail.

(iv) Proceed with the rest of the antecedents, i.e., education, employment, home circumstances.

(e) Make any application for costs that you are instructed to make and any application for a compensation or destruction order (usual in a drugs case).

Example:

'Your Honour, there is an application for a destruction order in respect of the drugs which form the subject of the charge and a further application for costs in the sum of £120.'

(f) Finish by informing the court that you have closed your case.

'That is the case for the prosecution.'

(g) It is now the turn of defence counsel to mitigate on his or her client's behalf.

(h) The judge will then proceed to sentence. See **Criminal Litigation and Sentencing Manual**, **Chapter 14**. Be ready to assist the judge on his or her powers of sentence and to remind him or her if he or she exceeds those powers.

Antecedents of: Jane FORRESTER   Dated: 10.6.2002

Charged with: Possession of controlled drugs, intent to supply (× 2)

Date and place of birth: 21.12.77 (aged 24); London

Nationality: British

Date of arrest: 1.6.02/On bail

Summary of convictions: 2 findings of guilt as a juvenile
                        8 previous convictions recorded

Education: Attended Bishop's Rock Comprehensive School; left aged 16 with no formal
          qualifications.

Employment since leaving school: Many occasional jobs of short duration.
                                Presently unemployed, not claiming benefit.

Address, home conditions: 264 Bath Street, Streatham, London
                          Lives with parents and receives £100 p.w.
                          from them. No financial commitments.

Convictions recorded against: Jane FORRESTER CRD No. 40457/96
Charged in name of   Jane FORRESTER

Date	Court	Offences	Sentence	Release Date
1.4.96	W. London M.C.	Soliciting	Fine £20	
2.6.98	W. London M.C.	Theft	Fine £400; Costs £75	
9.9.99	W. London M.C.	Obtain prop by deception (× 2)	(1) and (2) Fine £300; Costs £80	
5.1.02	Inner London Crown Court	Theft (× 3)	(1)–(3) 1 month's imprisonment concurrent. Suspended 1 year	

40.3   Procedure before Sentencing — a Flow Chart

The procedure before sentencing, once an accused, D, has either pleaded guilty or, having pleaded not guilty, is found guilty, is as follows:

D pleads guilty

D found guilty

The court may adjourn, e.g., to obtain reports or to await the outcome of a co-accused's trial. If the court adjourns for reports, there is still a *prima facie* right to bail: s. 4, Bail Act 1976.

Prosecution summary of the facts of the case. Note: (i) counsel for the prosecution should take a neutral stance and not suggest any particular sentence; (ii) if there is a substantial conflict between prosecution and defence as to the facts of the offence (which may have a significant effect on sentence), the judge, having heard submissions from counsel, will normally either accept the defence version (so far as possible) or allow both sides to call evidence on the matter (a '*Newton* hearing') and then reach a decision as to what happened.

The antecedents. The prosecution adduces evidence of D's character and antecedents using a copy of written antecedents prepared by the police. This covers such matters as age, education, past and present employment, domestic circumstances, income, date of arrest, remands in custody or bail and previous convictions. If the antecedents are not in dispute, the information is normally given by prosecuting counsel. Exceptionally, the evidence is given by an officer. If so, the normal rules of evidence are relaxed but the defence are entitled to cross-examine and if they challenge any of the officer's assertions, the prosecution must then provide strict proof.

Reports. The judge reads any reports prepared on D, e.g., pre-sentence reports, medical and psychiatric reports and assessments for suitability for community service.

Mitigation by defence counsel on behalf of D.

Sentence, taking into account any other offences which D wishes to be taken into consideration.

FORTY ONE

THE PLEA IN MITIGATION

41.1   Introduction

A plea in mitigation can be made:

(a)   either after a plea of guilty, following the prosecution's presentation of the case and defendant's antecedents; or

(b)   after conviction, following the verdict/s and the presentation of the defendant's antecedents.

The objective of a plea in mitigation is to ensure that a sentence is passed by the court which is appropriate both in the circumstances of the offence(s) and to the circumstances of the defendant. The aim is to obtain the most lenient punishment which can reasonably be imposed. It should be remembered (see **Criminal Litigation and Sentencing Manual, Chapter 15**) that very few crimes carry with them a sentence fixed by law and so in most cases there is discretion in the court to decide which of a number of possible sentences is appropriate (for example, whether to imprison or fine) and within a particular sentence, a discretion to decide where, within the upper and lower limits, the particular sentence should be fixed.

41.2   Preparing to make a Plea in Mitigation

Always begin your preparation by checking on the sentencing principles which apply to the particular crime. You should use Thomas's *Encyclopaedia of Sentencing Practice* to find the guiding cases. Your aim should be to identify the type of sentence or order which would normally be imposed (see **Criminal Litigation and Sentencing Manual, Chapter 15**).

Having identified the type of sentence, you should then identify any aggravating features which would normally encourage a court to take the view that a sentence at the higher end of the scale would be appropriate and then see whether you can dissociate the defendant from those features. The following list of features will often be seen as aggravating: ringleader, planned or premeditated act; serious injury caused; use of weapon; unprovoked; large sum of money involved; breach of trust; re-offending soon after a court order is made; elderly/young victim; poor response to supervision; lack of concern for injured victim; lack of remorse; and offence committed whilst on bail.

Your next task is to identify whether there are any mitigating factors which should be brought to the attention of the court. The following list of features will often be seen as mitigating: minor role; spontaneous; provoked; minor injuries; property recovered; severe domestic or emotional stress; little or no damage to the victim; dependent children; has the care of an ill or disabled spouse; exceptional help to others; previous good character; offence out of character; long time since previous offence; out of trouble since offence; pleaded guilty; good response to supervision; full confession; gave himself or herself up; recently married; secure job; cured of addiction to drugs or alcohol; paid compensation prior to hearing; compensation offered; other restitution made or offered to victim; expression of remorse; suffered loss or injury due to the offence; mental disorder; good work record; consequences unintended; low intelligence; signs of reform; in financial problems not of own making; offence committed out of loyalty; parity with co-defendants needed; in some sex offences — willing victim; offender forgiven by the victim; and that it is a long time since the offence was committed.

41.2.1 HOLDING A CONFERENCE WITH THE CLIENT

You should aim to arrive at court in plenty of time to obtain the information that you need to present the plea in mitigation. You may only get the papers in the case a short while before you are due to appear in court but you should always see your client in conference before starting to mitigate in court. If, for whatever reason, you have not had enough time to get full information, you should ask the court to put the case back in the list to be dealt with later that day. If you try to make a plea in mitigation with inadequate or incomplete preparation, this may raise professional conduct issues for you; it is also likely to jeopardise your client's human rights. Where the court is told that your preparation time has been inadequate, it should consider seriously whether to adjourn the hearing (see European Convention on Human Rights, Article 6(1) and (3)(b) and (c); *Goddi* v *Italy* (1984) 6 EHRR 457, *T and V* v *UK*, unreported, 16 December 1999, and *cf. F* v *UK* (1992) 15 EHRR CD 32).

During the conference with your client you should seek to establish the following facts and/or make the following assessments of your client:

(a) Your client's age (if relevant); and

(b) Whether your client's actual age should be ignored because he or she appears to be immature or is mentally disabled. You should also consider whether to apply to have the case adjourned for reports to be prepared.

(c) Your client's background: whether there are any circumstances which might excuse or explain the offence; your client's past character (you should get a form listing any previous convictions (usually on form MG16) from the Crown Prosecution Service and take your client through it); whether this offence is similar to or different from previous offences; whether there are any underlying problems, for example, drug or alcohol addiction; past instances of generosity or kindness.

(d) Your client's involvement in the crime: was your client a principal actor in the offence or did he or she take a minor role in it; was the offence premeditated or did it happen on the spur of the moment; what, if any, pressure was your client subject to; was it an isolated incident or does your client's criminal conduct extend over a long period; was your client influenced by another offender; if so was he or she unable to resist that influence because of age or experience; quantify how much damage was done, or money taken and establish whether any offences are being taken into consideration.

(e) Your client's present situation: here you are looking for evidence of your client's stability, a regular home, job and people who will be supportive to the defendant; compare the situation as it is now with the time when the offence was committed; ask what your client has done to help himself or herself — acts showing contrition are more important than words, so establish whether your client has made any attempt at restitution. When a fine is a possibility you need to obtain considerable detail about your client's financial situation in order to help the court fix the fine at a proper level. So, you need to know your client's income after tax etc., your client's outgoings out of income and his or her capital. You also need to take your client's instructions on how much time he or she will need to pay any fine imposed and the level of weekly instalments he or she could meet.

(f) You may want to call one or two character witnesses to speak on behalf of your client. This can be useful sometimes. You should call people who know your client well and who can say something about him or her which is relevant in either dissociating your client from the aggravating features of the offence or enhancing the mitigating factors in the case.

(g) Prepare your client for what will happen by giving him or her realistic advice as to the likely sentence which will be imposed and by describing the procedure in court.

41.2.2   READING AND UNDERSTANDING THE PRE-SENTENCE REPORT

Make sure that you have got any reports (usually from the court probation service), have read them and that you have noted the comments made about the defendant's background, the background to the offence and any recommendation on sentence. Note that you should comply with a request not to show a report (for example, a medical report or one relating to the defendant's mental health) to the defendant and that you should always ensure that material which is given to you in confidence is dealt with on that basis.

41.3   Presenting the Plea in Mitigation

41.3.1   THE LENGTH OF THE PLEA

It is very important to keep your plea in mitigation short. In an ordinary case, aim to keep your submission to no more than 10 minutes.

41.3.2   WITNESSES

After a guilty plea the defendant's instructions may be that his or her view of the circumstances of the offence are different from the case put by the prosecution; in these circumstances the court may decide to hear evidence to determine which version of the facts to accept (*R* v *Newton* (1982) 77 Cr App R 13; **Criminal Litigation and Sentencing Manual, 14.4.2**).

Any witnesses as to character may be called before making the substance of (or during) your plea. You can call your witness in the following way:

'May it please Your Honour, before I address you in mitigation on behalf of Ms Smith, I should like to call Mr Jones. Mr Jones please.'

You should ask witnesses to identify themselves and explain their relationship to the defendant. Then ask any questions which will provide relevant information to be used later on in your plea. For example, if you are seeking to establish that Ms Smith's criminal act is completely out of character, you will want to call a witness who can say, based on the witness's long and detailed knowledge of her, that this act was completely out of character. You could try to elicit this kind of information from the witness with one or more of the following questions:

'Do you know Ms Smith?'
'When did you first meet her?'
'How did you come to know her?'
'As her (employer, etc.) . . . have you had the opportunity of assessing her character?'
'How would you describe her character?'
'What are her responsibilities at work?'
'From what you know of Ms Smith, do you regard her involvement in this offence as in or out of character?'

41.3.3 INTRODUCING THE PRE-SENTENCE REPORT

Usually the pre-sentence report will have been handed to the judge or magistrates before the plea in mitigation starts and it is sometimes necessary for the court to adjourn whilst the report is read. However, before you can refer to the contents of the pre-sentence report you will want to be sure that the judge or magistrate has a copy of it and has had a chance to read it. You can introduce the report in the following way:

'May it please Your Honour, a pre-sentence report has been prepared, dated . . . which I shall refer to in the course of my plea in mitigation. Has Your Honour had an opportunity to read the report?'

41.4 The Content of the Plea in Mitigation

41.4.1 SUMMARY

You should start your plea with a summary of the main points you intend to make. You could say:

'The substance of my plea in mitigation is . . .' or

'I shall seek to persuade Your Honour that . . .' or

'Your Honour, the defendant accepts that this was a serious offence and has fully admitted his part in it. I do not propose to address Your Honour on the circumstances of the offence but will seek to persuade Your Honour that. . .'

41.4.2 SENTENCING POLICY

You may then want to bring in the matters of sentencing policy which will bear upon the case. For example, you could say:

'In my submission, as Your Honour will appreciate, the authorities state that sentences at the higher end of the scale are reserved for offences where . . . (state the aggravating features).'

Next you will want to explain (if you can) to the court why the defendant can be dissociated from these aggravating features, and how the evidence (what the prosecution have said, and what any witnesses have said) supports your contention. For example,

'I hope that Your Honour will accept that on the prosecution's case, the defendant can be dissociated from any aggravating features and that as a matter of principle, a sentence at the lower end of the scale is appropriate.'

In the early days, however, you may be concerned more with the appropriate type of sentence, rather than the scale.

41.4.3 MITIGATING FACTORS

You should then make specific, albeit brief reference to the mitigating factors which are relevant. For example, that the defendant pleaded guilty, confessed immediately or was previously of good character. Where relevant you should tie in your submissions on these issues with any evidence which has been given to the court, for example, the testimony of the antecedents officer, any witnesses as to the defendant's character and any statements in the pre-sentence report. The pre-sentence report should be referred to by page number and where on the page the paragraph appears, so that the court is able to follow the points you are making. You should then round off this part of your submission with a plea for a sentence at the lower end of the scale if that is appropriate. For example,

'It is my submission that when all these factors are borne in mind, a sentence at the lower end of the scale is justified.'

If your client has indicated genuine remorse to you, you should refer to what the client has said to you in conference. For example,

'Your Honour, in conference Ms Smith told me how terribly sorry she is for what she has done and she has asked me to repeat this to the court.'

If you can also point to concrete signs of remorse — e.g., helping the police, wherewithal to pay compensation — that will carry more weight with the court.

41.5 Conclusion

You will then be in a position to conclude your plea. For example,

'In conclusion, Your Honour, in my submission, both as a matter of principle and on account of the particular facts of this case, a financial penalty would be appropriate which can justifiably be put at the lower end of the scale.'

or:

'Your Honour, the defendant appreciates that a custodial sentence is justified in this case and I do not propose to seek to persuade Your Honour otherwise. However, this is a case where, in my submission, there are some mitigating features which could enable Your Honour to take a lenient view and (impose a short period of imprisonment) or (suspend any sentence of imprisonment) . . .'

41.6 Warning

Always make sure that you have prepared your submissions in a plea in mitigation and that they are realistic. There is no point in suggesting to the court that a case is not appropriate for a sentence of imprisonment if the sentencing guidelines make it clear that a sentence of imprisonment should be imposed. Equally there is no point in dwelling on aspects of the defendant's background which are no longer relevant to mitigating the defendant's conduct, for example, when the defendant is 45 years old, revealing that his or her parents divorced when he or she was eight years old! You will also be in some difficulty if you try to tell the court that the defendant is really sorry for what he or she did, when the plea in mitigation follows conviction after a not guilty plea.

The Court of Appeal has emphasised on several occasions that it is the duty of both prosecuting and defence counsel to know what sentences may in any particular case be lawfully passed, so as to correct the judge if need be and avoid unnecessary appeals on the basis that the sentence was not one that the judge had power to impose.

41.7 Further Reading

Hyam, Michael. *Advocacy Skills*, Blackstone Press (OUP), 4th edn, 1999.

APPENDIX A

PRECONCEPTIONS

A.1   What is a Preconception?

A preconception is an opinion or idea which is conceived or framed prior to actual knowledge: it is an anticipation in thought.

A.2   How Do We Preconceive?

Have you ever sat in a public place (for instance in a pub or restaurant) and found yourself assessing the people sitting opposite you on the basis of their physical appearance? Have you made any assumption about their intellectual level on the basis of what they are reading? If so, you are not alone! We are all guilty of preconceiving to varying degrees. We make generalisations and assumptions in everyday life without any rational foundation for them. We make judgments about people on the basis of what we anticipate they will be like before we actually meet them. Most of the time we do so subconsciously.

Preconceptions are normal and a necessary condition for society to exist. They are part of every culture, a product of socialisation and much social interaction is dependent on them. It is important to recognise and acknowledge them.

Our preconceptions may be positive or negative; they may be common or limited in their application. Preconceptions are triggered by a combination of factors and senses: our upbringing and conditioning; previous experience (good and bad); what we see, hear and/or smell; what we read; what we learn from others. We classify people in our minds according to their looks, ethnic origin, colour, sex, religion, dress, speech, education/intellectual ability, material wealth, employment, socio-economic back- grounds. We label people, we categorise them, we discriminate. We continue to do this even when we meet the person, particularly if our assumptions are reinforced by the initial meeting.

A.3   How Does Preconceiving Affect Us?

Preconceptions affect us in many ways, either consciously or subconsciously. They affect the way in which we label, assess and judge people, the manner in which we communicate with them. They influence our expectations, how we treat others, our tolerance levels. They influence the way we behave, the relationships we make, the products we buy.

Have you ever assumed that an attractive-looking person is pleasant and kind on the basis of his or her looks? Do you presume that men who beat their wives belong to the lower socio-economic groups? Without actual knowledge, how on earth can you tell? Any such assumptions you make are preconceptions.

A.4 The Dangers of Preconceiving

Obviously, the main danger lies in our assumptions being wrong. This is compounded when on occasion our original assumptions turn out to be right ('the self-fulfilling prophecy', for example, a teacher's negative expectations of a child's abilities). We then use that to justify those assumptions and reinforce our views. We rely on those assumptions to argue from a false premise on the next occasion.

Which of the following is more likely to be violent?

(a) a doctor;

(b) a businessman;

(c) a teenage girl.

Which of the following is more likely to shoplift?

(a) a teenage drug taker;

(b) a middle–class housewife;

(c) an unemployed man.

Which of the following is more likely to rape?

(a) an unmarried man;

(b) a married man with children;

(c) a married man without children.

Evidence might show that some **are** more likely than others. The important point here is **not** whether any are more likely, but whether you have reason to suppose that any **individual** member of the category may have committed such an act in the light of such a generalisation. Note also that labels ('skinhead', 'hippie', 'yuppie', 'punk rocker') are preconceptions in themselves. One preconception leads to another and therein lies the further danger of preconceiving!

A.4.1 THE DANGERS FOR A BARRISTER

The dangers of preconception are never more apparent than in the work of a barrister who may have to make important provisional judgments.

Is a client more likely to be guilty because he or she has irritating mannerisms?
Is a man charged with indecent assault more likely to be guilty because he wears old clothes?
Do you believe what a client tells you more easily if he or she is well dressed, articulate, educated?
Do you listen less easily to what a client has to say because he or she is inarticulate or poorly educated?
Does the fact that a client has a previous conviction for dishonesty mean that he or she is more likely to have committed a crime of violence?
Do you believe your opponent is trustworthy because she is attractive and initially friendly?
Do you assume your opponent is less competent than you because she looks younger than you? Or because she confides that she has not done a lot of this type of work before?
Do you believe your opponent is more competent than you because he looks older than you?
Do you let your opponent's bragging of her experience undermine your confidence so that you advise your client to compromise on less favourable terms?

Of course, the answer to all these questions is 'no'; yet, in practice, many barristers forget this. They fail to recognise their own preconceptions and the manner in which they affect their conduct of the case.

A.4.2   THE 'CAB-RANK' PRINCIPLE

As a barrister you cannot pick and choose your clients so that you only represent those whom you like to believe in. You are bound to observe the 'cab-rank principle'. Unless you recognise your preconceptions about the client, they are likely to affect your judgment; the way in which you approach, prepare and present the case; the way you communicate with the client, your opponent, the court; the way in which you advise, negotiate or argue the case. By relying on premature assumptions or beliefs, you will be less able to communicate effectively with the client; you may lose the confidence of the client and your solicitor; you are likely to convey to your opponent and the court, by gestures or body language, your apathy towards the client. With the growth of conditional fees the art of assessing the possible success of a case is growing. Make sure all your judgments are objective.

A.5   Dealing with Preconceptions

The most important factor in dealing with preconceptions is to recognise them, either in ourselves or in others. You must learn to differentiate between assumptions and actual knowledge, so that you can identify where you have anticipated without justification. You must be careful not to prejudge a client, an opponent or a tribunal.

Once you learn to recognise preconceptions you can then determine their possible effects and uses. Ask yourself:

Have they affected my judgment or approach to the case in any way?
To what extent?
Are they more/less/equally likely to affect my opponent/the court's approach/judgment?
Is my opponent proceeding on the basis of an assumption I haven't made?
Is it likely to undermine or support his or her case?
Is the court likely to proceed on the basis of any preconception?
Is it likely to influence the jury?
Can I use it to my advantage?
Do I need to dispel it?

It is only by being alert to these possibilities that you can ensure that you recognise the existence of preconceptions, their dangers, uses, advantages and disadvantages. So the next time you find yourself assessing the person sitting opposite you on the Tube, stop and think about what you are doing!

A.6   Exercises

1.   Your client works as a prostitute. She is charged with theft and assault occasioning actual bodily harm. She denies both the charges. How might her employment affect:

   (a)   Your conduct of her case?

   (b)   The jurors' deliberations?

2.   Your client is approximately 6 feet tall and weighs 18 stone. His wife is seeking a non-molestation injunction. Are there any assumptions which you may need to overcome during the hearing of her application?

3.   Write a list of your own personal preconceptions and prejudices. Include any assumptions or generalisations which you commonly make. Be honest! Do you think that anything on the list may need to be overcome in order to fulfil your professional obligations as a barrister?

APPENDIX B

EFFECTIVE COMMUNICATION

B.1   The Importance of Effective Communication

The ability to communicate effectively is vital. You will, throughout your professional life as a barrister, have dealings with and come into contact with all manner of people from all walks of life. While a good barrister will have knowledge of and expertise in the law, that barrister must also be able to communicate that knowledge and understanding to clients, and a range of other professional and non-professional people, with whom he or she becomes professionally involved in the conduct of a client's case.

The ability to communicate is a skill. It is a skill which can be learned, as with all other disciplines, by addressing, studying and analysing the component parts which go to make the skill effective. Good communication skills and techniques play a necessary part in every aspect of your working life. These skills, once learned, can be adapted and adjusted to encompass any situation that you may find yourself in. In this way, you will be best able to apply and practise the law which you have spent some years studying.

Note that in the diverse culture that now exists in the United Kingdom you cannot assume that English will always be a client's first language, or that clients or witnesses will necessarily use English in the same way you do. You should not let this stand in the way of proper communication. Ensure the client has an appropriate relative or friend to assist, or an interpreter if necessary.

B.1.1   COMMUNICATION IS CENTRAL TO YOUR PRACTICE

At every stage of your professional life, you will need to communicate with someone else, such as:

(a) lay clients — in conference in chambers, or at court;

(b) professional clients;

(c) other barristers;

(d) other professionals;

(e) witnesses;

(f) expert witnesses;

(g) judges;

(h) juries;

(i) magistrates;

(j) court clerks and officials;

(k)   police;

(l)   clerks in chambers;

(m) colleagues in chambers.

These all have different requirements and may present different problems. You need to appreciate the differences and be ready to adapt quickly. A diversity of backgrounds of race, class and sex amongst all those involved in a court case can make good communication challenging but essential.

B.1.2   METHODS OF COMMUNICATION

You should recognise that many different methods of communication will be involved and that communication skills are not only to be considered when dealing with a person face to face but, particularly with the advent of modem technology, by other methods as well. For example, a barrister may communicate:

(a)   in a written advice;

(b)   by letter;

(c)   by telephone;

(d)   by telex;

(e)   by fax; and

(f)   by electronic mail.

Each of these requires an appropriate adaptation of skills.

B.1.3   THE ESSENCE OF COMMUNICATION

In a wide variety of circumstances you must be able to use language appropriately and accurately to be understood. If, for example, you fail to establish a good rapport with your client, then the client may be unwilling to communicate to you some information which is crucial to the conduct of the case. In the early years of practice, some of you will spend much of your time in magistrates' courts, and being able to establish a good relationship with the court ushers and court clerks can assist you in many ways. For example, in finding you a quiet place to interview your client; or giving you additional time with your client before your case is called on; or even making sure that you get your case on first.

It is important to appreciate that communication is a complex process with several stages, any one or more of which can be undermined, leading to potentially dangerous misunderstandings. The accepted basic model for the communication process is that the 'sender' decides what he or she wishes to communicate. This is then 'encoded' using the personal experience and cultural background of that particular individual. The 'message' is then sent through words/silence/body language. This message then has to be 'decoded' by an entirely separate individual who is the 'receiver', who may have a totally different experience and background to work from.

To communicate most effectively it is vital to identify clearly who your audience is, what the purpose of the interchange between you is, and precisely what sort of vocabulary is appropriate in the circumstances. Failure to do so will inevitably lead to a breakdown in communications which will render your task much more difficult.

B.2 The Importance of Word Skills

The barrister deals in words — classically in the form of advocacy, but also in many other ways in speaking and writing. To communicate as fully as possible, the barrister will have to adapt vocabulary and the use of words to the audience in question — you do not talk in the same way to the client as you do to the judge. This may sound obvious — it is — but the fact that it is obvious does not make it easy, and does not mean that all barristers do it well. It is important for each student to work on their personal skills in improving and adapting use of words in the different situations in preparation for practice.

In addition to being understood, the barrister must be able to understand. This has two vital aspects — you must be able to understand a client and be able to understand a case. This involves dealing with a full range of problems, from the inarticulate client who cannot get a point across, to the client who showers you with technical terminology. If your client is a pig breeder you will need to be able to talk the language of pig breeders pretty rapidly if you are to understand what your client tells you and to tell the court what the case is about. If you do not, the client is not going to feel that you really understand the case and the judge is not going to be quick to find in your favour.

Understanding difficult terminology and different uses of words is not simply a matter of knowing what a word means. You need to be able to put a word in context. You need not only to be able to read and understand a set of papers, but also to be able to talk to the client effectively, to examine a client in court effectively, and to cross-examine the other side's witnesses, however complex the material involved.

The barrister is effectively the client's mouthpiece. You are paid to use words to the best effect for someone else. As such it is vital to be able to adapt quickly to talking the client's language and the language of the case. The barrister's role is to some extent that of the interpreter, to change the client's vocabulary to the court's vocabulary and vice versa! This includes not just the meaning of words but all the elements of non-verbal communication and differences of communication styles that can come from a variety of backgrounds and cultures.

B.3 The Proper Use of Language

B.3.1 EFFECTIVE ENGLISH

You may have been speaking English for years — so many years that you have almost certainly ceased to consider the vocabulary that you use and how you use words. You may have built up your own style in speaking and writing and you were not considering making any change — beyond possibly slightly improving your spelling! However, in becoming a barrister you are moving from using language personally to using it professionally, so it is time to review the words you use and how you use them, to ensure that you are building up a professional level of ability. You are no longer using language just for yourself but for others.

B.3.2 LEGAL TERMINOLOGY

Legal terminology must be used accurately and appropriately at all times, whether you are speaking or writing and whoever the audience is. However, attention must be paid to whether legal terminology needs to be explained to ensure that it is properly understood, for example when talking to a client.

B.3.3 TECHNICAL TERMINOLOGY

Technical terminology can arise in endless guises. It is difficult to prepare for unless you build a practice in a specialist area. The cases that arise in general practice can easily come from any technical area. Even the simplest contract has a context that you may not be familiar with.

If you do work regularly in particular technical areas you must obviously become fully familiar with their terminology. Outside a specialist practice you cannot easily prepare, not knowing what specialisation the next case will require, but you can prepare yourself to adapt. Rather than simply panicking or preparing a case superficially if you encounter technical language you must be ready to deal with it, whether by getting help from someone or finding a book on the subject.

B.4   Range of Audiences

The most important audiences that a barrister may have to communicate with are as follows.

B.4.1   THE CLIENT

Any practitioner is going to get a wide range of clients. This is not just a simple matter of needing to adjust to a criminal client or a distraught husband — even if your intention is to go into a solely commercial practice you will encounter a very wide variety of business people who talk in different ways and need to be talked to in different ways.

Many of those who start to train for the Bar have given little thought to the immense diversity of clients they will have. Some make rather stereotypical assumptions about the type of client that a particular area of work might involve. In fact the client base for any area of work, be it commerce, crime or matrimonial, is of course potentially as wide as the cultural make-up of the country. Whatever your own background it is likely that many of your clients will have a different background, and anyone who is to be really successful at the Bar needs to be able to deal positively, effectively and sympathetically with this range.

You will meet and talk to a client in a variety of situations. You will not only meet in conference, you will also meet outside court, both before and after a case. Even if you are not talking to the client directly you are effectively talking indirectly through the solicitor, which needs to be kept in mind when, for example, writing an opinion.

Whoever the person and whatever the situation, communicating with a client is fundamental to each case, requiring the right use of words to ensure that nothing is lost or misunderstood. Beware the obvious reaction to this point. All too often a barrister will explain a few legal terms and feel that the job is done, without going any further into ensuring real communication with the client. The barrister can thus come across as condescending or irritating without really helping the situation. Real communication with a client is not an easy skill, however good you are at talking, and requires awareness and work to get it right.

It must be stressed that proper communication with a client is not a matter of stereotyping a client (which is more likely to do harm than good), it is much more a subtle skill of being able to appreciate the factors that are relevant in finding the best way to communicate with an individual, from obvious things like age to much less tangible attributes like attitudes. The Conference Skills part of the Bar Vocational Course emphasises the need for real communication with the client, and provides opportunities for practice. Everyday life will give you other examples of people you might have to deal with as clients. (See also *Conference Skills Manual*, **Chapter 3**.)

B.4.2   THE SOLICITOR

You can assume that a solicitor will understand legal terminology. But a solicitor may take a case to a barrister because he or she is not an expert in that particular area, so the barrister must tactfully and without condescension check that the solicitor really does understand the more esoteric points of law.

In accepting that the solicitor does understand legal terminology, do not talk over the client's head. Too easily a conference can become simply a legal discussion between the barrister and the solicitor. While this may sometimes be necessary, it should only happen when it is appropriate and in the client's interest and not at the client's expense. You may need to adapt carefully and quickly in talking to both the solicitor and the client together, and in writing an opinion that goes to a solicitor and a client.

Also beware of the case when you are not actually dealing with a solicitor. At court someone from the office may be sent along to carry the file, and they will not necessarily understand legal terminology. If understanding is important, check that there is no error.

B.4.3   THE WITNESS

There are limited circumstances in which a barrister can talk to a witness before trial, though amendments to the code of conduct have widened the possibilities. Generally the barrister will simply be relying on a written proof of evidence from the solicitor at this stage. This probably reinforces the tendency some junior barristers have of preparing to question a witness simply by listing the questions they need to ask straight from the statement. If the witness at trial fails to give the 'right' answers the witness is blamed. It does not occur to all inexperienced barristers to think of how to construct and pitch questions to ensure that a particular witness really understands the question being asked and is thus more likely to provide a useful answer. If a witness is intimidated or confused by the words used and phrasing of the question he or she is hardly likely to give good evidence.

There is a limit to what can be done. You do not know much about a witness in advance, but you always know something, and initially you can use questions to find out more about the best way to communicate with each individual witness, building up as much rapport as possible. In adapting to a witness it is again vital not to appear condescending, especially in a jury trial. The real skill is sensitivity to a variety of factors rather than simplistic stereotyping.

B.4.4   THE EXPERT WITNESS

Whatever area of practice you are in, there will be complex areas where you need the assistance of expert witnesses. It is not the role of the barrister to say, 'Well, of course, I know nothing about pre-stressed concrete!'. If you have a case involving pre-stressed concrete, it is your job to find out about it. You must be able to become familiar with new and complex terminology quickly.

You will need the ability to be able to build up an understanding with an expert witness quickly without being confused or overawed by the words he or she uses. A barrister can see an expert witness in conference before a trial, to help comprehension of complex elements of a case. Use this to full advantage if you wish to appear fully in command of the case, and to cross-examine effectively.

B.4.4.1   The technical expert

You may need expert help in all sorts of ways — to deal with machinery, industrial processes, handwriting, . . . the list is endless. The first stage will often be to decide that you need expert help, and then to make it absolutely clear to the expert precisely what it is you need expert help with (without indicating what the expert should say!). You need to read the expert's report with care, to get real understanding, not just a vague idea. If you are to present the case in court, you must know what every word means.

It is not just a matter of simply being able to define the technical terms — you also need to know what underlies them and how to identify the strengths and weaknesses in them. It is this sort of knowledge that can win cases. There are all sorts of ways of achieving this, not least of which is simply asking the expert to help. A barrister may not find this easy to do, feeling that he or she is in charge of the case, but the expert witness will normally be quite happy to help if properly approached. Some experts will be experienced in giving evidence in court and may be particularly good at explaining the technicalities. An alternative is to get a book from the local library, if you learn more easily by reading.

B.4.4.2 The medical expert
For many sorts of practice, especially criminal and personal injury cases, a medical dictionary is vital. If you ever need to look at medical reports or deal with injuries, you need to know not only what the words mean, but also how serious the condition is and what the prognosis may be. For example, it is of limited use knowing that a particular long word means a problem with a muscle in the arm unless you also know whether such a condition is likely to stop a person playing darts for a week or for life.

B.4.4.3 The accountant
A barrister must be able to talk intelligently with an accountant. This is why there is an accounts element in the Bar Vocational Course (see the *Remedies Manual*).

B.4.5 THE COURT

It goes without saying that the barrister needs to be able to communicate in court, be it with a judge, a magistrate or a jury. Only a couple of points need to be emphasised: the need to adapt what you say to the appropriate tribunal — you would not need to give the same speech to the Court of Appeal as to a jury — and the fact that you do need to communicate rather than just talk. The good advocate will talk **to** the court rather than **at** the court. You need confidence to do this, but seeing a judge as a human being helps in the building of confidence. Also remember that you often have more than one audience in court.

Real communication in court is not easy in early practice. There are many individual ways of doing it, but remember that it is a matter of communication — you do not just write out a speech and make it, nor is a good speech necessarily a hectoring debating speech. Communication is a matter of finding the best way to get your points across to the particular tribunal — and being careful to pick up the reaction to what you are saying. Communication is a two-way process.

B.5 Range of Situations

There are many different circumstances in which the barrister will have to identify his or her audience and choose the correct vocabulary to communicate properly.

B.5.1 IN INTERVIEWING OR IN CONFERENCE

Communication here is with the client and the solicitor. It is important to consider both and talk appropriately to each rather than simply pitching remarks generally.

It is not just a matter of thinking you understand what the client says. You may need to check that you have really understood. For example, towards the end of an interview it may be valuable to summarise what you understood the client to have said to ensure that you understood correctly.

It is also not simply a matter of explaining something to the client. You need to judge carefully what legal terminology and other matters need to be explained. You also may need to check that the client has understood. It may not be enough simply to ask the client if he or she has understood. A worried or overawed client may well say that he or she has even if this is not true — you do not want clients asking the solicitor to explain something as they leave the room after a conference. If there is any doubt, tactfully ask the client to explain back to you what your advice is.

B.5.2   IN WRITING AN OPINION

The audience is the solicitor and client, but here inevitably to some extent both at the same time. You are writing primarily to the solicitor who has sent the brief, but you are also writing for the client, and many clients, especially business people, will want a copy of the opinion for themselves.

In writing primarily to the solicitor, you do not need to explain legal terminology — the solicitor can explain it to the client when running through the opinion. You do not address the client directly, but the client must always be kept in mind, and if necessary the solicitor should be asked to check a point with the client.

B.5.3   IN DRAFTING

The audience here is the lawyer on the other side and the judge. The language must be clear, accurate and the best possible English with appropriate legal terminology. This is brought out in detail in the drafting classes on the Bar Vocational Course.

There are, of course, some exceptions. For example, when preparing an affidavit for a client to swear, the affidavit should still be written in good clear English rather than colloquial English, but it should not normally include legal terminology when it would be inappropriate for the person swearing the affidavit to use it.

B.5.4   IN ADVOCACY

The audience could be the judge, a jury, a witness, or all of these. A number of relevant points have already been made. Perhaps the most important is the need to adapt your style of communication and vocabulary to each as required. The tendency may be just to steam ahead and to talk in the same way in speeches and questions, regardless of whether a witness or a judge is being addressed. Obviously everything you say and each person you address may require some adjustment in your approach for it to be most effective. Do not let either lack of confidence or overconfidence allow you to forget this.

B.6   Adapting What You Say

There are ways to alert the mind to the need to adapt the choice and use of words to communicate properly, even if it is not easy to do. Here are some very basic exercises to consider:

(a)   How would you prepare to talk in conference with a client accused of making a fraudulent misrepresentation? Does it make any difference whether or not you are told that the client owns his or her own business? Does the size of the business make a difference? Or the size of the alleged fraud?

(b)   You are to have a conference with a client who is seeking a divorce. She is from an ethnic minority whose culture you have little knowledge of. The solicitor has told you that her use of English is not very fluent and that she is very reserved and embarrassed about discussing her problems with her husband. How should you prepare?

(c)   How would you explain the meaning and effects of an interim injunction to a chairman of a residents' association? Are there any questions you would ask before or after your explanation to decide how to phrase it and to ensure that it was understood?

(d)   How would you prepare for a conference with an expert witness who is coming to talk to you in a case involving the faulty manufacture of silicon chips for computers?

(e) How would you prepare to deal with a complex medical prognosis when you need to cross-examine the doctor who made the report?

One final practical point. Students are often nervous in talking to clients, questioning witnesses or making speeches. One way this nervousness may be overcome is to shift your centre of attention from yourself to the importance of communication. If you are trying to build an understanding and rapport with a client, a witness or anyone else, your attention should be outside yourself and how you feel and more on how they feel. In any event, a real attempt at communication cannot but help your skills as a barrister.

B.7   Exercises

Exercise 1
Consider all the types of communication the barrister might use, and the potential advantages and disadvantages of each.

Types of Communication	Advantages	Disadvantages
Spoken		
Written		
Non-verbal		
Other		

Exercise 2

List here all the factors you can think of which may assist a barrister in communicating effectively.

List here all the things you can think of which may prevent a barrister communicating effectively.

APPENDIX C

YOU AND YOUR VOICE

C.1   Introduction

As advocacy is central to the working life of a barrister, it should go without saying that having a clear and effective voice is a vital professional tool. You will also need an adaptable voice to fill the largest court room or the smallest interview room. A few students will already have a voice of this quality, but many will not. This chapter provides suggestions and exercises for improving your voice. Do not dismiss the exercises on the basis that you did not choose the Bar to do exercises — you have chosen to be an advocate and you must do what it takes to become a good one. Also, do not dismiss any exercise if it initially sounds silly, as these exercises are used by many leading actors and professional speakers. The good barrister needs the quality of voice these exercises can help to produce.

A 'good voice' is a basic requirement for ease of communication. This does not mean you have to have the sonorous tones of one of our great Thespians or public figures in order to be a success within your chosen profession. However, an enlightened under-standing of your own individual instrument, and of ways and means to achieve a balanced and tuneful voice, can only enhance your work, particularly in court.

Good sound can work to your advantage. It builds a sense of trust and can be positively manipulative, leading to a general feeling of well-being. The technical knowledge required should be simply understood and then stored in your memory. This may take a while to bring about, but with a healthy attitude towards your vocal training much can be achieved in a relatively short space of time.

What follows is a basic explanation of the importance of good posture, relaxation and breathing, how voice works and how speech is formed. This is followed by a series of exercises for the development of good relaxation, posture, breathing, speech and vocal expression.

If you wish to learn to speak effectively, and without strain, some voice training is essential. You will be well advised therefore to work on your voice by yourself, preferably every day, and to seek specialist help if you have any particular problems.

C.2   Posture and Relaxation

The mainstay of a strong voice is breath. However, in order to find breath you must first look to the main support for that breath, namely your body.

The way you function in everyday life, in both your work and social environments, will affect the way you use your body; and indeed the way you use your body will have a knock-on effect on the way you function. It becomes a Catch 22 situation.

The primary focus should be the spine, which is the central support for our skeleton. Acquiring a fluidity and elasticity in the spine will enable the rest of your framework to follow suit. Both a collapsed or 'C'-shaped spine and an over-rigid 'S'-shaped spine will result in extremely bad posture, which in its turn can lead, in later life, to rheumatic and/or arthritic conditions. Just carrying a heavy bag over one shoulder regularly for any length of time can lead to a minor curvature of the spine, which, unless corrected, will become set.

It is strongly recommended that some work with an Alexander specialist would be highly beneficial. Alexander, as a movement principle and technique, works best on a 1:1 teacher-student ratio. It teaches you to know the strengths and weaknesses of your own alignment and how to handle them efficiently. There is a book you can read about the Alexander technique called *The Alexander Principle* by Wilfred Barlow.

At this stage it should be mentioned that swimming is an excellent way of stretching all the muscles and releasing body tension. Indeed, the art of swimming will be enjoyed more fully with a sound knowledge of correct breathing.

C.3 Breathing

A detailed analysis of the breathing apparatus seems unnecessary when you can find simple and clear explanations in the books on voice listed at the end of this chapter. *Your Voice and How to Use it Successfully* by Cicely Berry would be a good starting point.

The following points are worth remembering. The action of breathing is a reflex action from the brain. We require oxygen and so we breathe. When breathing for public speaking, we learn to increase and strengthen and, indeed, control the movements already made when breathing involuntarily during repose. The books on voice explain how this happens, and you will find a detailed description of the muscles used in breathing in the exercise section.

C.4 Phonation

During exhalation, air passes from the lungs into the windpipe (trachea), and continues its journey toward the mouth by passing through the vocal folds (larynx). It is here that phonation — the production of vocal sounds — takes place.

The larynx comprises several bony cartilages and is very intricate in its structure. The front bony cartilage of the larynx is your Adam's apple and can be felt between the finger and thumb at the front of your neck. The Adam's apple (thyroid cartilage) protects your vocal folds. These are two muscular membranes (white in colour) lying across the glottis (throat) inside the larynx. By a series of complicated muscular movements, the various cartilages are made to open and close these vocal folds. When breath passes through them in a closed position, they oscillate with the pressure and vibrate, so producing *note* or *phonation*. The greater the frequency of vibration and the greater the tautness of the vocal folds — the higher the pitch of the voice. It is therefore very important that the breath supply passing into the larynx is relaxed and sufficiently supported by the musculature of the abdomen and chest so as not to cause vocal strain or damage.

C.5 Speech

Strong regional accents do not always give a clarity of understanding which can be communicated worldwide. You need to produce sounds which will be generally understood without losing the originality of your speech. There is absolutely no necessity for a uniform pronunciation to emerge; merely a refining of the stronger characteristics of regional accents.

The consonant and vowel sounds listed are those of RP (received pronunciation), a neutral accent which is universally understood by English speakers. Also listed alongside each sound is the phonetic symbol in RP for that sound.

Phonetics is the language of sound and has an international alphabet. One symbol will represent one sound, no matter whether you are English, German or Japanese. It is widely taught in the application of languages, though not perhaps as widely as it ought to be in the British Isles!

Two books that will give you a greater insight into phonetics are listed in **C.11** at the end of this appendix.

C.5.1   THE ORGANS OF ARTICULATION/SPEECH

The following organs and structures are involved in articulation:

(a) lips;

(b) tongue (tip, blade and back);

(c) teeth;

(d) teeth ridge — bony ridge behind the upper front teeth;

(e) hard palate — the bony 'roof' of your mouth;

(f) soft palate — the soft muscular membrane at the back of your mouth. It is a continuation of the hard palate and acts as a trap-door between nose and mouth. When it is raised, the air passes into the mouth, as in most RP sounds; when lowered, the air passes into the nose as in /m/, /n/ and / ŋ /; (NG)

(g) nose;

(h) lower jaw — the upper jaw is immobile.

C.5.2   VOICED AND UNVOICED SOUNDS

Unvoiced consonants are made by air passing through the larynx when the vocal folds are at rest and in an open position. This is then shaped by the organs of speech. Voiced consonants and vowels are made by air passing through the active vocal folds and this vibrating air is then shaped by the organs of speech.

C.5.3   CONSONANTS

A consonant is made by a passage of air passing through the mouth, which is interrupted either completely or partially by two organs of speech, e.g., lips, tongue + teeth, tongue + soft palate, etc.

There are different families of consonants, categorised according to the **manner** of articulation for each sound.

F5.3.1   Plosives
These are made by a **complete** interruption of the air-stream.

Unvoiced	Voiced	Place of articulation
/p/ /p ɪ g/ pig	/b/ /bæt/ bat	both lips
/t/ /ten/ ten	/d/ /dɒg / dog	tip of tongue + teeth ridge
/k/ /kəʊ t/ coat	/g/ gɜː ɬ / girl	back of tongue + soft palate

C.5.3.2 **Nasals**

These are made by a partial and continuous interruption of the air-stream. The soft palate is lowered to allow air to pass down the nose.

Voiced			Place of articulation
/m/	/m aʊ θ/	mouth	both lips
/n/	/n əʊ z/	nose	tip of tongue + teeth ridge
/ /	/s ɪ ŋ /	sing	back of tongue + soft palate

C.5.3.3 **Fricatives**

These are made by a partial interruption of the air-stream, involving a narrowing of space, thus creating a friction.

Unvoiced			Voiced			Place of articulation
/f/	/fɒks/	fox	/v/	/vet/	vet	bottom lip + top teeth
/θ /	/θ ɪk/	thick	/ ð/	/ ð en/	then	tip of tongue + teeth
/s/	/si: t	seat	/z/	/pɪ ɡ z/	pigs	blade of tongue + teeth ridge
/ /	/ʃ ʊɡ ə/	sugar	/ /	/me ʒ ə/	measure	blade of tongue + front of hard palate
/h/	/hetp/	help				narrowing of the glottis with approximation of the vocal folds

F5.3.4 **Affricates**

These are made by a complete interruption of the air-stream, involving considerable friction at the point of release.

Unvoiced			Voiced			Place of articulation
/tr/	/trɪ p/	trip	/dr/	/dres/	dress	tip of tongue + back of teeth
/t /	/tʃ ɜːtʃ/	church	/dʒ/	/dʒʌdʒ/	judge	tip of tongue, blade, teeth ridge + front of hard palate

C.5.3.5 **Laterals**

These are made by a partial and continuous interruption of the air-stream, where the air escapes sideways over the tongue.

Voiced			Place of articulation
/l/	/l ʌ v/	love	tip of tongue + teeth ridge
/l/	/sɪ l iː /	silly	tip of tongue + teeth ridge
/ /	/f iː ɬ d/	field	tip of tongue + teeth ridge, and lifting of the back of the tongue towards the soft palate

C.5.3.6 **Rolled consonants**

These are made by partial and continuous interruption of the air-stream.

Voiced			Place of articulation
/r/	/red/	red	tip of tongue + back of teeth ridge
/r/	/skri : m/	scream	
/ r/	/veri :/	very	

C.5.3.7   Semi-vowels
These are made by a non-fricative glide from a vowel of close proximity, e.g., u-w, i-y

Voiced			Place of articulation
/w/	/w ɛə /	where, wear	middle of tongue + soft palate with lip-rounding
/j/	/j ɒ t/	yacht	middle of tongue + hard palate

C.5.4   VOWELS

A vowel is made by an uninterrupted passage of air passing through the mouth. The vowel is shaped primarily by the tongue, the tip of the tongue being positioned against the lower front teeth. Secondary articulation is sometimes required and this is produced by the lips. All vowels are voiced sounds.

There are various changes in tongue position from vowel to vowel and, indeed, there may be a change in position within the same vowel sound, as in a diphthong.

An open vowel is a vowel shape where the tongue lies in the bottom of the mouth.

A close vowel is a vowel shape where the tongue is raised close to the roof (hard palate) of the mouth.

A front vowel is a vowel shape where the centre of the tongue pushes forward in the mouth.

A back vowel is a vowel shape where the centre of the tongue pulls back in the mouth.

A central vowel is a vowel shape where the tongue lies in a relatively relaxed position in the centre of the mouth.

Thus, the vowel sound AH/ : / is an open, back vowel, and the vowel sound e /e/ is a half-close front vowel.

A pure vowel is a sound made with one shape (position) of the tongue.

A diphthong is a sound made by a glide between two single vowels sounds, e.g., /a ɪ / is made up of the two single sounds /a/ -le chat (French) and / ɪ / -pig. With Received Pronunciation, the accent of Standard English, the glide between the two shapes creates the sound.

5 long pure vowels	/i: /	/tr iː /	tree
	/ ː /	/b ɜː d/	bird
	/ ː /	/h ɑː t/	heart
	/ ː /	/w ɔː k/	walk (s.l.a.)
	/u: /	/f uː d/	food (s.l.a.)
7 short pure vowels	/ /	/pɪ g /	pig
	/e/	/hen/	hen
	/ / /	/ ð ə /	the
	/ /	/k æ t/	cat
	/ /	/l ʌ n t ʃ/	lunch
	/ /	/d ɒ g /	dog (s.l.a.)
	/ /	/b ʊ k/	book (s.l.a.)
8 diphthongs	/ eɪ /	/ple ɪ s /	place
	/ aɪ /	/fa ɪ t/	fight
	/ ɔɪ /	/b ɔɪ /	boy (s.l.a.)
	/ əʊ /	/b əʊ t/	boat (s.l.a.)
	/a ʊ /	/h a ʊ s/	house (s.l.a.)
	/ ɪə /	/h ɪə /	here
	/ ɛə /	/ ð ɛə /	there
	/ ʊə /	/p j ʊə /	pure (s.l.a.)

(s.l.a. = secondary lip articulation)

C.6 Posture and Relaxation Exercises

C.6.1 POSTURE BREAKDOWN

Stand with your feet hip-width apart, with the toes forward. Allow the knees to relax and your arms to hang by your sides. Try to keep your jaw relaxed, by not clenching your teeth. Gently bounce from the knees, allowing every part of you to move freely, rather like a rag-doll. Stop bouncing and allow your head to drop forward, so that your chin is almost resting on your chest and let the weight of your head gradually pull the upper part of your body towards the floor, so you end up hanging over from the waist, with your arms dangling towards the floor. Remain in this position and imagine you are trying to shake a large shawl from your shoulders, and shake it off on to the floor. Gently breathe in and out a few times, in through your nose and out through your mouth. Then slowly build back up to standing — as if your spine is a set of building bricks and you are carefully and evenly placing one on top of the other. Let your head be the last to come upright — to 'centre'. Gently breathe in through the nose and release your body and breath, quite fast, at the same time — so you feel like a puppet whose strings have been cut in the upper part of your body. You will quite quickly find yourself hanging forward again, from the waist. Gently, but firmly, build up again. Remember to keep your knees relaxed.

At this point, have a really good stretch right through to your fingers and toes and the top of your head. Let yourself yawn too, if you feel like it. With lots of sound! Then have a good shake, by imagining that you're shaking all your flesh off. Start with one leg, then the other, then the arms and then shake them all together, as wildly and crazily as possible and try to let your head go, too.

Stand again with your feet hip-width apart and imagine you have a heavy yoke across your shoulders, which is pulling your shoulders and neck forward and down. Really feel how uncomfortable it is and let your arms become part of the action, too, by stretching them out sideways, away from your body, with the palms facing downwards. Gradually get rid of the yoke by turning your palms to face the ceiling and rolling your shoulders up and out, so freeing your neck and head and feel your head floating to the ceiling, as if someone is pulling you gently by a string from the crown of your head. Finally, lower your arms to your sides and let the hands hang free. You should feel more open, without being rigid, across your chest. Then, keeping your arms down slowly roll your shoulders in a full circle, first forward, up, back and down and secondly back, up, forward and down. Each time let the weight fall on the downward movement, so it becomes quite rhythmical. Do this several times, keeping your arms and hands relaxed.

In a similar way, let your whole head complete a full, circular roll. Drop the head forward to begin with and slowly allow it to swing like a pendulum over to your left shoulder, keeping your eyes front. (If you find yourself looking over your left shoulder, you will have twisted your head, rather than rolled it. This is wrong, so start again. Your head pivots at the top of your spinal column; any twisting will only cause excess tension in your neck and shoulder muscles.) From your left shoulder, continue rolling your head back, allowing the mouth to open and the lower jaw to relax. You will now be looking at the ceiling, with the rest of your body still relaxed and central. Remember to keep breathing! Complete the roll, by continuing over to your right shoulder and then letting your head drop forward again. Rest here a moment, always breathing, then do a complete roll the other way, starting to the right shoulder and finishing over the left. It is important to work through this slowly, as we all store large areas of tension in our necks. At first, you may find it quite painful, especially when your head is dropped back. So do take your time and keep the movement fluid and continuous. Remember, this is not disco dancing! Once the head roll is complete, float your head back to centre, so that your eyes are facing front again.

This is a fundamental posture work-out and can gradually become more detailed, although only in the hands of a professional movement or voice teacher.

C.6.2   RELAXATION

One of the easiest ways of achieving positive relaxation is through massage. Make sure the person who is massaging you knows what he or she is doing. Don't allow them to experiment with walking up and down on your back. This is very dangerous, although there is no reason why you shouldn't go to a professional masseur and get the full benefit of his or her expertise. However, most people are capable of massaging necks and shoulders and it is best to be lying on a carpeted floor or thin, firm mattress for this. Lie on your front and keep your arms spread with your elbows bent and your palms to the floor. Probably the most comfortable head position is to one side with your cheek resting on the surface. Again, allow your jaw to be relaxed and don't forget to breathe freely.

Massage should be both firm and gentle using the thumbs and fingertips as the main activators. The thumbs should work in a circular motion, kneading the flesh in a positive rhythmical fashion. Remember to remove any clothing which is non-stretch, such as jackets and shirts. A T-shirt is fine, bare flesh is even better. Always start in the centre of the back, between the shoulder blades and work out across the shoulders, returning to the centre and moving up the neck. Work with two hands together, each mirroring the other's actions. About 10–15 minutes of this daily is ideal, preferably before your courtroom work commences!

Another way of relaxing without involving a second party, is to lie on a soft floor on your back, with your knees and your feet flat on the ground at hip-width apart. This position is known as semi-supine and should look like this:

It is the most relaxed position for the body, as well as being the most beneficial for breathing. It allows the spine to flatten naturally, without tension. If you find your neck and head are uncomfortable in this position, support your head on a book, no more than an inch thick; this will allow your shoulders and head to be free. Let your arms rest by your sides, with your palms facing the ceiling, so letting your shoulders roll out and down. If you find your knees falling outwards, turn your toes in slightly. Remember to keep your jaw relaxed by not clenching your teeth or sticking your tongue to the roof of your mouth!

At this stage, it is difficult to separate the relaxation work from that of breathing, as they go hand in hand. However, it is possible to put on some soothing music of your choice and just close your eyes and listen for 20–30 minutes. You will most probably fall asleep, though, as it is the breathing which keeps a positive energy force passing through you.

C.7   Breathing Exercises

So, you are lying in the semi-supine position.

EXERCISE 1

Allow yourself to yawn. Breathe in deeply and steadily through the nose until you feel like yawning, let your mouth open wide and fully, stretching your lip muscles in a circular fashion, rather like a lion, and let the air come flooding out. Don't worry if you make a lot of noise! Imagine you are slowly filling the room with your outward breath, so allow yourself to do this as many times as you like. Each time you do it, you should feel more relaxed and yet more energised.

Picture a really exotic flower and place it in front of you. Breathe slowly and deeply in, through the nose, smelling the exquisite perfume; this will help stir your senses and open both your nasal and throat passages. Then gently blow the air out again, through your mouth, pursing your lips, and imagine you are dispersing tiny pollen grains which have gathered on the petals of your flower. This must be a very sensitive process, so as not to ruin the flower's beauty. Do this three or four times.

EXERCISE 2

Imagine yourself lying on a beach. (If only!) You are very warm and relaxed. It is quite late in the day and you are quite close to the water's edge, so that you can hear the waves lapping gently on the smooth sand. Mirror the movement of the waves, ebbing and flowing, with your breathing in, silently, through an open, relaxed mouth, and as the waves flow, so you breathe out, again through your mouth. Only this time, use a continuous 'sshhing' sound on the outward breath, so it really sounds like the music of the sea. Where are you? The Mediterranean? Barbados? Thailand? Make sure you have a positive image. Remember, no two waves are ever the same, so really let your imagination have a free rein. Use your lips on the 'sshh' to focus the breath forward. If you choose to open your eyes, you can really see yourself sending the breath up and away from you, again steadily filling the room. You can do this for as long as your imagination lets you.

Floor work is by far the most beneficial for breathing, as you do not need to support yourself. You can achieve the best results this way, so make the best of it!

Now we get a little more technical. We need to make sure you are breathing from your diaphragm and lower ribs, and not taking the air into your upper chest. This is not easy, especially as old habits die hard, so persevere and don't try too hard to make it work. Remember breathing from your diaphragm is an involuntary action in repose and we need to extend this slowly for good voice production.

EXERCISE 3

Place your two hands palms down on your abdomen, just underneath the swell of your rib-cage and with your lower fingers over your belly button. Hold yourself firmly, using the whole of your hands and keep your elbows spread and resting on the floor.

Allow yourself to cough gently and indeed, laugh, and feel the movement of the muscles underneath your hands. The movement you will experience is the action of the abdominal muscles, the most inferior of these being the diaphragm (inferior meaning 'deepest'). You cannot actually feel your diaphragm moving, it is too deep within your body for that. What you will feel, is the relaxation of the various abdominal muscles as you breathe in, so allowing room for the diaphragm to descend and the lungs to expand from top to bottom, and the contraction of these same muscles as you breathe out, so aiding the diaphragm to rise again to its former position, helping the lungs to deflate slowly, releasing air up through the trachea (windpipe) and out through the nose and mouth. Consequently, as you breathe in (inhalation or inspiration), your hands will rise gradually and smoothly towards the ceiling, so increasing your capacity and size. As you breathe out, the reverse will happen, your hands will drop slowly away from the ceiling, back to their former position. Try to be aware of your upper chest and rib-cage moving as little as possible during this process, without forcibly holding them still. They are bound to rise more than necessary to begin with, but slowly, as you learn to breathe deeper the movement should lessen. A slight swelling at the lower end of the sternum (breast-bone) is quite alright, but an obvious heaving of the whole of the upper chest should be avoided at all costs. Indeed, should you find this happens, you will also discover an adverse movement underneath your hands. The abdominal muscles will suck in as you breathe in and harden slightly. Then, as you breathe out, they will relax and even push against your hands. This is completely wrong. If you find you are unable to stop this incorrect breathing pattern, with time (and patience!) it would be best to seek professional help from a voice teacher to put you right.

For all the following exercises, you need to get into a routine of breathing in through the nose and out through the mouth, imagining a free passage-way, like a ship's funnel, from the movement of your hands to your open mouth. The wider the ship's funnel is, the freer the air-flow through. The whole process of breathing which has been described above applies to every exercise described below. The more often you complete this sequence, the less you will have to think about it and the more spontaneous it will become.

EXERCISE 4

Breathe in to a mental count of 3 seconds (nose) and breathe out (mouth) to a mental count of 10 seconds. Really be strict with yourself over this. If you cannot manage 10 seconds, start with 6 and gradually build it up. Get a steady rhythm going and always make sure the inward breath is silent. On the outward breath, use 'sshh', very gently and freely.

EXERCISE 5

Breathe in for 2 seconds and out on a slightly voiced count. Start with 2 and build it by 1 count on each breath.

Breath IN 1, 2	Breath OUT 1, 2
1, 2	1, 2, 3
1, 2	1, 2, 3, 4
1, 2	1, 2, 3, 4, 5
1, 2	1, 2, 3, 4, 5, 6
	and so on to 10

Gradually add more voice — but never very loud. Imagine you are speaking to someone about 3 feet away from you.

You can swop the count for days of the week or months of the year; signs of the horoscope; a shopping list; 'This is the house that Jack built'; a legal definition or phrase!

Eventually you can take a speech you are preparing and break it into sensible breath phrases. Speak it quietly, allowing the meaning to carry the breath, and pausing at each phrase end to mentally breathe in for 3 seconds. Keep practising this discipline, until eventually you feel able just to allow the breath to drop in spontaneously without a mental count.

EXERCISE 6

All of these exercises can eventually be carried out sitting or standing. But you will soon discover that the moment you need to support your body again, the old habits will return. Remember, when sitting, to keep the bottom back in the chair and the spine supported. Keep both feet on the ground at least hip-width apart. This is a very positive way of sitting. Do **not** cross your legs; this throws your centre weight off balance. Place one hand on your diaphragm and the other on one front-side of your **lower** rib-cage. Encourage the movement to happen spontaneously and together, so that the lower ribs expand outwards as the abdominal muscles swell. This can take some time to occur satisfactorily. If any difficulties occur, consult a voice teacher. Remember you are looking for all-round expansion, so imagine, as you breathe in, that you are blowing up a rubber ring round your waist.

When standing, and before commencing, go through the posture breakdown and keep your feet firmly on the ground. Avoid shifting your weight from foot to foot, as this will throw you off-balance and is an over-casual attitude anyway.

C.8 Articulation Exercises

The aim here is to achieve clarity of diction. A good facial warm-up is the basis of a mastery of good diction. Have fun!

Sit down in front of a mirror.
Using your hands, massage your whole face, keeping jaw bone loose.
Screw your face up tight and then slowly stretch it fully. Widen your eyes as well.
Puff your face up with air and suck it in through the cheeks.
Slowly open your lips wide and then purse them in tightly to a small hole.
Smile slowly and hold it for 10 seconds.
Frown and try pulling your lip corners right down. Without your hands!
Blow air through your lips, loosely.
Place the tip of your tongue behind your bottom teeth and stretch your tongue out of your mouth, by raising the back of your tongue.
Point your tongue out of your mouth slowly. Try not to clench your tongue between your teeth or lips, but use only the muscles in the tongue. And then relax the tongue out of the mouth.
Repeat slowly several times. Then point your tongue in different directions. Up, down, left and right.
Repeat several times.
Release your tongue, by flapping it repeatedly against your top front teeth, keeping your jaw loose.
Roll your R's (don't worry if you can't).
Click your tongue against the roof or your mouth. Try to keep the jaw relaxed, but still. You can help yourself by lightly placing your hand under your chin to steady it, with your palm towards the floor.
Chew slowly, as if eating a large sticky toffee.
Lift the back of your tongue slowly up to your soft palate, with the jaw open and relaxed, so making the sound 'ng' / ŋ / as in *sing* and continue the sound into an open 'AH' / ɑː / and back again to 'ng' / ŋ /.

Repeat and slowly build the pace. The air passage will move from nose (ŋ) to mouth (ː). Really focus on the sound and sing it: ŋ – ɑː – ŋ – ɑː – ŋ – ɑː , etc.
Lastly, gently shake the face out, keeping the jaw and tongue loose.

There is a page of tongue twisters at the end of this chapter for you to try. Remember to keep relaxed and use only minimal voice. Start slowly and build the pace as you get more skilful. Try to keep the rhythm and rhyme of each tongue twister. There are also some extremely good articulation pieces in Michael McCallion's *The Voice Book*. They are mainly stories, so use them as such and don't forget to breathe.

Remember that for all articulation work your tongue is your main organ of speech and like many muscles in your body, it requires exercise. Don't spend more than 15 minutes, daily, doing articulation work, otherwise you will tire your tongue out. Gradually you can extend the time limit to 30 minutes as you get more skilful. You need to have full control over your organs of speech; especially because, when nervous, you will have a tendency to speak too fast and fall over your words. So, the greater dexterity you have, the more you will be able to disguise your nerves.

C.9 Resonance Exercises

These exercises will help to add 'colour' to your breathing and should only be added to your daily routine after your breathing has become established and centred. In other words, not before the end of your first year's practice. This may seem mad, but they will not work for you otherwise.

EXERCISE 1

When lying on the foor, imagine your voice mirroring the movement of a waterfall. Let the breath come in for the usual mental count of 3 seconds, imagine your yawn and indeed think of the flower, or your own favourite smell and gradually release the breath on a quietly voiced 'AH' /ɑː/ — shaping the waterfall from its height to its depth. This way you allow your voice to fall naturally and easily through its range. Stretch your range a little each time, so that you may start with a range of eight notes (an octave on a piano) and increase it to 16 (two octaves). Allow the voice to slide, rather than step down the range. You can even try beating your chest with your hands while doing this and listening to the sound it produces. Don't beat your chest too hard, though! Then reverse the image, like running a film backwards, and take the range from bottom to top; this is far more difficult and requires a greater breath capacity. Don't end in a squeak! Eventually as you begin to feel quite skilful at this, you can move the voice freely all around your range, changing your tongue and lip positions and experimenting with different sounds. Use different vowels, several on one breath AW /ɔː/, OO/u:/, EE/i:/, AY/eɪ /, or try humming. (Remember humming creates a vibration on the lips, as well as in the nose; keep the teeth unclenched and the tongue resting in the bottom of your mouth.) Humming 'mmm', will help to focus your voice to the front or 'mask' of your face. If you travel the hum through the range, feel the vibration travelling down and up the middle of your face. Alternating 'mmm' with 'AH' / ː / or, indeed, any vowel, will also focus the voice forward.

EXERCISE 2

Sit in a chair and paint a picture with your voice. Imagine your voice painting grey, flat clouds; yellow, tall sunflowers; red, fast cars. If you find this too childish, which hopefully you won't, then paint a courtroom scene, and paint all the different types of people within it. This exercise can do wonders for moving the voice, so be as silly and mad as you can.

EXERCISE 3

Take your count of 1–10 and vocalise a staircase with it. Move up and down it freely, remembering to breathe. Try to let your voice do all the action and not your head. You will be surprised how easily your head can move and therefore distract the listener.

EXERCISE 4

Take a prepared speech and really exaggerate it. Over-dramatise it, lifting and dropping the voice, so it sounds totally artificial. Be really ingratiating; speak it as if telling a story badly to children — speak down and be really nauseous. Exaggerate all the nasal sounds, m, n, ng / ŋ / and lengthen all the l's. Roll your r's!

EXERCISE 5

Stand up now and hum a song you know — a nursery rhyme if nothing else comes to mind, the 1812 Overture if it so takes your fancy! Remember to breathe and phrase it correctly. Some great tunes for resonance work are:

> Smoke Gets in Your Eyes
> I Only Have Eyes for You
> Blue Moon
> Strangers in the Night
> Summertime
> Stormy Weather
> Ferry Cross the Mersey
> Michelle (Ma Belle)

And if you enjoy singing — well, sing them!

EXERCISE 6

Then take one of your speeches and sing it, too! Try different styles: grand opera; Gilbert and Sullivan; crooning; a lullaby; soul; rap. Imagine yourself slowly winning the jury over to your way of thinking and alter the style and tempo to suit. You may find you have three or four movements within one speech! Just remember to keep breathing.

C.10 Projection Exercises

Achieving good projection, without risk of vocal damage, is a painstaking process. Again, it should really be an area which is left alone until the second year of voice training. It should be approached with caution and with a great awareness of relaxation and breath control.

Start any projection work by lying on the floor. If you lie on your front, this will both aid capacity in the back ribs and enable you still to feel the movement of the diaphragm against the floor. Lie, stretched out, with your forehead resting on your hands, palms down, with the elbows spread.

EXERCISE 1

Imagine yourself in a rowing boat, a team of eight, say, out for a practice on the river. Take time to establish the image of yourself, pummels (handles of the oars) at the ready. As you reach down to your feet, lifting the blades out of the water, you breathe in; as you smoothly pull the oars through the water by bringing the pummels up to your chest, you breathe out, initially using a 'ssshh'— lengthening the breath right through the movement. Start to get this working to a regular rhythm, allowing yourself to breathe in through the mouth. See yourself beginning to make progress down the river, gradually gathering momentum with each outward stroke and breath. When you get really skilful at this, the breath will drop in easily and quickly and you can put yourself into a racing situation, changing the 'ssshh' to a steady count of 1–10, which again gathers pace and intensity with each stroke. The important part of this exercise is not only learning to let the breath drop in, but also to 'ground' the voice, making sure you don't let the pitch rise with the speed and intensity. This means you're really allowing the breath to do the work and not letting constriction in the throat muscles take over.

EXERCISE 2

Another exercise is imagining yourself to be a dog! Get down on the floor again, place the body in an all-fours position, with the hand and knees shoulder- and hip-width apart, respectively. Your back should be flat and supported like a table top, with the head hanging free. But your 'undercarriage', your diaphragm and abdominal muscles, should be allowed to relax completely on the inward breath. This way the breath drops in, without any conscious effort. On the outward breath, imagine you are strongly blowing all the dust and muck off the floor. Do this several times, then gently collapse the whole body into a prostrate praying position. Let the bottom sit snugly on your feet and let the arms be extended, with the elbows resting on the ground. Your forehead should also be resting on the ground. Just gently breathe in and out in this position, to relax after quite a vigorous exercise.

Once you have rested a couple of minutes, start to use the 'building count' exercise described earlier. Only this time, don't only extend the count:

> 1, 2
> 1, 2, 3
> 1, 2, 3, 4
> 1, 2, 3, 4, 5
> and so on . . .

but also build the volume level, obviously starting very quietly. Try to let the muscles relax each time to let the breath come in quickly, but don't quicken the count. Keep this steadily contained in its place, so that you can really tap the breath supply.

EXERCISE 3

Another exercise, which you can do lying, sitting or standing, is to take a piece of poetry. Choose a lyrical poet like Tennyson or Swinburne and say the poem, or part of it, only shaping the vowel sounds ('The Lotus Eaters' by Tennyson is particularly good for this). Take away the consonants and make your tongue, and lips when necessary, really pass through the vowels, linking each one to give you the shape of the phrase. Make sure you are still conveying the meaning, even if it sounds rather odd. This will help give you a weight and length to your breath and voice. Go back to the top of the poem and speak normally.

EXERCISE 4

Lastly, take a particularly fiery political speech, or such like, and start by lying on your back, using only 'ssshh', throughout each breath phrase. You can emphasise the stresses this way, too. Work to make the breath return quickly. Eventually you can stand up and use the words, giving it the appropriate gusto and energy, but remembering where to breathe.

p Peter Piper picked a peck of pickled pepper, a peck of pickled pepper Peter Piper picked, if Peter Piper picked a peck of pickled pepper, where is the peck of pickled pepper Peter Piper picked.

b Bibby Bobby bought a bat, Bibby Bobby bought a ball, with that bat he banged the ball. Banged it bump against the wall, but so boldly Bobby banged, soon he burst the rubber ball. Boo sobbed Bobby, goodbye ball. Bad luck, Bobby, bad luck ball. Now to drown his many troubles, Bibby Bobby's blowing bubbles.

sts There were three ghosts,
Sitting on posts,
Eating buttered toasts,
And licking their fists,
Right up to their wrists,
Weren't they beasts.

fr You can have fried fresh fish, fish fried fresh, fresh fried fish, fresh fish fried, or fish fresh fried.

s-
sh Susan Schumann shot a solitary chamois and received a short sharp salutary shock from such shameless slaughter.

m She stood on the balcony inexplicably mimicking him hiccupping and welcoming him in.

h Heather was hoping to hop to Tahiti to hack a hibiscus to hang on her hat. Now Heather has hundreds of hats on her hat rack. So how will a hop to Tahiti help that?

b Betty Botter bought some butter, but she said this butter's bitter. If I mix it with my batter it will make my batter bitter. So she bought some better butter and she mixed it with her batter, and she made her batter better.

t A tutor who tooted the flute,
Tried to tutor two tooters to toot,
Said the two to the tutor,
'Is it easier to toot,
Or to tutor two tooters to toot.'

th Theo Thistler, the thistle sifter, sifted a sieve of sifted thistles into a sieve of unsifted thistles, then sifted a sieve of unsifted thistles into a sieve of sifted thistles, for Theo Thistler was a thistle sifter.

s-
sh To sit in solemn silence in a dull dark dock, in a pestilential prison with a lifelong lock, awaiting the sensation of a short, sharp shock. From a cheap and chippy chopper, on a big black block.

s, Sheila is selling her shop at the seashore,
sh, For shops at the seashore are sure to lose,
z At her shop on the seashore should Sheila sell shellfish?
Or should she sell sandpaper, sherry and shoes?

ng Sending a ring through the post was plain sailing,
Sending a ring through the mail was just fine,
Writing a note to his girl friend and hailing,
A taxi, to take it to Ealing on time.

w-
ch If a woodchuck would chuck wood, the wood that a woodchuck would chuck is the wood that a woodchuck could chuck, if the woodchuck that could chuck wood would chuck.

353

C.11   Further Reading

Berry, C. *Your Voice and How to Use it Successfully*, Harrap, 1986.
Rodenburg, P. *The Need for Words*, Methuen, 1993.
These two books will serve you best for all-round information.

McCallion, M. *The Voice Book*, Routledge, Chapman & Hall, 1988.
This is particularly good for articulation.

Berry, C. *Voice and the Actor*, Harrap, 1986.
Linklater, K. *Freeing the Natural Voice*, Drama Books, 1976.
These probably serve the actor mainly, but could nevertheless be interesting reading!

Gimson, A.G. *An Introduction to the Pronunciation of English*, 2nd edn, St Martin, 1970.
Wells and Colson *Practice Phonetics*.

APPENDIX D

LISTENING

D.1   Introduction

Barristers need to listen in many situations but particularly when holding a conference with a client, in negotiating and in advocacy. Listening can be difficult if a barrister feels bored, preoccupied, impatient, biased or just too familiar with the case. Try to be disciplined about listening; try to stop thinking about other things, be physically alert, concentrate on the speaker and what is being said. A central element of being able to listen effectively is being able to interpret behaviour accurately. The combination of listening and observing should enable you to 'hear' what is said (see also **Appendix F**). It is easy to appreciate that it is part of the barrister's working life to speak, but it is in fact almost as important to listen to gather the information you will then present.

Do not be deceived into thinking you need to do no work on your listening skills just because you have been listening to people for years. It is a constant complaint of clients that barristers fail to understand what they are told, or fail to remember what is said. Few people will have listening skills so good that they cannot be improved.

D.2   Importance of Understanding Different Listening Styles

The primary interest of the barrister in a conference will often be to obtain more detail about the facts of the case. A barrister may be tempted to take a very active role in the conference by asking a series of questions in quick succession in order to elicit those facts. The dangers of adopting this approach are twofold:

  (a)   the client will have little opportunity to develop a relationship with the barrister and hence to feel that the barrister empathises with the client's predicament;

  (b)   the barrister needs some insight into how the client perceives the situation in order to give the best advice to solve what the client sees as the problem and to present the case in the best possible light.

Listening effectively helps the barrister to hear what is really being said, both:

  (a)   about the facts; and

  (b)   about the client's emotional response to the situation.

D.3   Different Kinds of Listening

This section introduces different listening styles, passive listening, active listening and variations, such as responsive listening. The point is not to recommend any particular style of listening for a barrister, but simply to open your mind to the options. In each conference, or other situation where you need to listen, you should always consider what sort of listening is appropriate for the client and for the case. You will often need to change your listening style for different parts of the conference.

D.3.1   PASSIVE LISTENING

This gives the client space to say what he or she wants to say but gives no verbal indication to the client of the barrister's response or understanding of the tale that is being told.

The most obvious way to listen passively is to listen in silence. Do not feel uncomfortable about allowing short periods of silence; the client may need time to develop the story and may feel hurried and pushed if you start to fill in the silent periods with your own words. Silence can suggest that you are listening and invites the client to go ahead at a pace with which they feel comfortable.

A long silence which indicates that the client has finished telling the tale may leave the barrister needing to know more. Open-ended questions will encourage the client to resume the narrative, for example, 'What happened to you after you were arrested?'; 'What did you do next?'; 'Tell me more about the damage to your car'; 'How have you managed financially since your husband left you?'. These kinds of questions enable the client to retain control in telling the story and also allow you to hear what the client thinks is really important. The relevance in law of what is said is not all-important, since a major concern should be to understand your client's motivations in seeking your advice.

D.3.2   RESPONSIVE LISTENING

As a slight modification of passive listening, there is responsive listening. Whilst passive listening is quiet and provides no reaction, seeking to draw as much as possible from the person speaking without any intervention, this may lead to silence or may start to unnerve the person speaking. Where this may happen, responsive listening may be used, meaning that brief and non-committal responses are made, basically to encourage the speaker to keep talking.

The type of non-committal response that might be used for this purpose includes 'I see', 'Mmm', 'Quite', or even simply a nod of the head.

D.3.3   RECEPTIVE LISTENING

The receptive listening response has some overlap with passive listening and responsive listening, but it has a distinct purpose. The purpose of receptive listening is still to make no substantial contribution to the conversation, but to make minor contributions that are specifically intended to show clear understanding and positive support. You might for example say 'I do understand', 'I am sorry', or 'I'm sure that was really upsetting'.

This type of listening can be particularly useful in dealing with a client who is upset or lacks confidence. With the forthcoming client it may appear patronising or give a false impression of the prospects of the case.

D.3.4   ACTIVE LISTENING

This kind of listening gives a more positive response by conveying back to the client the thrust of what the client has just said. It makes explicitly clear to the client that the barrister has heard and understood everything that has been said (both verbally and non-verbally) but seeks to make no judgment about what has been said. For example:

Lay client
My husband became increasingly disinterested in me and the children. He stayed late at work and when I complained he said that he was doing it for us, he said he was trying to earn more money so that we could have just a few of the little luxuries in life. I never saw any extra money though. All the time he said he was working for us but now I know he was carrying on with her, his secretary. He never earned any extra to help our family but he spent plenty of the little we had on her. He was a real

pig and she was a right cow, she knew he had a wife and children, we had even had a little chat at the firm's Christmas party — and all that time she was carrying on with my husband and all the office knew. They made a right fool of me.

Barrister
Your husband lied to you. All the time he was having an affair with his secretary and everyone in his office knew about it, and he spent the family's money on her. I understand why you feel angry and upset.

Active listening requires you to listen for all the meaning which is being communicated, not just that which is obvious from the words used. Active listening helps to develop rapport with the client; it is intended to enable you to get the client to talk openly and fully about the problem. Once that rapport has been established, the extent to which you need to continue to reflect your client's feelings will vary with every case and depends on your own judgment. Active listening can also appear patronising if it is not carefully judged with the individual client.

D.4 Understanding What You Hear

The main purpose of listening is to gather information. For the barrister serving the client it is vital that every possible piece of information is gathered, and all relevant information is retained.

To gather all information provided in an interview it is vital to concentrate, and not to let your mind wander, or rush ahead to devise the next question. It is a common fault for barristers to push on quickly rather than taking time to deal with matters fully. While efficient use of time is important, you will not be efficient if you fail to listen properly. To retain information you will need to take appropriate notes, but this requires skill only to note essential matters and should not distract you from listening.

To gather information, it is necessary to understand fully what is being said. If you are in any doubt about something you are being told, do clarify it.

The fact that you are listening effectively and understanding what you are told should communicate itself to the client, not only through your listening style, but also through other things, such as the client not having to repeat information. Nothing undermines a client's confidence more than feeling that a barrister is not listening, or misunderstands what has been said.

D.5 Interpreting What You Have Heard

Listening is not a simple, superficial activity but a complex one. You cannot always accept face values, you may need to interpret.

The following merely suggests clues to interpretation and does not provide hard and fast rules upon which you can rely. However, it does give you a basis from which to explore with the client whether your interpretation is correct.

(a) The first words spoken by your client may give the largest clue to what the client wants to get from the conference.

(b) Shifts in conversation may often be defensive.

(c) Issues or matters which are constantly reintroduced into the conversation can indicate concern about them even when they do not obviously have any connection with what is being discussed.

(d) Going round in circles can suggest that there is something which the client (or barrister) wants to avoid discussing.

(e) Inconsistencies can suggest troubled feelings, perhaps guilt, or lies.

(f) Sometimes clients say one thing in order to avoid saying what they mean, for example, 'Whenever anybody says to me "It's not the money, it's the principle of the thing", it's the money'. (Martin and War, quoted in *Legal Interviewing and Counselling* by Shaffer and Elkins, 1987, p. 224).

(g) It is also important to look out for clues from non-verbal communication, such things as pitch, intonation, speed in speaking and pauses in the conversation. If the way in which a story is told suddenly changes, for example, the voice becomes higher or the speaker increases the speed of speech, etc., the observant/listening barrister will note the change and seek to tease out the reasons for it.

Never assume that the words, intonation or body language used by someone from a different cultural background have the same meaning as they would if used by you. Always consider the possibility of different meanings, and if in doubt check what is meant by sympathetic questioning.

D.6 Exercises

1. Consider each of the listening styles outlined above.

What are the potential advantages of each in different situations and with different clients?
What are the potential disadvantages of each?
Can you identify any further listening styles?

2. Your client tells you 'My husband just walked out after 30 years of marriage and three children'.

What do you think is the most appropriate listening response? Why?
If you think the response should be any other than passive, what precisely would you say?
Is there anything you would wish to know before deciding which listening response was appropriate?
Do you think that the following responses are good or bad, and in each case, why?

'I understand how you feel'.
'It's quite normal to feel bitter.'
'We'll be able to get maintenance for you.'

3. Think of a situation in which you tried to tell someone something but they did not appear to be listening.

What indicated to you that they were not listening?
What were your reactions?

4. Do you feel that in general barristers are good listeners? If not, suggest how they might improve.

5. What significance might your own ethnic origin/gender have on communicating with:

(a) female clients;

(b) male clients;

(c) ethnic minority clients;

(d) white clients?

APPENDIX E

QUESTIONING

E.1 Introduction

The use of language (i.e., the spoken word) is the most obvious way in which we communicate with each other:

> The final cause of speech is to get an idea as exactly as possible out of one mind into another. Its formal cause therefore is such choice of words as will achieve this end most economically.
>
> (G.M. Young, quoted in *The Complete Plain Words* by Sir Ernest Gowers.)

The way in which we find out what information is possessed by others is by questioning them. This involves a two-way process — the questioner requests information and the person being questioned supplies information. If the question has been asked correctly, the desired information is most likely to be supplied. If the question has been asked incorrectly, then the information supplied is unlikely to be that which was desired.

To ask a question correctly requires proper and appropriate use of language. You, the questioner, must communicate your request to your subject in such a way that he or she correctly divines what it is that you want to know. You must use language which is proper — that is, which obeys the rules of grammar and syntax — and the words that you use must be appropriate. What is appropriate is determined partly by who you are, partly by who your subject is and, finally, by your audience. If you use a vocabulary that is effectively foreign to your subject, you will be unlikely to elicit the information that you want.

The language that you use ought to be appropriate to your status as a barrister but, most importantly, it must be appropriate to your audience. One expert talking to another may use a lot of jargon which makes sense to them. Often, jargon is simply 'shorthand', used within a profession or special group for speed. But it is incomprehensible to outsiders. For a barrister, perhaps the simplest and best motto is: 'When questioning someone, use plain English'.

E.2 Types of Questions

For the barrister, questioning occurs in a variety of contexts — in conference, in chambers, in a courtroom — and with a variety of subjects — for example you could ask questions of your lay client, your solicitor, court welfare officers, judges or expert witnesses. The type of questions that you use will vary according to who is being questioned, where the questioning is taking place and with what purpose.

Questions can be divided into different classifications and many people have tried to do this. The most commonly accepted categories are outlined below.

There is further discussion of the use of different types of question in **Chapters 18** and **19**.

E.2.1   OPEN QUESTIONS

An open question is one which gives the broadest possible freedom to the person questioned as to the form, length and content of the answer, for example, 'What did you do yesterday?'. Such a question is particularly useful to gather information, as the fewer limits you impose on the person you are questioning, the more opportunity they have to tell you their own story and to provide the information they think is important. On the other hand, the open question gives little control to the person asking the question.

E.2.2   THE SEMI-OPEN QUESTION

There are different degrees of 'openness' in questions. You can ask a question which defines some parameters, but which still gives substantial choice as to answer, for example, 'What did you have for breakfast yesterday?'. Various researchers and theorists have tried to give different names to different degrees of openness in questions, but in simple terms one can just say that there are a wide variety of semi-open questions, depending on how clearly the parameters for answering are drawn, and it is important to choose the right degree of openness to get the information required. For example, a more defined question than that just given is, 'What did you have to drink for breakfast yesterday?'.

E.2.3   THE CLOSED QUESTION

The closed question closes in the options available to the person being questioned as much as possible. Normally the answer to a closed question can only be a single word or a short sentence. An example of a closed question is, 'Did you have coffee for breakfast yesterday?'. The closed question obviously gives more control to the questioner, and can thus be particularly effective in getting specific information. However, the closed question may equally mean that the person being questioned has no opportunity to provide other information which may be relevant (which may or may not be a good thing!). It is possible that a person who is asked a closed question may feel frustrated by this, and may not restrict themselves to answering the question asked. It is possible to 'dodge' a closed question, for example by talking generally about the qualities of coffee, a technique now widely used by politicians, and you may need to insist on an answer.

E.2.4   THE YES/NO QUESTION

This name is fairly self-explanatory. It is a type of closed question that simply allows a yes or no answer. Such a question can be useful in ascertaining precise details, but it suffers from the general drawbacks of closed questions. Some questions simply cannot be answered 'Yes' or 'No', or if the answer is limited to choosing one of these, that answer may really be incomplete or not entirely truthful.

E.2.5   THE ALTERNATIVE QUESTION

This name is slightly ambiguous, but is again fairly self-explanatory. Depending on context, it may be a type of closed question or a type of semi-open question. The question simply provides options of response, but those options may be one word or whole sentences. An example of a closed alternative question is, 'Did you have tea or coffee for breakfast yesterday?'. The alternative question may prompt arguments where the person being questioned does not feel that the options are appropriate, as may a yes/no question.

E.2.6   SIMPLE QUESTIONS AND MULTIPLE QUESTIONS

Simple questions are those which simply put one issue to the person being questioned. Multiple questions are those which put several issues at the same time. Simple questions should generally be preferred by the barrister, as they are more likely to yield a clear and unambiguous answer. However multiple questions may have advantages where they effectively act as open questions, or where they put several options and set off trains of thought.

E.2.7 LEADING QUESTIONS

The leading question is of course one which leads the person being questioned to a particular answer by suggesting that answer in the question itself. The question limits the information that is being provided by the person being questioned, as it is the questioner who essentially puts the information forward. Such questions are of course of particular importance to barristers as their use in court is restricted, because otherwise evidence would effectively come from the barrister rather than from the witness. An example of a leading question is, 'Is it not right to say that you had toast with butter and black coffee for breakfast yesterday?'.

Do note, however, that leading questions only need to be avoided in certain circumstances in court. They are quite permissible outside court, and they can be quite useful in checking with a client that you have properly understood what you have been told. However, even outside court you should always keep in mind the objections to the leading question — never use leading questions to impose your view on a client, or to sow thoughts in a client's mind improperly. It is, for example, unethical for a barrister to suggest a line of defence to a client if the client has not suggested it may exist.

E.2.8 RHETORICAL QUESTIONS

The rhetorical question is of course one that does not expect an answer. Such a question has no use in ascertaining information (unless you are simply looking to see someone's reaction), but it does have its role in advocacy, especially when addressing a judge or jury.

E.3 Choosing the Best Question

As a barrister, you will constantly need to choose appropriate forms for questions.

E.3.1 QUESTIONING OUT OF COURT

Away from the courtroom, you are trying to get information from people. This may involve getting instructions from your client, or occasionally supporting evidence from other witnesses. Usually, a barrister will not question potential witnesses but may suggest to the solicitor what questions to ask. This is stipulated as a rule of professional conduct. There is, however, now an exception in civil cases, where a barrister may discuss a case with a potential witness if he or she considers that it is in the interests of the lay client, provided the solicitor is present and the barrister has a proper proof of evidence. In such circumstances, the barrister will have to define very carefully the questions to be asked — sometimes this can be done in broad terms, e.g., 'Find out if Mrs Sharma was due for any wage increases in the two years since the accident'. Sometimes specific questions may be necessary, e.g., 'Was the witness with Mr Chan between 7 am and 9 am on 24 July 2002? If so, where were they?'.

The main exception to the rule that barristers must not question potential witnesses directly is when questioning an expert witness. Often, a barrister needs to question an expert witness in order to understand technical issues raised by the case or to establish what assistance the expert can offer.

When you question your client in an interview, courtroom rules do not apply. You may ask about hearsay matters — although you may not be able to use the information in court, it could initiate a line of enquiry (e.g., asking your solicitor to try to find the person who told your client that the other driver was driving on the wrong side of the road so that direct, rather than hearsay, evidence can be given), or it could simply help you to get a better understanding of what went on. Similarly, you may ask questions to get information which will not be relevant to proceedings in court, e.g., 'We only have a 25 per cent chance of success. How badly do you want to continue this case?'. You may play devil's advocate, that is, ask questions opposed to your client's interests rather than supporting them — this has three functions:

(a)   It gives you the information that your opponent is likely to get from questioning your client in court (and forewarned is forearmed!).

(b)   It gives your client the chance to experience cross-examination from a hostile barrister (it may prepare the client better for the real thing).

(c)   It lets you see how the client stands up to cross-examination (whether or not to use your client as a witness is an important decision, although the final choice belongs to the client).

When questioning your client in conference, you will frequently use open-ended questions. You want to extract information and often the best way to do this is to ask an initial question which gives a lot of freedom to the client as to the answer. For example, 'I know that you injured your arm at work, Mrs Brown. Perhaps you would tell me exactly what happened'.

After you have got a broad picture of the topic, you can continue by asking increasingly specific questions:

Q.   'Is the machine usually fenced?'
A.   'Usually, but it had been taken off before my accident.'
Q.   'When was the fencing removed?'
A.   'On the morning of my accident.'
Q.   'Who took it off ?'
A.   'I did.'
Q.   'Did anyone tell you do so?'
A.   'Mr Smith.'
Q.   'Is he your supervisor?'

Notice that in all these questions (except the last), the answer is not suggested. Some of them are semi-open questions; some could have been answered by yes or no. If yes (or no) had been the response, the barrister would then have had to ask a further question.

E.3.2   QUESTIONING IN COURT

In the courtroom, a barrister is bound by certain rules (either legal rules, rules of professional conduct or simply convention). These may oblige you either:

(a)   not to ask certain questions at all (examples of such rules are hearsay, relevance, questions based on your knowledge rather than your instructions); or

(b)   to ask questions in a certain way (e.g., using a witness's out-of-court statement which is inconsistent with his or her evidence in court; not asking leading questions without permission from the judge or your opponent).

Also, when questioning in the courtroom, the barrister should seek to fulfil a special function, depending on which party called the witness to give evidence — you or your opponent. For further discussion of this see **Chapters 18** and **19**. Also remember that in court the answer is important for the judge and the jury, not just for you.

E.3.2.1   Witnesses called for your client

With your own witnesses, you present your evidence (information) to the court. You should know what they are going to say before they go into the witness box. If things go well, the evidence should be put before the court in the manner you intended. This will mean that you try to use open questions, e.g., 'What happened next?' or 'What did he do then?'.

You should not repeat a question after receiving an answer — if your witness has responded, you must accept the answer, whatever it is. You must not cross-examine your own witness. You might ask a question to clarify a point about the last answer but you should not have a second go at getting the answer that you wanted, as distinct from the one you got. You cannot force a witness to 'come up to proof', and all too often a client will not say quite what was said in a previous statement.

Sometimes, one of your witnesses will threaten to run out of control. Perhaps you asked him or her, 'What happened next?' and he or she is now telling you the story of his or her life, straying off the point, introducing inadmissible evidence. Then you need to exert control and bring the witness back to the matter that you want him or her to tell the court. 'If I can stop you there, let us go back to the day of the accident. Did you speak to anyone after it happened?' Remember — you cannot ask leading questions but that does not mean that you abandon all control over your witness.

E.3.2.2 Witnesses called for the opposition

When questioning your opponent's witnesses, you are seeking information of help to your client, i.e., consistent with your theory of the case; or you are trying to attack the witnesses' credibility; or you are giving them the opportunity to agree or disagree with your theory of the case. This usually means that you try to control the witness — perhaps by the use of closed questions where the answer is suggested, often as yes or no. For example: 'You told her to take the fencing off the machine, didn't you?' 'The fencing was removed to allow the operator to work faster, wasn't it?'.

You will ask this sort of question often, not because you expect the witness to agree with you or give the suggested answer but because the allegation is part of your client's case.

You will use the open type of question rarely in cross-examination. This is for the simple reason that the open question allows the witness a lot of freedom and you do not know what the witness is going to say. The answer may be fatal to your client's case. This fear has led to the notion that you should avoid asking questions to which you do not know the answer. Of course, with your own witnesses, you should always know what the expected answer is, even though you sometimes do not get it! With your opponent's witnesses, you are taking a great risk in allowing them their head, for example:

Q. 'So if you didn't tell her to do it, why do you say she removed the fencing from the machine?'
A. 'In the hot weather, you get a nice breeze from the unfenced machines. I'm always telling her not to do it, but the minute my back's turned she does as she likes.'

It is not possible to adhere rigidly to the notion that you only ask questions to which you know the answers. Applied to cross-examination, this would lead to very few questions being asked. Again, sometimes you need to give the witness a little rope in the hope that he or she trips up on it. But you should only do so with caution and as part of a plan — you need to have another line of questions ready if you get an unfavourable answer.

E.4 Planning Questions

It may be tempting to take the cavalier attitude that the right question will occur to you when you need it, especially when you are conducting a conference with your own client. This attitude will suffice for day-to-day life, but it is not an attitude that will suffice for the efficient professional who proposes to make a living collecting and presenting information about a case.

Even for the simplest conference you will need some planning for questions, to ensure that everything is covered in an appropriate way. If you do not plan, time will probably be used inefficiently, and important information may be overlooked. Planning for a conference is dealt with in the *Conference Skills Manual*. Do not underestimate the importance of preparation out of laziness or over-confidence — proper forethought always shows in matters of detail and gives both solicitor and client belief in your ability.

It may be more obvious that you need to plan questions for examination and cross-examination in court. But beware of overdoing this. While sufficient preparation of lines of questions and specific questions is very important, too much preparation can make your performance unconvincing and inflexible.

E.5   Exercises

1.   Consider each of the types of question outlined in **E.2**.

What are the possible uses of each type of question?
What are the possible drawbacks of each type of question?
Can you identify any types of questions that are not outlined?

2.   Your client has been run over and injured by a car.

Frame three open questions to find out what happened.
Frame three closed questions to find out what happened.
Frame three yes/no questions to find out what happened.

3.   Your client is accused of causing grievous bodily harm by pushing a beer glass into the face of an acquaintance. Work with another student who will play the client for you and see if you can find out what happened:

(a)   using only open questions;

(b)   using only closed questions;

(c)   using only yes/no questions.

APPENDIX F

NON-VERBAL COMMUNICATION

F.1   What is Non-verbal Communication?

Non-verbal communication is a complicated combination of the way language and words, tone of voice, body posture and movement are used. It is important to remember not to interpret a single gesture as a major clue to understanding what is being said, since gestures, like words, come together in sequences and should be considered as a whole within the context in which they occur. Your perception of non-verbal behaviour can be distorted by many things: for example, you may have preconceived notions about a particular client, witness, opponent or judge, etc. (see **Appendix A**); you may see only what you want to see; you may focus on one particular aspect of another's behaviour and exclude all the other clues which are being signalled to you; or you may have influenced another's response to you by the manner in which you asked the question (see **Appendix E**). It should also be remembered that the more verbally fluent a person is, the less likely that person will be to use non-verbal communication and, on many occasions, the clues which you can gain from the use of non-verbal language are likely to be limited, but they will often have something to add to what is said.

F.2   Value of Understanding Non-verbal Communication

For the barrister, understanding non-verbal communication can be helpful in several ways. It can provide useful clues to aid in your assessment of the truth of what is said to you and in deciding whether the full story has been told. It will also help you to know whether what you are saying has been understood or not.

It can also help you to assess your audience before you start to speak and hence to pitch what you say in the right way and at the right level. It will help the barrister assess whether his or her advocacy is going down well with the judge and/or jury. Indeed with a jury non-verbal communication is normally all you can use to determine their mood. It will help you in assessing whether it is necessary to change the style of presentation in order to capture or recapture the interest of your audience, or whether to alter the complexity of the language used in order to make what is said easily comprehensible.

Be aware not only of non-verbal communication in others, but also in yourself. By learning to use positive open gestures instead of negative ones, the barrister will feel more comfortable with others (although negative gestures may be useful in a particular situation!). By learning about non-verbal communication a barrister may be able to control his or her non-verbal behaviour, although contradictions between verbal and non-verbal communication should be avoided because, as John Stefano has written:

> What it comes down to for the lawyer is this: if you have correctly understood the situation, if you know what you are doing, and if you believe in it, your body, voice, emotions, and intellect will work together in the act of communicating with other human beings . . .

If on the other hand, you do not know what you are doing or you do not believe in it, or you are afraid of revealing what you feel, your body and voice will betray you, no matter how much you attempt to manipulate them. You will either be acutely, painfully aware of both of them, as will your audience; or, if you choose to avoid the pain by not feeling, your audience will remain unmoved and unpersuaded.

I have argued that congruence of feelings and words is necessary for a communication to be accepted as potentially true. Direct attempts to produce this congruence — that is, attempts to manipulate the body and the emotions — will fail, as will most attempts to mask them. Congruence is achieved through integrity, not technique. But emotionless speech is ambiguous and unpersuasive. For those of us not addicted to Machiavellianism, that leaves only one alternative: know what you believe, and say it with feeling.

> (Quoted in *Effective Speaking*, British Columbia Skills Materials.)

Remember that attempting to fake your own body language is difficult and it is possible that others will see through your attempts, although it has been suggested that: 'Some people whose jobs involve lying, such as politicians, lawyers, actors and television announcers, have refined their body gestures to the point where it is difficult to "see" the lie and people fall for it hook, line and sinker.' (Alan Pease in *Body Language*: How to read other people's thoughts by their gestures, 1981, p. 18.)

You should think about your own body language because you can use it to emphasise what you are saying. Equally, being aware of your own body language should help you to avoid distracting habits, for example, drumming your fingers on the desk or biting your pen or pencil.

Do not underestimate the importance of non-verbal communication because of any initial reaction that it is not very important. Simply looking at a video of yourself should show you the importance of improvement of your own non-verbal communication. And failing to use skills at recognising non-verbal signs in a client, a witness or a judge is simply failing to use an important tool available to you. As in all skills do not be simplistic, but develop your ability to appreciate non-verbal communication as far as possible.

F.3   Interpretation of Non-verbal Communication

Several possibilities exist. When the verbal language and non-verbal language co-incide, a very strong and probably accurate message is being conveyed. Where the verbal and non-verbal language used portray entirely different and opposing or confused messages, research suggests that it is the non-verbal communication which is likely to be the more accurate and hence the more reliable in helping you to assess what is really being said. A word of warning – although some guidance to understanding body language is provided in this chapter, do not assume that all people are the same and that there are rules which can be applied automatically to everyone. Particularly remember that body language is likely to be different depending on the ethnic and cultural background of the individual concerned. You will learn from your own experience of the non-verbal behaviour of others when they respond to you what they are really saying; when the opportunity arises, test out whether your assessments are right.

F.4   Meaning of Various Kinds of Non-verbal Communication

The following merely suggests possible interpretations of the body language described. It is not intended to provide a set of rules which apply in all cases but only some guidance upon which you can build, using your own experience. These suggestions are based on substantial research, and many examples and explanations can be found in books such as *Body Language* by Alan Pease or *Bodytalk — a World Guide to Gestures* by Desmond Morris.

F.4.1   EYE CONTACT

Eye contact is centrally important to building up rapport with others, be it a client, a witness or a judge. Whether you are trying to form a relationship with a client or to force the truth from a reluctant witness, good eye contact is vital. Whoever you are talking to, you should try to look them in the eye quite frequently, rather than merely looking generally in their direction, or looking at something else. Eye contact can help to create a sense of trust and suggests interest. Avoiding eye contact may, for some people, suggest untrustworthiness or lack of confidence.

On the other hand, substantial eye contact can be disconcerting or even threatening. Staring at someone can make them most uncomfortable and may be used if this is the intention. It is important to be aware that in some cultures excessive eye contact is regarded as threatening or rude. You may need to adjust to this in appropriate circumstances.

F.4.2   BODY POSTURE

Good posture is important for the barrister. The profession may be rather different from that of the model, but how you look is still very important. The person who stands upright, stands square and keeps their head up appears confident and convincing. The person who slouches, looks down frequently and fidgets easily comes across as the opposite. You only have to watch a few barristers in court to appreciate the difference.

In a conference, body posture can also be important. Sitting so that your body faces the client, and perhaps leaning forward from time to time, suggests interest. Turning your body away, leaning back frequently or slouching in the chair can easily suggest lack of interest and lack of efficiency to the client. Such a posture in a client may suggest that they are nervous, or perhaps that they are not telling the truth.

F.4.3   HEAD MOVEMENTS

Holding the head square, upright and facing straight forward is most likely to appear strong and confident, in a barrister or in a client. Holding the head slightly to one side may suggest alertness or interest, but this depends on other factors too. Holding the head down tends to suggest a negative attitude. In court you can often see little more of a judge than his or her head and arms. The movements of the head can be a good indicator to the judge's view of your case.

F.4.4   ARM MOVEMENTS

Folded arms tend to indicate a barrier, but this barrier may be there for many reasons, and it is important to try to decide which is operative. Folded arms may indicate defensiveness, hostility or lack of confidence. A person who crosses their arms during a conversation may be indicating that they do not agree with what you are saying. Folded arms with clenched fists rather than relaxed arms are most likely to indicate tension or hostility.

In general terms, the way a person holds their arms and how much they move them may give real clues as to whether they are tense or relaxed, confident or lacking in confidence, or nervous and perhaps not telling the truth.

F.4.5   HAND GESTURES

Some hand gestures have fairly obvious meanings. The hand on the hips may well indicate aggression, as may waving a pointed finger. The open palm may suggest honesty and openness. However, beware hasty or superficial judgments, not least in that different gestures can mean different things in different cultures or different contexts. The two-fingered 'V' sign may be most unfriendly or may mean victory! Another gesture with a dual meaning is that of resting the head on a hand (common with judges!), which may mean boredom or may mean interest, especially if the index finger is extended up the cheek or is stroking the chin.

Research has suggested meanings for other hand gestures, but these perhaps may need to be used with care. It is suggested that putting a hand partly across the mouth is likely to indicate that a lie is being told, as this is a common gesture with children who are not telling the truth. It has also been suggested that scratching the nose may mean that a lie is being told, but all circumstances may need to be taken into consideration, such as the simple possibility that the nose itches!

F.4.6 LEG MOVEMENTS

Crossed legs may be a barrier in a similar way to crossed arms, though for cultural reasons this should perhaps be interpreted differently for a woman and for a man. Frequent leg movements while sitting or standing may well suggest restlessness, but the reason for this restlessness should be considered. The person may not simply be bored, but may wish to get off a subject because they find it uncomfortable — which may or may not be a good reason to pursue it!

F.5 Improving your Communication Skills Using Non-verbal Behaviour

F.5.1 PERSONAL SPACE

Attitudes towards personal space vary between cultures. Feelings about personal space should be borne in mind when setting up a conference with a client, be it in chambers or at the court. Consider how close you should be to your client and how close you want your client to come to you. If you get too close you will probably both feel uncomfortable and this will interfere with communication and your ability to build up rapport with your client. Remember, though, that you want to build up a close professional relationship with your client, so do not keep too far away.

F.5.2 HANDSHAKING

A handshake can communicate many things about you to your client, and about your client to you. As a general guide, a dominating handshake faces downwards in relation to the other person's palm, while the reverse is true of the dominated handshake. If you want your client to feel that you are in control, use the former; if you want your client to feel more comfortable with (equal to) you, you should use a handshake where your hand is at 90° to your body. It is a good idea to practise your handshake so that through it you can make the impression you want. Decide whether you want to use a handshake which is firm and just how firm it should be. Think about the impression which a 'wet' handshake can give; it could undermine your client's confidence in you. Always turn your body towards the person with whom you are shaking hands — it indicates openness and is welcoming. The one thing you should never do is hesitate for a long time wondering whether to shake hands or not. If you do not feel comfortable shaking hands, plan an alternative greeting in advance.

A tradition of the Bar is that barristers do not shake hands with one another, although quite often these days the tradition is ignored. So if a member of the Bar does not shake your hand he or she is not being rude or trying to gain a dominant position over you.

F.5.3 FOLDED ARMS

If your client has folded his or her arms you should try to alter this stance by being more open and welcoming and by trying to find out what you have said that has made your client feel negative. If your client keeps his or her arms folded it can colour the whole of the conference because this kind of body language encourages a negative view. If your client folds his or her arms in mid-conversation you should stop the conversation and ask, in an open and non-threatening way, whether he or she has anything to say about what you have said or any questions which he or she would like answered. These are merely suggestions of things you can do to check whether your interpretation of the body language of the client is a true reflection of his or her attitude. If it is not, you will have lost nothing; if it is, you will have the opportunity to retrieve the situation.

F.5.4   SUPERIOR BODY POSTURE

Avoid habits which suggest your superiority, for example, leaning back with your hands behind your head. Expressing superiority by sitting behind a large desk may have its attractions, but it may not be beneficial to how well you get on with a client.

F.5.5   EYE CONTACT

Avoid writing out in detail what you want to say or the answers to questions, and always keep your eyes on your audience — they may be fidgeting, resting their heads on their hands (that is, bored) or looking puzzled. If you are not watching them you will not be aware of the fact that you have lost them. Do not stare at the client as this is likely to make him or her feel uncomfortable. Remember that if you change the direction of your gaze your client will notice and might think that you are bored. Always think about where you are looking.

F.6   Exercises

1.   Pick a person in the same room as you. Try to pick up as many indicators as you can of their mood and what they are thinking from their posture, their arm and hand movements and their leg movements.

2.   Next time you are in a pub, restaurant or Tube carriage with a number of people you do not know, pick a single individual and try to analyse their body language. Would your analysis be the same if they were your client and if they were a witness giving evidence against your client? If not, why not? If possible, try to compare your analysis with that of a companion analysing the same individual.

3.   List as many messages as you can that you think it is possible to pick up from body language. Compare your list with someone else.

4.   Make a list of the 'rules' governing bodily contact in our society.

5.   Think of a situation in which you think someone was lying to you or not telling you the whole truth. What physical factors indicated to you that this was the case?

6.   Identify someone in your tutorial group who has a cultural background different from your own. Discuss with them what they identify as the most important aspects of non-verbal communication in their culture.

7.   When you observe someone from a different cultural background in a natural situation such as a café try to identify any non-verbal communication habits that are different from your own, and to identify whether any of these habits could be misinterpreted. Is a first impression that someone is bored, aggressive or self-confident necessarily a correct impression?

INDEX